MEDICAL MALPRACTICE IN NINETEENTH-CENTURY AMERICA

The American Social Experience Series

GENERAL EDITOR: JAMES KIRBY MARTIN

EDITORS: PAULA S. FASS, STEVEN H. MINTZ,

CARL PRINCE, JAMES W. REED & PETER N. STEARNS

MEDICAL MALPRACTICE IN NINETEENTH-CENTURY AMERICA

Origins and Legacy

KENNETH ALLEN DE VILLE

NEW YORK UNIVERSITY PRESS
NEW YORK AND LONDON
1990

Copyright © 1990 by New York University
All rights reserved
Manufactured in the United States of America

Library of Congress Cataloging-in-Publication Data
De Ville, Kenneth Allen, 1955–
Medical malpractice in nineteenth-century America : origins and
legacy / Kenneth Allen De Ville.
p. cm. — (The American social experience series ; v. 19)
Includes bibliographical references.
ISBN 0-8147-1832-9 (alk. paper)
1. Physicians—Malpractice—United States—History—19th century.
I. Title. II. Series.
[DNLM: 1. History of Medicine, 19th Cent.—United States.
2. Malpractice—history—United States. WZ 70 AA1 D4m]
KF2905.3.D4 1990
346.7303'32'09034—dc20
[347.30633209034]
DLC
for Library of Congress   90-5823
CIP

New York University Press books are printed on acid-free paper,
and their binding materials are chosen for strength and durability.

Book design by Ken Venezio

Contents

Illustrations

Preface

A nineteenth-century physician commenting on malpractice law suits observed that "[t]he remedy of these evils in the profession involves many and grave problems in sociology which I cannot now stop to consider."[1] The writer was correct. The malpractice phenomenon, like other legal issues, was and is a reflection of social, cultural, and professional trends that have yet to be identified and explained. Neither nineteenth-century observers nor modern scholars in legal, medical, or social history have attempted to document and interpret the development of medical malpractice in America. Instead, scholars have made only passing reference to the issue and have failed to exploit a rich and multidimensional topic.

The short tradition of malpractice history began with Hubert Winston Smith's lengthy 1941 study in the *Journal of the American Medical Association*.[2] Smith explained basic legal doctrine to his readers and traced the genealogy of a twentieth-century American malpractice decision to its English common law ancestors. Smith's most valuable contribution to the discussion was his tabulation of all the American malpractice appellate cases between 1793 and 1940. Other writers have followed Smith's approach and used state appellate court decisions to understand the history of malpractice.[3]

But appellate decisions tell only part of the story. The majority of trial cases never reach an appellate court. Although useful, the information gleaned from these higher court decisions is uneven. Appellate courts deal primarily with legal doctrine and seldom provide detailed information about the mechanics of the trial or the life of the litigants. Moreover, the writers who have used these materials have tended to treat law and legal development as an entity divorced from the cultural contexts of specific times. Strictly linear tracing of cases often results in important omissions and limited insight into the causes and development of malpractice suits.

Although a few writers have begun to study twentieth-century malpractice, professional historians have virtually ignored it.[4] In 1969, Chester Burns recognized the research potential of the topic, identified the 1840s as the first outbreak of malpractice suits, and implicitly called for an investigation into its nineteenth-century roots.[5] Unfortunately, no one has expanded on Burns's work. General medical and legal historians occasionally mention increased malpractice litigation in the nineteenth century, and they have provided clues to its origins. William Rothstein, for example, explained that nineteenth-century malpractice rates increased as scientific advancements made objective evaluations of physicians possible.[6]

For the most part, however, lack of resources, both primary and secondary, has handicapped attempts to understand fully the history of medical malpractice. There are no studies that consider trial court decisions or local peculiarities. Quantitative approaches to the problem are restricted by the nature of trial court activity. Nineteenth-century trial records have sometimes disappeared, while the surviving ones are often inaccessible and seldom in good condition. A systematic tabulation of trial court cases would require a search of hundreds, if not thousands of locations and would be, according to one writer, "practically speaking, impossible."[7] Ultimately, smaller scale studies of individual states may be warranted but they will never provide a completely accurate report of the number of cases in nineteenth-century America.

Until recently, the secondary literature in several fields was not sufficiently developed to support a viable study of the issues surrounding the topic. Malpractice is neither solely a medical issue nor a legal one. It also has social, political, and religious components. Before the 1970s medical historians (with some notable exceptions) concentrated on great doctors, major diseases, or specific events. While their work was competent and valuable, they generally did not explore the ways in which medical practice and thought interacted with the cultural and political environment.[8] Similarly, traditional legal historians tended to emphasize "great cases" and major constitutional changes while ignoring the law's relationship with society, the market, and contemporary intellectual developments.

In the past two decades, however, both legal and medical historians, using fresh approaches, have explored new areas of research. They have examined law and medicine not as self-contained disciplines but as part of the society in which they exist. These new works help provide a perspective from which to view malpractice litigation. In addition, the enormous growth in social history and anthropological studies has enhanced understanding of the nineteenth-century world and provided important new insights. Because of this prodigious increase in secondary literature in a wide range of fields, a synthetic study of the origins of medical malpractice is now feasible.

Problems remain, but many can be overcome. When malpractice became a perceptible problem in the 1840s, medical journals published accounts and editorials on scores of malpractice suits. Some of these articles contained portions of trial transcripts, detailed descriptions of the treatment involved, and contemporary commentary. Sometimes physicians or disgruntled patients published pamphlets containing partial or full accounts of trials. Nineteenth-century physicians often discussed malpractice in their memoirs, and state medical societies regularly appointed committees to study the problem. By midcentury, medical and legal writers produced entire treatises and compendia on the subject. And, despite their deficiencies, appellate court decisions are a crucial source of information.

I do not intend to provide a comprehensive history of medical malpractice in the nineteenth century. The issues are so numerous and rich and the country so large and diverse that a full history is far beyond the reach of any single book. I do, however, hope to offer a historical discussion of the origins of modern medical malpractice. I am interested in presenting close-up pictures of medical and legal life, but I am equally concerned with identifying, and at least partially illuminating, the fundamental and topical causes of the phenomenon in America.

Acknowledgments

I have always considered myself lucky. In completing this book I have been fortunate enough to incur a wide range of debts, which I take great pleasure in recognizing.

Rice University history department provided consistent intellectual and financial support for this project and my general academic development. I am sincerely grateful. Vali, Michelle, and Douglas in the Rice University Fondren Library interlibrary loan department performed remarkable feats in acquiring often obscure materials. Inci Bowman of the University of Texas Medical Branch at Galveston and Elizabeth White and Linda Davenport of the University of Texas Health Science Center at Houston also helped me gather research and illustrations.

Many individuals have offered various types of help at different points of the project. Randy Sparks, Matt Taylor, and Bill Warren provided regular and essential encouragement. John Boles, Albert Van Helden, and Mary Winkler contributed valuable insights on many of the issues discussed in chapter 5. Members of the 1988–1989 Rice University Legal History Seminar, including Brian Dirck, Randall Jamail, Charles Robinson, James Schmidt, Patricia Tidwell, and Charles Zelden, read each chapter as it was completed; their comments were both helpful and charitable. Baruch Brody, Chester Burns, Elizabeth Heitman, James Kirby Martin, Steven Mintz, Mark Steiner, Albert Van Helden, and Martin Wiener all read various complete versions of the manuscript. They provided enormous editorial and intellectual aid.

My deepest gratitude and most profound respect are reserved for Harold M. Hyman. Harold played an integral role in the conception and completion of this project. More importantly, he guided and shaped my general academic and professional development. His example and tutelage have convinced me that opportunity, hard work, and discipline can yield undreamed of results and satisfaction.

Finally, I want to thank Chris Moore De Ville (who clearly had better things to do) for her unremitting support and saintly patience.

•

CHAPTER 1

Before the Flood,
1790–1835

In March 1829 Dr. Asabel Humphrey instructed his student to vaccinate Harriet Landon for smallpox. The physician had been hired by the town of Salisbury, Connecticut, to vaccinate its citizens. Humphrey's student made two punctures just above Landon's elbow joint. After the treatment Landon found that her lower arm was almost paralyzed. When her condition did not improve, she sued Humphrey for malpractice. After several witnesses, including a medical school professor, testified that the vaccination punctures were in a "very unusual place" and had caused irreparable injury, the jury awarded Landon $500 in damages. In reporting the case for the *Boston Medical and Surgical Journal*, an editorialist "confess[ed]" that he was "somewhat incredulous as to the justice of the decision" and declared that the case should "excite the astonishment of every medical man."[1]

By the mid–nineteenth century commentators in medical literature rarely expressed incredulity or astonishment when a patient sued a physician. They had begun to view the malpractice suit as a ubiquitous and possibly permanent fixture of medical practice. Before the late 1830s and early 1840s, however, malpractice cases had been rare in the United States, and physicians did not consider lawsuits a significant threat to their income or status. The social, political, legal, technological, and professional transformations that would eventually incite and sustain the malpractice phenomenon were underway, but they had not

1

yet created the environment conducive to widespread prosecutions. The years from 1790 to 1835 were a period of relative judicial safety for the physician, and only isolated cases presaged the menace on the horizon.

"Not a Very Commendable Sight Anymore Than a Very Customary Sight"

While there is no accurate way to calculate the absolute number of malpractice suits in this or any other period, certain legal records, medical literature, and contemporary responses clearly illustrate the relative frequency or infrequency of the litigation. Soon after the American Revolution, individual compilers began publishing reports of all the cases decided in the appellate courts of the respective states.[2] Appellate reports did not record cases decided at the trial level but provided state supreme court rulings on lower court judgments. Appellate decisions were accepted elaborations and, occasionally, alterations of the common law and could be used as precedents in subsequent trial and appellate court cases. Therefore, appellate decisions are valuable sources of legal theory and doctrine.

Unfortunately, they are less useful for determining the exact number of malpractice cases at the trial level. A variety of legal, social, financial, and historical factors contributed to the decision to appeal a trial court ruling, and only a small percentage of trial judgments terminated in appellate court rulings. One writer developed a formula that suggested there were nine malpractice charges filed at the trial level for each reported appellate decision. Another study estimated that the proportion was 100:1.[3] The 9:1 ratio is an unreasonably low conjecture.[4] The 100:1 figure corresponds with some known nineteenth- and twentieth-century rates and is probably a better estimate. For example, an 1860 Ohio medical commentator on malpractice reported that there had been over 200 malpractice cases in the state while the Ohio supreme court had reported only two appellate court decisions regarding malpractice.[5] Still, the vagaries of appellate jurisprudence rob even the 100:1 figure of much of its certitude and utility.

Nevertheless, reported appellate decisions serve as a broad measure of the frequency of malpractice litigation. There were 216 appellate malpractice cases reported between 1790 and 1900. Out of the 216 total, only 5 cases, or 2.3 percent, were reported before 1835.[6] Despite the uncertainty involved in correlating appellate decisions to trial court judgments, the insignificant number of malpractice cases in the first third of the century contrasts sharply with the acceleration of reported decisions after 1840. Although the rate of increase intensified in the course of the nineteenth century and continued to soar in the twentieth, the initial increase in the late 1830s and early 1840s represented a fundamental break with the past. In the early part of the century malpractice suits were virtually nonexistent; after 1840 they became a prominent feature of the medical world.

The contrast between malpractice rates before and after the first third of the century is even more striking when these rates are compared to population increases. Between 1790 and 1840 the United States population grew 334 percent, from 3,929,214 to 17,069,453. During this period, the number of appellate malpractice decisions remained almost constant: 7 appellate decisions were scattered over fifty years. However, between 1840 and 1880 the population increased 194 percent, from 17,069,453 to 50,155,783, but the total number of appellate malpractice decisions jumped 1228 percent, from 7 cases as of 1840 to 93 cases by 1880.[7] While the rate of appellate malpractice decisions was seemingly unaffected by a 334 percent population increase between 1790 and 1840, the rate of reported cases far outstripped population growth over the next forty years.

TABLE 1 [8]

Appellate Court Malpractice Decisions, 1790–1950

Years	# of Decisions	% Increase in Cases	% Increase in Population
1790–1830	2	—	227
1830–1860	21	950	144
1860–1890	117	457	100
1890–1920	485	308	68
1920–1950	1,143	136	43

In fact, the interval between 1790 and 1840 has been the only period in American history in which the proliferation of appellate malpractice decisions failed to surpass the growth rate of the population (see table 1). These observations suggest that the increase in reported suits in the last two-thirds of the nineteenth century was not directly related to population increases, and they reinforce the conclusion that the late 1830s represented a critical turning point in the history of American medical malpractice litigation.

The low frequency of reports of malpractice in early nineteenth-century medical journals corroborates the rarity of suits before 1835. Physicians developed their views about malpractice suits in medical publications, where they communicated their attitudes to other doctors. Detailed malpractice reports helped physicians gauge the frequency of litigation, speculate on the causes of the suits, and suggest possible remedies. These commentaries, while virtually absent from early journals, were published at a furious rate beginning in the late 1830s. For example, between 1812 and 1835 the *New England Journal of Medicine and Surgery* and its successor, the *Boston Medical and Surgical Journal*, reported on only three malpractice cases. These three cases included one suit each from France, England, and the United States.[9] In contrast, between 1835 and 1865 the *Boston Medical and Surgical Journal* published forty-eight reports and editorials on malpractice.[10] Other journals exhibited a similar disparity between the number of suits reported before and after 1840. In New York (the state considered the center of the new malpractice phenomenon in the 1840s) the medical society reported on only one malpractice incident before 1835 in its *Transactions*—and that involved an illegal abortion, not a lawsuit.[11] Similarly, the *Medical Examiner*, founded in the 1830s, did not report a single malpractice case until the next decade. Publishers did not attempt to provide a comprehensive list of suits, but the scores of malpractice reports between 1835 and 1865 reflected the general trend of litigation and the level of professional concern. While these later articles were filled with the medical community's concerns regarding the frequency of malpractice suits, the few existing reports in the *Boston Medical and Surgical Journal* and other publications from the years 1790–1835 reflected little anxiety and treated the cases as regrettable, but isolated incidents.[12]

Although the field of medical jurisprudence blossomed in the early nineteenth century, legal scholars seldom, if ever, addressed the issue of malpractice before 1835.[13] Two of the most widely circulated works in America were Theodoric Beck's *Elements of Medical Jurisprudence* (1823) and Joseph Chitty's *A Practical Treatise on Medical Jurisprudence* (1834). Neither Chitty, a lawyer, nor Beck, a New York physician, contributed a word of advice or information on malpractice.[14] When R. E. Griffith added an American chapter to Michael Ryan's work on medical jurisprudence in 1832, he merely noted that there were three types of malpractice: willful, negligent, and ignorant. He did not cite any cases or suggest that such litigation was prevalent.[15] Timothy Walker, a professor of law at Cincinnati College, published an extensive *First Book for Students* in 1837. Walker described *malpractice* as the attempt to produce an abortion. He did not include the incompetent practice of physicians that resulted in permanent injuries to patients in his definition.[16] When physicians and lawyers discussed malpractice in the first third of the century, they were most likely referring to nonlicensed practice, ethical violations, or criminal abortion. Civil lawsuits for damages after treatment received scant attention and generated no concern.

The Law

When late eighteenth- and early nineteenth-century American lawyers brought malpractice suits against physicians, they were able to refer to a slowly expanding body of legal literature for guidance, but no specialized works. Lawyers at the time of the American Revolution read William Blackstone's or Edward Coke's commentaries, referred to scattered English court decisions, and learned from assisting their preceptors. After Independence Americans published their own law journals, case reports, treatises, and legal handbooks.[17] Despite this relative outpouring of reference material, the essential mechanics of malpractice prosecutions remained relatively unchanged.

American lawyers eagerly bought Blackstone's *Commentaries* when they first became available in 1765. The first American edition printed in 1771–1772, and St. George Tucker's annotated version published in 1803, made the commentaries accessible to virtually every lawyer in the country. In fact, for those lawyers who trained in the late 1700s and practiced into the mid-1830s Blackstone was the most important legal resource.[18] Blackstone categorized *mala practice* not under *contract* or *mercantile law*, but under the heading of *private wrongs*. He defined *malpractice* as an injury or damage to a person's "vigor or constitution" sustained as a result of "the neglect or unskillful management of [a] physician, surgeon, or apothecary." Blackstone declared that malpractice was an offense because "it breaks the trust which the party placed in his physician." The injured patient possessed a remedy for damages with the special legal action, or *writ*, of "trespass on the case."[19]

The trespass on the case writ was the technical name of the action in a malpractice suit.[20] This writ served as the common law remedy for all cases in which one person purportedly caused another an injury without the use of force. The scope of trespass on the case included damages sustained as the result of breach of duty, negligence, or carelessness. An attorney had to convince the judge and jury that the accused physician had failed to live up to the common law definition of professional responsibility and that this lapse had resulted in an injury to the defendant. Judges and lawyers drew on English precedents to form the American standard for malpractice. While the law did not demand that physicians implicitly guarantee effective treatment, it required that they exercise "ordinary diligence, care, and skill."[21] Although the precise wording of the requirement varied and was occasionally qualified in significant ways, the essential standard remained. Doctors were expected to possess and apply an ordinary and reasonable degree of care, skill, and diligence in their work with patients. Individual physicians' performance would be measured against the therapeutic conventions, or standards of "ordinary" or average members of the profession.

The common law reserved an important role for the jury in malpractice cases. While trial judges articulated the legal standards by which juries were required to assess physicians, jurors were asked to determine "questions of fact" such as what constituted carelessness and the standards of the profession at large. Although expert medical testimony was required to guide the jury's deliberations, laymen were entrusted with the tremendous power to designate the boundaries of acceptable medical behavior. Since juries made these decisions on a case-by-case basis, acceptable standards of care, skill, and diligence were highly sensitive to popular conceptions of the medical profession and medical practice.[22] Similarly, the use of physicians as medical witnesses provided an official inlet for the personal or professional prejudices of rival medical practitioners. These provisions, contained in the common law, would play a role in the multiplication of suits in the 1840s and 1850s.

The Cases

Malpractice suits were such an uncommon occurrence before 1835 that it is difficult to draw many confident generalizations. Still, some trends do appear. The lawsuit was neither a common nor a completely acceptable response to personal misfortune. Generally, only in cases of severe injury or death did individuals overcome tradition and sue physicians. Patients and their families rarely won in court. Although malpractice suits of all kinds were infrequent before 1835, cases that did not involve death or amputation were especially rare. Fractures that did not result in amputations—which would become the most common source of suits after 1835—were seldom the source of litigation.

For example, in 1767 a physician was accused, but not charged, of malpractice when a patient died as a result of a blood-letting procedure.[23] The earliest reported American appellate decision, *Cross* v. *Guthery*, was decided in 1794.[24] Cross, a Connecticut physician, amputated one of Mrs. Guthery's breasts; she died three hours later. Her husband sued the physician, asking £1,000 for "his costs and expense, and deprivation of the service and company of his wife." Although the jury ruled in favor of Guthery, they awarded him only £40 in damages.[25] In 1825, Michael O'Neil accused Dr. Gerard Bancker of infecting his four-year-old son with a fatal dose of smallpox during a vaccination and sued for $5,000. A New York City jury refused to award the father any damages.[26] A third case from this period that resulted in death occurred in Ohio in the early 1830s. A physician, using a knife and hook to remove a fetus, injured the mother, who subsequently died. The patient's husband sued the physician for malpractice, but the trial court judge dismissed the case as a nonsuit.[27]

In addition to cases involving deaths, patients also sued physicians in this early period when they believed that improper treatment had resulted in an amputation or a severe deformity. Another obstetric case in the first decade of the century involved a man who, having been a merchant, a grocer, a dancing instructor, and a fencing master, claimed proficiency in medicine, surgery, and midwifery. During a difficult delivery he violently used a pair of scissors and his hands to remove a fetus, presumably to save the mother's life. In doing so, he produced an "irreparable injury to the internal parts of the mother" and caused her "great and unnecessary pain." The prosecution presented evidence to show that the defendant had received no form of organized medical training. Several physicians testified that the defendant's procedure was unusual and unwarrantable, and a Connecticut jury found him guilty of malpractice.[28] The defendant appealed the verdict to the state supreme court, claiming that the prosecution had no right to introduce evidence concerning his previous occupations and lack of training. In 1812 the state supreme court noted that any "attempt to practice in cases of this sort, without the necessary previous qualifications, clearly manifests extreme depravity, and evinces a general hostility towards the human race," and it upheld the verdict.[29] In a Pennsylvania suit in the late 1820s, a patient accused a physician of improperly treating his broken leg. The limb remained swollen and inflamed for twelve months after the injury until amputation was the only remedy. Although the patient won his case at the trial level, the Pennsylvania state supreme court overturned the judgment.[30] As a final example of the character of these early, rare suits, in the 1832 case of *Landon* v. *Humphrey* there was confrontation between a physician and a woman who reportedly suffered a paralyzed arm after an improper vaccination procedure.[31]

The narrow range of cases prosecuted in the early nineteenth century provides a clue to, and a preview of, the subsequent increases in malpractice suits. The suits before 1835 generally involved obstetrical or vaccination cases or profound deformities such as amputations, and it is notable that at this time the public viewed obstetrics and vaccination procedures as having a mechanical certitude. For example, a judge in 1827 noted that a "physician may mistake the symptoms of a patient;

or may misjudge as to the nature of his disease; and even as to the powers of a medicine; and yet his error may be of that pardonable kind, that will do him no essential prejudice." But, the judge observed, while a physician often was part of a profession "beset by great difficulties, the employment of a man midwife and surgeon for the most part, is merely mechanical, and therefore held to a higher standard of performance."[32]

By the 1820s and 1830s smallpox vaccination was widely considered a predictable, almost routine, procedure. Statistics from European countries convinced Americans of the value of vaccination, and several state legislatures required counties to provide the procedure for all citizens.[33] These attitudes toward particular medical treatments engendered a false sense of certitude and confidence. Both obstetrics and vaccination were still uncertain fields subject to the vagaries of individual patients and practitioners. But public perception was more important than reality: If a physician did not perform a seemingly mechanistic, simple procedure with success, then the public often assumed that he must have been guilty of a lapse in care or skill.

The image of the body as a machine and the physician as a mechanic grew out of the triumph of Cartesian thought in the eighteenth century. The mechanistic view of the body and of certain medical practices did not have a major impact on the frequency of malpractice litigation until advancements in medical technology created a reasonable, yet illusory, expectation of success.[34] More important, however, the complex of social and professioinal factors necessary for widespread litigation had not entirely coalesced in the first third of the nineteenth century. An early suit in Maine illustrates the social, medical, and legal environment of this period and suggests some of the reasons for the increase in malpractice suits after the first third of the century.

Lowell v. Hawks and Faxon

In September 1821, Charles Lowell, 30, was riding in the country near the village of Lubec, Maine. Lowell's "young and restive" horse threw him from the saddle and then fell across his legs. Lowell's companions carried him home and called for Dr. John Faxon. Although Faxon, according to Lowell, was "not a thorough bred physician," he was the only doctor in town and had treated Lowell's family for several years. Faxon examined Lowell and discovered that the man's left hip was dislocated and that the left leg was twisted at a forty-five degree angle from the right leg. Using a ball made of a large sheet as a fulcrum and the dislocated limb as a lever, Faxon attempted to force the hip bone back into the socket. He could not correct the injury, so he sent a messenger to the nearby village of Eastport to bring Dr. Micajah Hawks.[35]

During the three-mile journey from Eastport, Hawks told the messenger that Faxon "was not fit to doctor a sheep or a hog, much less a human being." However, when Hawks reached Lowell's house, he was courteous and allowed Faxon to assist him. Hawks directed several men to pull on Lowell's good leg, others to pull at his arms, and ordered Faxon and three additional men to manipulate the injured leg. Without anesthesia this was a profoundly painful procedure that Lowell referred to as "torture." Witnesses heard "a kind of grating," and Hawks declared that the hip was in its proper position. Hawks tied a handkerchief around Lowell's knees and told him to lie still for fourteen days. Hawks said that he would not come back but that he would tell Faxon how to proceed. Hawks spent a total of fifteen minutes with Lowell.[36]

Lowell repeatedly sent messages to Hawks asking to see him. Hawks refused to visit. Neither Hawks or Faxon were concerned when Lowell discovered a mysterious indentation near his hip joint. Hawks visited Lowell in late October 1821, and, though Lowell had reported that the injured leg was very painful and three inches shorter than the other one, the physician refused to examine it. Hawks finally told Lowell that he had "gotten to be a cripple for life and all through Faxon's ignorance and quackery." Even though Lowell had been in bed with his legs bound together, Hawks claimed that Faxon had allowed the patient to reinjure the hip. Now Lowell was in constant pain and was unable to walk without crutches.[37]

In December 1821, about four months after the accident, Lowell traveled 250 miles to Boston aboard a cargo ship to meet with Dr. John Collins Warren, easily the most distinguished physician in the country. Warren had studied at schools and hospitals in London, Edinburgh, and Paris. He was an accomplished surgeon, held the chair of anatomy and surgery at Harvard medical school, and had helped found Massachusetts General Hospital and the *New England Journal of Medicine*. Warren examined Lowell first in a public coffee house in Boston. The physician informed Lowell that he had suffered a simple hip dislocation, but that because the injury had been left untreated for such a long time, nothing could be done to remedy the deformity. He declared that it "was nonsense for Hawks to say he ever reduced the dislocation and that [Lowell had] displaced the bone again lying in

LETTER

TO THF

HON. ISAAC PARKER.

CHIEF JUSTICE OF THE SUPREME COURT OF THE STATE OF MASSACHUSETTS,

CONTAINING REMARKS

ON THE

DISLOCATION OF THE HIP JOINT,

OCCASIONED

BY THE PUBLICATION OF A TRIAL

WHICH

TOOK PLACE AT MACHIAS, IN THE STATE OF MAINE, JUNE, 1824.

BY JOHN C. WARREN, M. D.

PROFESSOR OF ANATOMY AND SURGERY IN HARVARD UNIVERSITY, AND ACTING SURGEON IN THE MASSACHUSETTS GENERAL HOSPITAL.

WITH AN APPENDIX

OF

DOCUMENTS FROM THE TRIAL NECESSARY TO ILLUSTRATE

THE

HISTORY OF THE CASE.

CAMBRIDGE :

PRINTED BY HILLIARD AND METCALF

1826

Title page from John Warren's 142-page pamphlet explaining his role in the Lowell malpractice case (1826). (Courtesy of the Truman G. Blocker, Jr., History of Medicine Collections, Moody Medical Library, Galveston, Texas.)

bed." Warren consulted four other physicians from the hospital, and they all agreed that Lowell's deformity and handicap were the result of an untreated simple dislocation. Although Warren said that nothing could be done to repair the limb, Lowell begged the physician to intervene, explaining that he depended on his leg for a living. Lowell announced that he was "prepared in mind and body for the pain of [an] operation," had a family to support, and convinced Warren and his associates to try and treat the leg.[38]

Since the coffee house did not contain the necessary equipment for the procedure, Warren had Lowell taken to Massachusetts General Hospital. The physician consulted a medical text written by the English surgical pioneer Astley Cooper, who specialized in fractures and dislocations. Following Cooper's direction, Warren began. He provided tartar emetics to induce vomiting, "that deadly sickness, which relaxes the whole muscular system." Warren's associates placed Lowell in a hot water bath "at as high a temperature as he could bear" for an hour. Warren employed a series of pulleys, bandages, and cords suggested by Cooper's work, in an attempt to force Lowell's leg back into its proper position. Medical assistants tied Lowell to a table. A band of leather was placed around his thigh and attached to a pulley, another around his leg and above his knee. Warren placed additional bands around each thigh and attached them to the walls of the operating theater. The pulley on the upper thigh would draw the leg away from the body; the pulley above the knee would wrench it from its frozen position. Immediately before the procedure, according to Warren, "a vein was opened in the arm, and blood drawn as rapidly, and in as large quantities, as the faintness of the patient would allow." Then Warren ordered several men to pull simultaneously on the ropes attached to the various pulleys.[39]

He conducted the operation with the pulley device between one and two hours in front of one hundred students and physicians but could not improve the condition of the leg. According to Warren, Lowell submitted to the painful ordeal "most courageously, and never uttered a complaint."[40] Lowell consulted one or two other Boston physicians before returning to Maine but all the doctors told him that there was little they could do to restore his injured limb. Returning to his hometown, crippled and bitter, Lowell declared, "I am aware of the necessity of kissing the rod, and him who hath anointed it; and were it purely an act of God, I would accept it without a murmur." But after leaving Boston, he "was satisfied that [his] ruin had been brought on by ignorance, stupidity, and unpardonable neglect."[41]

Lowell sued Faxon and Hawks for malpractice and asked for $10,000 in damages. In March 1823 a jury for the Court of Common Pleas found Faxon and Hawks guilty of malpractice and awarded Lowell $1,962, an extraordinary sum in the early nineteenth century. The physicians appealed the case and won the opportunity for a retrial. The jury in the second trial could not decide on a verdict and passed the case to the trial judge, who awarded Lowell only $100. The defendants appealed this verdict too, which led to a third trial.[42]

In the third trial, as in the earlier hearings, John Warren and his associates from Massachusetts General supplied the most damaging evidence against the defendants. The physicians gave sworn depositions in Boston that were presented to the Maine court. Warren disagreed with the primary physician on the specific type of injury Lowell had suffered. He repeated his assertion that Lowell's injury was a simple dislocation, downward and backward, that could have been corrected with prompt treatment. He said that a physician of "ordinary skill" ought to know that a limb that was three inches shorter than the other was dislocated. Warren also agreed with Lowell's attorney that "common and ordinary attention" would lead to regular examinations, comparisons of the lengths of the patient's legs, and concern over any chronic pain. Warren also contended that if "naked hand force" was not sufficient to reset the dislocation, then it was improper treatment to neglect the use of some mechanical means such as pulleys. Warren concluded by stating that he believed that physicians of high standing would agree with his diagnosis and treatment in the case. Several other doctors testified that dislocations were easy to diagnose and treat.[43]

Faxon and Hawks' attorneys countered Warren's testimony by introducing Dr. Nathan Smith, a well-known New England physician and the founder of Dartmouth and Yale medical schools. Warren's father had been instrumental in the establishment of Harvard's medical program, which may have generated rivalry between the two men. When Smith heard Warren's deposition, he called the Boston doctors "a pack of old grannies." Smith blamed the near unanimity of the evidence against the defendants on Warren. "I suppose Warren said

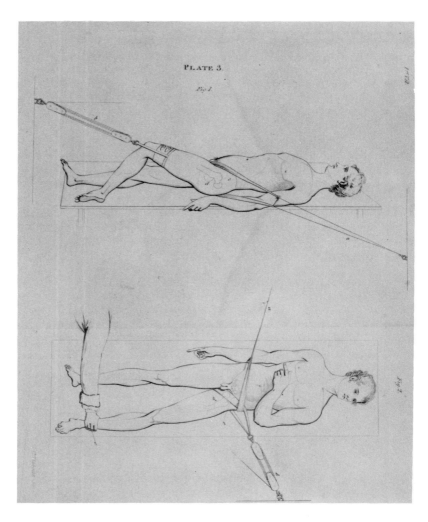

Apparatus to relocate dislocated hips. From Astley Cooper, Surgical Essays *(1821). (Courtesy of the Historical Research Center, Houston Academy of Medicine, Texas Medical Center Library, Houston, Texas.)*

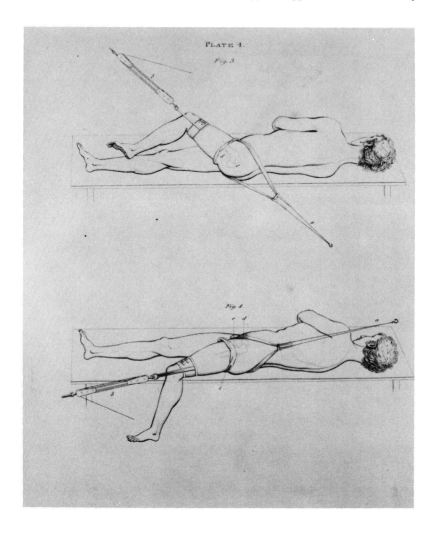

so, and all the rest fell in with his opinions." Smith had examined Lowell's leg in June of 1822. He testified that Lowell did not have a dislocation but had broken the bones of the joint in his fall from the horse. In such a situation, Smith argued, nothing could have been done to cure the injury. Smith declared that pulleys such as Warren used were not necessary and that they had often been injurious. When Lowell's lawyers cross-examined Smith, the physician admitted that he knew Hawks and that he had once told Lowell that "he had better drop his action [malpractice suit] and try and get well, which would be better than to try to get damages out of the doctors."[44]

In his short closing statement Lowell's attorney declared that it was a "known principle of law" that he "who undertakes any business for another shall conduct that business with ordinary skill." Nothing would be more just, he continued, than "that one man should not suffer of the carelessness of another." According to Lowell and his lawyer, Hawks was negligent because he left a patient in the care of Faxon, a man he did not consider fit to treat a "sheep or a hog." Hawks had been hasty in his treatment of Lowell, careless in not noticing the shortened leg, and negligent in allowing Faxon to treat patients. The lawyer asked the jury to award Lowell enough damages to support the injured man for life.[45]

John Davies' closing argument for the defendants filled over fifty pages of text. Davies portrayed Hawks as a modest but committed physician. Hawks did not claim the highest powers and honors of his profession but he had used the best means at hand to reduce a difficult dislocation. According to Davies, Hawks did not expect to cure Lowell completely because he was always "satisfied that there was some interior injury which his art could not reach and which he thought best to be trusted to the healing power of nature." Davies noted that malpractice cases were rare and difficult to adjudicate because "[t]he work of a physician is all tentative and experimental . . . [n]ew observations and discoveries are continually enlarging the field and changing the instruments of professional power." Therefore, Davies reasoned, "The same degree of skill cannot be expected in all places nor exacted of all persons. A young physician cannot be equal to an old one, nor a village apothecary set up to rival a college professor."[46]

After arguing that physicians' skills should be judged on the standard of care in their locality, Davies tried to persuade the jury that the quality of medical care in rural Maine was probably preferable to the scientific advances of Boston. According to the lawyer, Hawks and Faxon did not try to adjust Lowell's leg further because they believed that he was beyond help and did not wish to subject him to more pain. Davies' sarcastic tone throughout the closing argument was designed to create resentment in the small-town jury against the pretensions of big city medicine. Davies told the jurors that John Warren and the "learned faculty of that eminent institution [Massachusetts General]" came together to examine "the case of an unfortunate victim of village quackery." Davies described the Boston doctors as "[c]radled in the love and honor of our society, nursed in the laps of ease, enjoying the patronage of power and opulence, having walked perhaps one after another the hospitals of Europe . . . a Boston jury would hardly permit the winds of Heaven to visit them too roughly." In contrast, Davies contended, Hawks's "opportunities" were more limited.[47]

While "persons of loftier standing" than Hawks might be "a little more adventurous," "it behoove[d] such humble individuals as himself to be cautious and circumspect in their conduct . . . [and] not to perform experiments at random." In Boston, Davies declared, they were less cautious. Warren and his colleagues had argued that Hawks and Faxon should have used mechanical means to treat the dislocation. Davies lampooned the scene in Boston as Warren prepared to treat Lowell. "The rising usefulness of this grand institution [Massachusetts General] was about to be attested by a decisive achievement—and a day of glory was about to dawn upon Massachusetts General Hospital." Davies described how Warren had administered powerful cathartics and nauseating doses of antimony and had bled Lowell as freely as possible.[48]

Davies compared Warren's use of a pulley on Lowell to seventeenth-century torture. He quoted medical books that discouraged the use of mechanical devices and declared that the treatment was so painful and dangerous that "[t]he wonder is not that the operation was unsuccessful but that the patient survived." Yet, Davies reminded the jury, Hawks and Faxon were being persecuted because they had not used the dread pulley device. Finally, Davies asked the jurors to consider the impact of a guilty verdict on the community since Hawks and Faxon were the only physicians in their respective villages, demanding, "What is the consequence of a limb like Lowell's . . . compared with the usefulness of such a physician as Dr. Hawks, entirely lost to the present scene from his practice?"[49]

After Davies finished his argument, Judge Nathan Weston instructed the jury on the applicable law. Accepting Davies' description of the legal responsibilities of surgeons, Weston declared:

> It is not to be expected of a Surgeon or a Physician in a country or obscure village, that he will possess the skill of a surgeon in the city of London, or any large city—this would be unreasonable to expect . . . all that is required is ordinary skill according to the general state of medical science in the section of the country in which he lives.

Judge Weston was clearly partisan. He said that he did not think the leg had ever been dislocated. While he believed the Boston physicians "spoke with too much certainty," he knew of no reason why the jurors should not believe the witnesses for the defense. The Boston physicians had testified that Hawks and Faxon should have used a pulley. Weston followed the defense attorney's lead and suggested that mechanical devices might be dangerous. But, according to Weston, even if the pulleys were the most appropriate treatment, "it did not appear that anything of the kind could be had" in Lubec.[50]

The jury could not decide on a verdict, and Judge Weston convinced Lowell to drop the malpractice charge permanently. Lowell later felt that he had been coerced and published a twenty-nine-page pamphlet exposing "the official conduct of Judge Weston and the candor and intelligence of the Jurors of this county." In addition a 117-page account by a friend of the accused physician and a 142-page report by Warren were published.[51] The volume of literature on this case far exceeded the literature published on any other suit in the century and underlines the rarity of the litigation in this period. Lowell claimed that Weston had "instructed the jury in the most novel and extraordinary way" and that the public "excitement and prejudice was so great that there would be no probability of getting an impartial trial." He forsook any further legal action and lamented that "[the trials] doomed me to a miserable existence, through the residue of my mortal life for every step I take, I am reminded of my now irreparable misfortune."[52]

The Lowell drama generated intense national interest and haunted the central characters for years. The series of trials reportedly cost Lowell $2,000 and left him in financial ruin. Dr. Hawks spent between $2,000 and $3,000 on his defense and labored for years to overcome his debt. Ironically, a postmortem examination of Lowell's injury revealed that all the diagnoses offered at the trial had been wrong. Lowell had indeed suffered a dislocation, but of a character not anticipated by his physicians or Warren and Smith, two of the best medical minds in America.[53]

The suits and their aftermath generated unwanted public attention for Warren and Massachusetts General Hospital. Soon after the publication of the first two pamphlets on the case in 1825 and 1826, Dr. Hawks's hometown newspaper carried a lengthy attack on Warren and the Boston institution. The author speculated that patients of the hospital must be in the "most deplorable of any situation that I can imagine" and added that Warren "must take a high rank among the detestable class of men who pretend to[o] much and know but little."[54]

In response to the pamphlets and the subsequent attacks, Warren followed with his own account in 1826. Although his testimony seemed unequivocally to favor Lowell's contention that Hawks and Faxon had acted incompetently, Warren claimed that his evidence and actions thoughout the trial had been badly misconstrued. He complained that the publications had brought discredit and ridicule upon himself, his colleagues, and his institution. One of the pamphlets contained the defense attorney's mocking description of the hospital and Warren's treatment. After praising the credentials of the institution and its physicians, Warren asked: "Are the names of such persons proper subjects for the jeers of a lawyer, to be thrown out in a court of justice, and afterwards distributed through the community?"[55] While some observers had accused Warren of causing the suit, he argued that "nothing could be further from the truth." From the beginning, he explained, he had informed Lowell that it was a difficult injury. He recalled telling Lowell that the first physicians had done the best they could and that there were many aspects of medical practice that laymen did not understand. Warren claimed that he had discouraged the suit, told Lowell that a victory in court was unlikely, and then refused to testify. He ultimately had provided a deposition only because he believed that the law required his testimony. Finally, Warren explained that many of his more damaging statements against the defendants had been made before he realized that a suit was underway and were later added to his official statement.[56]

The *Lowell* case was an anomaly for its time, but it foreshadowed the imminent onslaught of suits and helps illustrate some of the factors that would instigate future litigation. By 1824 the social, religious, and political assumptions of colonial society were well on their way to being destroyed. Early America had been characterized by the existence of organic communities in which individuals were bound together by common interests and dependency relationships. The good of the community was often placed above the good of the individual, and stability and consensus were the order of the day. Most communities were small, and emigration was relatively rare. Local issues remained local. Since relationships among citizens were intimate, mediation of disputes through community opinion was both possible and necessary. Stability and order were maintained by a network of hierarchical and familial relationships that emphasized deference and compromise over conflict. These orderly, closed, communal relationships began to break down under the stresses of economic development, emigration, and the growth of egalitarian ideas, especially after 1776.

Although social upheaval and fragmentation of communal structures continued unabated after the American Revolution, a decisive break with colonial structures did not occur until the second third of the nineteenth century.[57] Therefore, remnants of many colonial assumptions, though dramatically undermined, persisted into the period embracing the 1824 *Lowell* lawsuit. Several factors in this unusual and transitional case anticipated the foundations of increased malpractice prosecutions later in the century.

Judge Weston had charged the *Lowell* jury that a physician practicing in an "obscure village" was not required to possess the same degree of medical knowledge as a practitioner in a large city. The jury was asked to compute a physician's acceptable degree of skill according to the state of local medical practice. This doctrine, which became known as the *locality rule* in the latter part of the century, reflected the condition of both the medical profession and the nation in the first part of the nineteenth century.[58] Rural practitioners were usually isolated from urban centers of medical progress, and in 1824 there were few medical schools and journals to disseminate knowledge on a national scale. When juries judged physicians by local standards, they expressed the more general commitment to localism and antiurbanism of the period. Davies, Hawks's attorney, manipulated this strain of local pride in his description of the elite Boston physicians who testified for the prosecution. He also argued that malpractice suits were difficult and uncommon partially because "the work of the physician is all tentative and experimental; it is all as it were underwater."[59] Unfortunately, these sentiments could also work against medical advancement and proper care by putting a low premium on superior skill, protecting incompetent physicians, and discouraging suits. The arguments and result of the Lowell case reflected the country's diverse medical culture and were an explicit legal toleration of lower medical standards.

Three decades later, at midcentury, both the country and the medical profession looked quite different. The assumptions of the judge, defense attorney, and jury were no longer as obviously applicable. Much of the public was willing to hold physicians to a higher standard of accountability after 1835. Physicians' performances were seldom measured against only the standard of care in their own community. Thus, in 1860 Stephen Smith, one of the patriarchs of nineteenth-century American medicine, argued that while it may have once been proper to gauge the amount of skill required by physicians by the locality in which they lived, it would be "manifestly dangerous" to accept the practice. It was ludicrous, Smith declared, for a physician to plead ignorance of generally recognized knowledge "in our time when communication is so rapid, and books and periodicals are abundant and cheap."[60] Reality, however, did not match perception. While medical care had improved nearly everywhere by midcentury, it had not developed uniformly. Physicians' and patients' inflated expectations in the wake of medical advancements between 1820 and 1840 contributed to dissatisfaction with medical treatment and undermined the development of realistic standards of care.

The defense attorney also warned the jury that a guilty verdict would hurt more than just the physician. Medical practitioners were crucial members of society. "The consequences [of a verdict] extend therefore to the community, which is hardly less interested in the result." The attorney urged the jury to consider "What is the consequence of a limb like Lowell's . . . compared with the usefulness of such a physician as Dr. Hawks, entirely lost to the present scene from his practice?" He argued that though their natural sympathy may be with the injured parties, the physician's importance should also be weighed. The lawyer exhorted the jury to "[r]ise then above the influence of prejudice, and restore him [the physician] to society."[61]

Both Hawks and Faxon were the only physicians in their respective communities, and the prospect of their loss following a successful malpractice prosecution undoubtedly influenced the jury's decision. Lowell, in fact, had charged that jurors from Hawks's community had consistently protected him. Lowell lived in Lubec, Hawks in Eastport. The towns were in the same county, and jurors were drawn from both communities. At the first trial the one Eastport juror held out eight hours after the other eleven men had decided in Lowell's favor. In the second trial three Eastport men held out against the others and forced the trial judge to decide the case. He awarded Lowell the much reduced sum of $100. Lowell and his attorney claimed that community leaders from Eastport had talked to the jurors from that town and convinced them to vote in favor of their sole local physician.[62] In the early years of the nineteenth century physicians were scarce in rural areas.[63] As physicians became significantly more plentiful later in the century, however, patients, juries, and judges could afford to charge and convict malpractice defendants without the fear that the community would be left without a medical man.

Finally, the *Lowell* case illustrated that the decision to sue a physician also depended on complex cultural preconditions. Lowell's terse apologia affirming the religious necessity of accepting adversity by "kissing the rod and him who hath anointed it" suggests that much of society still believed that misfortune emanated from the hand of God rather than from the irresponsible actions of humans.[64] The proper response to an act of God was humble acceptance, not a lawsuit. As religious beliefs concerning divine providence evolved, victims of misfortune were freed to search for temporal causes and blame human actors.[65] Hawks's attorney had observed, "It is not a very commendable sight anymore than very customary sight to see a patient prosecuting his physician. It is rather doubtful whether the intensity of moral obligation can be increased in such a case by legal action."[66] Davies contended, rather, that "public judgment" was the "proper tribunal to regulate this species of responsibility."

In the closed, parochial communities of the late eighteenth and early nineteenth centuries Davies was probably correct. For example, Ephraim McDowell became legendary for performing the first ovariotomy in 1809. His small, backwoods community of Danville, Kentucky, however, vehemently opposed the historic operation. Local physicians, including his nephew and partner, questioned McDowell's judgment and morality. Ministers attacked him from their pulpits. While McDowell operated, an angry mob waited outside, not with lawyers and writs, but with a rope swung over a tree. At one point the indignant crowd attempted to burst into the patient's home to stop the surgery.[67] This type of communal enforcement was common in the small, cohesive settlements of early America. Citizens often relied on extralegal remedies, coercion, group action, and moral suasion in various areas of public life. Davies, Hawks's attorney, appealed to this tradition when he declared that "legal action" was not appropriate "in such a case." These attitudes may have limited the public acceptance of suing physicians well into the 1830s, and even later in some areas of the country. As social, economic, and geographic mobility began to destroy the basis of communal "public judgment," however, disgruntled patients were more likely to turn to courts for satisfaction.

By the 1840s episodes like the *Lowell* case were common, and medical men felt they were in the midst of an unprecedented malpractice epidemic. Suits disrupted professional relations, injured individual reputations, and burdened physicians with legal fees and damage awards. The unorganized medical profession of the first half of the nineteenth century was unable to devise an appropriate response to this new threat. Malpractice law was in a state of flux and sensitive to various social pressures. Judges and lawyers relied on English precedents with minor alterations, but the resulting changes in legal doctrine were not responsible for the sudden outbreak of suits.

American patients began to sue their physicians on a wide scale because of specific social, medical, and technological developments in the first half of the nineteenth century. The antistatus, antiprofessional sentiment of the Jacksonian period increasingly turned the lay public against orthodox, trained practitioners. In addition, Americans, with a long tradition of self-cure, home remedy, and folk healing, had little patience with doctors who demanded deference and privilege but offered few cures. Physicians' authority and public respect also declined as a parade of alternative medical practitioners offered their services to antebellum Americans. Physicians exacerbated their own descent in esteem and contributed to the litigious trend. As medical men of all types became more plentiful in the 1830s and 1840s, intraprofessional competition generated conflict, and many medical men incited suits against fellow practitioners. Dramatic advances in several areas of medicine created unrealistic expectations in both physicians and patients and blurred standards of care.

These immediate causes, however, would not have engendered widespread suits without concurrent fundamental cultural changes. Many Americans decisively changed their views on divine providence in the first half of the nineteenth century. This transformation allowed individuals to seek earthly causes for their misfortunes, assign blame, and demand compensation. At the same time, a variety of forces combined to make Americans dramatically more concerned with physical well-being and significantly more confident that they could do something about it. Finally, the erosion of traditional community customs inhibiting litigation and a transformation in individualism allowed patients to attack their physicians in court more frequently. These changes in the larger culture did not cause malpractice suits, but without them widespread litigation would not have been possible.

The patterns set in the first half of the century continued through 1900. Many of the inciting causes of the 1840s disappeared, but new technological, social, professional, and legal factors arose to take their place. More importantly, the underlying cultural trends that made the suits possible continued to develop and provided an increasingly hospitable social environment for malpractice suits.

CHAPTER 2

The Deluge,
1835-1865

In 1844 a writer for the *Boston Medical and Surgical Journal* warned that qualified physicians were "constantly liable to vexatious suits instituted by ignorant and unprincipled persons."[1] In 1853 the *Western Journal of Medical and Physical Sciences* reported that malpractice suits "occur almost every month in the year and everywhere in our country."[2] These writers were not exaggerating, and their suspicions and fears were well-founded. They and their contemporaries were witnessing the first symptoms of a professional disease that would plague the medical community for the next 150 years.

Although medical malpractice suits were virtually nonexistent between 1790 and 1835, thereafter patients suddenly began to sue their physicians at an increasing and unprecedented rate. As early as the 1840s the frequency of suits in some parts of the country had filled doctors with a mixture of anger, panic, and confusion. The suits and the alarm increased as the decades passed. Frank Hamilton, a New York physician, claimed that between 1833 and 1856 "suits for malpractice were so very frequent in the Northern states" that many men "abandoned the practice of surgery, leaving it to those who, with less skill and experience, had less reputation and property to lose."[3] By 1860 John Elwell, a physician and a lawyer who wrote a book on the subject, could claim that "[t]here can hardly be found a place in the country, where the oldest physicians in it have not, at some periods in their lives, been actually sued or annoyingly threatened."[4]

The rate of prosecutions in this period was probably not as great as in comparable periods later in the century, and certainly not as intense as in the twentieth century, but the initial explosion of litigation in the 1840s represented a basic, fateful, and irrevocable shift in attitudes toward the practice. While a variety of technological, intraprofessional, economic, and social changes would push litigation rates to soaring heights over the next century and a half, the profession and the country crossed over the critical threshold in the 1840s and 1850s.

"An Incubus upon the Profession"

Every available indicator suggested that the doctor-patient relationship was entering a dramatic new phase. Of the 216 reported appellate malpractice decisions in the nineteenth century, only 5 had occurred before 1835. In contrast, state supreme courts ruled on 42 malpractice cases between 1835 and 1870, 45 cases from 1870 to 1880, and 47 cases from 1880 to 1890.[5] The period between 1835 and 1870 also marked the first time that the increase in appellate malpractice decisions outran the increase in the nation's population. State supreme courts continued to rule on malpractice cases at a rate faster than that of the growth of the population through the twentieth century. Although the numbers of appellate cases represented only a small fraction of the total number of actual prosecutions, they underscore the sudden prevalence of the practice after 1835.

Similarly, medical journals printed hundreds of accounts and comments on malpractice cases between 1835 and 1865. The editorials, rare in the first third of the century, reflected the novelty and intensity of the phenomenon. As Alden March, a prominent New York physician, reported in an 1847 issue of the *Boston Medical and Surgical Journal*, "Legal prosecutions for mal-practice occur so often that even a respectable surgeon may well fear the results of his surgical practice."[6] A writer for the *Medical Examiner* in 1851 lamented that "[m]ischievous prosecutions for some years have alarmed medical gentlemen in various parts of the country to such a degree that many have concluded to let all surgical patients go unassisted in their afflictions."[7] Worthington Hooker, the Connecticut doctor who wrote the influential *Physician and*

Patient in the 1840s, declared that "the professional reputation of medical men seems to be considered by common consent as fair game for the shafts of all, whether high or low, learned or unlearned. Although the charge of mal-practice is a serious charge . . . it is exceedingly common to hear this charge put forth without any hesitation."[8]

Observers believed that the new and dangerous trend began in western New York in the late 1830s and early 1840s and quickly spread both east and west. A writer for the *Boston Medical and Surgical Journal* noted in 1847 that the malpractice "fever" first became popular in western New York "a few years since," and then spread through other eastern states, into Vermont, and even into Canada.[9] Frank Hamilton told the 1843 graduating class of Geneva Medical College that he knew of over twenty malpractice prosecutions against "respectable and eminent" New York state surgeons in 1840 and 1841 alone.[10]

These commentators were probably correct. New York accounted for the lion's share of the publicized cases in the 1840s. One 1839 New York case gained national attention and opened a widespread debate in the pages of the major medical journals. When one of the medical witnesses in the trial was subjected to a retaliatory suit two years later, a commentator warned that western New York was the country's hotbed of medical malpractice.[11] In 1844 Dr. James White of Erie County, New York, treated William Tims, who had suffered an oblique fracture of his thigh bone after falling from the roof of a railway depot. When Tims's limb healed, it was crooked and had a bony protuberance at the point of the injury. He sued White for malpractice but the jury refused to reach a verdict. Tims sued White again the next year with the same result. Finally, in 1848 a jury decided the case in favor of the physician. During the trial, Dr. Trowbridge of Buffalo, who served as one of the medical witnesses, testified that while he had never been sued, the frequency of malpractice prosecutions in the state had driven him from practice. The editor of the *Buffalo Medical Journal* congratulated Trowbridge for his "timely and judicious course in laying down the scalpel" and reported that "in this city [Buffalo] there are but a few surgeons of years or reputation in the profession, who have not been latterly crowned with the accompanying honors of a public prosecution for malpractice."[12]

When Adolphus Gates, a German laborer in Buffalo, was awarded $600 after his fractured wrist healed in a frozen position, an editorialist in the same journal wrote in the early 1850s that "the whole system of trials for malpractice is so radically wrong that the defendant must be mulcted in every case where he is not sustained by the entire professional evidence." According to the author:

evidence of a single man, contradicting all surgical experience, and evidently based on an egregious error in diagnosis, outweighed the opinions of older and better surgeons, and subjected a poor, hard-working and intelligent practitioner to a judgment and costs heavy enough to sweep away the greater portion of the small earnings of many years.[13]

New York physicians became more preoccupied by the phenomenon as the suits multiplied. In 1853 a reviewer for the *New York Journal of Medicine* barely mentioned the two books he was ostensibly reviewing and used the occasion to rail against malpractice litigation in the state. "The disposition to institute legal proceedings against the surgeon for the treatment of fractures has become so strong, that prosecutions have been made where there was not the slightest ground for complaint." "And," he observed, "this spirit of persecution is stimulated and more widely disseminated on every repetition of these trials."[14] In less than fifteen years, from 1839 to 1853, malpractice suits in New York went from being rare and unimportant to being common and a major concern to all New York physicians.[15]

New York may have been the apparent source of the malpractice "fever" in the 1840s, but the disease did not spread to other states by imitation alone. While patients and physicians in other regions may have been aware of the growing malpractice epidemic in 1840s New York, the practice could not have spread to other states unless the complex of social and professional factors that favored its existence were already present.[16] Intraprofessional rivalry, numerous medical sects, and low public esteem fueled by particularly strong Jacksonian sentiment made doctors in New York somewhat more vulnerable than their colleagues in other states. These factors and others, albeit in slightly diminished intensity, quickly provided the environment necessary for the more frequent prosecution of physicians in other states.

By 1850 suits began to appear at an increasing rate in western states such as Ohio. Several malpractice cases surfaced in the state in the

1830s but the prosecutions did not alarm the profession until midcentury.[17] The appearance of suits in some counties for the first time in the late 1840s heightened physicians' fear. Washington County, Ohio, reported its first malpractice case in 1849, when a patient asked for $10,000 in damages after his thigh fracture resulted in a shortened limb (he received only $200). According to the *Western Lancet*, Meigs County, Ohio, suffered its first malpractice suit in 1850.[18] During one week in 1855, four cases were tried in four separate Ohio counties. The same year, the Ohio Medical Society created a committee to investigate the sudden onslaught of suits in the state. The committee published accounts of seven cases and called the phenomenon "a standing and cumulative evil bearing with the weight of an incubus upon the profession."[19] The *Ohio Medical and Surgical Journal* published numerous such accounts between 1850 and 1865, and as in New York, doctors reportedly left the profession because of the frequency of lawsuits. One editorialist claimed in 1861 that "from first to last there have been over 200 prosecutions in Ohio."[20] While many counties in the state had recorded their first suits as late as 1850, lawsuits were common enough to be considered a major threat as early as a decade later.

Within ten years of the first outbreak of malpractice suits in 1840s New York, other eastern physicians began to complain of the malady. William Wood, a Pennsylvania physician, warned in 1849 that "the principles of law, intended for the protection of the community, are perverted into powerful instruments of wrong and injustice." Echoing the claims of observers in New York and Ohio, Wood reported that "[s]ome of the most competent young men are driven off, and such as remain refuse to take the responsibility of surgical cases." To illustrate the situation in Pennsylvania, Wood chronicled the plight of Charles Brandes, a young German physician who set up practice in the late 1840s. Almost immediately he was plagued by malpractice suits and threats of suits. He was charged twice for the improper vaccination of patients and once for the unskillful treatment of a thigh fracture.[21] Like those in Ohio, local Pennsylvania medical societies established committees to investigate this new threat to the profession.[22] The malpractice litigation phenomenon reached even such isolated states as New Hampshire and Vermont. Dixi Crosby, a prominent Vermont physician, was sued for $5,000 after offering advice to another physician on a thigh fracture in 1853. After the jury awarded the patient $800 in damages, a judge exclaimed that in Vermont "a man had better be in any other profession than in the medical."[23]

The experience of physicians in Massachusetts more than anywhere else demonstrates the timing, rapidity, and amplitude of the initial increase in malpractice litigation. A medical writer commenting on an 1842 Vermont malpractice case regretted that the defendant "could not have had a hearing before an enlightened jury of Massachusetts, where his high attainments in medicine and surgery would have been appreciated."[24] This writer believed that Massachusetts was not fruitful ground for the widespread prosecution of physicians. Through most of the 1840s this judgment appeared sound, and there were few lawsuits. As late as 1847, the *Boston Medical and Surgical Journal* could confidently assert: "Here in Massachusetts the trick has been attempted on a small scale two or three times, but the result has not been sufficiently encouraging to induce many to embark on it." The writer believed that "there happens to be too much intelligence here, for such depradators to succeed."[25]

The medical journalist's optimistic certainty that Massachusetts was immune to the "mania" that was sweeping the Northeast was unfounded and short-lived. By 1853 the tone of the Massachusetts medical commentators had changed from sympathy for their colleagues in other states to concern for their own professional safety. After a spate of cases in the state, the *Boston Medical and Surgical Journal* warned that "[e]very surgeon in the community is liable to a lawsuit for damages." Even more ominously, the journal observed that "[j]uries appear to have been particularly sympathizing with plaintiffs."[26] In 1853 another writer declared: "A fresh disposition to prosecute physicians for alledged [sic] malpractice is manifest in Massachusetts. It is becoming a hazardous enterprise to give surgical assistance in this ancient Commonwealth. It is even worse in some respects, than in western New York or Vermont."[27] A flood of suits struck the state as suddenly and dramatically as it had in other areas of the country. Between 1850 and 1856, for example, there were five malpractice suits in Middlesex County alone.[28]

By the mid-1850s Massachusetts physicians, like those in New

TABLE 2
Sample Malpractice Cases, 1835–1865

Type	Example
fracture	*BufMJMR* 4 (August 1848):131–54
hernia	*StLMSJ* 3 (May 1846):529–63
amputation	28 Me. 97 (1847)
laceration	*NWMSJ* 5 (1848–1849):536–46
abandonment	*MNL* 6 (May 1848):60
obstetric	*OMSJ* 2 (September 1849):6–10
dislocation	*WL* 11 (1850):763–68
vaccination	*AJMS* 22 (July 1851):43–50
calomel	*WJMPS* 24 (1851):168–70
aneurism	*BMSJ* 35 (12 August 1846):43–45
patent medicine	OMSJ 6 (November 1853):182
death	12 *Howard* 323 (1855)
bleeding	Elwell, *Treatise*, (1857), 142–62
misdiagnosis	21 *Tx.* 111 (1858)
chloroform	Smith, *Doctor in Medicine* (ca. 1860), 277–78
ocular	*BMSJ* 32 (2 April 1845):185
tonsils	*BMSJ* 28 (15 February 1843):29–33

York, Ohio, Pennsylvania, Vermont, and New Hampshire, were being sued in all parts of the state. In fact, malpractice charges had become a recognizable and urgent problem throughout the North, even though they remained rare in the South.[29] The actual number of lawsuits between 1835 and 1865 is impossible to determine without a courthouse-to-courthouse search of every state. It is clear, however, from appellate court reports, medical journals, and contemporary commentaries that these years represented a fundamentally new era in the history of medical malpractice.

The types of treatment that engendered lawsuits between 1835 and 1865 also broke with the patterns of the past. As noted earlier, in the first third of the nineteenth century malpractice cases typically involved severe deformity, vaccination, or obstetrics; less severe injuries seldom led to lawsuits. After 1840, however, patients began to charge physicians for malpractice involving a wider range of treatments (see table 2).

In addition, patients regularly sued physicians for less severe injuries than they had before 1835. For example, in 1839 a New York man
sued his physicians when his badly fractured leg healed, but was 1¼
inches shorter than his other limb.[30] In an 1843 case, John Basset of
Independence, New York, injured his thigh when his wagon overturned and crushed his leg. Two weeks after the accident, doctors
John Collins and Anthony Barney examined Basset and after noting
his shortened leg and out-turned toes, decided that the injury was a
dislocated hip. They used ropes and pulleys to adjust the hip to its
proper position. When the physicians heard the characteristic "pop"
that generally accompanied the relocation of bones and the leg was
restored to its natural length, they dismissed Basset as cured. Within a
year his leg was shortened 1½ inches, and he charged the physicians
with malpractice. After two trials and four years a jury decided in
favor of Collins and Barney.[31] Dixi Crosby was sued and fined $800
for providing consultation in a fracture case in which the patient's
injured leg lost a quarter of an inch in length.[32] Although these disfig-
urements may have been traumatic for the individuals involved, the
cases were significantly less serious than the typical case in the first
third of the century.

The increased variety in the types of cases brought to trial after
1835 and patients' marked tendency to sue for significantly less severe
injuries were both products of a transformed attitude toward malpractice. The increased willingness of individuals to sue and society's
accompanying acceptance of the practice encouraged litigation of all
types. Unrealistic public and professional expectations, born of technical advancement, particularly in fracture treatment, helped fuel the
trend.[33] Before 1835, when personal and public reservations concerning malpractice prosecutions dampened the flow of cases through the
courts, injuries and complaints generally had to be serious enough to
overcome traditional doubts about the practice. Therefore, death and
amputation cases dominate the small sample of early suits. As personal
doubt and public disapprobation regarding the litigation dissipated,
patients felt justified in suing physicians for injuries that resulted in
minor deformities, pain, or even inconveniences.

After 1835 deformities following fractures and dislocations suddenly became the major source of malpractice prosecutions. In his

1860 *Treatise on Medical Malpractice* John Elwell claimed that "nine-tenths of all the cases of malpractice that come before the courts for adjudication arise either from the treatment of amputations, fractures, or dislocations."[34] Although Elwell was correct in noting the predominance of fracture-dislocation cases, his estimated proportion was probably inflated. The wide variety of suits prosecuted after 1835 make it unlikely that fracture-dislocation-amputation cases could account for 90 percent of the total. Elwell also misled his audience by combining amputation cases with fractures and dislocations. Suits involving amputations were rare after 1835, and lumping them together with other orthopedic injuries masked their insignificant contribution to the total number of cases. Stephen Smith, also writing in 1860, countered Elwell's claim by using statistics that he had gathered from "several hundred suits for malpractice." He argued that 142, or a "little over two-thirds" of the cases he studied, grew out of amputations, fractures, and dislocations. Of these 142 suits, only 8, or about 4 percent, of the approximately 213 in his study originated from amputations, while 102 suits grew out of fractures, and 32 suits stemmed from dislocations.[35]

Smith's figures are in general agreement with the distribution of suits and the rate at which they were reported in contemporary medical literature. Fracture-dislocation cases accounted for about two-thirds of the malpractice cases between 1835 and 1865, with the rest of the suits represented by the causes listed in table 2. While fracture-dislocation cases did not account for 90 percent of the litigation as Elwell had claimed, they did constitute a majority of the suits in the nineteenth century. The particular propensity to sue physicians for the maltreatment of fractures and dislocations aggravated an atmosphere that was already conducive to widespread litigation and played a role in making the initial increase in suits more profound. Suits were, for a variety of reasons, becoming more socially and morally acceptable by the middle of the century. Because individuals did not feel the same compulsion to justify their actions to themselves and their community, they were freer to demand monetary remuneration even when their injuries were relatively minor, as in the type of results that often followed fracture treatment. Therefore, the general tendency to sue physicians after 1835 and the new found inclination to sue for fracture type-injuries interacted and pushed the climbing malpractice rates higher.[36]

"Shocking Outrage[s] on Professional Humanity"

Most patients, of course, chose not to sue their physicians. At the same time, many incompetent doctors escaped guilty verdicts and even prosecution. While innocent physicians were sometimes sued for minor or fabricated injuries during the first half of the century, a variety of legal rules and procedures protected ignorant and careless medical men from the grasp of justice. John Ordronaux, a frequent midcentury commentator on medical-legal issues, confirmed that "strange as it may seem, one might, through unskillfulness, sacrifice a human life with more impunity than he could mutilate or deform a toe or a finger."[37]

When patients died, it was particularly difficult to sustain a suit against the offending physician. The wronged patient could not present himself or herself to the jury as was possible in fractures and other visible injuries. Rarely was the actual cause of death readily apparent or easily demonstrable. And, as Ordronaux explained, "who would presume to say, in the case of a patient's death, that he had not naturally reached that 'last illness' foreordained to all men and of which the physician's unsuccessful treatment is the only official testimony?"[38]

Medical journals commonly chronicled egregious episodes of medical incompetence. In 1850 the parents of a young girl who was suffering from a tumor on her arm sought the advice of the most distinguished physicians available. The physicians agreed that the growth was malignant and, because it intertwined with major blood vessels, could not be removed without amputating the limb. The parents consulted a less respected, less experienced physician, who agreed to excise the tumor and save the arm. During the operation, performed in a dimly lit room, no tourniquet was employed and no pressure applied to stop the flow of blood. The doctor clumsily cut into the growth instead of removing it whole. To stop the "frightful" bleeding, the physician tied off the main artery and large veins and "bandage[d] the arm tightly from the fingers up." According to one editorialist,

"This extraordinary and unheard of proceeding, was well calculated to insure [sic] the fatal result that followed." Despite breaking several rules of established practice, the surgeon apparently escaped legal action.[39]

Physicians at respected institutions also committed "shocking outrage[s] on professional humanity." In the mid-1850s doctors at the New York Academy of Medicine and Bellevue Hospital experimented with the injection of silver nitrate into the trachea and lungs to cure bronchitis, tubercular symptoms, and other pulmonary maladies. The treatment, performed primarily on charity patients, resulted in suffering and death within a few days. *Scalpel*, a New York medical journal, alerted the district attorney to the "utterly absurd, and highly reprehensible" procedures, and pleaded with its readers to "forever guard our public charities against such cruel experiments."[40]

One of the most grotesque episodes of medical incompetence occurred in the late 1860s. A physician struggling with a difficult birth prescribed ergot to a woman to induce contractions and the expulsion of her child. The drug did not help, and during the protracted labor the woman's uterus ruptured. The physician dissected the fetus to save the patient's life, but the severed head escaped the uterus into the abdominal cavity. The doctor frantically removed the fetus and afterbirth to relieve the patient. The attending midwife suddenly noticed adult intestines intertwined with the removed placenta and infant body parts. When the physician realized his error, he told the patient that "if she had anything to say she had better say it." She asked for her minister and died several hours later. Despite the gross incompetence of the physician, he never faced a malpractice jury. The woman's husband accepted $300 in lieu of litigation.[41]

The nineteenth-century common law doctrine and statutes governing wrongful death made it difficult to convict a physician for the death of a patient. When a person died under a physician's care, the doctor might theoretically be charged under criminal or civil law. *Criminal charges* generally refer to offenses against the public, while *civil charges* pertain to private wrongs. Criminal charges were nearly impossible to sustain against physicians. The patient's consent to the fatal treatment virtually eliminated the chance of a murder or manslaughter conviction.

The most important precedent for manslaughter charges against a physician was the 1809 Massachusetts case of *Commonwealth* v. *Samuel Thomson*. Thomson, the founder of the immensely popular Thomsonian medical sect, was called to the home of Ezra Lovett, a young man who had been confined to his bed for several days with a severe cold. Thomson wrapped Lovett in hot blankets and gave him dose after dose of powerful emetics, which induced violent vomiting. In addition, Thomson supplied his patient with a concoction that induced profuse sweating. Thomson prescribed dozens of emetic and sweating procedures over several days. When the emetics ceased to work, Thomson administered a cathartic (laxative) concoction, and Lovett went into convulsions—at which point Thomson's assistants held the thrashing Lovett so that Thomson could administer yet another emetic dose. After three days of almost constant convulsions, Lovett died.

Acting on reports that several of Thomson's patients had died after severe treatments, the Massachusetts attorney general brought murder charges against the practitioner. The chief judge of the state supreme court acknowledged that it was clear that Lovett had died as a result of Thomson's treatment, but he explained that that charge of murder required that "the killing must have been done with malice, either express or implied." He held that there was no evidence that suggested that Thomson intended to kill or injure his patient. The judges on the court also ruled that Thomson could be convicted of manslaughter only if the death had been the result of an unlawful act or "gross negligence." If a physician "acted with the honest intention and expectation of curing the deceased," he could not be found guilty of manslaughter. *Commonwealth* v. *Thomson* served as the shield that protected even ignorant physicians from criminal prosecution for much of the century. Defense attorneys could argue that almost any form of treatment was performed with the honest intention of curing.[42]

Similarly, the nineteenth-century doctrine of *wrongful death*, a civil offense, also tended to benefit medical men whose treatment resulted in the death of their patients. In the English common law of the seventeenth century, under the doctrine of *acti personalis moritur cum persona*, a claim for personal injury could not survive the death of the victim. In other words, the deceased's family could not sue for damages inflicted while the victim was still alive. When a person died as a result of injuries, it was considered a felony, and the family of the victim received a proportion of the perpetrator's property. Since the criminal law provided an award for the victim's family, the common law allowed no other remedy for wrongful death. Death was a public, not a private wrong. This doctrine forbade noncriminal awards for wrongful death long after the practice of confiscating the convicted felon's property was abolished. Even though the original justification for the rule had disappeared, an English court in *Baker* v. *Bolton* (1808) reaffirmed the doctrine that the death of a human being was not grounds for legal action for monetary damages.[43]

In several early decisions it appeared as if American courts would not accept the English rule.[44] Even after the 1808 *Baker* v. *Bolton* decision, which explicitly overruled wrongful death actions, some American courts in the early nineteenth century allowed nonfelon suits for wrongful death damages. American judges argued that the original justification for the doctrine was superannuated and had no place in American law.[45] The new environment and an informal sense of justice temporarily prevailed over formal doctrine.

In the first half of the nineteenth century the industrial revolution swept across the eastern seaboard, leaving a wide variety of unnatural deaths in its wake. Innovations in manufacturing and transportation generated a revolution in the scale and gruesomeness of accidental injury. Fatal railroad and steamboat accidents were common. The development of these industries would be severely hampered by frequent and costly wrongful death claims. State judges who in effect favored the expansion of industrial capitalism devised a variety of doctrinal innovations and adjustments that limited the personal injury liability of these enterprises. For example, between 1842 and 1850 Massachusetts Chief Justice Lemuel Shaw transformed the nature of legal liability by championing the *fellow servant rule, contributory negligence,* and *assumption of risk.* In addition he shifted the notion of legal responsibility from strict liability to no liability without fault. These modifications benefitted venture capitalism and decreased the likelihood of personal awards by requiring a higher degree of proof from injured parties.[46]

In the same spirit, Shaw's court in the landmark *Carey* v. *Berkshire R.R.* (1848) ignored three decades of American precedent, cited the

English *Baker* v. *Bolton* case, and ruled that there was not, and never had been, a common law action for wrongful death. Appellate courts after 1848 followed the *Carey* decision's lead and began to deny families of accident victims the right to sue for damages. In railroad law, it was cheaper to kill than to injure. To remedy this omission, from 1840 to 1887, numerous state legislatures passed laws allowing wrongful death actions against common carriers such as railroads and steamboats. Although these statutes in many cases were written to remedy the specific problem of railroad death, many contained wording that seemed to support other kinds of death actions.[47]

In cases involving physicians, trial court judges sometimes allowed juries to use the new statutes to award damages to the families of dead patients. In June 1863 Albert Braunberger was working at a tannery in Pittsburgh, Pennsylvania. His leg "came into contact" with the machine he was working on and an exposed piston shaft about two inches in diameter crushed the limb below the knee. Braunberger crawled twenty feet from the engine to the door and called for a fellow workman. Dr. George Cleis examined Braunberger at home, declared that the injury was "only a flesh wound," sewed up the gash, and told the man's family that he would soon be back to work. Braunberger maintained that his leg was badly broken.

After seven days Braunberger developed a severe fever, his abdomen became distended, and his leg began to swell and discharge profuse and offensive matter from the wound. The injured man asked for another physician. When the second doctor arrived, the odor in the room forced him to cover his face with a handkerchief. He removed the stitches and surveyed the injury. The muscles below the knee were "lacerated and broken," those of the thigh separated from the bone. The bones of the knee and lower leg, according to his account, "were not simply broken, they were absolutely ground." The physician declared that the rule of practice of "every intelligent civil and military surgeon" would have been to amputate the leg immediately after the accident and not sew up the wound. A team of physicians attempted to nurse Braunberger back to health and to amputate his mangled leg, but he died nine days after the accident.[48]

Braunberger's wife sued Cleis for wrongful death for ignorantly sewing up the wound, misdiagnosing the obvious injury, and failing to amputate the leg at the proper and customary time. Her attorney argued that these actions had led to Braunberger's death. The trial court judge explained to the jury that the law required physicians to exercise a "reasonable degree of care and skill in the treatment of this patient." He held that though there had been no common law action for wrongful death, the Pennsylvania legislature had passed a statute declaring that when death was caused by "unlawful violence or negligence," the survivor of the deceased could sue and recover damages for the death. The physician's attorney admitted that the treatment may have constituted malpractice, but argued that "mere malpractice" was not "unlawful violence or negligence as [was] contemplated by the act." Therefore, there should be no award granted for wrongful death. The local trial judge and jury, however, believed that the statute applied to medically induced deaths and awarded Mrs. Braunberger $3,250.[49]

Wrongful death awards for incompetent medical treatment often depended on how trial court judges and juries interpreted the new statutes. In flagrant instances of medical ineptitude or carelessness, local courts sometimes relied on the statutes and a subjective sense of justice to award the victim's family compensation. When defendants appealed to state supreme courts, however, appellate judges, insulated from local pressures, sometimes applied a narrower, more formal interpretation of the statutes and relied on the general notion that there could be no recovery after death, even in the face of flagrant incompetence. Though Cleis apparently did not appeal the verdict, the Michigan case of *Hyatt* v. *Adams* illustrated the unsettled nature of wrongful death law.[50]

In 1865 Lucinda Adams visited Dr. Loften Hyatt complaining of pain in her abdomen. Hyatt diagnosed the pain as a uterine tumor and assured Adams that he could safely remove the growth in half an hour. Hyatt performed the operation in the presence of three women, in the bedroom of the Adams' farmhouse. Using morphine and chloroform, Hyatt struggled for an hour with his hands and forceps to pull the tumor free. Hyatt abandoned the forceps and told the witnesses that he needed some instrument "bent like a fishhook." After in fact attempting to use a large fishhook, the physician bent a large knitting needle into the desired shape and sharpened the end on a grindstone. The futile attempts to remove the tumor lasted several hours over two days. Adams' husband later said that he could hear her screams several acres away. Hyatt declared that he had shredded the tumor sufficiently so that it would pass naturally, but Mrs. Adams died the following day.[51]

Adams sued Hyatt for *loss of consortium*, or the loss of the service, comfort, and society of his wife. He also claimed damages for his and his wife's mental suffering. During the trial, Mrs. Adams' body was exhumed, and an examination revealed that despite the energetic attempts of the physician, the tumor had not been touched. Instead, the operation had injured the woman's pelvic cavity and had resulted in infection, shock, and death. Several physicians testified against Hyatt and his mode of treatment. The Michigan jury deliberated only a short time before granting Adams an award of $2,000 plus $159 in costs.[52]

Hyatt and his lawyers appealed the case to the Michigan supreme court. While the jury was supposed to award Adams damages only for his loss of consortium, it had granted what amounted to death damages. The physician's attorney argued that "at common law the death of a human being cannot be made the ground for legal action." The lawyer concluded that defendants could be held liable only for damages incurred in the interval between injury and death. In this instance, Mrs. Adams lived three days after the initial surgical procedure.[53]

Chief Judge Christiancy, who wrote the majority decision in *Hyatt v. Adams*, observed that while "total want of skill" and a high degree of carelessness could have made Hyatt guilty of manslaughter, he was charged only with depriving Adams of his wife's services and companionship. Any claim that Mrs. Adams had against the physician died when she did. Citing the 1848 *Carey v. Berkshire R.R.* case, Christiancy declared that it "is admitted on all hands, and can not be denied" that at common law there was no civil action for the death of a human being "or for any damages suffered by any person in consequence of such death."[54] The Michigan judge, like other appellate jurists after the *Carey* case ignored the early American decisions that suggested that there was a common law wrongful death action.

Christiancy discusssed at length why he believed that there was no civil law death remedy. Conventional wisdom held that there was no action because under the old common law, relatives were provided for by felony confiscation rules. Christiancy offered a more fundamental explanation. The judge declared that there was a "natural and almost universal repugnance among enlightened nations to setting a price on human life." He argued that Christian people found the notion of compensating loss of life with money revolting. Christiancy admitted that Michigan had passed a wrongful death statute (almost identical to the one in Pennsylvania), but he implied that it was necessary only to meet the demands of "the new modes of travel and business" and could not apply to all forms of death. He believed that it was the role of the appellate courts "to prevent the best and most benevolent feelings of our nature from clouding the judgment of jurors and prompting them to intemperate verdicts in the vain endeavor to give money compensation for that which, in its very nature, is incapable of valuation by any such standard." He warned that the idea of pecuniary compensation for human life would tend to render it less sacred in the public estimation.[55]

Finally, Christiancy condemned the concept of mental anguish of the husband as indeterminate. If a husband could recover for mental suffering, then why not a mother, a friend, or a neighbor? In concluding, Christiancy agreed with Hyatt's attorney and ruled that there could be no award for the death, or for the husband's mental suffering. Adams, however, did deserve to be compensated for the loss of his wife's services and companionship for the three days from the initial surgery to her death. The court determined her service at $.50 day and calculated Hyatt's total legal liability at $1.50.[56]

Suits for the wrongful death of patients were legally and substantively different from other forms of malpractice litigation. These factors undermined attempts to sue physicians in fatal cases through the first two-thirds of the century. Consequently, death suits did not play a significant role in the initial increase of suits against physicians, and many of the worst cases of medical incompetence probably went unpunished.

Dissatisfied Patients
and the "Noble Sister Profession"

When patients received permanent injuries after treatment for fractures or other maladies, different factors precipitated the initial decision to hire a lawyer and begin a lawsuit. Often patients acted on their own without any apparent prodding from friends, lawyers, or other physicians. For example, in the mid-1850s, after an Ohio man suffered a compound fracture of his lower leg, his family summoned a physician who set and wrapped the victim's seriously injured leg. Within days the leg became inflamed and swollen, so the physician removed all the wrappings from the limb. The family, believing that the physician was neglecting the fracture, dismissed the doctor after two weeks. The patient suffered in bed for almost a year. His first action upon leaving his bed on crutches was to visit, and hire, an attorney.[57] In a similar case in 1856, Nathan Varner was riding his sleigh, drunk, about two miles from his home in Zanesville, Ohio. Varner lost control of the horse, fell from the sleigh, and broke his lower leg. When Dr. Thaddeus Reamy was treating the injury, he told Varner that there was almost always shortening after these types of injuries and asked his patient if he was going to sue if the leg did not heal perfectly. Reamy replied that he would be "damned if he wouldn't" and warned that he would make the physician "pay like hell." Varner believed that his patient was joking. He was not, and when his injured leg healed $1\frac{1}{8}$ inch shorter than normal, Reamy found a lawyer and sued the physician for $3,000.[58]

Although there were many instances in which patients began litigation on their own initiative, outside parties and the physician himself often played important roles in the decision to file malpractice charges. When a young New York man's fractured elbow mended but froze in a rigid position in 1845, his friends convinced him to sue for damages; he won an award of $450.[59] In the late 1830s in another New York case members of the community began a subscription drive to raise money to help an injured man sue his doctors.[60]

Some malpractice suits arose out of cross-complaints after a physician sued his patient for fees. Other patients used the threat of malpractice to intimidate physicians into dropping their claims for fees.[61] Patients who were sued by their physicians for nonpayment of fees could effectively use a cross-suit of malpractice because of the loosening of traditional legal pleading rules in the late eighteenth and early nineteenth centuries and the civil procedure reforms of the late 1840s and early 1850s.[62] In 1850 a Kentucky patient refused to pay his medical bill, claiming that the physician had infected his family with smallpox while treating them for typhus. The physician sued for fees, and the patient, on a cross-complaint, sued for malpractice damages.[63] In the 1850s Dr. William Gautier sued Texas slaveholder William Graham for $187.57 in fees for treating ten slaves who died. Gautier had treated the slaves for cholera. Graham, however, claimed that the physician had wrongly diagnosed the slaves and caused their deaths and demanded $10,700 for the costs of the slaves.[64]

Even though disputes over fees surfaced regularly in malpractice cases, reluctance of patients to pay medical bills alone cannot explain the sudden appearance of numerous suits in the 1840s. Patients would have been able to file cross-suits well before 1840. Suits for delinquent medical bills did indeed reflect the general popular antipathy that formed part of the environment responsible for engendering malpractice prosecutions. But disputes over fees provided only the precipitating incident of an occasional suit rather than the cause of the dramatic increase of litigation.

Medical fees became an important issue in the nineteenth-century malpractice debate because they helped characterize the type of patient whom physicians most distrusted. Because so many malpractice plaintiffs had not paid their bills, physicians began to believe that their poorer patients were the most likely to sue. Undoubtedly, many patients refused to pay because they were dissatisfied with their treatment. But, these plaintiffs' poverty was substantiated by the fact that in many cases they could not pay their court costs either. Physicians regularly observed that a disproportionate number of malpractice plaintiffs could afford neither the doctor's bill nor the legal costs of the suits. This "class of persons," physicians argued, constituted the profession's biggest malpractice risk.[65] An 1878 survey of malpractice in Maine discovered that the vast majority of malpractice plaintiffs could not pay court costs.[66] Even if indigent patients constituted a majority of malpractice plaintiffs, they were not the "cause" of the malpractice phenomenon. Physicians treated poor patients before the outbreak of malpractice fever, and the inability to pay bills did not spark lawsuits on a broad scale.

In contrast to many twentieth-century physicians' claims that lawyers incite malpractice suits either directly or indirectly, mid–nineteenth-century doctors believed that attorneys were mostly honorable and more guilty of misunderstanding than malevolence. Stephen Smith was convinced:

Could the capable and the conscientious legal adviser clearly understand and be thoroughly impressed with the inherent difficulties in the practice of medicine, he would be slow to counsel prosecutions of medical men; and had the court the same knowledge, we believe that a nonsuit would be the summary termination of many a trial for alleged malpractice.[67]

Frank Hamilton, a respected New York surgeon and a perpetual expert witness, maintained that while there may have been a few who undertook malpractice suits, "honorable and intelligent lawyers seldom countenance these prosecutions."[68] Joshua Spencer, a New York attorney, explained in 1855 that while he had frequently served as counsel for physicians in malpractice cases, he had never worked for the plaintiff/patient. "My brethren," he noted, "generally, look upon the complaints with suspicion and refuse to meddle with them."[69]

Physicians acknowledged that lawyers regularly refused to represent undeserving clients and often withdrew from cases when they discovered the true nature of the injury involved. One physician in 1856 exhorted his colleagues, "[L]et us be thankful that the poor and unenlightened will often find counsellors actuated by higher motives than the paltry profits of a suit, and so honest as to use the influence which they possess over their clients to prevent rather than forward so ill-judged an action."[70] Samuel Parkman, a surgeon at Massachusetts General Hospital, examined the physician's relation to the law at midcentury and concluded that "the practitioner of medicine has no cause of complaint against the law or its ministers."[71] Most accounts seemed to confirm this judgment. A report on malpractice in Ohio recounted suits in which "some difficulty was experienced in finding a lawyer to undertake the case."[72] The *Boston Medical and Surgical Journal* reported an incident in 1860 in which a New York man searched his county for a lawyer to sue his son's physician. Despite the physician's treatment for a degenerative hip disease, the boy's hip had frozen in one position. "To the honor of the legal profession," the journal observed, "no attorney in the County could be induced to engage in the suit." However, "[a]n obscure 'limb of the law' was found in an adjoining county" to handle the case.[73]

Elwell argued in his *Treatise on Medical Malpractice* that lawyers were hampered by the lack of relevant medical and legal materials on the topic. "[T]he attorney," he explained, "experiences the greatest difficulty, doubt, and perplexity, in preparing cases involving the question of Malpractice."[74] Through the 1860s law journals rarely contained articles or commentary on malpractice, and lawyers had to rely on their own scant knowledge of medical issues and on legal authorities scattered, undigested, through appellate law reports. Many writers seemed to believe sincerely that most lawyers would decline or drop illegitimate cases once they were apprised of the intricacies and uncertainties of the medical world. One Worcester, Massachusetts, lawyer helped a patient sue a physician whose supposedly inept treatment had resulted in a withered and deformed arm after what was allegedly a simple fracture. After listening to several medical witnesses, the attorney rose in court and declared that the case would proceed no further. He had mistakenly believed that the injury was a simple fracture, but the evidence had demonstrated that the injury had been compound and was very difficult to treat. He "handsomely" and "honorabl[y]," according to one medical journal, praised the physician's treatment and abandoned the suit.[75]

Despite the general era of good feeling between the professions, some writers foreshadowed the more negative attitude that became prevalent in the late nineteenth and early twentieth centuries. In 1854 Dr. T. J. Pray observed that in trials for malpractice, "it seems to be the great forte of legal gentlemen to make an abusive tirade upon the medical profession at large." He warned that "*Braying* and *sound argument* are two different kinds of action, and originate generally not from the same species of animals . . . A man may put on a lion's skin, but too often certain long appendages will peep out from under their concealment, and betray the wearer."[76] Pray's observations, however, did not reflect the majority position among physicians. Admittedly, lawyers served as an essential tool of the malpractice plaintiff. But the lowering standards for entry into the profession had only slightly increased the number of attorneys in practice. Some lawyers used contingency fee arrangements, but physicians did not directly attack the practice as an evil incitement to litigation.

Although change was already underway, physicians and lawyers often came from the same social class and held similar interests. In addition, lawyers were commonly believed to exert a restraining influence on the antielite, antiprofessional sentiments of the period. Alexis de Tocqueville reported that Jacksonian lawyers provided "the strongest barrier against the faults of democracy." When the common people "let themselves get intoxicated by their ideas," de Tocqueville explained, "the lawyers apply an almost invisible brake which slows them down and halts them."[77] Lawyers and physicians, along with the clergy, constituted the "liberal professions," which, in the eyes of members of these groups, provided enlightenment, order, and cohesion to American society.[78] Consequently, between 1835 and 1865 physicians did not believe that lawyers were unredeemable villains but felt instead that they constituted a misguided, underinformed, but "noble sister profession."[79]

Physicians usually laid most of the blame for inciting suits on other heads. Many physicians believed that other doctors played a central role in convincing patients to sue. During the nineteenth century *allopaths*, or *regular* doctors, were joined by a variety of alternative healers, or *irregular* practitioners, such as *Thomsonians*, *homeopaths*, and *hydropaths*, who followed radically different treatment regimes. Occasionally irregular practitioners encouraged patients to sue regular physicians. Most observers agreed, however, that regular physicians stirred up more suits than their irregular counterparts. Regular physicians frequently incited suits against their own kind. They competed bitterly with their colleagues and purposefully advised patients to sue rivals in order to ruin their reputations and gain patients.[80]

An "Ordinary Standard of Care, Skill, and Diligence"

No matter how a patient made the initial decision to sue his physician, through friends, a lawyer, a rival practitioner, or his own initiative, the path afterward followed a fairly standard pattern. True, legal rules of evidence and procedure varied from state to state and from decade to decade. Nevertheless a model of a typical case may be imagined.

Most malpractice plaintiffs were men; when women were the victims of supposed medical malpractice, their husbands or fathers generally sued the physician. After an injured patient, usually with a fractured or dislocated limb, decided to sue his physician, he hired a lawyer. Sometimes lawyers made contingency arrangements and prosecuted a case for a percentage of the anticipated damage award. In other cases, attorneys merely deferred payment until after the trial or were paid at the time of their employment.

With rare exceptions, malpractice cases were heard by a jury in a county court house. Although physicians occasionally favored the use of arbitrators to decide malpractice complaints, by the 1840s it was an uncommon practice.[81] Jury trials were the almost unalterable rule. Until the late 1840s the lawyer and his client filed a writ of *trespass on the case* or *action on the case*.[82] After the late 1840s various states abolished the writ system, and thereafter all civil offenses, including malpractice, fell under the rubric of a catch-all civil action writ. Law reformers had hoped that this civil procedure reform would simplify the complex, traditional pleading requirements. However, with the exception of abolishing the category of specific writs, most of the pleading requirements remained, and the reforms did not significantly alter the broad outlines of malpractice procedure.[83]

The common law required that the plaintiff prove that a doctor-patient relationship had existed between him and the physician/defendant. This point was seldom in dispute. Physicians usually admitted to treating the patient, and treatment was enough evidence to establish that a *duty-filled* relationship existed. After confirming the existence of a doctor-patient relationship, the court would examine whether the physician was legally liable for the permanent injuries or pain of the patient. The physician was always held legally responsible for everything that he explicitly promised to do. For example, if a physician claimed that he could save a patient's badly crushed leg and "make it as good as new" yet was unable to fulfill his promise, the injured man would have a strong case against the practitioner.

However, such simple situations constituted a very small proportion of the suits against physicians in the nineteenth century. Physicians rarely guaranteed their work, and if they did so orally, the existence of such a promise would be very difficult to prove in court. In fact, liability based on a promise to cure constituted an entirely different type of case from the typical medical malpractice charge. Responsibility based on promises to cure involved an explicit, conscious agreement between doctor and patient, an ordinary contract. The theoretical and doctrinal source of most malpractice liability was more ambiguous.[84]

The more common situation did not involve a physician's promise to cure patients. In such situations the common law did not require a complete cure. In 1833 an Ohio man tried to bring charges against a physician under a writ of assumpsit, or breach of promise, for failing to deliver safely the plaintiff's baby. The trial court judge dismissed the case because "the law does not raise from the fact of employment, an implied undertaking to cure."[85]

The element of explicit contract to cure aside, when trial court judges held or even implied that physicians guaranteed cures, appellate courts consistently overturned the decisions and granted physician/defendants new trials. For example, an Ohio man who charged a physician with malpractice in the 1830s declared to the court that he had retained the physician to "manage, take care of, and *cure*" (original emphasis) his fractured leg. Although the physician "promised" to set and *cure* his leg, the plaintiff insisted that he had lost his limb to amputation because of the doctor's failure. The physician asked the trial court judge to tell the jury that the law required proof of the existence of an explicit promise to cure. The judge, however, explained to the jury that because the defendant had held himself out to the world as a physician, there was no need to prove an explicit promise to cure; the law assumed the existence of that duty. The jury found the physician guilty of malpractice. The Ohio supreme court summarily reversed the decision, ruling that physicians did not implicitly promise to cure every case and they would not be held responsible for such a promise.[86]

Few trial court judges ignored the clear common law precedents regarding implied promises to cure, but when they did, state appellate courts invariably reversed the decisions. In 1853 one rogue Pennsylvania trial judge went so far as to tell a jury that the defendant/physician was required to use the skill necessary "to set the leg so as to make it straight and of equal length with the other." The judge even suggested that "if suits were more frequently brought, we would have perhaps fewer practitioners of medicine and surgery not possessing the requisite professional skill and knowledge." Although the trial jury ruled against the physician, the state supreme court overturned the decision and reiterated the common law precedent that "the implied contract of a physician is not to cure—to restore a fractured limb to its natural perfectness—but to treat the case with care, diligence, and skill."[87]

The bulk of the legal arguments, evidence, and testimony centered not on promises and guarantees to cure, but rather on the meaning and requirements of the terms ordinary *care, diligence,* and *skill*. Before malpractice juries retired to make their decisions, trial court judges would instruct them on the common law rules. Judges across the country drew on virtually the same precedents, and their essential requirements varied little from state to state. In 1833 a trial court judge told a Connecticut jury that "if there was either carelessness, or a want of ordinary diligence, care, and skill, then the plaintiff was entitled to recover."[88] The Maine supreme court declared in 1848 that "[t]he [malpractice] defendant is not liable for a want of the highest degree of skill, but for ordinary skill. And of course only for the want of ordinary care and judgment."[89] The Illinois supreme court enunciated one of the clearest and most enduring renderings of the doctrine in an 1860 case in which Abraham Lincoln was an attorney for the patient. Justice Walker wrote:

The principle is plain and of uniform application, that when a person assumes the profession of physician and surgeon, he must, in its exercise, be held to employ a reasonable amount of care and skill. For any thing short of that degree of skill in his practice, the law will hold him responsible for any injury that may result from its absence. While he is not required to possess the highest order of qualification, to which some men may attain, still he must possess and exercise that degree of skill which is ordinarily possessed by members of the profession.[90]

The first American treatise on tort law, published by Francis Hillard in 1859, reinforced the essential permanence of the ordinary skill and care doctrine, as did Amasa Redfield's important *Treatise on the Law of Negligence* in 1870.[91]

Although the formal legal definitions of standard of care over the first half of the nineteenth century were similar and fairly consistent, in actual operation the principles of malpractice liability were anything but "plain" and of "uniform application."[92] The unornamented simplicity of the maxim "ordinary diligence, care, and skill" engendered ambiguity. In addition, the requirements of the trial process and the prerogatives of trial judges complicated the ostensibly simple "ordinary" care standard.

The "Glorious Uncertainty of Legal Justice and Medical Testimony"

The plaintiff/patient was required to present expert witnesses to prove that his physician had not exercised "ordinary" skill and care. In rebuttal, the defendant/physician could offer testimony from his own expert witnesses. Witnesses testified to both fact and opinion. However, an expert was not allowed to make a judgment on whether the treatment constituted malpractice. Expert witnesses were required to give their opinion on whether the plaintiff's injury was permanent and whether the treatment provided by the defendant was standard. They were also asked whether the type and the degree of the plaintiff's permanent injury would have occurred after competent medical care. The first question rarely generated much controversy. Permanent injuries were usually readily apparent and not disputed by the defendant. Most of the disagreement among witnesses, and, indeed, the central issue in most malpractice cases, derived from problems in determining what constituted ordinary care in each instance. Precedents applied only to legal doctrine and not to technical information. Medical practice was evolving. Every injury was ostensibly unique. Therefore, this phase of the trial was unpredictable.

Expert witnesses complicated the determination of what constituted an ordinary degree of skill and acceptable results. Since medical licensure was mostly a dead letter by the late 1830s, courts allowed any practicing physician, licensed or unlicensed, educated or not, to serve as an expert witness. According to one text, "Extra knowledge on questions of science, skill, trade, business or other matters requiring special knowledge, qualifi[ed] the person thus informed to give opinions in courts of justice."[93]

Practitioners from different schools of medicine, regular physicians, homeopaths, hydropaths, and Thomsonians were allowed to testify interchangeably at each other's trials. This practice was remarkable because therapeutically, competitively, and socially, the various schools of medicine were generally at odds with one another. Complicating the matter further, even though a variety of types of practitioners could testify at a trial, the defendant was required to exercise ordinary skill only according to the standards of his own school of practice.

For example, in the late 1840s an Iowa man sued a Thomsonian physician because he had caused the man's wife pain and injury during and after the delivery of a child. The Thomsonian had failed to remove the placenta following the birth, and the mother suffered a massive loss of blood and great pain. The afterbirth was finally removed by a regular physician, who testified at the malpractice trial. He explained that it was standard practice to remove the placenta at a much earlier period and that a delay was injurious and created the risk of puerperal fever. Several other regular physicians concurred and testified against the defendant.[94]

The Thomsonian physician attempted to prove that his school of medicine considered it improper to remove the placenta until it was expelled by nature. The trial judge, however, refused to allow the introduction of the evidence, and the jury found the Thomsonian guilty. He appealed the judgment to the Iowa supreme court, which overturned the decision. Writing for the majority of the court, the chief judge explained that because there "is no particular system of medicine established or favored by the laws of Iowa, . . . [t]he people are free to select from the various classes of medical men." "While a regular physician is expected to follow the rules of the old school in the art of curing, the botanic physician must be equally expected to adhere to his adopted method."[95]

Paradoxes multiplied. Courts strictly followed the doctrine that physicians were accountable for injuries resulting from the failure to supply ordinary skill and care only according to their respective systems of treating diseases. Yet, through the first half of the century judges continued to accept any practicing physician as an expert witness. Not until the early 1860s did state legislatures and appellate courts begin making changes in the rules of evidence so that physicians from different schools could not testify against one another. Regular practitioners appeared to suffer much more from this practice than their irregular counterparts. While irregular practitioners were rarely sued, regular practitioners bore the brunt of the majority of the suits and routinely had to face their hostile counterparts in court.[96] For example, in 1849 a young doctor was sued after he failed to save a patient's life following a difficult fracture and amputation. While two regular physicians testified on his behalf, a homeopath and a Thomsonian were aligned against him as expert witnesses for the prosecution.[97]

Although testimony from rival schools of medical practice contributed to the confusion and antipathy in the witness-box, evidence presented by regular physicians against regular physicians constituted the majority of the proof in malpractice trials. The same features that characterized irregular practitioners' testimony applied equally to regular physicians' testimony in court. The competition among regular physicians was nearly as vigorous as that between regulars and irregulars. Often this contention among regulars carried over into court, and physicians found their rivals testifying against them.[98]

In addition, medical evidence on appropriate treatment for injuries or illnesses was not always consistent, even when all the witnesses were regular physicians. Many times the expert witnesses came from radically different regions of the country; sometimes expert witnesses practiced in areas quite different from those of the defendant/physician. Elwell recounted the episode of a rural Ohio man who had lost his leg to amputation after crushing it while building a log cabin in a new settlement. Several years later, the man and some friends recovered the bone, cleaned it, and used it as the basis of a suit against the physician who performed the operation. The bone was shipped to Philadelphia, New York, and Washington, D.C., where physicians examined it and provided depositions. Another trial, for the mistreatment of an eye ailment in Cleveland, elicited expert opinions from physicians who practiced in Boston and New York.[99] Although the physicians won the several trials related to these cases, the incidents demonstrate how witnesses were sometimes drawn from diverse community and medical surroundings and asked to judge the competency of a medical defendant. Often, however, defendants had more to fear from local colleagues. Keen competition for patients or personal animosity could influence the testimony of local practitioners.

Even when expert witnesses were not competing with the defendant for patients or practicing in a center of medical excellence, their testimony seldom clearly delineated the acceptable standards of the profession. The unspecific nature of the malpractice doctrine allowed even disinterested medical witnesses to disagree on what constituted ordinary care. The state of medicine between 1835 and 1865 also contributed to the frequent dissension among medical witnesses. The difficulty in defining standard practice once a case was taken to court was aggravated by attacks from irregular practitioners, the growth of statistical scrutiny of procedures, and universal recognition of the considerable uncertainty in medicine. As John Elwell noted in 1860:

While the uncertainty of medicine is readily admitted, the reasons of this uncertainty, and the unsolved state of the science, are far from being understood; and not being understood, more blame is often thrown upon the physician or surgeon than if there existed an intelligent knowledge of the real inherent difficulties of his profession.[100]

Even in the treatment of fractures, where significant progress had been made in the first third of the century, competing theories and expectations were more prevalent than many practitioners realized.[101] A single trial often yielded several opinions on the correct procedure for setting a broken leg.

Similarly, obstetric treatment, where physicians claimed to possess scientific advantage over midwives, was far from standardized. In 1864 a Pennsylvania man sued a physician for injuring a child during its delivery. Six years earlier the plaintiff's wife had suffered a difficult labor. She bled profusely and lay for nearly eight hours with only the arm of the baby protruding from the birth canal. The woman pleaded with the physician to "take away the child and save her [the mother's] life." Finally, the doctor amputated the arm claiming that he believed the baby was dead and that he feared for the life of the mother. Immediately after the amputation, however, the woman delivered an otherwise healthy girl. During the trial, at which the six-year-old girl was present, medical witnesses presented greatly divergent views on the case. One physician criticized the defendant saying that the practice of amputation in such cases had been long abandoned. He also contended that ether, then available, could have been used to ease delivery and turn the child so that a natural birth would have ensued. Other witnesses testified that the amputation did nothing to ease delivery and that other methods would have been preferable. Still other physicians favored the use of morphine or other relaxants. The witnesses who testified for the defendant, however, opposed the use of anesthesia in such cases, praised the doctor's treatment, and claimed that both mother and child would have died in any other circumstances. After hearing the wide range of medical opinions, the plaintiff's attorney informed the judge that he wished to drop charges against the physician.[102]

Conflicting expert testimony did not always work in favor of the defendant. Both malicious and innocent disagreements of medical witnesses extended the already wide latitude of discretion left to the jury. A medical editorialist in 1847 condemned the "glorious uncertainty of legal justice and of medical testimony" and warned that conflicting testimony "bewildered" lay juries.[103] Jurors were not bound to accept the evidence of expert testimony even when it was unanimous; disagreement among medical witnesses gave jurors even freer rein. As one irate New York doctor reported in 1854, "A single dissenting voice among the surgeons on the stand is enough to turn the scale in favor of the plaintiff, toward whom the sympathies of the jury invariably run."[104]

Juries frequently found against the defendant even when the bulk and quality of the expert testimony supported the physician. The jury's social beliefs and attitudes toward the profession surfaced in many ways. If a juror harbored a general antipathy toward the medical profession at large, as much of society did in the period, he might vote against the physician regardless of the evidence to the contrary. If a juror used the service of an irregular practitioner, he might have been more likely to believe a homeopathic witness for example, or less likely to rule against a Thomsonian defendant in a malpractice case.

The Locality Rule

The nature and development of national medical practice further complicated the determination of what constituted an "ordinary" standard of care. In the 1824 *Lowell* v. *Faxon & Hawks* case, the trial judge instructed the jury that a physician in an "obscure village" was not required to possess the same degree of skill as his urban counterpart.[105] Instead, he need only possess and exercise the degree of skill that was ordinarily possessed and exercised by other rural practitioners in similar communities. This notion, which became known as the *locality rule* in the late nineteenth century, was a recognition of the decentralized nature of the medical profession and the nation. The locality rule was unknown in English common law and until the 1870s, unsupported by any state appellate court decision. In the first third of the century some judges instructed juries to abide by its formula. Other juries, because they understood and sympathized with the plight of the rural practitioner, probably often applied an informal version of the locality rule when they considered the "ordinary" care requirement.

The locality rule, however, did not become a general feature of malpractice law until the last third of the nineteenth century. Between 1835 and 1865, national medical journals multiplied, and transportation and communication improved. As Stephen Smith argued, it was "manifestly dangerous" to accept the locality rule in 1860 because every physician now had the opportunity and the duty to keep abreast of medical advancement.[106] Much had changed since the first part of the century. Judges only irregularly instructed juries to calculate the required medical competency by community standards. Jurors, with less general sympathy for physicians and under the mistaken impression that the American medical world was becoming homogeneous, were more willing to hold parochial physicians to the standards of their better educated and more practiced cosmopolitan counterparts. Plaintiffs would summon medical experts from larger cities, other communities, and even other states without regard to the relative standards of practice. In the case of small communities, urban physicians usually served as witnesses to the detriment of the defendant/ physician.

Medical practice in America, however, had not become homogeneous. Despite the proliferation of medical journals and schools and the increased interconnectedness of the rest of society and the economy, physicians' skill in different geographic locations and social surroundings varied greatly. Hospital-based physicians with thriving urban practices, for example, were exposed to a wider range and greater number of injuries and illnesses. Some writers and jurists recognized the still decentralized and uneven nature of American medicine and the need for adjusted standards of care. One observer argued in 1849 that there was only one remedy for the wave of malpractice prosecutions. He demanded, "Let judges make themselves acquainted with what should be the qualifications required of medical men, according to the *standard justified by their location*, and charge juries definitely and clearly upon that point."[107] Elwell agreed that it was sometimes difficult to define *ordinary* degree of skill:

It may vary in the same state or country. There are many neighborhoods, in the West especially, where medical aid is of little attainment; yet cases of disease and surgery are constantly occurring, and they must, of necessity fall into the hands of those who have given the subject but little if any thought.[108]

Therefore, Elwell believed that the locality rule, or *community standard doctrine*, should be applied in all malpractice cases.

Only a few trial and appellate court judges invoked the locality rule between 1835 and 1865, and when they did, it was not in forums that would set doctrinal precedent. In 1857 a patient sued two Ohio oculists for malpractice after treatment that left him in bed for two months and unable to read for two years. The oculists had bled the patient and dosed him with cathartics for several weeks. The trial court judge instructed the jury that "[a]n absolute necessity requires that the wants of the community be supplied with the best medical knowledge its means and location will command."[109] The jury was unable to reach a verdict. In a similar instance, a patient sued his physician in Massachusetts for a deformity following a severe hip injury. Although the medical witnesses for the defense and the prosecution both agreed that the results of the treatment were the best that could be expected, the jury returned a verdict against the physician for $365. The physician appealed the decision to the state supreme court, which overturned the verdict for being against the weight of the evidence. In writing the opinion for the court, the eminent chief justice of Massachusetts, Lemuel Shaw, noted that the defendant/physician had "shown a degree of skill beyond what is usually expected of surgeons residing in the country."[110] Since Shaw's comment did not clearly articulate the principle, and was incidental to the decision in the case, it was probably considered *obiter dictum* and therefore not binding as precedent. At any rate, the decision was ignored by other courts and had no impact on the law of malpractice.

Elwell's comment and the Massachusetts and Ohio cases are important as points of contrast. Most judges and the majority of society were not inclined to measure physicians only against community standards even though geographic location and professional atmosphere could have a profound impact on the intellectual and technical development of individual practitioners. The failure of the locality rule to take hold between 1835 and 1865 was the result of two developments. First, the public and most judges misunderstood and overestimated the degree of change in the medical profession in the first half of the century. Despite the substantial development of a more integrated national economy, the establishment of a national medical organization for regular physicians in 1846, and increased communication among national medical practitioners, the profession could still best be characterized as a diffuse collection of small groups of doctors of varying knowledge and skill.

Second, the acceptance of the locality, or community standard, rule would have been out of harmony with developments in other areas of American law. Between 1780 and 1860 state and federal judges transformed many aspects of the traditional common law in ways that reflected and encouraged the growth of national economic development. For example, Joseph Story, in his career as a treatise writer and Supreme Court justice (1811–1843), devoted much of his time to creating and fostering a uniform federal common law to neutralize the pluralistic tendency of the states. He attempted to formulate a uniform national commercial law and worked on schemes to adjudicate conflicts of laws among states.[111] The John Marshall court (1801–1836), of which Story was a member, and the subsequent Roger Taney court, made numerous "nationalizing" decisions calculated to facilitate economic integration by extending federal oversight.[112] In one of them, *Swift* v. *Tyson* (1842), the Taney court ruled that federal courts were bound to follow state court commercial law decisions only in strictly state matters. Other economic issues could be decided by federal courts on the basis of general principles of commercial law.[113] The intent of the ruling was to open the door to national commercial uniformity. Changes in such areas of the law as contract also reflected the same nationalizing tendencies. For example, in the late eighteenth and early nineteenth centuries courts began to scrutinize contracts less by community standards of fairness and more according to the explicit terms of the agreement. This new view of contractual liability was designed to facilitate long-distance, future-oriented agreements with strangers rather than immediate exchanges between individuals in parochial communities.[114]

Story wrote in 1837, "I am myself no friend to the almost indiscriminate habit . . . of setting up particular usages or customs in almost all kinds of business and trade, to control, vary or annul the general liabilities of parties under the common law."[115] The application of the locality rule in malpractice cases was incompatible with this sentiment and with the general context of jurisprudential thought in antebellum America. The locality rule stressed diversity while economic development and law were bolstering national uniformity.

Unfortunately for malpractice defendants, the nationalizing tendency in law arrived long before the medical community could deliver a consistent level of care nationwide. Physicians in isolated communities could not acquire the same training, education, and experience as physicians in thriving urban centers. The failure of judges and the public to understand or to admit this fact did not cause the wave of malpractice suits in the 1840s and 1850s, but it clearly aggravated an already complicated situation. The use of the locality rule between 1835 and 1865 could have softened the blow of the initial increase in suits. Instead, judges continued to allow expert witness from centers of medical excellence to testify at the trials of rural practitioners without instructing juries to consider their relative theaters of practice. The confusion that resulted from admitting testimony from a variety of witnesses with differing standards of practice played a role in enhancing the discretion of the jury.[116]

Disgrace, Vexation, and Ruin

It appeared to many physicians that they had little chance in a courtroom once they were sued for malpractice. As one physician noted,

"[T]he defendant must be mulcted in every case where he is not sustained by the entire professional evidence."[117] Other writers, however, actually believed that there was no escape from conviction even if all the witnesses supported the defendant. "The fact is," reported an editorialist in 1855, "that sometimes surgeons have been mulcted in damages simply because the jury believed from the united character of the medical testimony that it was a conspiracy and the more conclusive the testimony, the more certain with some jurors is the defendant to suffer."[118] These two varying viewpoints both reflected the prevalent belief among medical practitioners that the "sympathy of a jury of citizens is not generally with the doctor, but rather on the side of the poor, ill-advised, unfortunate victim of incurable injury."[119]

These writers exaggerated juries' inclination to rule against physicians. In the majority of medical malpractice trials reported in the medical literature, juries ruled in favor of the defendant/physician. Although many patients were more willing to sue physicians, it is not clear that all of society approved of the practice in these early years. Thus, when suits did come to court, juries could have demonstrated their disapproval by finding for the defendant. Jurors, some already skeptical about the propriety of suing physicians, would be especially hesitant to penalize a defendant where the plaintiff had received only a relatively minor deformity, like those from unsuccessful fracture treatments. Some contemporary estimates of acquittal rates are remarkably high. An Ohio physician in 1859 estimated that while the tendency to prosecute physicians was increasing, "[t]his certainly has not originated from the success connected with these prosecutions. In not one instance in twenty as far as my observation extends—have they been successful."[120] While the Ohio writer's estimate was unrealistically optimistic, it provided a counter to the gloomy predictions of other physicians. Even when physicians lost their cases in the initial trials, they often received favorable verdicts in retrials or at the appellate level. Appellate ruling victories in the nineteenth century were fairly evenly split between physicians and patients.[121] State appellate courts overturned trial verdicts against physicians when the trial judge had improperly instructed the jury on the "ordinary" care requirement, when juries awarded excess damages, and when evidence was improp-

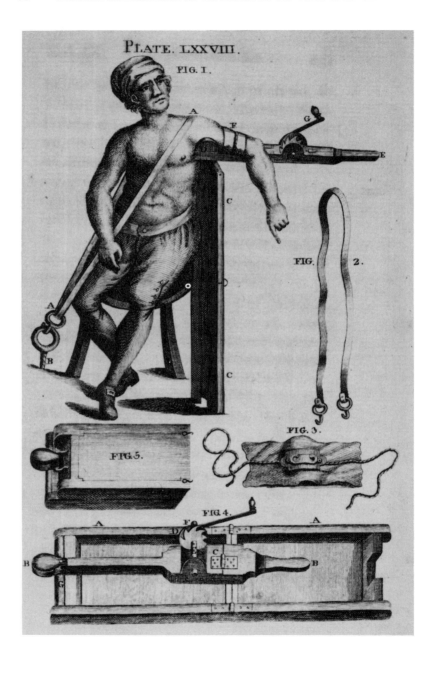

erly admitted or rejected. Including acquittal verdicts gained by malpractice defendants in retrials and on appeals, physicians probably prevailed in well over half the malpractice suits of 1835–1865.[122] Yet, these successes were small consolation to a profession that felt deluged by prosecutions and believed, as did John Elwell, that "[v]ictory in these cases is in one sense, defeat because the disgrace, vexations, and cost are generally ruinous."[123]

When judges incorrectly or prejudicially instructed juries or juries flagrantly ignored evidence, physicians could either ask the trial judge for a new trial or appeal their case to a higher state court. Indeed, the typical legal battle between a patient and his physician consisted of multiple trials involving numerous witnesses and covering several years. For example, when Lorenzo Slack first accused Dixi Crosby of malpractice in the spring of 1851, it had been nearly six years (two days before the statutory limit) since Crosby had treated the man's broken leg. The first trial, in which Slack asked for $5,000 in damages, was delayed until 1853. The jury awarded Slack $800 plus $300 in costs. A second trial yielded similar results, and it was not until nine years after the incident that a third trial jury acquitted Crosby.[124] Another fracture case in New Hampshire began in 1850 and was not concluded until 1855, after a long procession of trials, hearings, and negotiations. At the first trial the patient was awarded $1,500 plus court costs. A jury at the second trial awarded him only $525 plus costs. The physician appealed the decision to the New Hampshire supreme court, which overturned the decision on the basis of the trial court judge's instructions to the jury. A third jury again ruled against the physician in 1854, but the state supreme court overruled this verdict because some of the jurors had shared some brandy the night before they reported their decision. Finally, the patient and the physician settled the dispute out of court for an undisclosed sum of money.[125]

These two cases were the rule, not the exception. The number and length of the trials growing out of each malpractice charge were significant because the litigation subjected the physician to more anxiety,

Device to relocate dislocated shoulder. From Benjamin Bell, A System of Surgery *(1788). (Courtesy of the Historical Research Center, Houston Academy of Medicine, Texas Medical Center Library, Houston, Texas.)*

cost, and publicity. The trials of the New Hampshire physician lasted several days each and played to regularly packed courthouses. One trial employed sixty witnesses. Although the legal costs and attorneys' fees undoubtedly varied greatly, five trials in Massachusetts in the mid-1850s generated $10,000 in trial costs and fees. One of the defendants reportedly paid $2,000 of that total, an enormous sum in the mid–nineteenth century.[126] This figure was abnormally high, but costs often approached the amount of damages awarded to the patients.

When a jury found a defendant guilty of malpractice, it was asked to calculate the monetary value of the damages to the plaintiff. The injured patient could receive money for all the consequences of the injury, past and future. In addition, the jury was authorized to take into account the effects of the injury, including pain, personal inconvenience, and decreased income capacity. The award, however, could not exceed the amount claimed by the plaintiff at the beginning of the trial.

Patients invariably asked for damage awards of $5,000, $10,000, $20,000, and $25,000. Juries' awards, however, never approached the damage claims of the patients. While there were several awards between 1835 and 1865 in the $1,000 to $3,000 range, the typical malpractice damage judgments fell between $200 and $800 (see appendix A).[127] If an appellate court believed that an award was excessive, it could overturn the judgment, as did the Maine supreme court in 1848. A patient had accused a physician of malpractice because he failed to amputate the plaintiff's leg high enough. Consequently, the man required two more operations to remove progressively more of the stump of the leg. A jury returned a verdict for the plaintiff in the amount of $2,025. The physician appealed the verdict, claiming that it was excessive and against the weight of the evidence. The state supreme court demanded that the patient agree to remit $500 of the judgment because "surgeons should not be deterred from the pursuit of their profession by intemperate and extravagant verdicts." If the patient refused to accept $1,525, the court threatened to grant the physician a new trial. The court justified its decision by explaining that "[t]he compensation to surgeons in the country is small, . . . and an error of judgment is visited with a severe penalty, which takes from one a large share of the surplus earnings of a long life."[128] On the low end of the awards scale, a Pennsylvania jury in 1847 granted a black man only $30 for a permanent injury to his shoulder.[129]

These awards seem almost insignificant by mid– and late–twentieth century standards. But they shocked nineteenth-century physicians. Eight hundred dollars was no inconsequential sum in 1850, even for a physician. Wages were low, and the majority of physicians had to pursue sideline occupations to support their families. While a handful of physicians might have earned as much as $6,000–$8,000 per year, the *Boston Medical and Surgical Journal* considered $500 normal for an established, full-time doctor in 1833. Expenses could have depleted that figure to as low as $350. Many rural doctors earned less, and a portion of their income usually included payment-in-kind rather than money.[130] Second, nineteenth-century physicians were not shielded from malpractice claims by any form of insurance. Malpractice insurance and group defense schemes did not surface until the last decade of the nineteenth century and were not an established feature of medical life until the early twentieth century.[131] Before then, physicians had to fend and pay for themselves.

Finally, the dollar amount of early damage awards was of secondary importance to both antebellum physicians and to the overall development of medical malpractice in America. When a physician was charged with malpractice, he felt as if his professional future had been put in jeopardy even if the damage award against him was small, or even if he won his case. Many malpractice suits were highly visible local events. After an Ohio suit in 1849 in which the courthouse had been crowded for four days, one observer declared that "there has been no case [of any kind] tried within the county during the last ten years which has elicited so much attention."[132] Members of the community could sit and listen to a parade of witnesses testify that the accused physician was unskillful, incompetent, or careless. Members of the patient's family, rival or more accomplished physicians, and the prosecuting attorney could all join in the attack.

In the highly competitive medical environment of the mid–nineteenth century, an era when public trust of regular physicians was tenuous at best, attacks on a doctor's competency could have significant fallout. A writer for the *Ohio Medical and Surgical Journal* in 1861 affirmed that a malpractice suit was a "grave matter" to both the accused physician and the profession. As he explained, "The reputation of the physician is his stock in trade. He cherishes it beyond all price." A physician could bear the loss of property, arduous labors, obscurity, and poverty, but the "formal and public attack on his reputation, and the concurrence of twelve disinterested members of the community," struck at the core of his, and his colleagues', professional respectability. "It is not very difficult to see that the event, from its very inception casts a long shadow upon the future, pregnant with fears, uncertainties, apprehensions, and future forbodings."[133]

The writer's prophetic statement expressed the profession's well-justified impression that the sudden and dramatic appearance of widespread and frequent malpractice suits was an augur of things to come and a fundamental threat to the medical community at large. As he predicted, "The public knowledge of a verdict for the prosecution will beget a brood of new cases, in which, quite as likely as otherwise, the most skillful and diligent of the profession will be the victims."[134]

While damage awards were smaller than in later years, they were not inconsequential. In addition, it is important to remember that most patients did not sue their physicians. Those who did, however, broke decisively with the past. But a focus on the amount of the awards or the percentage of patients involved obscures the more important contemporary and historical issues. The first malpractice "crisis" of 1835–1865 was the genesis of a modern professional epidemic, the first step over a threshold into a new era of American medicine. Many nineteenth-century physicians saw it as such and desperately tried to unravel the twisted social and professional motives behind the suits. The questions of the size of the damage awards or who won the majority of the cases are important; but they are dwarfed by the need to explain why the suits originated in the first place and how the phenomenon's origins continued to generate suits for the next 150 years.

CHAPTER 3

Schools for Scandal

The increase in malpractice suits and threats of suits in the early 1840s was sudden and dramatic. Contemporaries identified several factors as the underlying cause of the phenomenon. Medical society committees on malpractice in Pennsylvania in 1850, Kentucky in 1853, Massachusetts in 1854, and Ohio in 1855, plus scores of individual physicians, agreed that the status of the profession was deteriorating.[1] However ill defined, a view prevailed that the increase in malpractice suits was inextricably related to this decline in public confidence. In addition, physicians contended that the specific agents of the decline, aspects of medical treatment, competition, and antiprofessional sentiment were also the specific causes of the litigation crisis.

These perceptive commentators accurately explained physicians' low status. But they were unable to recognize and interpret the long-term cultural trends that created the environment conducive to widespread litigation. Instead, observers in the mid–nineteenth century mistook important topical factors for fundamental causes. These immediate factors may have incited suits in the 1840s and 1850s, but they cannot explain why the number of suits continued to increase into the twentieth century. Indeed, frequent malpractice litigation persisted long after the so-called causes identified by mid–nineteenth-century physicians had disappeared.

The immediate causes of the increased incidence of malpractice prosecution were usually apparent to contemporary observers. Although their social standing in America had never been high, most doctors were painfully aware of the medical profession's abysmal status in the first half of the nineteenth century. At a meeting of the American Medical Association in 1848 Nathan Chapman noted that the "once revered" and "venerated" profession has become corrupt, and degenerative to the forfeiture of its social position."[2] In 1858 a physician confirmed that the medical profession had "been losing its hold on the respect and confidence of the people" for fifty years. Since the early part of the century, the physician lamented, the profession had lost its favored position, when children had been "taught to raise their caps, if boys; and drop and curtsey, if girls, in token of respect, when they met their family physician on the street . . . even when that physician was under the influence of intoxicating drink."[3]

Alexander Garnett, writing for the *Medical and Surgical Reporter*, outlined the causes of the profession's meager social standing. According to Garnett, by 1854 doctors were held in low public esteem because of "defective medical acquirements," the "want of union and harmony among physicians," and "the radical and progressive proclivities of the present age."[4] Garnett's three factors deserve closer analysis for they explain physicians' low status, accurately characterize the medical environment of the first half of the nineteenth century, and provide insight into the source of many malpractice suits.

"Defective Medical Acquirements"

In the late eighteenth century American physicians attempted to introduce the English institutions that bestowed a unique, elevated social status on physicians. They organized medical schools, founded professional societies, and convinced state legislatures to pass licensure laws. But despite these temporary successes, American physicians were unable to inspire widespread confidence and respect and gain a monopoly over medical practice.[5]

Physicians' inability to demonstrate the superiority of their methods of treatment was one of the central components of this failure. Americans had a long tradition of domestic medicine. Although full-time physicians existed, much of the medical practice in the eighteenth and early nineteenth century was dispensed by part-time practitioners and lay persons.[6] Since the family served as the center of economic and social activity, it was not surprising that medical care was often dispensed by a mother, a grandmother, or an aunt. In addition, self-care reflected the geographic isolation of families living in rural areas and on the frontier as well as the shortage of trained physicians in the eighteenth century. Before the proliferation of medical schools in the first half of the nineteenth century, a single physician might serve several communities. Even in large cities physicians' time was divided among a large clientele and charitable service in almshouses and dispensaries. The periodic, and sometimes regular, unavailability of a family physician forced many sick to look for help within their own families. Often, even when a trained physician was obtainable, poor immigrants or farmers could not afford his services. Armed with folk remedies and widely available patent medicines, many people served as their own doctors. Lay practitioners could also refer to the nearly ubiquitous handbooks on home health care. William Buchan's *Domestic Medicine*, for example, was reprinted in 142 editions between 1769 and 1871.[7] Since many families had supplied their own medical care for generations, much of the public had little respect for pretentious physicians who offered what were recognized as ineffective, unpleasant, and sometimes dangerous therapies.

Conventional medical theory in the late eighteenth and early nineteenth centuries was dominated by the *heroic* treatments popularized by Benjamin Rush. Rush contended that all disease and illness was the result of "morbid excitement" of the capillaries and vascular tissue. He advocated the copious use of emetics and cathartics to induce vomiting and evacuation and advised the massive bleeding of patients to ease this capillary tension.[8] Although the centuries-old system of humoral pathology included bleeding and employed agents that induced vomiting, diarrhea, and perspiration, heroic practitioners, under Rush's inspiration, disregarded traditional restraints and employed active agents in immense quantities. Physicians removed blood using small cuts, or *scarification*, and suction cups. In other instances they resorted to leaches placed, internally and externally, on literally every part of the body. For larger volumes, doctors opened major blood vessels with a small-bladed knife, or *lancet*. Often, patients were bled until they fainted. Rush suggested that in some cases four-fifths of all the blood in the body might be removed. He epitomized the typical physicians' commitment to heroic bleeding when he declared: "I would sooner die with my Lancet in my hand . . . than to give it up while I had Breath to maintain it or a hand to use it."[9]

Physicians applied similarly enormous doses of cathartics and emetics. As one nineteenth-century doctor recalled, "If vomited, they did not come up in gentle puffs and gusts, but the action was cyclonic. If perchance, the stomach was passed the expulsion would be by the rectum and anus, and this would be equal to a regular oil-well gusher."[10] Calomel, a mercury-based cathartic, was often prescribed until the gums bled (a sign of mercury poisoning). Patients lost hair, teeth, tongues, palates, and in some cases sections of their jaw bones as a result of over zealously prescribed mercury-based remedies. As one disgruntled patient complained in 1832, "I was in the first place bled 3 times & Physicked almost to deth." He acknowledged that "the Doctors have got an idea into their heads that they must give calomel for evry complaint[;] they have fed me so much on it since I been hir that I have lost all my hair from my head and a good share of my teeth."[11] Blistering served as another weapon in the heroic armory. Physicians used caustic substances and heat to raise blisters on various parts of the body, in theory to draw poisons from the patient through the expulsion of pus. Similarly, they purposely incited infection in some cases by inserting foreign substances in open wounds.[12]

Heroic therapy won converts in wide circles, but it was also the object of considerable derision and one of the main sources of public antipathy toward the profession. A physician in 1835 claimed that the injudicious use of heroic treatments "has produced, does continue, and will perpetuate (unless obviated), the fear, jealousy, and suspicion that exists between . . . the community, and the profession at large."[13] Physicians also weakened public confidence by their conflicting and inconsistent diagnoses and therapies. Doctors not only employed depletive therapies like bleeding in varying degrees, but prescribed drugs and tonics such as opium, quinine, antimony, and arsenic in a fickle and unsystematized fashion. Because they did not understand the pharmacological working of their "remedies" and possessed no diagnostic tools except their senses, physicians favored drugs and doses that induced visible results.[14] Because the same remedies often produced different effects in different patients, medical practice appeared to be unsystematized and erratic. Moreover, the same remedy prepared by different physicians usually tasted and acted differently in various cases. This problem was compounded by a lack of consensus among physicians about appropriate practice.[15]

Much of the public accepted heroic methods, but impatience, opposition, and skepticism grew as physicians and alternative practitioners questioned the practice. By the 1830s and 1840s, physicians themselves had begun to distrust the efficacy of their medical treatments. Empirical statistical studies inspired by Pierre Louis in Paris demonstrated that heroic treatments were generally useless and sometimes harmful.[16] Medical writers began to stress the "uncertainty" of medical practice, the healing powers of nature, "self-limiting" diseases, and the merits of "conservative" treatments.[17] Still, physicians' gradual abandonment of heroic therapy did not improve their image significantly. Instead, intraprofessional resistance to the regime helped undermine the legitimacy of the medical community in general. The public distrusted and was increasingly unwilling to support a profession that first endorsed harsh heroic therapies and then began to abandon them within three decades.[18]

These therapeutic fluctuations were relevant to the malpractice phenomenon in two respects. On the one hand, the absence of widespread agreement on the diagnosis and treatment of most maladies precluded the establishment of an "ordinary standard of care." Even when physicians agreed on a remedy, they followed the dictum of *specificity*, a theory that held that medicines acted differently on different patients.[19] Therefore, malpractice suits for purely medical, as opposed to surgical, treatments were rare and usually unsupportable. On the other hand, therapeutic inconsistencies subverted physicians' general status as competent public servants and left them more vulnerable to malpractice charges for treatments in which they did claim proficiency, like orthopedics. In 1854 a Kentucky Medical Society committee on the causes of malpractice suits noted: "During the last half century, the relative position of our profession to the public has undergone a marked change. Implicit confidence, amounting in some instances to blind credulity, has given place to widespread skepticism as to the powers and capabilities of the healing art."[20]

Other professional activities contributed to public fear and distrust. Physicians' and medical students' quests for cadavers for anatomical study helped to brand members of the profession as unfeeling ghouls. The public was repelled by the use of cadavers for instruction. Some early medical schools obtained their dissection subjects from other states or countries, but many merely retrieved recently buried corpses from the local cemetery or relied on professional grave robbers. Attempts to introduce dissection into early anatomy classes often met with violent opposition. Thus, for example, rioters, believing that William Shippen had robbed graves to acquire teaching aids, attacked his Philadelphia School of Anatomy in 1765. By the mid–nineteenth century, similar riots had occurred in Maryland, New York, Vermont, Massachusetts, Ohio, Illinois, and Connecticut. Three rioters were killed in a Baltimore disturbance and seven in a New York uprising.[21]

Violent opposition to "body-snatching" and dissection continued far into the nineteenth century and encouraged state legislatures to establish penalties for grave-robbing and to criminalize the use of human cadavers for instruction. The dissection controversies colored the public's perception of the medical profession at large. A group of enraged Ohioans in 1845 passed a resolution "That we most solemnly believe that those who have no regard for the dead, can have but little respect for the living, and those who respect neither the dead nor the living, should never receive the confidence of the public."[22]

The reaction to the study of anatomy both damaged the medical community's status and hindered the acquisition of anatomical knowledge. Medical societies and contemporary observers argued that physicians would be subject to malpractice suits if they did not understand the workings of the human body and yet were being denied the primary source of that knowledge.[23] In one of the rare nineteenth-century malpractice cases decided by arbitrators, a panel of Michigan physicians refused to award damages to a plaintiff because they found that the injury resulted from defective medical knowledge, and declared that it was unfair to hold physicians responsible for insufficient training when "the study of anatomy essential to the proper treatment of such cases, is by the laws of the state of Michigan a penitentiary offense."[24]

Although judges never appeared to consider the lack of access to proper training as a mitigating factor in malpractice cases, physicians often complained. Josiah Trowbridge, a Buffalo, New York, physician, reported in 1848 that he abandoned his twenty-five-year medical practice in protest because the state legislature criminalized human dissection as a method of teaching anatomy and surgery. Since physicians would be "mulcted with ruinous damages" if they did not possess this knowledge, Trowbridge resolved "not to serve the public on such conditions."[25] John Elwell, in his 1860 treatise, stressed that a physician "may be a good theorist without it [dissection of cadavers], but he cannot be a ready, practical practitioner; and he will be very liable, at some stage of his life, to be awakened to his defective education, by having to respond, in damages, for Malpractice." Elwell contended that it was wrong to punish ignorant physicians if it was impossible to attain proper training. "The court should either permit the student of medicine and surgery to obtain all the subjects they may require . . . or it should cease to punish those who are guilty of Malpractice, by reason of the great difficulty in obtaining subjects for dissection."[26] Although several state legislatures passed laws allowing dissections under certain circumstances, most soon repealed these statutes. By 1860 only two states allowed the use of human cadavers.[27]

Physicians in the late eighteenth century had hoped that they could use improved medical education to increase the ability and the status of their profession. Before 1765 most aspiring American physicians trained as apprentices to established practitioners. These preceptorships varied in quality and length. Some physicians required their trainees to read the important medical texts, but others merely used them as a source of cheap menial labor. Relying on the many self-help medical books or on experience, still other physicians were entirely self-trained. A few wealthy medical students were able to study in the universities of Britain and Europe.[28]

Earlier reformers had believed that Americans could improve the quality of medical care as well as physicians' social standing by introducing the London guild system to the colonies. Medical practice in London was theoretically regulated through three royally chartered corporations: the Royal College of Physicians of London, the United Company of Barber Surgeons, and the Guild of Apothecaries. Under this scheme, the rights and duties of physicians, surgeons, and apothecaries within a seven-mile radius of London were strictly defined.[29]

In this system the physician was an aloof and gentlemanly advisor who did not sully his hands with the task of manually dealing with patients. In fact, physicians were not allowed to do anything but diagnose, prognose, and prescribe. Surgeons, however, were not permitted to carry out any of these responsibilities, and were limited to manual treatments. Apothecaries, who were formerly associated with the grocer's guild, mixed and sold pharmaceuticals and potions. Both surgeons and apothecaries were forbidden to act without a physician's direction.[30]

When any member of a group performed a function reserved for another, he could be prosecuted. While each of the three required specialized training, only physicians were required to possess a university education. Physicians could not charge or sue for fees, but had to accept the payment that was offered. This hierarchical arrangement applied only to the London area, but even in this setting it was theoretical rather than actual. Nevertheless, this arrangement was important because it supported the image of the physician as an elite, gentlemanly public servant who was uninterested in financial gain.[31]

This system was not transplanted to the American colonies. The majority of the immigrants to New England did not come from London, where at least the ideal of the elite physician existed. Instead, colonists came from rural farming communities like East Anglia, where the highest percentage of practitioners was comprised of physicians who diagnosed, prescribed, performed surgery, and mixed drugs. In addition, many of the practitioners in these areas also served as cobblers, wheelwrights, ministers, and innkeepers. Most emigrants had no experience with and saw no reason for the specialized, educated, full-time physicians of London.

Virtually all colonial physicians were generalists. They eschewed the distinctions of London because of the type of practitioner common in rural England, because of the scarcity of university-educated physicians in the colonies, and because they could make more money by prescribing and preparing medications than by prescribing alone. It was this image of the physician as generalist practitioner that would influence American attitudes toward medicine.[32]

The prevailing attitudes toward physicians in the mid-1700s did not stop physicians from attempting to raise the standards and change the image of the profession. John Morgan, born of an upper-class Philadelphia family in 1735, served a medical apprenticeship in America and studied medicine in London and Edinburgh. When he returned to America in 1765, he attempted to organize the medical profession into the hierarchical guilds he had seen in London. More importantly, he met with the board of trustees of the College of Philadelphia (now the University of Pennsylvania) and convinced them to establish the first medical school in America. The school adopted formidable entrance requirements and demanded four years of study for a doctorate. Morgan also called for strict licensure and separation of medicine from surgery and pharmacy.[33]

Despite Morgan's stature, his proposals did not have the desired impact. Some colonies passed licensure laws in the last half of the eighteenth century, but these laws did not effectively limit or proscribe practice.[34] Although Morgan promised to forgo all surgery and pharmacy, most physicians could not afford to make that sacrifice and continued to practice in all three roles.[35]

Morgan's campaign to transform medical education also failed. In fact, the effort to improve medical education succeeded only in institutionalizing poor training. Several schools copied the College of Philadelphia model, but the institutions were unable to maintain its high standards. By 1789 even the Philadelphia medical school had lowered its entrance requirements and reduced the length of study to one year. Other schools followed suit. Morgan and his supporters introduced medical schools into America to enhance the status of the profession. Other American physicians had the same idea, and by the early nineteenth century, medical schools began to proliferate. In 1834 there were over twenty. By 1850 forty-two schools, as well as many diploma mills, had been established in the United States.[36] Many of these institutions were proprietary schools, and in their competition for students they had low entrance requirements and graduation standards. Even earnest medical administrators were forced to forgo enhanced standards. Admission was open to any student who could pay the fees. By 1850 the typical program at American medical schools was comprised of two identical, four-month terms of lectures. At Harvard, one of the better schools in the country, students were required to pass only five of nine five-minute oral examinations. As late as 1870, perhaps one-half of Harvard's medical students could not write.[37]

Alfred Stillé, a professor of pathology at the University of Pennsylvania, admitted in 1847 that the medical profession had become "[d]egraded in its position and authority" and forfeited "public confidence" as a result of the state of medical education.

By an extraordinary multiplication of medical schools a vulgar rivalry has arisen in spirit and conduct similar to that displayed in the competitions of steamboats, and railroads, with the same means resorted to for reaching success. Education is cheapened, the period of study abridged, or lightened—no irksome examinations are to be endured, and degrees acquired easily and assuredly.[38]

The proliferation of medical schools and diplomas, and the accompanying deterioration of educational standards in the first half of the nineteenth century affected physicians' status and their vulnerability to malpractice suits in two ways. First, the mediocre education offered at most schools left graduates ill prepared to deal with the complexities of the human body. Physicians' resulting deficiencies often led to bungled diagnoses and treatments, which in turn generated law suits. An editorialist for the *Medical Examiner* admitted in 1841 that while "malignity and sordid calculation are no infrequent instigators of prosecutions for malpractice, it is quite possible for medical men, in these days of easy graduation and multiplied professorships, to be guilty of culpable neglect or—in the existing condition of many medical schools—scarcely blamable neglect."[39] Alden March, a nationally known specialist in surgery and a professor at Albany Medical School, agreed. Although he condemned the wave of malpractice suits that threatened even "respectable surgeons," he confessed that "too many ignorant and careless men get into the ranks of our profession, who are liable to commit errors, for the consequences of which, the law holds them responsible. This would seem to indicate the necessity of higher attainments in our profession."[40] Individual doctors who were the product of cursory medical educations that were devoid of clinical experience and anatomical instruction were more likely to make mistakes and become defendants in malpractice suits.

Second, the farcical educational process debased the status of the medical profession as a whole. Physicians had hoped to use education to establish professional credibility and overcome the multitude of home practitioners, folk healers, midwives, and irregular practitioners who practiced in the early nineteenth century.[41] Indignation with this attempt arose from contradictory sentiments. The popular democracy of the Jacksonian period was accompanied by an anti-intellectualism that elevated native intelligence over education and common sense over expertise. This feeling informed attitudes toward politics, law, religion, and medicine. Andrew Jackson personified the unschooled, uncorrupted, unassuming wisdom that captured the imagination and hearts of the country.[42]

Jacksonian Democrats resented the pretension of physicians who endeavored to place themselves above other practitioners and the common people. Worthington Hooker, a Connecticut doctor who wrote in the 1840s, lamented that "education in the science of medicine is practically despised by quite a large portion of the community." According to Hooker, many people demonstrated a "readiness to put the quack on a level with the thoroughly-educated physician, or even above him," because they felt that "[m]any a man has arisen to eminence in other professions by his own exertions, without any great amount of education, and why should this not be the case in the practice of medicine?"[43] Jacksonian antipathy toward educated elites was undoubtedly compounded by the fact that even properly trained physicians could cure only a few maladies with any consistency.

A Pennsylvania physician, William Wood, commented on the phenomenon in 1849 and linked it to the profession's malpractice woes. He explained that physicians had customarily defended medical education despite the facility with which diplomas were granted "on the ground that it is better to provide the people with imperfectly educated physicians, than with those not educated at all." However, the experience of "some few years" had led Wood to change his position. He now believed that in light of many of the malpractice suits: "It is better to be without a diploma; for then besides having the sympathies of the community, the practitioner can say, 'I make no pretensions, I offer no certificate of ability, and only gave my neighbor in his sufferings such aid as I could.' "[44] It is unlikely that the abolition of medical degrees would have immunized the profession from accusations of malpractice, but Wood's assertion underscored the public's attitude toward education and the profession: The physician was at greater legal peril because he had undemocratically claimed expertise through education.

Ironically, physicians could be maligned for possessing both a medical education and a defective medical education. Although Jacksonians resented the ostentation of the medical degree, they were appalled by the insufficient education of most physicians. As Alfred Stillé reported in 1847, the "diploma [M.D.] has lost its value. Everyone knows of its prostitution, and has ceased to regard it as in itself deserving attention."[45]

Stillé cited another important product of the burgeoning number of American medical schools: a burgeoning number of doctors. He speculated that "the annual number of graduates, in medicine, is at present probably larger in the United States, than in the whole of the residue of the civilized world."[46] Other physicians shared Stillé's concern over the flood of physicians entering practice in the first half of the nineteenth century. One writer reported in 1858 that "[e]very little hamlet has now two or three physicians, where one physician, forty years ago did the entire practice of half a dozen such hamlets."[47] Between 1765 and 1800 the five existing American medical schools produced less than 250 physicians. Many communities subsisted without the benefit of a formally educated practitioner.[48] But most figures suggest that the supply of physicians between 1790 and 1850 grew from scarcity to surfeit.

With the medical school "mania" of the early 1800s, the number of graduates increased dramatically. During the 1830s medical schools granted approximately 6,800 degrees. In the 1850s almost 18,000 physicians received their M.D.'s. Although most early estimates are imprecise, the total number of practicing physicians grew from between 3,500 and 4,900 in 1790, to 40,564 in 1850.[49] Some of this increase reflected the medical needs of the growing population. However, the ratio of physicians to inhabitants increased between 1790 and 1850 from between 1:800 and 1:1,100, to about 1:570.[50] In some areas of the country the density of physicians was greater. In 1846 a speaker before a graduating medical class bemoaned the crowded state of the profession and argued that the country did not need more than 1 physician for every 2,500–3,000 inhabitants.[51] It was said that in 1845 there was 1 doctor for every 400 persons in Buffalo; in St. Louis, the proportion reached 1 to 274.[52]

Despite these figures, the "surplus" of physicians was regional and not national and may have represented a maldistribution, rather than an overall excess of practitioners.[53] For example, communities on the western frontier continued without adequate numbers of trained physicians. Still, physicians in the areas with an oversupply of medical practitioners suffered in several ways. The over abundance of physicians had played a major role in diminishing the respectability and status of the profession since 1800. One physician who had practiced for forty-seven years complained in 1858 that the medical profession was "greatly overstocked; and it is a natural consequence, that where there is an excess of a commodity in the market, its value should be proportionally diminished."[54]

F. Cambell Stewart, a midcentury physician, offered an additional interpretation of the relationship between an increase in numbers and the decline in status. He explained that, despite the generally low status of the physicians as a group, many individual doctors were held in high esteem by their respective communities. The elevated social status of these physicians could "excite the ambition of many of the thousand applicants for admission to our ranks, some of them thus see a road opened for access to a society which it might be much more difficult for them to reach by other more laborious and circuitous routes."[55] As unworthy social climbers crowded the profession, the overall image of the profession deteriorated further. The decline of public trust and confidence emboldened patients and made it easier for them to accuse their physicians of mistreatment.

"Want of Union and Harmony"

The rise in the number of medical practitioners created another pitfall for potential malpractice defendants. In the 1824 *Lowell* malpractice case, the defense attorney asked the jury to weigh the patient's injury against the two defendants' importance to their communities. "What is the consequence of a limb like Lowell's," the lawyer demanded, "compared with the usefulness of such a physician as Dr. Hawks, entirely lost to the present scene from his practice?"[56] Hawks and his codefendant, Faxon, were the only doctors in their respective towns. The jury could not decide on a verdict, and the trial judge issued a nonsuit ruling.[57] The prospect of losing the sole practitioner in the village may have intimidated the judge and jury and influenced their decision.

If other late eighteenth- and early nineteenth-century juries were influenced by physicians' value to their communities, as suggested by the *Lowell* case, they were probably less likely to charge and convict physicians and risk denying their villages medical aid. The alteration of legal rules regarding contract, tort, property, and corporations between 1780 and 1820 encouraged the expansion of commercial enterprises that would presumably serve the public interest.[58] Similarly, the attitudes of juries and judges in medical cases may have represented the socially "instrumental function" of law by protecting and allowing the development of another resource vital to the welfare of the public: medical care. But by 1850 the number of physicians in some areas had increased to the point of a glut. If a malpractice suit destroyed a physician's career, there was always another doctor, or more, ready to take his place. In this situation, juries and judges were less likely to shelter physicians from unhappy, litigious patients.

The surplus of physicians in many parts of the country also subverted the medical profession's status and gave rise to malpractice suits by engendering and exacerbating competition among regular practitioners. Competition, however, did not arise merely from the excess of doctors. Physicians often fought bitterly over control of local medical societies and against rival organizations. Other intraprofessional disputes centered on issues such as fee bills and consultations. Local medical societies set price guidelines for physicians to follow. When practitioners undercut or overpriced, quarrels ensued.[59] Physician-owned and operated medical schools were also the source of open economic conflict.[60] One physician, writing in 1846, admonished his colleagues that they "too often pursued a course in furtherance of their own individual interests which was calculated to impair that of the body [medical profession] generally." If the profession did not stem the tide of dissension, the writer warned, conflict would "lessen the estimation in which [the profession] should be held by the public at large."[61]

The founders of the American Medical Association recognized that the lack of internal cohesion and low education standards damaged public confidence in the profession. Representatives from various state medical societies met in 1846 to attack the problems of the national medical community. A second convention in 1847 finalized the form of the organization and devised a code of ethics that reflected the concerns of elite physicians. The code enumerated the reciprocal obligations of doctor and patient and condemned fraternization with irregular practitioners and quacks. It also devoted considerable attention to relations among regular physicians and their impact on public confidence and respect. It advised that since

the feelings of medical men may be painfully assailed in their intercourse with each other, and which cannot be understood or appreciated by the general society, neither the subject matter of such differences nor the adjudication of the arbitrators should be made public, as publicity in a case of this nature may be personally injurious to the individuals concerned, and can hardly fail to bring discredit on the faculty.[62]

The authors hoped both to encourage internal peace and to portray a harmonious front for the public. The AMA, however, wielded little or no coercive power. It was comprised of only a small number of physicians and a multitude of local and state societies that jealously retained their sovereignty. Consequently, the warnings in the code failed to restrain the competition and strife that were seemingly endemic to the profession.

Large numbers of physicians streaming out of medical schools in search of patients added to the discord. The competition for patients became so vigorous that a young student was advised in 1836 that the "only way to get practice would be to underbid those already practicing."[63] Conversely, established practitioners considered new physicians trespassers. As one writer confirmed, "[A]ny new comer is looked upon as an intruder upon vested rights."[64] Many doctors believed that conflict indirectly encouraged malpractice suits by marring the physician's public image. But they also contended that competition, born of the physician surplus, directly incited suits.

The burgeoning number of regular physicians was joined by a wide range of medical sects, or irregular practitioners. Thomsonians formed a self-taught sect that used only botanic remedies. Samuel Thomson, the founder, was a New Hampshire farmer who claimed that all illness was caused by an imbalance of the four bodily elements of antiquity: earth, air, fire, and water. Specifically, he believed that illness was synonymous with loss of bodily heat. Thomson remedied this imbalance with large doses of botanic concoctions of cayenne pepper and other sweat-producing herbs. He frequently used steam baths or hot bricks and blankets to produce the same effect. He also employed powerful "natural" vomiting and laxative agents, specifically lobelia, to purge patients. Thomson patented and sold the rights to his medical regime, making it widely available. Despite the severity of his cures, Thomson and his followers viciously attacked regular physicians for their use of harsh, "heroic" treatments. They were able to take this seemingly hypocritical stance by successfully branding regular physicians enemies of the common man and democratic, egalitarian ideals. Thomsonian writers condemned regular physicians for their supposed aristocratic pretensions and supported popular political movements of the Jacksonian era. Thomson claimed that his medical theories were the most democratic because they made each American his or her own physician. Although there were certainly many regular physicians who also held some of these cultural and political beliefs, the Thomsonians were able to create the impression that they were the exception rather than the rule.[65]

Regular physicians also faced threats from homeopathic practitioners. Homeopathy was based on the doctrine that "like cures like." Samuel Hahnemann, the founder of the movement, cataloged substances that would produce effects similar to various maladies. The homeopathic practitioner then provided patients with the designated substance in minute doses. According to the theory of *infinitesimals*, concoctions would be diluted sometimes as much as one part to a billion or even one to a trillion. The sect believed that these virtually microscopic amounts of medication could be fortified by *dynamization*, or the vigorous shaking of the preparation, an enormous but well-defined number of times. Homeopaths were generally educated and sincere practitioners. Their treatment regime was extremely benign and harmless—a major advantage over regular physicians and Thomsonians. In addition to orthodox physicians, homeopaths, and Thomsonians,[66] Americans could choose from a medical potpourri of alternative practitioners including hydropaths, who stressed the therapeutic virtues of water in all its forms, as well as natural bonesetters, mesmerists, root doctors, and phrenologists.

Irregular physicians, especially Thomsonians and homeopaths, became enormously popular in the first half of the nineteenth century and created significant competition for regular physicians. They battled orthodox practitioners not only for patients but also for the mantle of medical legitimacy. Regular, orthodox physicians could only tenuously claim therapeutic superiority and tried to overcome their irregular rivals by mocking their techniques and lobbying state legislatures for restrictive licensure. The multitude of irregular, alternative practitioners abounding in the period may have indirectly aggravated the malpractice problem. By offering several reasonable, and in some cases viable, alternatives to orthodox treatment, irregulars helped envelop the regular medical community in a cloud of doubt and distrust.

Thomsonians and homeopaths occasionally encouraged patients to sue regular physicians for malpractice and testified against them in court.[67] Most physicians agreed, however, that irregular practitioners stimulated few suits and played only a small role in the patient's decision to bring charges. The real enemy was inside the orthodox medical community. In fact, between 1835 and 1865, doctors identified intraprofessional competition among regular physicians as the primary source of the malpractice affliction more often than any other cause. In 1847 Alden March claimed, "In most of the prosecutions of physicians and surgeons for malpractice, it is fair to presume, from a pretty extended observation, that they originate in, or grow out of an unwarrantable rivalry, or perhaps jealousy, between two neighboring practitioners."[68] The 1853 Massachusetts Medical Society committee on malpractice concluded that "the jealous eyes of rivals" were the "most important" cause of the prevalent suits.[69] Similarly, in 1854 a writer decried, "We too often find the viper within our own ranks; those who from envy or rivalry seek to destroy the hard earned fame of one in every way their superior."[70] One of the patriarchs of mid- and late–nineteenth-century medicine, Stephen Smith, concurred in 1860 that his "own experience in suits for alleged malpractice has led to the conclusion that both the source of the evil and the remedy lie within the pale of the profession itself. The secret history of the vast majority of these cases reveals the humiliating fact that they were instigated by medical men."[71]

Some physicians inadvertently generated suits with offhand remarks while examining patients. Samuel Parkman, a frequent commentator on malpractice, reported that sometimes "a medical man is entrapped into the examination of a case which he afterwards discovers involves a legal investigation." Parkman explained that a patient who believed he had been mistreated by a physician would consult a second practitioner in hope of securing evidence. "The second surgeon soon discovers that he is summoned as a witness in a trial in which the first surgeon is the defendant and the patient is the plaintiff."[72] In one such case a New York man broke his leg when he was pinned under a falling tree. A local physician set the leg, but since it was planting time, the man hobbled about in the field trying to work. About six months later he visited a second doctor who examined the limb and remarked that "the attending physician ought to be ashamed of it; and that he ought to pay him for a year's work." The farmer sued the first physician for malpractice.[73]

When physicians testified as expert witnesses in court, they attempted to display their medical superiority to the audience, often to the detriment of the defendant. In their endeavor to appear knowledgeable and competent, they often claimed or intimated that their methods of treatment were safer, more advanced, or more effective than the defendant's. As one observer noted, when physicians were "called into court, one is pitted against another, like two roosters in a cock pit."[74] Other physicians genuinely attempted to protect the defendant when they testified in malpractice trials. But under the rigorous cross-examination of the prosecuting attorney medical witnesses often found themselves giving more damaging evidence than they had intended.[75]

Some physicians, however, deliberately used malpractice suits against competitors. When Dr. Sargent was sued by a New Hampshire man in 1852 for the treatment of a broken leg, the medical witnesses separated into two camps according to their place of practice. The two expert witnesses for the prosecution were local physicians who undoubtedly competed with Dr. Sargent for patients. All the physicians who testified for Sargent came from surrounding communities. Sargent lost two trials relating to the case, won on appeal, and finally settled out of court.[76] Physicians sometimes urged patients to sue their professional antagonists in order to ruin their reputations and destroy their practices. Often the accuser served as an expert witness for the prosecution. Covetous, aspiring physicians used suits to discredit established practitioners. Established practitioners used them to discourage new competitors. Occasionally, these suits inspired retaliatory litigation.

The Crosby case is once again illustrative. In 1847 a Vermont man sued his two physicians for malpractice. They had treated the patient for a broken tibia, the smaller bone in the lower leg, which healed in a twisted position. Dixi Crosby, a local medical man, served as the key witness for the prosecution. He argued that the defendant physicians should have visited the patient more frequently, perhaps even daily. He questioned the defendants' treatment and declared that they had failed to diagnose an accompanying fracture of the fibula. The jury ruled against the defendants and charged them $500. In reporting the case for the *Boston Medical and Surgical Journal* an editorialist noted that the defendants were Crosby's competitors and that the plaintiff had previously been a patient of the star witness. The editorialist, carefully avoiding libel, remarked that "Dr. Crosby, no doubt, intended to do justice to all parties, although his testimony was strongly for the plaintiff, as evidently were his feelings." While all the other medical physicians in the case "expressed no doubt" as to the propriety and quality of the defendants' conduct, Crosby's "testimony upon the main points, method of treatment, and attendance, was at variance with the testimony of the other witnesses."[77]

While the reporter tempered his analysis of Crosby's motives, the message remained plain. Crosby had used his position as expert witness to undercut his competitors. A Vermont appellate court overturned the conviction of the physicians, and in May 1851 a subsequent jury found them innocent of any malpractice.[78] The same month, Crosby found himself the target of a malpractice accusation for an injury and treatment that had occurred six years earlier. When a jury convicted and fined Crosby $800, medical editorialists rushed to his defense and speculated that a "scheme is imagined to have been devised for breaking down the professor [Crosby] . . . in other words, by driving off an old surgeon, there is a chance of dropping into his place."[79] The coincidental timing of the suit against Crosby also suggests that it may have been a reprisal for his role in the previous malpractice trial.

A young physician in the 1840s complained that he was plagued by accusations and suits for malpractice as soon as he arrived in Erie, Pennsylvania. The suits, he said, were instigated by local practitioners "who regarded his advent with a jealous eye." The same practitioners who encouraged patients to sue the newcomer served as expert witnesses for the prosecution. The strategy worked. After being sued for two smallpox vaccinations and one fracture treatment, the doctor "wearied of vexation . . . [and] left his suits, his property, and his family, to seek a more generous home and better rewards, in the golden valleys of California." The physician eventually returned to Erie County to face trial. He was acquitted on two charges, but fined $1,450 in the third trial.[80]

Even powerful and famous physicians were vulnerable to suits incited by professional enemies. William Beaumont became world renowned in the 1830s for his historic studies on digestion gained by observations through the chronically unhealed wound in Alexis St. Martin's stomach.[81] In 1844 Beaumont, practicing in St. Louis, Missouri, took a public position in a dispute between two rival medical schools. The opposing faction convinced two patients to sue Beaumont for malpractice. In one case he was charged, along with a codefendant, with an incompetent hernia operation that left the young woman patient with a small, open incision. Beaumont neither assisted in the surgery nor advised the attending physician. Although he was only one of several physicians to view the patient during her long convalescence, his name was added to the $10,000 suit. A local physician claimed that some doctors "resolve to attain practice at any cost, whether of professional principles or of a brother's character." They were willing to use "unholy means" and "calculated success by others' downfall, and by means of detraction will sap the reputation of a professional brother, with the hope of building up a practice in his ruin." Beaumont was ultimately exonerated, but a vicious pamphlet debate continued for many months.[82]

Medical literature counseled physicians against playing either an accidental or a malicious role in inciting litigation. An editorialist in 1847 gently advised that a "difference of opinion between two or more physicians, where the spirit of kindness and courtesy controls the intemperate expressions of vanity and malevolence, may often lead to the best results."[83] Another writer, commenting on malpractice cases for fractures, observed, "These cases should lead members of our profession to be kind, generous, liberal to one another, and not to impute to ignorance or inattention, that which is the result of a generally incurable accident."[84] Other writers encouraged harsh reprisals against physicians who purposefully instigated litigation. As one physician declared in 1854, "Those puny strife engenderers, who stir up these unnatural suits, deserve the execrations of all classes and conditions." He recommended that "they should be shunned and left to wallow in their own filthiness."[85]

"Radical and Progressive Proclivities"

The medical profession's open competition within itself, combined with its lack of a respected and distinct social status, reflected the social and political environment of Jacksonian America. The roots of the crisis are somewhat earlier. Although the stratified nature of society had been under attack since the early eighteenth century, the republican rhetoric of 1776 hastened the process. Between the American Revolution and 1800, the traditional ranks of society rapidly blurred, and social hierarchies weakened. Plain, unlettered men started to believe that they were the equals of men of any rank and began to resent and hate any emblem of hierarchical privilege or status.

Professional monopolies reeked of aristocratic privilege and were inconsistent with the growing notion of equality and democracy because they interfered with free and open competition. The late eighteenth-century attempts of elite physicians to organize the profession failed because they could not provide efficacious care and because their reorganization plans mirrored the hierarchical, tripartite arrangement of the London medical profession. Consequently, when physicians lobbied early state legislatures to pass licensure laws, they met with limited success. Virtually every state had passed some type of licensure statute by the late eighteenth century but the laws were inclusive rather than exclusive. Many of the statutes did not forbid unlicensed practice but merely provided certificates of legitimacy to "qualified" doctors. In some states unlicensed physicians were only prohibited from suing in court for unpaid fees. Unlicensed physicians in these jurisdictions could mitigate this handicap by requiring payment in advance.[86] Even in states where licensure laws provided penalties for unsanctioned practice, juries generally would not convict violators. For much of the public, physicians' education and results did not justify the establishment of a medical monopoly. Many Americans, especially in the working classes, believed that a physician's status should be determined by his performance and not by legislation.[87]

This trend of decreasing respect for traditional authority and status accelerated after 1800. Physicians were continually frustrated in their attempts to retain their social status and to establish a market monopoly by licensure. They lost ground as democratic, antistatus feelings grew. Alexis de Tocqueville, one of the most eloquent and opinionated observers of Jacksonian culture, concluded that democratic revolutions were generally followed by an attack on symbols of social aristocracy and an increase in individualism.[88] The old order was changing rapidly. These new sentiments glorified the image of a society of common, hard-working individuals operating without legal or institutional restraints. This philosophy had no room for aristocratic, intellectual, or economic privilege and was accompanied by widespread attacks on various forms of authority. Jacksonian Democrats praised free trade and competition and condemned monopolies and chartered corporations. They attacked professional licensure as an injustice as odious as the monster U.S. Bank.[89]

Critics of the profession argued that physicians were no different from merchants or craftsmen. Medical sects such as Thomsonians, homeopaths, and hydropaths claimed to embody the free-market, common-man mentality of the Jacksonians and joined in the attack on the desires of regular physicians for a privileged legal position. An antebellum Ohio journalist exemplified the mood of much of the working class when he declared that "[w]e go for free-trade in doctoring."[90]

State legislatures responded. Beginning in 1838, jurisdiction after jurisdiction abolished already weak licensure laws. By 1850, only New Jersey and the District of Columbia retained any effective controls over medical practice.[91] There was "free trade in doctoring." These were the "radical and progressive proclivities" that Alexander Garnett believed "induce[d] every street urchin or illiterate mechanic, to entertain the belief that he has not only the unquestionable right to fill, but that he is eminently fitted for any station or position in society."[92]

Physicians saw an intimate connection between Jacksonian rhetoric, their decline in status, the abolition of licensure, and the increase in malpractice suits. William Wood noted in 1849 that "the general influences leading to these perversions of justice [malpractice cases] can be readily perceived by all." According to Wood, the efforts to limit the practice of medicine to those who "have the abilities and acquirements essential to its proper understanding" had failed. The public, Wood held, considered the limitation of medical practice to those with "scientific attainments" as an attempt to "monopolize rights and infringe on the greatest liberty." As a result, "ignorant and impudent pretenders, under a great variety of humbugging titles, come before the public with equal rights and a better chance for public favour, than the regular practitioners." Meanwhile, the medical doctor was forced to pursue his profession "under risks and hazards no prudent man could encounter."[93]

Stephen Smith saw a direct correlation between the lack of medical licensure in the United States and climbing malpractice rates. Smith pointed out that Britain, France, and Germany had enacted stringent licensure laws that were designed "to develop, foster, and advance true scientific medicine." The physicians in these countries, Smith noted, suffered fewer malpractice suits than their American counterparts.[94] In the absence of any limitation on medical practice, malpractice became the only way to protect the public from incompetence. Thus, in 1847 one writer recognized that the lack of effective licensure in most states left "to the common law the task of guarding their citizens by suits for malpractice."[95]

The use of market forces and individual malpractice cases to oversee the medical profession was a characteristically Jacksonian approach to regulation. Licensure, in the Jacksonian mind, represented regulation from the top down and appeared to benefit the physician by creating an unfair monopoly and relying on artificial measures of merit. Malpractice suits, however, represented regulation from the bottom up. Individual patients could choose which practitioner to patronize, and individual juries could decide if the medical treatment had been competent. This arrangement was consistent with regulating patterns in other areas of early nineteenth-century life. Most regulation was "local and self-sustaining." States made few overarching efforts to enforce existing regulations, and if an individual did not initiate a lawsuit, the statutes were not enforced.[96] Indeed, one of the hallmarks of the Jacksonian movement was the desire to make the courts and the law more accessible and responsive to the common person.[97]

While patients increasingly accused regular physicians of malpractice, Thomsonians and homeopaths, who espoused the social and political equalitarianism of the working classes, were seldom sued. The Pennsylvania medical society committee investigating malpractice found that irregular physicians, who are "gross and ignorant pretenders, [and] whose whole existence is a continued system of mal-practice, pass unnoticed and unharmed." A judge interviewed during the investigation confirmed that although he had seen many suits against regular physicians, he knew of only one malpractice charge against a "quack doctor." The committee concluded that irregular physicians avoided law suits because "they act on popular prejudices." The regular physician "is hunted as the victim of popular prejudice, while the quack who has complied with that prejudice goes free."[98] Other writers agreed. In 1853 the *Western Medical and Surgical Journal* reported "that the chances are all together better for the acquittal of an ignorant, uneducated pretender to medical knowledge, who is really guilty, than that of an intelligent, well-educated surgeon to whom no fault can justly be charged."[99]

Physicians recognized that they were at greater risk from the poorer segments of society and blamed political and class antipathy for many of the suits and subsequent convictions. Malpractice suits offered injured farmers and laborers an outlet for antistatus, antiprofessional sentiment. A writer alleged in 1847 that "the people, or, at least that class of persons who are most exposed to accidents, and the least responsible, either for the surgeon's bill for professional attendance, or for the costs of a suit for mal-practice seem to require high surgical attainments."[100] And, as a physician claimed in 1849, "the interests and prejudices of the whole class are against the acts and doings of the regular practitioner."[101]

Prosecuting attorneys sometimes exploited this prejudice in their arguments to juries. In an 1848 New York case the patient's attorney condemned the medical profession as an "oppressive and aristocratic monopoly." While the trial court judge cautioned the jury to disregard the remarks, and while they returned a verdict for the physician, other physicians were not so lucky.[102] One layman observed that

[a] jury of laboring men . . . go into the jury box with feelings excited against the surgeon, because they think his business should produce no better pecuniary returns than his own; the surgeon's bill is always deemed exorbitant by them; and he is generally looked upon as almost a swindler, and living luxuriously upon their hard earnings; therefore they are always inclined to render a verdict against your profession, and in favor of one of their own class.[103]

The lay observer also described the reaction of a working-class jury to expert witness testimony. According to the narrator, "after a few questions are answered, they sneer and laugh at you [physicians], and make up their minds long before they leave the box." A medical editorialist verified the characterization and confirmed that a "great number of these trials in various parts of the Union, but especially amongst farmers, are terminated in this way."[104] A writer in 1856 concluded, "The trial of a professional man for an alleged malpractice by a jury of laborers is a farce and a disgrace to our country."[105] All malpractice juries, however, were not composed solely of doctor-hating laborers and farmers. Otherwise physicians would not have won as many cases as they did.

Corporations and physicians shared working-class resentment and distrust. The Massachusetts Medical Society committee on malpractice concluded that patients "from whom the least remuneration is to be obtained" were responsible for most of the suits. The committee believed that the sympathy of the jury was generally with the plaintiff. According to the study, "this sympathy for the seemingly oppressed and misused has influence in all cases where a corporation, civic or otherwise is the defendant; and it cannot be denied that it is an important element in the patient's decision to bring a suit against his physician."[106] Corporations, specifically railroads, were also suffering through their first wave of lawsuits in the early 1840s and 1850s. In personal injury cases against corporations, plaintiffs' attorneys often described the cases as battles between oppressive, powerful corporations and virtuous, hard-working laborers.[107]

Declining social status of physicians, "defective medical acquirements," the "want of union and harmony," and "radical and progressive proclivities" were central elements in the increase of malpractice suits between 1835 and 1865. These factors clearly helped to generate, directly and indirectly, many of the suits in the period. However, they do not provide the fundamental explanation for the malpractice phenomenon. Poor medical training and therapy, intraprofessional competition, and Jacksonian sentiments were immediate causes of the dramatic increase in litigation and help to explain why these three decades contrasted so starkly with the pre-1835 years. Yet, as important as these elements were in 1835–1865, their gradual disappearance did not retard the rate of malpractice prosecutions.

Appellate malpractice decisions multiplied at a rate faster than the population through the early twentieth century. During this time the therapeutic, educational, professional, and social trends that played an important role in promoting suits during the 1835–1865 period faded and in some cases reversed. The malpractice epidemic did not.

In the 1870s, medical education started its long trek toward excellence and respectability. The new medical school produced more competent physicians and slowly raised respect toward the profession.[108] Much of the competitiveness and divisiveness that had afflicted the profession in the Jacksonian period dissipated by the first decades of the twentieth century. Statistical revelations and scientific discoveries of the last half of the nineteenth century helped standardize and unify medical beliefs and treatments, as did the standardization of medical education. Medical societies, which were weak and contentious in the 1840s, settled their differences, increased their membership, and successfully promoted professional harmony by 1900. Likewise, a reorganized AMA had a unifying and pacifying effect on the profession.[109] Finally, the Jacksonian antipathy for corporations, monopolies, and professions declined. In the 1880s and 1890s states instituted effective medical licensure laws that helped limit access to the profession. By 1900 the public still distrusted the intellectual, but recognized and often deferred to the authority of experts. These developments, the improvements in therapy in many areas of medicine, and the promise of the future significantly raised the status of the medical profession by 1920.[110]

Malpractice suits continued to rise in spite of the general improvement in the status of the profession and the disappearance of many elements that had incited litigants between 1835 and 1865. Contemporary observers were correct in blaming these factors for the wave of malpractice suits. However, litigiousness persisted because these factors were only the immediate and topical causes of suits in a specific historic period. The presence of these elements alone did not automatically lead to runaway litigation.

Despite the existence of many of the same elements that encouraged litigation in the rest of the country, medical malpractice suits in the South were rare. Antebellum southern physicians were also poorly organized and educated. Irregular practitioners, especially Thomsonians, were prevalent and popular there. Southern state legislatures abolished licensure about the same time as their northern counterparts. But, southern society had not yet undergone the cultural transformations that provided the fundamental preconditions for widespread malpractice prosecution. Therefore, even though many of the immediate factors that inspired suits in the North existed, they did not produce the same results.[111]

Suits continued to proliferate in the rest of the country long after the immediate causes of the Jacksonian period dissipated because the social and cultural foundations for the litigation continued to evolve unabated. Immediate factors such as low status, antiprofessionalism, and competition were responsible for provoking the first malpractice crisis of the 1840s. Without these elements, medical malpractice rates may have risen more gradually, but they cannot completely explain the flood of suits in the years 1835–1865 nor the unremitting litigation since.

CHAPTER 4

"The Expression of a Wellmade Man"

The expression of a wellmade man appears not only in his face,
It is in his limbs and joints also. . . . it is curiously in the joints of
   his hips and wrists,
It is in his walk . . . the carriage of his neck . . . the flex of his waist
   and
knees. . . .
                          —Walt Whitman, "I Sing the Body Electric" [1]

Malpractice suits arising from the treatment of fractures and dislocations constituted most of the increased litigation after 1835, and continued to be the major complaint through the early decades of the twentieth century. [2] Lay and professional attitudes toward orthopedic practice
and the development of fracture treatment, like physicians' low status,
intraprofessional rivalry, and Jacksonian sentiment, represented one of
the immediate causes of the first dramatic leap in malpractice rates.
But at the same time the impact of technological developments illustrates an underlying cultural attitude that helped cause suits into the
twentieth century. Malpractice suits were, in part, an expression of a
transformed view of the human body and an unprecedented concern
for physical well-being.

"The Mechanic's Hand"

Before 1835 fractures accounted for a small percentage of the total malpractice cases unless they resulted in a severe deformity or amputation. Malpractice suits were neither a common nor an entirely acceptable practice in the first third of the century, and patients generally refrained from bringing charges for milder injuries. As the practice of suing physicians became more acceptable and prevalent, patients freely sued on the basis of more moderate physical damage. Fractures and dislocations were the type of injuries most likely to have permanent but not grievous physical results such as shortened or deformed limbs, frozen joints, and long periods of convalescence. These injuries left the prospective plaintiff with a physical manifestation of the defendant/physician's supposed incompetence to display to sympathetic jurors. The long recovery period usually required for orthopedic injuries provoked potential plaintiffs by keeping them out of work and causing them long-term discomfort.

In spite of the protracted healing process, however, patients sometimes left their beds and went to work before doing so was safe or sensible. Occasionally, patients would loosen or remove painful or restrictive splints and bandages. Premature activity and interference with the physician's treatment could hamper the healing process, distort the results, or even worsen the patient's injury. In these instances physicians could ostensibly protect themselves in court with the doctrine of *contributory negligence* by arguing that the patient was responsible for the bad results of treatment.

In one such case in 1856 an Ohio man was thrown from a sleigh near his home. He severely fractured both bones in his lower leg. A year later, when his leg healed with some shortening and deformity, he sued his physician for malpractice. The defense attorney introduced a parade of witnesses who affirmed that the patient had been careless and did not follow the physician's instructions. One witness testified that he had accompanied the patient, still on crutches, on an all-night, whiskey-drinking raccoon hunt. Another witness had drunk with the patient until he became "pretty well sprung." Then the injured man "said he could walk as good as me; jumped over a manure pile by aid of his cane; [and] tried to walk curb stone without [his] cane." According to one witness, the plaintiff admitted that "the leg had been set straight and he had hurt it running about." The jury returned a verdict of not guilty after only three minutes of deliberation.[3]

Patient complicity was not always so obvious. Contributory negligence was a "complete defense" and a potentially powerful weapon for defendants. If the defendant/physician could demonstrate that the patient was in any way responsible for the failure of the treatment, the injured party would receive no award. However, contributory negligence was not always easy to prove and could be ignored by juries. Additionally, juries may have been hesitant to accept contributory negligence as a defense because it so thoroughly absolved the physician of liability. Therefore, it is difficult to determine the impact of the doctrine in the early nineteenth century.

When malpractice suits for all types of injuries increased after 1835, it was not surprising that fracture cases became the predominant subject of litigation. Fractures and dislocations were common in a society dominated by manual labor.[4] They yielded less severe, but often permanent injuries, which, in a culture increasingly sympathetic to malpractice charges, were considered legitimate subjects for litigation. Moreover, orthopedic injuries were occurring at an increasing rate in the first half of the century because of the newly mechanized and dangerous workplace. By 1860 arms and legs were being torn, crushed, and mutilated at an unprecedented rate on railways, in textile mills and mines, and by powerful steam engines.

Fracture and dislocation suits multiplied after 1835 not only because of burgeoning injuries and the general increase of malpractice cases of all types. The relationship between orthopedic treatment and contemporary malpractice rates was interactive. Before 1835 suits fell into two categories: severe injuries and mechanical treatments. By 1800 and through the first two decades of the nineteenth century, physicians could offer several moderately successful medical procedures. They were able to administer smallpox vaccinations, amputate limbs, set simple fractures and dislocations, excise superficial growths, and remove foreign objects.[5] Blood-letting was considered a relatively standardized procedure. By the third decade of the nineteenth century, male physicians had displaced many midwives by touting their scientific and technical expertise. Early obstetricians championed the advantages of superior physiological knowledge, drugs such as opium and ergot, and instruments like forceps and the crochet to ease painful and dangerous births. This new, but still primitive technology gave physicians a competitive advantage over the traditional midwife.[6]

Even though their successes were tenuous, physicians asserted technical expertise in these treatments, and patients began to expect mechanical, predictable results. As an 1827 judge explained, the physicians often exercised a profession "beset by great difficulties, [but] the employment of a man midwife and surgeon, for the most part, is merely mechanical."[7] These areas, especially vaccination, amputations, and obstetrics accounted for most of the scattered malpractice cases before 1835.

Even though orthopedics was in some respects considered a mechanical enterprise, fractures and dislocations generated very few cases in the early part of the nineteenth century. Physicians were moderately adept at restoring simple fractures, and even when they failed, the resulting deformity was usually too minor to warrant a suit in an atmosphere that was generally not conducive to malpractice charges. Severe compound fractures and dislocations, on the other hand, usually required amputation. Benjamin Bell's *System of Surgery*, a widely used textbook in the early part of the century, advised that "[f]rom the difficult treatment and uncertain event of compound fractures practitioners have been very universally disposed to consider the amputation of the fractured limb as necessary."[8] In his 1819 treatise on compound fractures Percival Pott noted that a surgeon often "showed much more rashness in attempting to save a limb, than he would have done in the amputation of it: The amputation would have been the more justifiable practice."[9] Similarly, Samuel Cooper, author of an 1813 handbook on surgery, warned that although "apparently desperate cases [of compound fracture] are sometimes cured, . . . every man also knows, that such escapes are very rare to admit of being made precedents and the majority of such attempts fail."[10] The standard of good practice before the 1820s demanded that physicians amputate badly broken limbs early instead of risking losing the patient to subsequent complications in an ill-advised attempt to save an arm or leg.

Amputations did not generate a large number of suits. By its nature,

PLATE III.

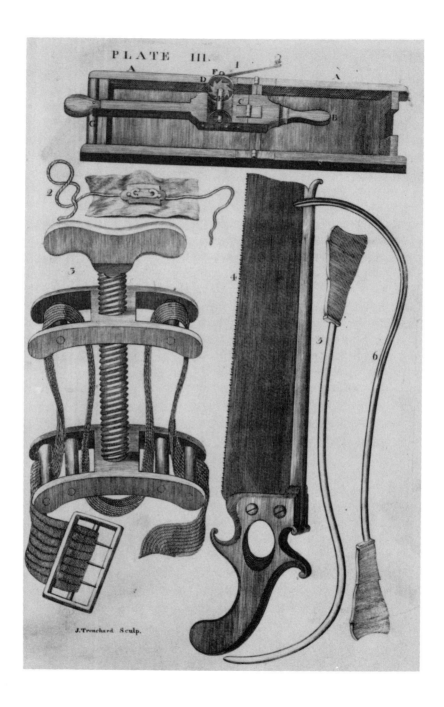

J. Trenchard Sculp.

amputation complicated the prosecution of a physician. Often, medical experts, juries, and judges could not examine the excised limb to determine if it truly required the operation. Even if the patient died during the procedure, as many did, there were limited legal remedies before the 1850s, when state legislatures enacted wrongful death statutes.[11] Even compound and complicated fractures in which patients kept their limbs yielded very few cases before 1835. Although the profession and the public were beginning to view procedures such as childbirth, vaccination, and amputation as mechanical and expected mechanical predictability, the treatment of complicated fracture injuries did not inspire the same confidence, and hence, the same demands.

Physicians were making dramatic improvements in the treatment of compound fractures and dislocations between 1820 and 1840, and these would change the basis of prognosis for fractures and dislocations, transform professional and lay attitudes, and provide the raw material for malpractice suits. During this period evidence rapidly accumulated against the desirability of frequent and perfunctory amputation. Astley Cooper, a surgical pioneer, declared in 1835:

Formerly, and with my recollection, it was thought expedient for the preservation of life, by many of our best surgeons to amputate the limb in these cases, but from our experience of late years, such advice would in a great majority of instances be now deemed highly injudicious.[12]

Physicians had developed new techniques, such as excising jagged pieces of exposed bone with saws and roughing the exposed ends of bones to facilitate union. They developed new bandaging and splinting procedures that allowed them to save both limbs and lives. Although antiseptic practices were not popular until the 1870s and 1880s, antebellum physicians also devised methods to counter the deadly infections that often followed compound fractures. For instance, innovative packing procedures ensured that wounds healed from the inside to the outside and diminished the number of severe internal infections. Consequently, during the 1830s and 1840s medical journals reported case

Machine for adjusting dislocations; screw tourniquet for amputations; seventeen-inch amputating saw; and grooved staffs for lithotomies. From Benjamin Bell, A System of Surgery *(1806). (Courtesy of the Historical Research Center, Houston Academy of Medicine, Texas Medical Center Library, Houston, Texas.)*

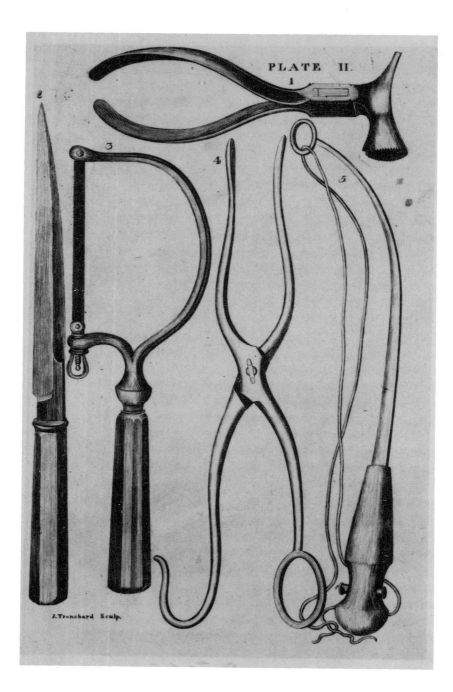

PLATE II.

J.Trenchard Sculp.

after case where compound fractures healed with the only bad effect being some shortening or deformity of the patient's limb.[13] William Walker presented a lengthy paper to the Massachusetts Medical Society in 1845 celebrating the advancements made in the treatment of compound and complicated fractures.[14] Finally, with the advent of anesthesia and painless surgery in the late 1840s, physicians could work longer and more carefully on patients and save rather than amputate limbs.[15]

Concurrently, a strong revulsion developed against amputations on other grounds. American physicians, under the influence of foreign clinicians such as Pierre Louis, scrutinized the treatment's efficacy statistically and discovered that the procedure was dreadfully dangerous.[16] In 1838 George Norris published a statistical appraisal of amputations, reporting that "[t]he endeavors that have been made for many years past, to save limbs under almost desperate circumstances . . . ha[ve] almost imperceivably produced a great unwillingness with us as to the performance of amputations." Moreover, Norris noted that amputations were hazardous. An 1833 survey of a St. Louis hospital found 13 fatalities out of 21 amputations. Norris conducted a survey at the Pennsylvania Hospital between 1831 and 1838 and discovered that 21 of 55 amputees died.[17]

Finally, physicians who embraced the move toward the "conservative medicine" of the late antebellum period were abandoning heroic medical and surgical procedures and placing a greater trust in the healing powers of nature. Austin Flint, a prominent surgeon, wrote in 1862 that the history of surgery in the first third of the century was characterized by the "introduction and frequent performance of numerous formidable operations." But, Flint remarked, "The change that has taken place is marked. We hear now comparatively little of the terrible operations of that sort which is associated with bloody deeds. What would have once been considered as a degree of courage to be admired is now stigmatized as rashness."[18] As William Walker recom-

Forceps for removing skull bone in trepanning; twelve-inch amputating knife; small spring saw for amputating fingers and toes; forceps for removing nasal polyps; and ligatures for removing uterine polyps. From Benjamin Bell, A System of Surgery *(1806). (Courtesy of the Historical Research Center, Houston Academy of Medicine, Texas Medical Center Library, Houston, Texas.)*

mended, physicians began to "estimate the powers of nature and of art in resisting and surmounting injuries."[19]

Not surprisingly, wholesale amputations had become less acceptable by the 1850s. As John Elwell declared in his 1860 work on malpractice, "An amputation that would have been justified by the rules of surgery and the operator protected in court, twenty years ago or even less time than that, would now be repudiated by the best authority and the operator justly chargeable with malpractice."[20] Physicians were caught in a double bind. The treatment of fractures had improved dramatically over the first half of the century, and they were more often able to save, rather than amputate limbs. However, badly injured limbs, even if spared, usually healed with some shortening or deformity. By the late 1830s patients were willing to sue physicians for treatment that saved profoundly injured limbs, albeit with some accompanying imperfection. The less than perfect results following compound fractures and dislocations were the single most common source of malpractice suits in the nineteenth century.

Physicians who exercised the most up-to-date techniques and preserved badly injured limbs often found themselves in greater legal danger than those practitioners who followed the archaic practice of perfunctory amputation. For example, in 1853 a New Hampshire man who had suffered a compound fracture-dislocation of his ankle and lower leg sued his physician after the joint became frozen in an awkward position. Despite testimony from expert witnesses that this type of an injury would have previously required amputation and that the patient should have been "glad to get off with any foot that would do to walk on," the jury found the physician guilty of malpractice.[21]

Though unnecessary or incompetent amputations were seldom penalized, physicians who saved limbs with compound or complex fractures were regularly sued. In 1856 the *Medical News* reported a typical case in an article titled "Legal Robbery of a Physician." A man had crushed his leg so badly that "the first question was as to the propriety of primary amputation." A doctor saved the man's leg, but as in other cases, some deformity resulted. The patient sued for malpractice and won a substantial award.[22]

The irony of physicians being placed at greater risk because of medical advancements and successes in saving limbs was noted by

Abraham Lincoln during his legal career. In 1856 Lincoln, a successful lawyer, represented two physicians against a charge of malpractice. An elderly man had badly broken his leg, which had shortened as it healed. Lincoln searched out physicians to coach him on fracture treatment and used a chicken bone at the trial to demonstrate the comparative brittleness of young and old bones. During his closing address Lincoln chastised the plaintiff: "Well! What I would advise *you* to do is get down on your *knees* and thank your heavenly Father, and also these two Doctors that you have any legs to stand on at all." Lincoln declared that the injury might have easily warranted amputation but that the physicians had exercised their skill and saved the leg. He reasoned that "[t]he slight defect that finally resulted, through Nature's methods of aiding the work of surgeons, is nothing compared to the loss of the limb altogether." The jury ruled in favor of the physicians and charged the trial costs to the plaintiff.[23]

Although physicians continued to practice the new fracture and dislocation procedures, the vagaries of malpractice litigation could have diminished the quality of medical care in individual cases by making it more attractive to condone amputation than to follow the safer and more effective procedure of saving limbs. Often, then, the best treatment for the patient was not necessarily the safest treatment for the surgeon. In fact, physicians were left more vulnerable by medical progress that frequently provided patients with visible, bodily evidence for malpractice lawsuits.

After the introduction of ether in 1846, amputations became less horrible and encouraged some physicians to operate indiscriminately. As a physician in 1851 noted, "anesthesia has its drawbacks and evils." Patients were too easily persuaded to submit to the knife of "what are called promising young men who carve their way into practice."[24] This small, but not insignificant, problem arose at the same time that methods for saving mangled limbs were improving and malpractice suits were increasing. Irresponsible practitioners had sufficient motivation to avoid the chance of a suit and enhance their image as heroic physicians with a few strokes of an amputating saw. Faced with a difficult fracture, an unethical or unscrupulous doctor might recommend a dramatic amputation to portray himself as a courageous surgeon and, at the same time, sidestep the prospect of an imperfect result and possible malpractice charge. As one writer suggested after observing a dispute between two physicians over treatment in the late 1830s, "In the absence of every other motive, one might almost suppose that amputation was desired to get rid of a troublesome case, and the more effectively to conceal a bad piece of surgery."[25] In this case, as in other scattered instances, the fear of prosecution may have encouraged the physician to ignore improvements in medical practice while more responsible surgeons saved limbs and left themselves open to attacks in ways that would not have been possible before the 1830s.

The prominence of fracture malpractice suits highlights an additional reason why regular physicians were more susceptible to malpractice charges than alternative practitioners. Thomsonians, homeopaths, and hydropaths were more likely to espouse the cultural, equalitarian sentiment that much of the public found lacking in the regular physician. They portrayed themselves as anti-elitist friends of the common people. Irregulars were also often less likely to treat the orthopedic injuries that generated the bulk of suits. Many focused their attention on medical therapeutics rather than surgery. Consequently, regular physicians treated more of the legally hazardous medical problems. This factor, however, only aggravated the regular physician's already vulnerable position. Irregulars did not completely eschew fracture treatment. Indeed, some irregulars specialized in orthopedic injuries. "Natural bonesetters" claimed to possess divinely-endowed, innate skill to manipulate and cure fractures and dislocations and actively competed with regular physicians. Bonesetters were competent, but not unerring practitioners.[26] Their failures, however, seldom resulted in lawsuits.

Worthington Hooker, a regular physician, repeatedly attempted to discredit the bonesetters by recounting episodes of the practitioners' ineptitude and mismanagement. In one case, a bonesetter had violently rebroken a man's nearly healed, fractured wrist. Complications from the treatment rendered the entire arm useless for life. Hooker noted, "If this man had been treated by an educated surgeon instead of an infallible bonesetter, he could undoubtedly have recovered large damages for such mal-practice."[27] Hooker explained that while bonesetters were quite willing to accuse regular physicians of malpractice, they rarely suffered the same fate themselves. Patients and juries treated bonesetters' shortcomings more gingerly than those of regular practitioners. According to Hooker, in some parts of the country "no jury could be found sufficiently unprejudiced to inflict any just penalty upon a bone-setter for mal-practice; though they would inflict it to the full if the same facts were proved to them in regard to any educated surgeon."[28]

The state of fracture treatment played a major role in the multiplication of suits, but it did not affect regular and irregular practitioners equally. While regular physicians' disproportionate share of the orthopedic cases may have increased their chances of being sued, it did not completely explain their near monopoly over malpractice suits. The various sources of cultural antipathy and intraprofessional rivalry were equally important in making regular physicians the prime target for malpractice accusations.

The dramatic advancements in fracture treatment technology of the first third of the nineteenth century contributed to the leap in malpractice rates in another way. Through much of this period physicians and the public recognized the uncertainty in the treatment of complex orthopedic injuries and refrained from characterizing the procedures as "mechanical." Regular physicians began to use the image of a machine to counter the claims of irregular physician competitors. Worthington Hooker, who usually stressed that medicine was a mixture of art and science and inherently uncertain, abandoned this view when discussing orthopedics. Hooker wrote that the public should realize that "the joints of the body are constructed upon *mechanical* principles, and that they are to be understood just like any other *machine*."[29] After the improvements in treatments proliferated, physicians and the public alike began to conceive of orthopedic practice in mechanistic terms. Many physicians were dazzled by recent advancements and seduced into unrealistic expectations.

Physicians and medical writers began to believe that mechanical, standardized treatment yielded consistent, faultless cures. An Ohio medical society committee studying malpractice concluded that the absence of a realistic and accurate standard of success was responsible for the outbreak of fracture-related suits. "There is little in our text-books, or courses of instruction, from which the beginning practitioner would be led to expect anything but perfect results." The committee explained that doctors called to examine possible instances of malpractice were often misled by unrealistic expectations of cures. If their colleagues did not attain their ideal standard, they could "by the honest convictions of right" be "drawn into the service of the prosecution."[30] An antebellum surgery text introduced into evidence in an 1850 suit advised that "in such cases [compound fractures], . . . where shortening [of a limb] took place, it was owing to the carelessness of the surgeon, or the use of improper apparatus, and need not be so in these days, with the modern improvements."[31]

As the public began to perceive the physician as a technician in specific areas of medicine, the range of injuries open to lawsuits widened. A New Yorker wrote in 1848 that "there is but one method of setting a limb, of taking up an artery, or of extracting a bullet, and upon this method all well-educated surgeons are agreed."[32] In the same year, a plaintiff's attorney confidently told a malpractice jury that a "fracture is a simple thing to cure . . . there are no arbitrary rules on the subject."[33] Vaccination, obstetrics, and amputation were considered mechanical practices in the first third of the century and therefore dominated the small number of cases before 1835. After, the dramatic improvements in severe fracture and dislocation treatment contributed to the development of the image of the physician as a technician. Accordingly, the expectation of standard treatment and predictable, near perfect results intensified. Technological advancement and the accompanying expectations of complete proficiency have always helped fuel significant increases in malpractice rates. The malpractice rate between 1835 and 1865 was particularly sensitive to the improvements in fracture treatment because they occurred at the same time that factors such as competition and antiprofessional sentiment were also driving the litigation rates up.

Despite the growing view of both the public and the profession, it is clear that fracture treatment at midcentury was neither standard nor predictable. No one approach or device dominated practice. The point

Method for setting thigh fracture with adjustable tension. From Samuel Cooper, First Lines of the Practice of Surgery, *vol. 2 (1830). (Courtesy of the Historical Research Center, Houston Academy of Medicine, Texas Medical Center Library, Houston, Texas.)*

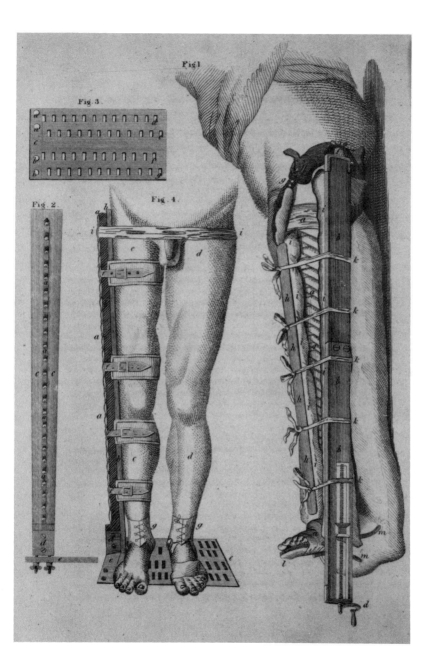

Fig 1.

Fig. 3.

Fig. 2.

Fig. 4.

was not lost on perceptive observers. Frank Hamilton, a Buffalo, New York, physician, served as an expert witness in dozens of malpractice trials. Hamilton believed that the misunderstanding surrounding the results of fracture treatments was the principal cause of the sudden increase in malpractice suits. He lamented that "surgeons themselves have believed, and taught, and testified, that in a large majority of cases, broken limbs may be made perfect, while the fact is not so!"[34] He reasoned that lower expectations from both physicians and patients would curb the seemingly rampant litigation. Using statistical methods he had learned in France in the 1840s, he compiled data on the treatment and results of hundreds of fracture and dislocation cases. Hamilton carefully measured and recorded imperfect alignment, shortening, or other deformations and matched the results with the treatment each patient had received.[35] He discovered that despite the claims of many practitioners, perfect restorations were uncommon. For example, one study revealed that forty of fifty fractures of the lower extremities healed with either deformity or shortening.[36] Hamilton began publishing his results in pamphlets, medical journals, and books in the late 1840s and by 1860 had reached a wide audience.[37]

Medical writers exclaimed that Hamilton's study had "revolutionized the opinion of surgeons the world over" and would "influence courts and juries, and constitute an imperishable defence and refuge, making his name and his fame immortal."[38] Defense attorneys and expert witnesses relied on Hamilton's findings. In an 1857 Ohio case in which the plaintiff had broken both bones in his lower leg, Hamilton's figures demonstrated that out of seventy-two similar cases, only thirty-two yielded perfect results.[39] The jury refused to award damages to the patient. Other defendants successfully used the fracture tables. Occasionally Hamilton himself would appear at trials to present and explain his findings.[40]

Hamilton's approach implicitly suggested that the bulk of malpractice suits represented a technological problem that could be cured with a technological solution. He was partially correct. Reasonable expectations of cure might have prepared patients for imperfect results. Physicians could consult statistical studies and choose the most effective treatment for the particular class of fractures. One reviewer hoped that Hamilton's work would "erect something like a standard which

TIBIA AND FIBULA.

No.	Age when it occurred.	Time since it occurred.	Sex.	Right or left side.	Character of the fracture.	TREATMENT.	RESULT. United or not.	When united.	Amount of shortening.	Remarks.	Perfect or imperfect.
					UPPER THIRD.						
1	25 y.		M.		Simple; frag. of tibia never displaced.	Gutta percha splint.	U.		none		P.
2	21 y.	5 y.	M.		Simple.		U.		⅝ in.		Imp.
3			M.		Simple.		U.		¼ in.		Imp.
4	35 y.	4 m.	M.	R	Simple.	Lateral splints, &c.	D. U.	119 d.	¾ in.	Slight forward projection of upper fragment of tibia.	Imp.
5	39 y.	6 y.	M.	R.	Simple.		U.		1½ in.	Tibia bent back at seat of fracture; anchylosis of knee (partial).	Imp.
6	30 y.	40 d.	M.	L.	Compound.	Felt splints and double inclined plane.	U.		none	Result uncertain; (see case).	
7	25 y.	5 y.	M.	R.	Simple and comminuted.		U.			Result uncertain; (see case).	
8	34 y.	8 y.	M.		Compound.		U.		¾ in.	Tibia bent at seat of fracture.	Imp.
9	50 y.	28 m.	M.		Compound comminuted.	Side splints, box, starch bandage, &c.	U.	63 d.	¾ in.	Several fragments removed.	Imp.
					MIDDLE THIRD.						
10	38 y.	36 d.	M.		Simple.	Paste bandage.	U.	35 d.	none		P.
11	16 y.		M.		Simple; frag. of tibia never displaced.		U.		none		P.
12	17 y.	40 d.	M.	L.	Simple oblique of tibia.	Double inclined plane; paste bandage, &c.	U.	40 d.	none		P.
13	10 y.	15 y.	M.	L.	Simple.		U.		none		P.
14	19 y.		M.		Simple; tibia transverse.	Paste bandage.	U.		none		P.
15	15 y.	27 d.	M.	L.	Simple; tibia oblique.	Gutta percha and double inclined plane, &c.	U.	21 d.	none	Straightened on 21st day.	P.
16	20 y.	2 y.	M.		Simple.		U.	22 d	none	Ankle occasionally painful.	P.
17	31 y.	6 w.	M.	R	Simple; frag. of tibia never displaced.	Paste bandage, &c.	U.	42 d	none		P.
18	70 y.	4 w. & 5 d.	M.	L.	Simple.	Side splints, &c.	U.	33 d.		Lower fragment of tibia slightly in front of upper.	
19	63 y.	4 m.	M.		Simple.		U.		none	Ulcer over point of fracture after 4 mos.	P.
20	30 y.	5 w.	M.	L.	Simple; frag. of tibia never displaced.		U.		none		P.
21	14 y.	5 w. & 2 d.	M.	L.	Simple; tibia transverse; fragment of tibia never displaced.	Paste bandage.	U.	40 d.	none		P.
22	41 y.	3 m.	M.	L.	Simple; tibia oblique; broken by muscular action; frag. of tibia never much displaced.	Copper splints; laid in Pott's position.	U.		none		P.
23	38 y.	8 m.	M.		Simple.	Paste bandages, &c.	U.		½ in.	Lower frag. of tibia in front of upper; unable to walk without crutches after 8 months.	Imp.

TIBIA AND FIBULA.

No.	Age when it occurred.	Time since it occurred.	Sex.	Right or left side.	Character of the fracture.	TREATMENT.	RESULT. United or not.	When united.	Amount of shortening.	Remarks.	Perfect or imperfect.
					MIDDLE THIRD—*Continued.*						
24	18 y.	46 d.	F.		Simple; tibia oblique.	Paste bandage, &c.	U.	48 d.	¼ in.	Upper frag. of tibia in front of lower.	Imp.
25	25 y.	11 w.	M.		Simple; tibia oblique with concussion of spine.	Side splints and a box.	U.		1 in.		Imp.
26	18 y.	5 m.	F.	R.	Simple; tibia oblique.	Side splints, &c.	U.		1 in.	Upper frag. of tibia upon outside of lower; began to walk in 5 months.	Imp.
27		6 w.	F.	L.	Compound.	Gutta percha side splints; pillow.	U.	42 d.	none	Fistulous discharge after 6 weeks.	P.
28	35 y.	4 m.	M.		Compound.		U.		none		P.
29	65 y.	47 d.	F.	L.	Compound; tibia oblique.	Pott's method 2 weeks, and then double inclined plane; gutta percha.	U.	26 d.	½ in.	No deformity	Imp.
30	35 y.		M.	R.	Compound (both legs).	Double inclined plane.	D. U.		¾ in.	Frag. of tibia bent forwards; slough on heel at end of 7 weeks.	Imp.
31	25 y.	12 d.	M.	L.	Compound (with other fractures).		U.		½ in.		Imp.
32	4 y.	23 y.	M.		Compound.		U.		½ in.	Paralysis of lower ext. produced by healing ulcer of 22 years, over seat of fracture.	Imp.
33	22 y.	3 m.	M.	L.	Compound; tibia oblique (with other fractures).		U.		1½ in.	Upper fragment of tibia in front; ulcer on heel, &c.	Imp.
34	8 y.		M.	R.	Compound; tibia transverse.	Side splint, pillow, cold water, &c.				Died in 3 months.	
35	19 y.	5 w.	M.	R.	Comminuted (both legs); tibia oblique.	Starch bandage, &c.	U.	35 d.		Not crooked; whether shortened or not cannot determine.	
36	14 y.	40 y.	M.	L.	Compound comminuted.		U.		none		P.
37	28 y.	37 d.	M.	L.	Compound comminuted; tibia oblique.	Double inclined plane, &c.; paste bandage after 7 weeks.	U.	56 d.	¼ in.		Imp.
38	33 y.	3 y.	M.	R.	Compound; tibia transverse.	Mayor's dressing. cool lotions. a box, &c. &c.	U.		½ in.	Upper frag. of tibia in front of lower very much; useful limb.	Imp.
39	48 y.	5 w.	M.	L.	Compound comminuted, with other complications.	Box, paste bandage, and later double inclined plane.	U.	35 d.	½ in.	Stiffness in ankle after 9 months.	Imp.
40	23 y.	4 w.	M.	R.	Compound comminuted (both legs); rupture of art.	Side splints; flexed position at first, then box, swing, &c.	U.	28 d.	¾ in.		Imp.
41	20 y.		M.	R.	Compound comminuted: rupture of art.	Gutta percha; wired fragm'ts together.				Died on 5th day.	
42	31 y.	7 w.	M.	R.	Compound, with fracture of femur of same side.	Straight splint.	U.		½ in.		Imp.
43	40 y.		M.	R.	Compound comminuted.	Box, cool water, &c.	N. U			Gangrene; amputation on 13th day; death on 16th day.	
44	32 y.		M.		Compound comminuted.	Box, side splints, &c.	U.		¾ in.	Slightly bent at seat of fracture.	Imp.

Plates from Frank Hamilton's "fracture tables." From Frank Hastings Hamilton, "Report on Deformities after Fractures," TAMA *10 (1857): 239–453. (Courtesy of the Historical Research Center, Houston Academy of Medicine, Texas Medical Center Library, Houston, Texas.)*

may be generally agreed upon for the protection and satisfaction of all parties who may hereafter be involved . . . in the miseries of a prosecution for 'malpractice.' "[41]

However, Hamilton's statistics were not conclusive, and his preferred treatments were not unanimously supported. No approach regularly produced either cures or failures. Even the reviewer who anticipated that the studies would establish a medical "standard" disagreed with several of Hamilton's surgical procedures. Quantification of several hundred cases helped guide physicians, but practitioners still had to treat each fracture individually, and uncertainty remained. In addition, fracture treatment was still in flux, with physicians continually developing new approaches. Reliance solely on the procedures enumerated in the statistical studies would have slowed medical progress and blunted beneficial innovation by encouraging doctors to use only familiar procedures.

Some physicians contended that the vast number of imperfect cures in statistical studies demonstrated the need for more effective treatments. These practitioners hoped that a technological breakthrough would limit the litigation. In 1851 a writer declared that "[t]he statistics of dislocations and fractures, display the limping gate of modern surgery, and we are solicitous to do all in our power to remedy the evil." He believed that "if surgeons used the proper means, in the reunion of fractured bones, no justifiable claim for mal-practice would live long before a jury." The physician commended the Jarvis adjuster, a mechanical device with gears that stretched, then compressed, fractured limbs, into their proper position. He claimed that "a correct understanding of its merits, and the use of its powers, would do much toward stopping those suits for malpractice."[42]

The writer's hopes were in vain. Within five years the Jarvis adjuster was generating suits instead of preventing them. The AMA condemned the mechanism, and Massachusetts General Hospital forbade its use. In 1856 a man sued a physician for breaking his wife's arm when the woman had dislocated her shoulder and the physician had used a Jarvis adjuster to relocate it. An expert medical witness claimed that the injury was caused by the machine: "The power of this adjuster is very great. We have considered it, in the Hospital [Massachusetts General], as a dangerous instrument, and it has not been used with us for four or five years."[43]

Confidence in technological solutions, such as Hamilton's tables or Jarvis' adjuster, was unfounded because technology could not stand still. Progress and advancement heightened expectations. Physicians' optimism for finding a technological cure for the profession's malpractice woes was illusory because the roots of the phenomenon were more complex than the development of fracture treatment. The new proclivity to sue physicians between 1835 and 1865 reflected, in part, the new way that Americans had come to look at their bodies.

"Song of Myself"

A committee on malpractice in 1850 argued that the principal source of malpractice suits was the popular misunderstanding of the nature of medical practice.

From this prevailing ignorance and misconception, the medical practitioner is expected to be the bold controller of nature instead of her vigilant observer, faithful follower and intelligent assistant . . . The jury is, perhaps told that the work of a mechanic is rejected, unless it comes up to a standard of perfection, so the work of the physician and surgeon must come to a like perfection; and such illustrations are received as parallel and analogical. By such reasoning, the mysteries of vitality, of that machine fearfully and wonderfully made in the image of its Maker, and living by the breath of the Deity, is reduced to a level with inanimate wood, stone, and iron, obedient to the mechanic's hand.[44]

These sentiments were the result of the mechanistic mentality that pervaded the first half of the nineteenth century. In 1800 the United States was still relatively untouched by the technological advances already transforming England. Within fifty years, however, profound changes had altered the landscape of the countryside and the contours of the American mind. From 1800 to 1830 entrepreneurs dug dozens of canals covering thousands of miles and built hundreds of roads in every part of the country. After 1840 railroad construction accelerated at a tremendous rate, fanning west from the business centers of the East Coast. A long series of inventions, including improved seed-drills, plows, reapers, and threshers, engendered unprecedented agricultural productivity. Similarly, water turbines, steam engines, mechanical drills, saws, pumps, and sewing machines sparked an accompanying boom in manufacturing.[45]

The tremendous advances in the physical sciences, industry, and transportation transformed the relation between humans and nature. As mechanization and transportation transcended the previous limits of the environment, humans felt a new power over nature and their destiny. By the 1840s many Americans felt that these material achievements made their society greater than any in the past, and they saw no reason why advancements would stop or even slow. Social commentary in every circle was filled with the enthusiastic expectation of perpetual material progress.[46] Some contemporary observers even believed that the democratic society accentuated and directed these attitudes.[47]

During the first half of the century society shifted much of its esteem from the divine wonders of nature to a fascination with the marvels of technological innovation.[48] The feeling was inspired by humans' growing ability to manipulate the natural environment in which they lived and their enhanced confidence that nature conformed to mechanistic laws. Similarly Americans gradually gained the ability to look at the human body as if it were a thing that could be manipulated and fixed, like any other machine and like other aspects of the natural world. Mechanistic mentality had its roots at least as early as the work of Issac Newton and René Descartes but began to reach its full expression in the early nineteenth century when it yielded widespread applications in a variety of fields.[49]

Some observers noticed that this newfound mechanistic mentality was accompanied by unfortunate side effects. Since "[m]en have grown mechanical in head and in heart, as well as in hand," Thomas Carlyle, the English social critic, warned "it is no longer the moral, religious, spiritual condition of the people that is our concern, but their physical, practical, [and] economic condition."[50] De Tocqueville confirmed that Americans were increasingly concerned with the material world. "Everyone," he noted, "is preoccupied caring for the slightest needs of the body and the trivial conveniences of life." He concluded that "[d]emocracy favors the taste for physical pleasures. This taste, if it becomes excessive, soon disposes men to believe that nothing but matter exists."[51] De Tocqueville speculated that "[i]n aristocratic ages the chief function of science is to give pleasure to the mind, but in democratic ages to the body."[52]

In the first half of the nineteenth century nearly every segment of Anglo-American culture expressed this unprecedented preoccupation with physical well-being. Concern with the body intensified to the point where many people were willing to believe that all health— intellectual, spiritual, and moral—began with bodily health.[53] Fitness promoters warned that Americans were suffering from widespread physical degeneracy.[54] In 1830 one observer suggested that the society was becoming a "weakened" one characterized by the "puny arm and shrinking sensibility of dyspepsy."[55] Even writers who concentrated on spiritual and intellectual matters exhibited a heightened concern over the state of the body and physical well-being. William Channing, a leading Unitarian minister in the 1830s, warned that the "puny, half-healthy, half-diseased state of body is too common among us," and he counseled that "nothing can be gained by sacrificing the body to the mind." Transcendentalists, who might have been expected to empha-size the spiritual above the material, were affected by similar senti-ments. Ralph Waldo Emerson declared that "bodily vigor becomes mental and moral vigor." Other Transcendentalists concurred that a strong, healthy body was an important prerequisite to higher con-sciousness.[56]

Popular writers agreed. In an 1858 article in the *Atlantic Monthly* titled "Saints and their Bodies," Thomas Higginson explained that "the mediæval type of sanctity was a strong soul in a weak body." Saints in previous eras had emaciated bodies. "But happily," he wrote, "times change, and saints with them." The new American image of the saint, he continued, now included a vigorous and well-developed physique. Higginson declared, "We distrust the achievements of every saint without a body."[57] Similarly, Walt Whitman filled his 1855 *Leaves of Grass* with dozens of paeans to flesh and blood. Lines such as "If life and the soul are sacred the human body is sacred," and "Who degrades or defiles the human body is cursed" expressed the poet's regard for the physical nature of humankind.[58]

While none of these writers spoke for the entire population, they represented a broad spectrum of cultural and intellectual life in ante-bellum America in which materialistic sentiments were becoming in-creasingly common. Colonial Calvinists would have considered regu-lar, organized play frivolous and unproductive. But by the 1830s and 1840s, Americans had initiated for the first time formalized physical fitness programs.[59] The antebellum physical education movement was only one expression of the new materialism and the changing view of the body.

Although de Tocqueville chronicled Americans' growing material-ism and concern with bodily worries and pleasure, he simplified, if not mistook, the basic cause of the transformation. Democracy may have encouraged materialistic attitudes, but it did not create them. Origins of a transformed vision of physical well-being can be found as early as the eighteenth century, but two interwoven developments between 1820 and 1860 heightened awareness of and concern with the body. The mechanization of the body encouraged physicians and laymen to believe that physical ills were understandable and remediable. Mechanical successes in manufacturing and transportation generated an atmosphere of optimism and a faith in material progress. Optimism was fortified by evolving religious beliefs in the 1830s and 1840s that supported the idea of a benevolent God. Many northern evangelicals began to believe in both social and individual perfectionism. Individuals felt that they had access to spiritual and bodily salvation.[60]

A variety of health reformers reflected this trend and exhorted Americans to revere and care for their bodies. They argued that good general health was within reach of all Americans. Sylvester Graham, one of the most prominent representatives of this movement, contended that the human body conformed to a set of rational yet divinely endowed rules. With proper diet, exercise, and temperance, Americans could preserve and improve their health. Bodily improvement was theoretically possible because reformers believed that the natural laws of health had been uncovered and because God wished humans to work toward both physical and spiritual perfection.[61]

It was clear that the mechanical workings of the body had not been completely explained. Many Americans, however, came to expect health and physical vitality in those areas in which science and medicine appeared to have unraveled the laws of the physical world. In preventative health, physical education, and some areas of surgery, physical problems and solutions seemed simplest and most mechanical. Grahamites explained that if individuals lived life according to human nature—practicing temperance and following a diet of whole grains, fruits, vegetables, and little meat—health would inevitably result. Fitness enthusiasts introduced a series of exercises carefully designed to benefit specific parts of the body. In medicine the process developed more slowly. Obstetric and vaccination treatments were widely, although wrongly, considered mechanical, predictable procedures by the early nineteenth century. During the next forty years fracture treatment sparked widespread optimism. In other areas of medicine, however, progress and the accompanying expectations did not come until the late nineteenth century or later.

Heightened public concern for physical well-being, combined with real progress in fracture treatments, created unrealistic expectations and demands. Suits for fracture treatments were uncommon before the late 1830s for three reasons. First, the general unacceptability of malpractice accusations discouraged many prospective plaintiffs. Second, fracture treatment was not developed enough to engender high expectations in either physicians or patients. Finally, America's preoccupation with material well-being was not sufficiently developed to provoke public comment, inspire health and fitness movements, or generate anger over minor bodily deformities. Before then, suits for treatments that resulted in only minor deformities were unsupportable.

The social and cultural factors that focused individuals' attention on their bodies did not disappear. Instead, they matured. Secularization, affluence, and the nascent consumer culture continued to evolve, and individuals became even more concerned about their health, comfort, and appearance.[62] As other medical treatments became mechanical and routinized, expectations grew, patient tolerance for imperfection decreased, and physicians were sued for a wider variety of medical treatments.

Community, Providence, and the Social Construction of Legal Action

Malpractice litigation flourished for the first time in the Jacksonian period because the social and medical environments were conducive to the frequent prosecution of physicians. The contributing causes in the first malpractice "crisis" were intraprofessional rivalry, and the decline of the professional and social status of the physician. Additionally, dramatic technological advancements blurred previous conceptions of standards of care and created unrealistic expectations in both patients and physicians. These immediate causes increased the impact of Americans' long-term growing concern for physical well-being. But these factors alone still do not account for the sudden and unprecedented appearance of large numbers of malpractice suits.

In an 1824 malpractice trial a defense attorney castigated the plaintiff in front of the jury. The lawyer declared that "it is not a very commendable sight anymore than a very customary sight to see a patient prosecuting his physician." "[P]ublic judgment," he argued, was the "proper tribunal to regulate this species of responsibility," and it was doubtful that a lawsuit would increase the "intensity of moral obligation."[1]

The lawyer's comments illustrate that potential litigants are often constrained by more than just legal rules. Cultural and community attitudes, habits, and customs define socially acceptable ways to re-spond to grievances and disputes. As modern legal anthropologist Carol Greenhouse observes, "Before a person can sue, he must have not only a legally justiciable issue and a legal forum, but also a personal conceptualization of conflict that is adversarial in structure and reme-dial in orientation."[2] Individual action is shaped by community beliefs and informal moral codes about the type of wrongs that warrant legal action. Changing cultural beliefs can make recourse to courts either more or less acceptable.

The initial burst of suits in the late 1830s and the subsequent "crisis" of the 1840s and 1850s would not have been possible without complex psychological and cultural developments. The two essential preconditions for the rise of malpractice suits were the dissolution of community stigmatization of certain types of litigation and the decline in belief in the concept of providence that held misfortune to be an expression of divine will. Without these two underlying, long-term developments, the widespread prosecution of physicians would have been inconceivable.

The Role of the Community and the Decision to Sue

The nature of the community an individual belongs to and the notion of community he or she holds determine the amount of influence that custom will have on that individual's behavior.[3] Throughout much of America's early history, community custom relegated many types of disputes to extralegal forums, but by the mid–nineteenth century, communities' coercive power had weakened. As a result, disputants were able to bring previously unlitigated forms of conflict into court, among them an expansion of medical malpractice claims. This change in legal culture did not cause malpractice suits. Without this develop-ment, however, and its subsequent expansion, widespread prosecution of physicians could not have occurred.

Although there is no effective or accurate way to measure the existence of community, seventeenth-century New England towns provide a convenient model.[4] A *community* may be defined as a group of people living in a defined geographic area who share the same basic values and view of the world. The early settlements were Christian, closed, corporate communities.[5] The demands of economic survival and old-world farming patterns encouraged cooperation. The citizens of the town were bound tightly by economic interest and also by family ties and religious beliefs. Indeed, part of the function of the social unit was to glorify God on earth. In the quest to create a "city upon a hill," colonists created integrated, organic, social systems. Individualism was both socially and religiously condemned.

Social relations in these settlements were dominated by face-to-face, personal relationships with a limited number of neighbors. Dissension was rare because the interests of the colonists were relatively homogeneous. They did similar work and worshipped the same God in the same way. In an effort to maintain social and spiritual peace, community members discouraged conflict in general and litigation specifically.[6] Scholars have suggested that the "relational distance" between members of a community influences their willingness to rely on legal remedies: When the "distance" is great, law will be relied on more frequently; when people live in tightly knit, kinship-based, corporate communities, the social costs of disrupting the order are greater, and litigation is relied on less frequently.[7] In early colonial America individuals were tied to one another in an interlocking network of family, church congregation, and community relationships.

Colonists were remarkably successful in discouraging disruptive litigation in the first half of the seventeenth century. Disputes were settled more often through arbitration, mediation, and mutual agreements. Often the entire church congregation judged conflicting claims of disputants. The inhabitants of Dedham, Massachusetts, for example, were largely able to avoid the use of courts in disputes through the 1680s. After that point, land hunger, population increases, generational conflict, and economic diversification had begun to undermine the homogeneous nature of colonial existence. Consensus weakened, disputes multiplied, and colonists more frequently resorted to courts. Community opinion and collective self-interest were no longer strong enough to keep public quarrels out of courts completely. Internal dissension was never eliminated, but the use of alternative means of settlement—arbitration, for example—had helped resolve quarrels without litigation.[8]

Despite the incipient breakup of communal structures, many patterns remained, and colonists were able to retain a relative degree of uniformity of thought through much of the eighteenth century. Although litigation was increasingly common, many communities were able to control access to their towns through "warning out" unwanted outsiders. Religious attitudes were changing, but they still stressed selflessness and restraint, compromise instead of conflict, and encouraged conformity to prevailing social standards. This ethos was reinforced by everyday relations, which were still dominated by face-to-face communications.[9] Uniformity and consensus were undermined significantly by the religious tumult and factionalism of the Great Awakening in the early eighteenth century, increased economic growth and political activity, and ever-growing geographic mobility.[10] Even though it was not static, in many cases community life in the eighteenth century remained stable, relatively insular, and maintained many of the customary prohibitions against the use of courts.

A study of fourteen Massachusetts towns suggests that shared ethical values and a respect for consensus retarded widespread litigation into the early nineteenth century. William Nelson discovered that the people in towns still "shared assumptions about how 'good people' lived . . . These assumptions were prescribed at the level of moral ideal by church doctrine and confirmed at the level of practice by geographic, demographic, and technological realities that precluded most people from adopting styles radically different from the one they knew." In these towns, it was not until 1790–1825 that the seventeenth-century methods of accommodation and consensual dispute settlement broke down significantly and yielded increased litigation.[11]

Although the first signs of the breakup of communal consensus were visible as early as the mid–seventeenth century, the most profound shocks to old ways of thinking occurred in the late eighteenth and early nineteenth centuries. The change took place at different rates in different communities and regions, but there is a clear overall movement from the communalism of colonial America to Jacksonian individualism and pluralism.

The crucial break with colonial communal habits was especially evident after the first third of the nineteenth century. As Michael Frisch notes, in the early nineteenth century "the fading of this homogeneity in fact had not yet disturbed the dominance of older patterns of social leadership and socialization—the accepted articulation, rather than the importation, of community standards, values, and practices by the social establishment." [12] But the massive geographic dislocation from westward expansion, the growth of a national economy, and advances in transportation severely undercut the insularity of community life. In addition, the democratizing effects of the American Revolution and the impact of economic competition helped both to nurture the growth of and to transform individualism. The expansion of the village economy increased the number of contacts with the outside world and led to specialist production. People no longer did the same kind of work and were more likely to form interest groups. Increasing religious diversity and a decline in piety also undercut the consensus that had characterized early America. De Tocqueville recognized the increasing fragmentation of community life, the accompanying weakening of personal ties, and the decline in the influence of custom over the individual in the 1830s. [13]

Community was not destroyed, nor was individualism created in the first third of the century, but the nature of both changed. Recent studies have suggested that the nature of community and individualism can influence the type and rate of litigation. According to David Engel, in communities more completely dominated by face-to-face relationships and economically self-sufficient farmers and merchants, such as those of eighteenth-century America, "it was considered inappropriate for injured persons to transform their misfortune into a demand for compensation or to view it as an occasion for interpersonal conflict." [14] Contract or defamation of character cases, for example, would have been more acceptable than personal injury suits; slander suits reflected the importance of reputation in communities dominated by face-to-face relations. [15]

However, in this form of cooperative, communal, individualism, it would have been inappropriate to sue for personal injury for three reasons: such suits disturbed the peace of the community; they contradicted notions of self-sufficiency by demanding compensation; and they violated other religious-based community strictures against suing for misfortune. Prohibitions against conflicts and certain types of suits were reinforced by the influence and coercive power of living in a closely knit community. The opinion of the community could not stop litigation, but it could discourage it by viewing those persons who initiated unacceptable types of suits with suspicion.

By the Jacksonian period much of America had moved toward a different world and a different vision of individualism. On the one hand, individuals were less self-sufficient than their predecessors. Farmers and merchants were connected to larger markets, and the economy was becoming more integrated. On the other, migration and social mobility had made individuals less integrated into the traditional organic and hierarchical society and less bound by ever-weakening public mandates. In this form of society, a "rights-oriented individualism," in Engels' term, "is consistent with an aggressive demand for compensation (or other remedies) when important interests are perceived to have been violated."[16] "Rights-oriented individualism" is illustrated, for example, in Jacksonian Democratic demands for more access to the benefits of law. Self-sufficiency was slowly fading into the realities of market economy. Individuals felt freer to sue for personal misfortune because recourse to law did not contradict their feelings of self-sufficiency. Although community proscriptions against suing remained, albeit in attenuated form, the power of community opinion lost influence as towns became increasingly heterogeneous and anonymous. This gradual transformation became especially evident in the first third of the century and was a prerequisite for the growth of personal injury suits. The shift from cooperative, self-sufficient individualism to competitive, rights-oriented individualism continued and allowed a wider scope of litigation as the decades passed.

Rod in the Hand of God?

Communal discouragement of certain types of litigation was based partially on religious grounds. Personal moral codes, formed largely from fundamental religious beliefs, however, may have kept potential litigants out of courts even in the absence of those community pressures.

The relationship between religious change and increased litigation during this period was subtle, not overt. The gradual secularization of

American society, combined with a growing confidence in material progress and a glorification of individual will, led to a search for the temporal, human agents of misfortune. When God no longer ordained specific social or physical ills, it became acceptable to search for human culprits, assign responsibility, and demand reform or restitution through the courts.

In the seventeenth and eighteenth centuries doctrines of direct, divine providence were common among America Protestants. The most powerful churches and the majority of the public subscribed to the Calvinist 1647 Westminister Confession, which proclaimed that "God the great creator of all things, doth uphold, direct, and dispose, and govern all creatures, actions and things from the greatest even to the least by his most wise and holy Providence."[17]

Providence theory reflected the prevalent belief that God both created the world and sustained it from moment to moment. Nothing in heaven or earth occurred by chance.[18] Puritan objections to card games, dice, and lotteries were based on the premise that they trivially abused divine providence.[19] God might manipulate events to punish sinners and reward saints, or he might rain misfortune on the holy to test or teach them. This intervention was known as *special*, or *specific, providence*. God's will brought lightning, bad crops, earthquakes, epidemics, a sick horse, or the death of a child.[20] John Winthrop, who helped found and govern early seventeenth-century Massachusetts, filled his journals with examples of colonists punished or rewarded by "a special providence of God." Individuals suffered or were spared the effects of fire, drowning, smallpox, Indian attacks, birth defects, and accidental injury because of the "righteous hand of God."[21]

In this setting the proper response to God's will was submissive acceptance. Human resignation to providential misfortune was defended on the grounds that human beings could not possibly hope to understand God's plan, and faith demanded that they believe that the Lord ultimately worked toward only good ends. More importantly, suffering and misfortune on earth were often rewarded in heaven.[22]

After the American Revolution many northerners began perceptibly to shift their view of the impact of providence on human affairs and moved gradually away from their fatalistically minded predecessors. Colonial engineered lotteries in the eighteenth century were one "symptom" of the gradual waning of conventional piety. Concurrently, the growth of insurance companies which reimbursed losses for such events as fires and storms reflected the gradual move away from the notion of "acts of God." Potential victims now sought protection, as well as strength and patience, when faced with misfortune.[23] By the beginning of the nineteenth century the belief in direct providential intervention was attacked overtly by Unitarians, deists, and liberal clergymen from various Protestant denominations.[24]

Still, fatalistic sentiments and the submissive acceptance of misfortune as God's will remained common throughout the first three decades of the nineteenth century. In 1823 a writer for the orthodox Presbyterian magazine *Christian Spectator* claimed that providence "extends to all beings that have existed, or ever will exist;—to all events that have occurred or ever will occur." "The impious scoffer will tell us that all is the result of accident; and he will misname the signal interpositions of heaven by the epithets of 'good fortune' and 'good luck' but the humble Christian will discern in them all the hand of a wise and holy God."[25] Another writer in the same magazine declared that "without [God's] permission, no power can harm, no ill can befall us; and every afflicting stroke is meant for our good."[26]

A belief in providence affected potential malpractice claimants. A "humble Christian" patient who discerned the wise hand of God in his broken leg would be unlikely to sue his physician if the leg healed with a deformity; to do so would be to question God's wisdom. The doctrine of providence according to the writer in the *Christian Spectator* turned "tears into gratitude."[27] Similarly, "humble Christian" juries would not be willing to hold physicians responsible for bad results that were most likely ordained by God either as a punishment or as a test. During the first three and a half decades of the nineteenth century, when a belief in specific providence was still strong, medical journals and state supreme courts reported only a handful of malpractice cases, and writers commented on the rarity of the litigation.

The apparent contradiction between human free will and God's providential control fueled theological debates in the 1820s and 1830s. Many groups who attacked the notion of direct providence claimed that it undermined the responsibility of the individual. Other writers argued that providential ideas left the status quo untouched by encouraging the acceptance of remediable ills. During the first half of the nineteenth century those theologians who saw God's direct intervention in every event lost ground to more liberal thinkers. A growing segment of the population believed that God operated only through universal, natural laws and influenced world events on the grand, historical level.[28] Instead of causing each particular event, God created an overall scheme, the environment for the unfolding of his will. The trend away from a belief in direct or special providence varied from person to person, denomination to denomination, and region to region. But through the course of the nineteenth century, progressively fewer Americans accepted social and physical ills as purely God's will.

Malpractice and God's Will

Malpractice suits were rare in the transition period of the 1820s and 1830s, before a large proportion of the population began to hold human agents responsible for human misfortune. When patients did sue their physicians, the cases generally involved only severe injuries or death.

One of the few cases before 1835 illustrates the relationship of providential belief to medical malpractice of the period. In 1824 the city dispensary of New York hired Dr. Gerald Bancker to vaccinate for smallpox all the citizens within an assigned urban district. For a $100 fee, Bancker vaccinated 870 patients without incident. In April 1824 the physician vaccinated the four-year-old son of Michael O'Neil. Eight days after the visit, the boy became dreadfully ill. When the symptoms worsened, O'Neil called in another physician who diagnosed the case as smallpox. The child's health deteriorated. He went blind, a brown crust covered him, and he began to lose his hair and skin. The boy's lower jaw disintegrated and fell out of his mouth, and he developed an ulcerous hole through his neck and into his throat. Finally, after four months of profound suffering, the child died. O'Neil sued Dr. Bancker for malpractice and demanded $5,000 in damages.[29]

O'Neil's lawyer and several medical witnesses claimed that Bancker had infected the child with smallpox by inoculating instead of vaccinating him. In a *vaccination* a physician took material from a cowpox sore and inserted it into a patient's arm. This process effectively immunized the patient against smallpox. For an inoculation, an already obsolete practice, material was extracted from a smallpox sore and inserted into the subject's arm. Inoculation was often effective, but patients contracted a form (usually mild) of the disease from the procedure. O'Neil's lawyers argued that Bancker had carelessly and negligently drawn material from a smallpox, instead of a cowpox, sore and had infected the boy with the dread disease.[30]

The doctor's lawyers argued that the O'Neil boy's disease was nothing short of miraculous. The physician had vaccinated scores of patients, and none had contracted this seemingly virulent form of the disease. Medical witnesses for Bancker testified that while some of the symptoms resembled smallpox, they knew of no instance from experience or literature in which such ravages followed an inoculation. The disease, though occasionally fatal, did not exhibit features such as the loss of the jaw or the frightful ulcer in the patient's neck. Therefore, the defense attorney claimed, providence, not the vaccination was responsible for this tragedy. "In a word," Bancker's attorney explained, "we expect to prove the child died of smallpox, proceeding from the visitation of God, and not from any negligence or any want of skill on the part of the defendant." The jury retired after the testimony and found the physician not guilty.[31]

The defense attorney's use of a divine explanation for the disease to defend his client suggests that much of society accepted the notion of a specific or direct providence. The apparent success of the lawyer's strategy helps to confirm this view. Moreover, O'Neil likely had to overcome personal reservations concerning God's will and misfortune before he sued Bancker. Where other victims of medical accident or incompetence may have been less willing to question God's visitations and considered malpractice litigation an improper, or irreligious, remedy, perhaps the horrific nature of the affliction wiped away O'Neil's misgivings. Indeed, the majority of the scattered suits before 1835 involved severe injuries or death.

Charles Lowell, who sued his physician in 1823, having suffered a severe, permanent hip deformity after an accident, felt uncomfortable enough with blaming the physician for his injury to justify his action to his community.[32] In a pamphlet describing the trial Lowell explained that "I am aware of the necessity of kissing the rod and him who hath appointed it; and were it purely an act of God, I could submit to it without a murmur." But since he had suffered this "calamity" only through the "ignorance and unprecedented fraud of the physicians," he claimed that he could force himself to sue. Even after losing his case in civil court, Lowell comforted himself that the physicians would "be brought to a higher tribunal than that of their country" in the afterlife.[33] Lowell's comments suggest that although he had abandoned a strict definition of direct providence, he, like much of society, still felt its influence enough to defend his legal action against religious questions. Over the next two decades many more Americans were able to shake off their nagging doubts and hold other people responsible for their misfortune.

Judges rarely openly revealed their beliefs about divine providence and malpractice. However, in explaining why physicians did not implicitly guarantee the results of their work, one judge noted, "The event is in the hands of *Him* who giveth life and not within the physical control of the most skilful [sic] of the profession." Even these types of statements were absent from judges' decisions after the 1830s.[34]

Few contemporary observers grasped the underlying theological changes that were making the litigation acceptable. The 1850 Pennsylvania Medical Society committee on malpractice argued that while medical science had advanced rapidly in the previous fifty years, the public and physicians had to acknowledge that there was a "mysterious agency of vital laws which are hidden by providence from the scrutiny of man." God still occasionally played an active role in the affairs of humans. Despite the medical community's progress in discovering physical laws, "occasionally all the arrangements and protections of science and philosophy vanish before the Deity . . . It is an ignorance of, or want of reflection upon these principles which forms the foundation for the prevalence of quackery, and of the unjust persecutions which pursue the regular practitioner, and display themselves in groundless suits."[35] The committee's insightful comment on the impact of attitudes toward providence on malpractice rates was unique in nineteenth-century medical literature. Most writers concentrated their attention on more immediate, concrete, and presumably remediable causes, such as low status or the strife created by intraprofessional competition.

The precise moment of the decisive shift in the notion of direct providence, which opened the door to widespread prosecution of physicians, is impossible to pinpoint. Several factors suggest that a critical transformation occurred in the decade and a half between 1835 and 1850—the same period that bore America's first malpractice "crisis."

This shift resulted from a variety of changes during the Enlightenment and the scientific revolution of the eighteenth and nineteenth centuries.[36] American intellectuals and theologians, especially Unitarians, were influenced by European philosophers of the 1830s and 1840s, including John Stuart Mill and Auguste Comte. These writers' conception of God, as Charles Cashdollar notes, "forced man away from the pietistic or providential to a naturalistic view of social problems, from prayer to human action."[37] The providential view of earthly events was inherently conservative; the naturalistic view was unreservedly reformist. The new perspective made it more difficult to claim that poverty, for instance, was a punishment for a sinful life.[38] What before had been divinely ordained burdens or punishments for sin became remediable ills. A Romantic belief in perfectionism, the ability to improve the individual and society, swept much of the country.[39] During this period a vast number of broadly humanitarian movements flourished for the first time in history, movements that were eager to address human suffering with human intervention. The social improvement efforts that arose included abolition, prevention of cruelty to animals, child protection, and prison reform.[40] Beginning in the late 1830s and contemporary with the outpouring of social reform and the theological debates over the nature of providence, physicians reported a massive, unprecedented attack of malpractice prosecutions.

Scientific and naturalistic explanations of specific phenomena accelerated the decline in the perception and acceptance of different varieties of misfortune as divine will. Medical researchers in the late eighteenth and early nineteenth centuries explored the mechanical aspects of the body and explained more and more functions in biological or physiological terms.[41] In addition, statistical analyses of diseases, treatments, and cures, as well as of other areas of society, began to engender the hope of scientifically predictable medicine.[42] Perceptions of scientists and physicians diverged from the views of many theologians and the general public, but the new attitudes slowly permeated much of society.[43]

Religious Reform

In the 1830s and 1840s liberal theology, embodied in ministers such as Horace Bushnell, William Channing, and Charles Grandison Finney, began to gain the upper hand in the battle against orthodox Calvinist views of providence.[44] Finney, a minister from New York, believed that God was the creator of the world and governor of natural law but contended that the Almighty did not interfere with the day-to-day life of human beings. Finney's 1835 *Lectures on Revivals of Religion*, according to one writer, "clearly marks the end of two centuries of Calvinism and the acceptance of pietistic evangelicalism as the predominant faith of the nation."[45] Finney explicitly denounced the precepts of the Westminister Confession that supported the notion of specific providence and the Christian's humble acceptance of misfortune.

The appearance of *Lectures on Revivals* in 1835, almost the exact point at which malpractice suits suddenly increased, does not suggest a direct causal connection between the work and the frequency of lawsuits. However, the success of Finney's book and career does reflect the widespread public acceptance of the religious and social beliefs that were the necessary precondition for intensified litigation. Finney glorified the individual will and expressed an optimistic belief in human progress.[46] He preached that humans, using their own free will, could achieve sanctification on earth; they could become morally perfect. This idea nourished the belief that other aspects of life on earth could and should be made perfect and fed the evangelical and health reform movements of the period. The body and the soul could be molded into almost ideal forms.[47] Moral and physical perfectionism made it much easier and more acceptable to assign human responsibility to earthly ills. These ideas were also compatible and intertwined with the individualistic tenor of Jacksonian democracy. Finney's theology appealed to the so-called working classes, whom physicians found most likely to sue, by stressing the individual's ability to make a personal peace with God and hew out his or her own place in the world.[48] These sentiments marked a further breakup of the hierarchical and communitarian attitudes that had played a role in discouraging early lawsuits.

Finney's brand of Protestantism had swept through western New York in a series of revivals in the late 1820s and early 1830s. These revivals were so frequent and did so much damage to Calvinist tradition that the region became known as the "burned-over district."[49] After an 1831 revival in the area Finney's enthusiastic perfectionism moved west into such states as Ohio and Michigan and east into the towns of New England. Within a few years much of the North accepted the importance of human action in the improvement of physical and moral life.[50] By the early 1840s observers had begun to identify this same burned-over district of western New York as the source of the malpractice "fever" that was sweeping the Northeast.

Finney's revivalism alone did not make western New York the seedbed of medical malpractice, or carry the phenomenon to other states. The political and social elements of Jacksonian democracy were particularly strong in the area, medical sectarians were popular and prevalent, and regular physicians competed and fought continually among themselves. Yet, combined with the transformation of religious attitudes, these factors undoubtedly propelled the state to an early lead in the field of malpractice suits. The revivals, however, did promote ideas that made the litigation more acceptable. As religious attitudes evolved in other areas of the country, conditions there also became conducive to the suits.

Epidemics, Providence, and the Role of Medicine

American attitudes towards epidemics serve as an important gauge of the nature and timing of religious changes in the nineteenth century. In the 1790s Philadelphia suffered a series of devastating yellow fever epidemics.[51] During the 1793 affliction one inhabitant revealed that "[m]ost, if not all [of the population] were convinced it was a judgment sent by the immediate hand of God."[52] When, in 1822, a yellow fever epidemic hit New York, public opinion had changed significantly.[53] While most of the population of the city still viewed the epidemic as moral retribution, the scientific camp had gained many converts. The yellow fever crisis of 1822 inspired an open debate over its divine or earthly origins, a debate that represented, according to one scholar, "an intellectual cameo, the miniaturized playing out of a national drama of the mind." Orthodox ministers still preached jeremiads and called for days of fasting, but other civil leaders had already begun to demand clean streets, pure water, strict shipping regulations, and proper disposal of bodies.[54]

The reaction to the 1822 New York yellow fever epidemic represents one transition point in the evolution of public attitudes toward divine providence. The majority of Americans had not yet abandoned the notion of direct intervention, but an increasing minority was willing to entertain alternate explanations for malevolent events.

Cholera, which swept through most large cities in America between 1832 and 1834, was also, according to most ministers and lay persons, "a rod in the hand of God."[55] They called for fast days to demonstrate their contrition and belief. Despite the arguments of physicians and various liberal clergymen, who rarely explained epidemics in supernatural terms, the majority of society believed that the disease, like yellow fever, was a punishment for social or individual sins. Although materialism and Enlightenment rationalism were already eroding traditional piety in 1832, they had not seeped into the consciousness of a sufficient proportion of society to affect the predominant view of misfortune. And during the 1832 epidemics the debates among theologians over special providence were still undecided.[56]

By the time cholera struck the country again in 1849, the notion of special providence had faded considerably. Orthodox clergymen, trying to hold a conservative line, warned that Americans had "lost sight of nature's divine Author and Govenor [sic]."[57] By the 1840s a significant percentage of clergymen had abandoned the idea of direct intervention and much of America had accepted a materialistic philosophy which embraced the goals of scientific, economic, and social progress. A decade later an 1857 article in *Harper's* on the "causes and prevention of epidemics" did not mention God, providence, or religion; instead it outlined the secular, scientific debate over whether contagion or infection was the cause.[58]

By the time of new epidemics in 1866 the transformation of the public's view of cholera was apparent. During the late 1850s John

Snow had demonstrated that cholera was transmitted through contaminated water and had encouraged Americans to work to remedy the scientific and physical causes of the disease.[59] Physicians and government officials used statistical surveys to determine that clean streets, ventilated housing, and pure water were more effective health measures than prayers and fasting days.[60] Secular interpretations of specific misfortunes that originated with scientists and physicians influenced other segments of society as soon as the interaction of religious views, medical interpretations, and effective cures made other explanations untenable. This process began at least as early as the eighteenth century and affected different physical events and ailments at different rates, but the scientific and religious developments in the first half of the nineteenth century contributed to a profound shift in public attitudes on a wide variety of subjects.[61]

Pain and Providence

The timing of this transformation and its relevance to malpractice suits are also supported by the concurrent shift in public attitudes toward pain and suffering. The secularization of pain was brought about by the same combination of religious, philosophical, and biomedical factors that changed the public perception of various diseases. Through the eighteenth century pain, like other forms of physical misfortune, was accepted as divine will and as such was both explicable and bearable.[62] There are numerous biblical justifications for the notion that pain was a punishment for original or earthly sins. Paracelsus experimented with ether on animals in the early sixteenth century, but fearing clerical reaction, did not use it on humans.[63] By 1818 scientists had discussed the clinical benefits of hypnotism, nitrous oxide, and ether, and yet none of these procedures gained popular acceptance until after 1830. Ether was not "discovered" until 1846.[64] Many writers have claimed that available analgesics were not employed because most individuals accepted pain as a divinely ordained fact of life. They have argued, moreover, that between 1780 and 1845 pain sensitivity may have increased as individuals began to view the phenomenon less as a message from God and more as a physiological mechanism.[65]

According to Nathan Rice, a prominent nineteenth-century physician, "[t]he curious ground of opposition to the use of ether[,] that of religious scruples—[was] based on the argument that, as man was condemned by Providence to suffer pain, it was wrong in him to endeavor to palliate the decree." Some patients consulted clergymen before accepting analgesics. Rice offered an anecdote that underlined the transitional, interrelated nature of attitudes toward providence and pain in this period.[66] In 1850 Rice was present when a messenger called on a fellow physician and explained that a local farmer had cut an artery in his hand. The physician sent the man back to tell the farmer that a minor operation would be necessary and that he would bring some ether to ease the surgery. While waiting for the physician to arrive, the farmer and his wife knelt, prayed together, and decided not to use the ether because they both considered it wrong. The farmer declared that he "would not endeavor to escape any of that punishment which had been ordained by sin."[67]

When the physician arrived, the farmer lay down on the kitchen table and his wife left the room. As soon as the physician began the operation, however, the man cried out in pain. "Doctor do you think that it would be really wrong to take it; of course you don't. You are a good man and you wouldn't do anything wrong I know; besides if you recommend it to me, the blame ought to fall on you . . . Well wicked or not I guess I'll have the ether." The farmer's wife came into the room soon after the surgery and began to chastise her husband for his weak faith while the farmer, drunk with ether, staggered around the room and vainly tried to defend himself from the woman's verbal onslaught.[68] His stream-of-consciousness justification for using ether symbolically encapsulates the more general shift in society's attitude toward pain and providence. Although this couple ostensibly retained traditional beliefs about the role of providence later than much of the population, their experience illustrates the complex religious change in the middle decades of the century. The farmer was a devout Christian. Yet, when faced with the opportunities presented by modern science, he formulated a justification for exemption from the restrictions of his beliefs. This adaptation, however, was not simply an acknowledgment and acceptance of the existence of scientific explanations and the availability of technology over and above religion. Scientific progress and theological evolution were both responsible for the decline of the role of special providence in everyday life.[69]

As with attitudes toward disease, the changing perception of pain was a product of a popularized concept of Enlightenment rationalism and scientific optimism that permeated much of Western society in the early nineteenth century. For example, social philosophers such as Jeremy Bentham and John Stuart Mill, in contrast to previous thinkers, portrayed pain as an "inherent evil." Pain was neither punishment, nor redemption.[70] In addition, significant advances in anatomy and physiology between 1800 and 1850 illuminated the physical mechanisms of pain to such a degree that physicians and lay persons began to view it as an essentially biological function that could and should be controlled by any available scientific means.[71]

Society's new sensibility regarding pain was reflected in many of the movements that had themselves been inspired by the possibility and advisability of reform. A variety of groups campaigned against cruelty to animals, flogging, capital punishment, vivisection, and blood sports such as bull-baiting, and cock- and dog-fighting.[72] When William Morton effectively publicized the clinical use of ether in 1846, the public and the medical profession were for the most part ready to accept the innovation. Still, many physicians and ministers condemned the use of ether during childbirth on the grounds that labor pains were a divinely ordained punishment for the sins of Eve.[73]

The Case of the South

The importance of the secularization of public attitudes toward misfortune as an essential precondition for the rise of the malpractice suit in the Jacksonian era is confirmed by the relationship between the two phenomena in different areas of the country. The change in the popular view of providence, pain, natural disaster, disease, and social reform did not occur throughout the entire country at the same rate; neither did malpractice litigation.

New England and western physicians, assailed by an increasing number of malpractice suits in the 1840s and 1850s, marveled at the apparent rarity of such litigation in the South. Of the 216 state supreme court malpractice decisions reported between 1790 and 1900, only eight originated from the eleven states of the Confederacy.[74] Even considering the relative populations of the North and South, there is a significant difference in the frequency of litigation. The *Boston Medical and Surgical Journal* reported that the first malpractice case in Tennessee did not occur until 1855.[75] By that time suits were a common occurrence in states such as New York, Pennsylvania, Massachusetts, and Ohio where hundreds of cases had been reported. Frank Hamilton, speaking to the Medico-Legal Society in the 1870s, observed that while "suits for malpractice were so very frequent in the Northern States—they were always less frequent in the Southern States."[76]

At an American Medical Association conference in 1873 a Pennsylvania physician noted this disparity and asked a Mississippi colleague to explain the phenomenon. The southern physician acknowledged that malpractice suits were not a problem in the South and that he had never heard of a case in his state. He suggested that strong medical societies had discouraged intraprofessional rivalry and prevented suits.[77] While his interpretation was plausible, it is not clear that southern medical societies were better organized or less contentious than their northern counterparts. Even if the explanation were valid, it alone could not account for the vast disparity in suits.

Most of the immediate factors that incited suits in the North also existed in the South. Homeopaths and especially Thomsonians enjoyed a booming business. In 1835 a Mississippi governor estimated that half the citizens of his state relied on Thomsonian therapy. Antebellum medical sectarians wooed patients away from regular practitioners in states as diverse as Virginia, South Carolina, Louisiana, and Texas.[78] Just as in the North, the practice of southern sectarians thrived as the reputation of orthodox practitioners declined. Public scorn and distrust emanated from the same sources as in the North. Although deceased slaves provided a somewhat more accessible pool of dissection subjects, southern physicians and medical students were often forced to rely on grave-robbers to acquire research and teaching cadavers.[79] The medical community's standing was undermined by highly visible incidents such as one in 1838 in which a prominent New Orleans physician was accused of using bodies of patients who had died at the charity hospital for dueling practice.[80]

Southern physicians employed different and less severe remedies than other doctors, but many people continued to associate regular practitioners with the horrors of heroic practice. J. Marion Sims, a southern physician, reported that some "[p]atients were bled, purged, administered tartar emetic, and given fever mixtures every two hours during the twenty-four . . . Those who were bled and purged the strongest died the quickest."[81] Jacksonian antiprofessional sentiment was equally strong in the South and added impetus to the delicensure movement that occurred the same time as in the North. The evils of inadequate education, defective therapies, and soaring public disdain helped inspire the many malpractice suits in the North. The existence of these factors alone, however, was not enough to produce widespread litigation in the South because the region had not undergone the cultural transformations that were the preconditions for large numbers of malpractice suits.

Southern culture grew out of and maintained the hierarchical rural communities that resembled and reinforced the old world and colonial order. Face-to-face, kinship, and community-based relationships continued to dominate social life in the South. Community opinion was much more important than legal action in settling quarrels.[82] The existence of such hierarchical, communal settlements in colonial late–eighteenth-century New England had to a certain degree discouraged extensive litigation. While the social, economic, and political turmoil of the first three decades of the nineteenth century destroyed this communal base in much of the country, southern culture retained many of its features and continued to distrust legal redress as the most appropriate solution to conflict.[83]

The relative infrequency of malpractice litigation in the South may also be explained by the absence there of the religious and cultural changes that were preconditions for the malpractice phenomenon in other parts of the country. Southerners retained traditional, eighteenth-century views of divine providence much longer than northerners, and these beliefs shaped southerners' attitudes toward misfortune, disease, pain, and reform.

The antebellum years were probably the most religious period in the history of the South. During the era of the American Revolution the intellectual leaders of the South shared Enlightenment ideas about humanity and society, but these ideas never penetrated much below the upper class. The popular evangelical churches had slowly begun to take root in the decades before the revolution, and after the Great Revival of 1800 they came to dominate the popular mind of the South. By the third decade of the nineteenth century, for example, even the aristocrats of Virginia had essentially accepted the evangelical ethos with its emphasis on human depravity and belief in the concept of direct providence.[84]

Conservative religious views that stressed providence were useful in the defense of slavery and encouraged southerners to retain traditional interpretations of providence.[85] Unitarians, Transcendentalists, and other liberal sects that assailed the notion of direct providence in the North were virtually nonexistent in the South. Southerners believed that their God supervised day-to-day life on earth to such a degree that He willed each sparrow's fall. They were resigned to the fact that a certain part of life and nature would always remain inscrutable and must be accepted as God's will.[86] In an ultimate sense God's will, not human action, determined the timing of one's fate, and neither the patient nor the doctor was finally responsible for healing or death.

The transformation of the concept of providence from a specific to general one, which encouraged society to prevent and remedy earthly ills in the North, had virtually no impact in the South. Southern evangelical fervor had a different face. While the rest of nineteenth-century America grew increasingly optimistic and confident of the prospects of human and social perfectibility, the South remained pessimistic and stoical. It did not search for cures for every evil because it did not believe they existed.[87] The region was relatively untouched by almost every reform movement of the early nineteenth century: abolitionism, feminism, humanitarianism, prevention of cruelty to animals, and prison reform.[88]

The history of the discovery of ether suggests that people living in the South may have held a considerably different view of pain and misfortune than most of their northern counterparts. In the early 1840s, before Morton's famous demonstration in 1846, Crawford Long, a Georgian physician, experimented extensively with ether. Despite his moderate successes, he failed to convince patients or other physicians of the value or propriety of his work. Long even noted that his colleagues advised him to abandon his experiments. When Morton demonstrated ether to a group of physicians in Boston just two years later, the northern medical world hailed him as a hero. Long lived and worked in a stronghold of orthodox Protestantism where an eighteenth-century view of pain was still prevalent. Morton, on the other hand, presented ether to a liberal, progressive society that believed pain was a biological function that should be remedied. While other conditions contributed to Long's failure and Morton's success, the divergent views of pain in their respective communities may have been a factor in the reactions of their colleagues.[89] A final barometer of southerners' perception of pain was their continued enjoyment of so-called blood sports such as cock- and dog-fighting, ring tournaments, and vicious man-to-man battles.[90] It may also have been expressed in their willingness to discipline their slaves physically.

The views of two physicians, one northern, one southern, reflected the sectional disparity in attitudes towards God's role in the world. Samuel Gross, one of the most revered surgeons in nineteenth-century America, lived and practiced medicine in Philadelphia. In his 1887 autobiography Gross declared that "God cannot be said ever to have killed or willfully afflicted any human being." On the contrary, Gross argued that people suffer and

die by and through natural laws, none by and through God's interposition or direct agency; and the same is true whether life is destroyed by disease or by accident, by the upsetting of a carriage, by the pistol's bullet, by a railway collision, by a boiler explosion, by a tidal wave, by a cyclone, or by an earthquake.[91]

Gross's position typified the worldview that accepted and stressed scientific rationality and perfectibility.

In contrast, Edward Warren, a physician who had been born and raised on an antebellum North Carolina plantation, held a different view of divine intervention. Warren explained in his 1885 memoirs that medicine had brought him into "daily contact with the misfortunes of humanity," and had left him with an "exalted faith." He was "compelled to attribute the harrowing scenes . . . [to] the attributes of a God having as a purpose the ultimate rectification of a work which he is compelled to do in the vindication of his governmental policy."[92] Warren, like many of his fellow southerners, believed late into the century that providential interposition sometimes guided, taught, and tested humankind.

Southern attitudes toward direct providence, natural disaster, reform, and pain suggest that they had a fundamentally different response to natural and physical misfortune than most northerners of the same period. Historians have consistently agreed that the culture of the American South "grew out of a fatalistic world view which assumed that pain and suffering were man's fate."[93] Fatalism formed an integral part of the southern worldview and encouraged individuals to accept society and their lives as they were. This resignation, born of religious conviction, may have played an important role in discouraging malpractice suits in the nineteenth-century South.

The history of a small, predominantly Baptist community in Georgia reveals that both communal and religious sanctions against legal conflict discouraged litigation into the 1970s.[94] Residents of the town maintained what they believed was a "community of Christ." Local Baptists' aversion to the adjudication of adversarial conflict in civil courts, outside the local church community, reached back into the first half of the nineteenth century and persisted through the twentieth. Their substantial rejection of the use of civil courts was based on the notion that God is the judge of humanity and that resorting to an earthly power questioned divine wisdom.[95] Consequently, as late as the mid-1970s, residents of the town considered personal injuries, accidents, automobile wrecks, and even personal violence as examples of God's will, and community members generally refused to seek legal redress. To do so would have violated both God's will and community customs that emphasized Christian and social harmony.[96] While this consensus is probably possible only in small socially and religiously homogeneous societies, it suggests a reason why malpractice suits in the American South remained relatively rare through the nineteenth century.

Jacksonian society's secularized, scientific view of general misfortune, disease, and pain was the psychological backdrop for the dramatic increase in malpractice suits in the late 1830s and early 1840s. Moreover, it was the foundation for the continued rise in suits through the twentieth century. Since the 1830s social and physical misfortune has been perceived more and more as preventable or at least remediable. While there was an array of complex causes for the initial increase in lawsuits, Americans' faith in the benefits of science and their new-found certainty that God did not intend man to suffer on earth freed them to blame physicians for incomplete cures. Widespread lawsuits would not have been possible without a fundamental shift in public attitudes about divine providence in everyday life. Although the trans-formation of public belief was gradual, and not complete by 1865, the threshold point had been reached as early as the 1840s.

Religious attitudes continued to evolve through the nineteenth cen-tury as the notion of providence lost its grip on the American mind. Providence was replaced by a secularized, optimistic view of the merits and promise of material and social progress.[97] Broad public confidence, however, was accompanied by higher expectations and increased de-mands. When these demands were not met, individuals increasingly blamed people and institutions for their personal misfortune. Although the decline in the importance of providence in the public mind paved the way for beneficial and humane reform, it also encouraged the proliferation of lawsuits by removing the possibility of divine intent and highlighting human culpability. This process, beginning in the late eighteenth century and continuing through today, helps explain the perpetual increase of malpractice suits in the face of profound and unceasing medical progress.

CHAPTER 6

"Dangerous Ground for a Surgeon"

"Western New York is becoming dangerous ground for a surgeon" a writer complained in 1844. According to the observer, qualified physicians were "constantly liable to vexatious suits, instituted by ignorant, unprincipled persons, sometimes urged on, it is presumed, by those who have a private grudge." This editorialist warned "that unless a better state of things could be brought about, the medical practitioners in that part of the country would unitedly refuse to render any assistance in cases of fractures and dislocations."[1] One physician claimed that between 1833 and 1856, "[t]here was scarcely a surgeon in the State of New York, of any respectability, who had not been prosecuted one or more times; and probably not one who had not been often threatened."[2] In 1853 Frank Hamilton estimated that nine out of every ten physicians in Western New York had been forced to defend themselves against malpractice charges.[3]

This apparent malpractice epidemic reflected the confused professional and political position of embattled doctors in Jacksonian America, especially in New York. Irregular practitioners were numerous and popular in the state, and they eroded the status and political power of regular physicians. Western New York was a stronghold of Jacksonian sentiment, which was incompatible with the type of monopoly privilege represented by medical societies and licensure laws. Competition among regular practitioners and disputes over therapeutic procedures weakened professional solidarity and sabotaged public confidence. Physicians' social status and lack of professional cohesion encouraged disgruntled patients to sue their doctors. Western New York, in the wake of Charles Finney's revivalism, was also one of the first areas of the country to feel the impact of the notion of perfectionism and the accompanying decline in the belief in special providence. Perfectionist sentiments helped create the optimism and expectations that underlay the new demands for physical well-being and were an essential precondition for widespread personal injury suits.

Once instituted, malpractice litigation exposed and exacerbated the fundamental weaknesses of contemporary medical professionalism in the Jacksonian era. Individual physicians, professional journals, and local medical societies were faced with dilemmas they could not solve. No matter how they reacted to the crisis, they contributed to either public distrust, professional competition, or physicians' incompetence. In turn, this suspicion, divisiveness, and medical ineptitude aggravated what seemed to be an ever-increasing wave of malpractice prosecutions. One New York malpractice case in the early 1840s demonstrates how destructive litigation could be and how the crisis confused professionals.

Doctors and Politics

New York physicians in the early 1840s suffered under even greater debilities than their colleagues in other states. In 1836 the *Boston Medical and Surgical Journal* reported that New York was filled with "troops of quacks [and] foreign pretenders of all grades, from pill makers to magicians."[4] John Thomson, the son of the founder of the Thomsonian sect, organized the New York opposition to the licensure laws in the state. He forged a temporary alliance between the Thomsonians, Homeopaths, and other irregular practitioners against the regular physicians and helped make the licensure struggle more intense than in any other state. Job Haskell served as the medical sects' spokesman in the New York state assembly. In 1834 he presented the legislature with a petition with forty thousand signatures that called for an end to restrictive medical legislation. Haskell claimed that licensure laws encouraged "privileged physicians" to "depend on their diplomas and legislative enactments to advance them instead of worth and merit."[5] The obvious popularity of irregular practitioners in New York indicated the public distrust of the regular practitioners.

The political atmosphere in New York also worked against the regular physicians. Thomsonians were natural allies with the Jacksonian Democratic party and its Loco Foco spin-offs. New York was a Democratic state and "served as an acknowledged Democratic tutor for the newer western states."[6] The party's anti–National Bank, antimonopoly philosophy fit well with Thomsonian goals. The Loco Focos, a radical strain of Jacksonian Democrats, were especially strong in New York. They opposed all privileged or aristocratic pretension and declared that "every profession, business, or trade not hurtful to the community, shall be equally open to the community."[7] It was not surprising that Haskell, the Thomsonians' advocate in the legislature, became a Loco Foco supporter. These forces were successful, and the New York legislature repealed the licensure statute in 1844.

Even in the face of these outside threats to the medical profession, the state's physicians failed to put aside their intraprofessional battles. In the *New York Journal of Medicine* F. Campbell Stewart wrote in 1846 that the New York medical profession was marked by "a degree of jealousy and unkind feeling which ought nowhere to exist."[8] Doctors fought each other over therapeutic doctrine, fee schedules, and the profits and prestige of controlling medical education in the state. To reduce conflict, competition, and jealousy among themselves, some New York physicians tried to strengthen the influence of medical societies and associations. For example, the state medical society adopted a code of ethics that stressed the need to avoid disputes within the profession. These active professional organizations sometimes provided an enlarged and more public forum for dispute. Historian Daniel Calhoun has characterized the unsuccessful efforts to create a united front of physicians in Jacksonian New York as "the clash between community consciousness and individual ambition." Local and state medical societies served as new bases of professional discord and were often used as weapons in the battle of physician against physician.[9]

New York physicians' tendency toward professional "suicide" as well as their declining social status and weakened political position encouraged dissatisfied patients to seek relief or revenge in court. Many observers believed that New York was the source of the malpractice "fever" in the 1840s that later spread into New Hampshire, Vermont, Pennsylvania, and Massachusetts.[10] The *Boston Medical and Surgical Journal* reported in 1847 that public sentiment in Western New York was so much in favor of "breaking down surgeons" that the most distinguished physicians "were hardly willing to give advice in surgical practice." New York physicians regularly ran the risk of "being prosecuted by some unprincipled fellow, who either expected to gain more money by it than he could get by honest industry" or sought revenge "for some supposed injury, by ruining the surgeon in purse and reputation."[11] Relatively unsensational malpractice cases of little legal doctrinal importance often disrupted professional relations, distorted standards of care, and further damaged physicians' status in society.

Smith v. Goodyear and Hyde

William Smith was fifty years old, had a "strong and robust constitution," but, by all accounts, was "addicted to intemperance." On 4 July 1839, while working on a house in Cortland, New York, Smith fell from a scaffold and injured his leg. Witnesses sent for Dr. Azariah Booth Shipman, who lived several miles away.[12] Shipman, who was thirty-six had, since his late teens "determinately g[iven] his odd leisure to studying medicine." He later spent two years working under his brother, who was a physician. Though he never studied at a medical school, the county medical society granted Shipman a license in 1826. He earned a good reputation for surgery and was called for nearly all the important operations for miles around, including such difficult procedures as the removal of tumors, tracheotomies, and lithotomies. At the time of Smith's accident, Shipman was president of the Cortland County Medical Society.[13]

Shipman examined Smith two hours after the accident and discovered that Smith had broken both bones in his lower leg about two inches above his ankle. The jagged edge of the fibula had penetrated the skin, puncturing Smith's boot and pants' leg. Despite the severity of the compound fracture, there was little damage to the nerves, blood vessels, or leg muscles. Shipman cleaned the wound, removed a small piece of bone, and was able to place the bones in their proper positions, by "extension and counter-extension," the procedures by which physicians stretched a broken limb, either manually or mechanically, to make the adjustment of broken bones easier. Smith also prescribed an anodyne of sulfate and morphine for pain. Shipman closed the gash with adhesive plaster, and put three padded splints on Smith's leg.[14] The next day, 5 July, Smith was sent to the county almshouse and put under the care of doctors Goodyear and Hyde.

Miles Goodyear had graduated with the first medical class at Yale in 1816. He moved to Cortlandville and became "a man of large influence in the city." Fredrick Hyde "read medicine" under several private physicians, attended three medical lecture courses in the early 1830s, and was granted a county license in 1833. In 1836 he received a diploma from Fairfield Medical College in New York. Two years later he married Miles Goodyear's daughter and joined the older man's established practice. In addition to their private patients, Goodyear and Hyde were responsible for the sick and injured clients of the county poorhouse.[15]

Goodyear and Hyde competed with Shipman for patients and prestige in Cortlandville. Though Goodyear and his partner advertised in the *Cortland Republican & Eagle*, they were careful not to impugn the ability of other local physicians. The partners claimed to specialize in "practical and operative surgery," but they cautiously noted that their "treatment of all surgical cases shall not be inferior to the ordinary practice of this country."[16]

By modestly professing to provide only "ordinary" care instead of claiming superior ability, Goodyear and Hyde were attempting to avoid public quarrels with other practitioners. Though competition among regular physicians was a fact of life in the 1830s and 1840s, the profession collectively faced the greater threat of a hostile public, sectarian rivals, and decreasing legal legitimation. Therefore, many physicians strove to portray a united front to the public and downplay professional dissension. Inevitably, individual doctors broke ranks and destroyed this artificial professional solidarity. Shipman was one of these physicians. Through most of the 1830s his advertisement appeared immediately adjacent to the modest claims of Goodyear and Hyde. In it Shipman confidently promised that he could provide "the best treatment which the art can afford." His willingness to proclaim his technical superiority and to compete openly for patients antagonized other physicians and set the stage for more bitter disputes.[17]

On 13 July, nine days after the accident, the superintendent of the almshouse visited Shipman at his office and asked him to help Goodyear and Hyde amputate Smith's leg. When Shipman arrived, he discovered that the splints and dressings had been removed from the limb. Smith's foot was swollen and twisted to one side and his leg was in a double-inclined plane, a device with a joint in the middle that supported the leg in a 45-degree, bent-at-the-knee position. Worst of all, the broken end of Smith's fibula was again protruding nearly two inches out of the original wound. He was in considerable pain and part of the bone had begun to decay. Smith's general health, however, was fairly good. Part of the wound had healed, there was little pus, his pulse and appetite were normal, and he was free from fever.

Goodyear and Hyde argued that Smith's age and alcoholic habits convinced them that immediate amputation was necessary. In addition, they held that the hot weather might induce a dangerous fever. Shipman disagreed. He contended that the physicians should remove the dead portion of the bone, close the wound, and replace the splints. Goodyear, who had apparently helped Shipman in his early practice, cursed the physician and warned, "[D]on't mention the villain's [Shipman's] name, I have been a father to him." Nevertheless, Shipman held to his contention that Smith's leg should be saved and declared that "a man would be a ——— fool to propose amputation in this case." Shipman explained later that the abusive language from Goodyear had prompted his strong response.[18] Three other local physicians joined the debate. Three of the six physicians opposed the amputation, one doctor believed that amputation might be "talked of," and Goodyear and Hyde supported the operation. Shipman refused to assist in the amputation and left the almshouse.[19]

The leg remained untreated for ten days until on 23 July the superintendent of the almshouse allowed Smith to choose his own doctor. Smith dismissed Goodyear and Hyde and sent for Shipman. When Shipman arrived, he found that Smith's condition had deteriorated. Following the course of treatment he had recommended ten days before, Shipman removed about an inch of the decaying end of the

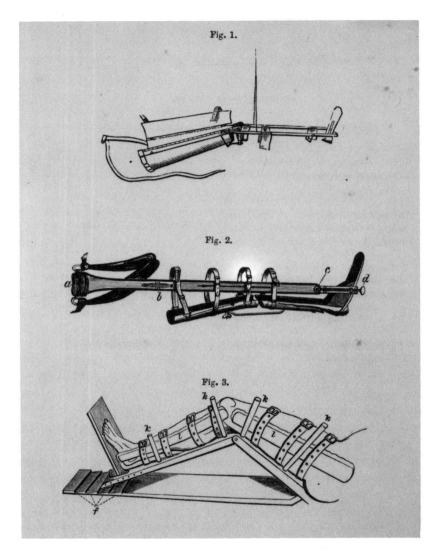

Various double-inclined planes for fractures. From Frank Hastings Hamilton, "Report on Deformities after Fractures," TAMA 10 (1857): 239–453. (Courtesy of the Historical Research Center, Houston Academy of Medicine, Texas Medical Center Library, Houston, Texas.)

protruding bone with an amputating saw and set the leg in splints. He also cleaned the wound of pus and maggots and closed it with adhesive plasters. Throughout Smith's recovery Shipman or one of his colleagues visited the almshouse daily to clean and dress the wound and keep the bone in place. Smith's leg healed slowly but steadily, and he was able to leave the poorhouse in the spring of 1840. His leg was an inch and a quarter shorter, but it was strong and "he walk[ed] without difficulty and without much lameness."[20]

During the summer of 1840 local residents collected money to help Smith hire an attorney.[21] In February 1841 Smith sued Goodyear and Hyde for malpractice. Smith asserted that they had been negligent in allowing the bone to become displaced and in failing to keep the wound clean and dressed. They were also negligent, Smith claimed, for refusing to perform the resection of the decayed bone ultimately carried out by Shipman. Shipman was Smith's strongest witness. He and three other physicians testified that Goodyear and Hyde did not regularly attend Smith and that the broken end of the bone was left untreated until Shipman reset it nearly three weeks after the accident. They also claimed that amputation would not have been the proper treatment.[22] Dr. Lewis Riggs, a member of the U.S. House of Representatives, had examined Smith in the almshouse. Imputing sinister motives to Goodyear and Hyde, Riggs declared that a physician should never "deprive a poor patient of a leg or an arm, or subject him to any other severe and cruel operation, to gain a reputation as an operative surgeon, or to rid [him]self of the trouble, care or expense of a protracted cure."[23]

Goodyear and Hyde presented a strong defense. Six local physicians, plus James Webster and Frank Hamilton, professors at the Geneva Medical College, testified on their behalf. Webster and Hamilton had long and respected careers. Hamilton was an authority on fractures whose later tabulations on the results of fractures led doctors to lower their expectations of complete cures.[24] In the Smith case, Hamilton and Webster testified that Shipman's resection of the end of the bone was improper and that an amputation would have been the correct treatment. After the witnesses for both sides testified, Smith's lawyer withdrew the complaint and agreed to drop the suit.[25]

Professional Reaction. This aborted suit from a small town eventually gained national attention. Ironically, Shipman, the star witness for the prosecution, and not the defendants, Goodyear and Hyde, suffered most from negative publicity. Local physicians, who were already antagonized by Shipman's aggressive advertising campaign, attacked him in the county newspaper both for his medical treatment and for his role in the trial. Anonymous letters published in the *Cortland County Whig* praised the character of Goodyear and Hyde, questioned Shipman's medical ability, and insinuated that he had encouraged the lawsuit. During the trial, under cross examination, Shipman had admitted that he had remarked to some of the town's residents that Goodyear and Hyde's treatment constituted malpractice.[26]

On April 20 1841, about two months after the trial, the *Whig* published a letter signed by "Justice." The writer explained that Goodyear, a twenty-year resident, had raised his family in Cortland and had distinguished his professional life by "faithful, disinterested and laborious service." These attributes gave "him a hold on the affections of the people," which grew stronger with the "lapse of time." The letter characterized Hyde as a young but thoroughly educated and talented physician with a bright future. The author recounted the events leading to the litigation and reported that the trial was a "triumphant vindication of the professional merit and private worth" of Goodyear and Hyde. The pseudonymous observer "Justice" was, however, "indignant at the foul spirit, that instigated the groundless prosecution" and warned that the "vain," "secret machinations" against the defendants would, "return 'to plague the inventor.' "[27]

One week later, a response, signed by "Truth," defended Shipman in the pages of a rival paper, the *Cortland County Democrat.* "Truth" contended that he did not have "any feelings of prejudice against either of the parties," but that the articles in the *Whig* had been "calculated to lead the public mind to erroneous conclusions, and to reflect dishonor upon the professional judgement and practice of the leading surgeons of our country." The letter-writer argued that common sense and "successful precedent" supported Shipman's treatment. If Shipman had not removed the diseased part of the bone, then the patient would have been "lying around for months with the bone projecting through the wound waiting for it to rot off before the limb could be straightened and properly adjusted." "Truth" questioned the value of the testimony of the famous medical professors Webster and Hamilton, who had spoken in defense of Goodyear and Hyde. The writer for the *Democrat* argued that the newspaper attacks on Shipman had relied on the testimony of the "learned professors" "who were summoned from a distance" and ignored the evidence presented by the intelligent, local physicians who were acquainted with the case and "therefore the most competent to decide." In sparkling Jacksonian rhetoric, "Truth" exclaimed that he was confident that

our community profess[es] too much intelligence to be awed by titles and induced to hold the mere opinions of such men ["learned professors"] paramount to the actual knowledge of men of equal talents who have lived among and in the community and proved their judgement and skill by their practice.[28]

The *Whig* and the *Democrat* continued the debate through the following year, the *Democrat* consistently supporting Shipman, the *Whig* reviling him. Shipman may have represented to the editors of the *Democrat* the prototypical democratic physician. He excelled by his superior abilities, did not rely on conspiratorial professionalism, refused to protect incompetent practitioners, and was willing to engage in "free trade in doctoring." When in April 1842 the editors of the *Whig* and the *Democrat* both received an anonymous article entitled "Medical Ethics," the editor of the *Democrat* refused to print the piece because it "was a wanton and malicious attempt to injure Dr. Shipman" written by a "vile" and "low blackguard." The *Whig*, however, printed the article even though the editor later admitted that it had been "written with an express design to cast ridicule and reproach upon him [Shipman]—to injure his reputation as a citizen, and to impair and ruin his business as a practitioner."[29] According to one medical journal, the case had "been extensively misrepresented in the neighborhood, and rumors circulated in every direction touching the professional character of [Shipman], and the gentlemen associated with him in the treatment."[30]

Shipman complained that "[t]he 'miasma' of falsehood ha[s] been permitted to go out in every direction, and as yet no antidote ha[s] been offered." He charged that the accounts of the trial and treatment in local newspapers "abound in grandiloquent and bombastic bursts of rhapsody, evidently proceeding from the brain of some conceited attorney."[31] To vindicate himself, Shipman had the *Cortland Democrat* publish a thirty-five-page pamphlet chronicling the case and his medical treatment and sent copies to major medical journals around the country.[32] In his attempt to win a local battle against rival physicians, Shipman escalated the debate to a national level and risked undermining public confidence in the profession as a whole. But Shipman's action was consistent with his willingness to engage in open competition with his local rivals.

An editorialist for the *Boston Medical and Surgical Journal* was the first to respond to Shipman's pamphlet, in November 1841. The writer attempted to maintain professional solidarity at all costs and took the opportunity to rail against litigious patients. He noted judiciously that all the witnesses were "[s]urgeons of respectability and skill" and that they had testified ably to the expediency of both modes of treatment. Shipman's pamphlet, the writer believed, presented "sufficient authority . . . for his choice of treatment to prevent any stigma attaching to his reputation as a surgeon." The editorialist was careful to add that his comments were not intended to reflect on the ability or performance of Goodyear and Hyde. He noted candidly that "[i]n all trials for mal-practice . . . our sympathies are in the first place enlisted on the side of the defendant." Continuing, he asserted:

Prosecutions for malpractice are pretty much of a piece with those for a breach of promise of marriage, and are looked upon by the discriminating public in a similar light. They are in general a pretext, and that is all, for sponging, a little money out of someone who has got more than the plaintiff . . . the public good, humanity, benevolence, philanthropy or any other praiseworthy object, is in most cases entirely out of the question.

The writer hoped that Shipman's pamphlet would "have the effect of putting surgeons on their guard against unprincipled patients and their special friends."[33] It was not clear whether "special friends" referred to lawyers, or if the term masked criticism of Shipman and the other physicians who testified against Goodyear and Hyde.

This writer's comments demonstrated the lengths to which some physicians would go to avoid criticizing other practitioners. He did not question Goodyear's and Hyde's methods, though they left Smith's wound open, pus-filled, and maggot-infested with a protruding bone for nearly three weeks. Rather, he implied that both modes of treatment were acceptable even though the respective results would have been radically different. Moreover, he ignored the growing body of medical opinion that increasingly questioned the wisdom of amputations.[34]

But while the writer endeavored to preserve the dignity and legitimacy of the profession by refusing to disparage other physicians, he was also damaging the profession's image by confirming the prevalent belief that physicians closed ranks to protect their own monopolistic interests. The writer's refusal to support one treatment over another was more suspicious in light of an article published in the same journal two months before about a man who had suffered an injury identical to Smith's. The two bones in his lower leg were broken about two inches above the ankle and the fibula protruded from a wound in the leg. The physician sawed off about an inch of the bone and set the leg. The patient recovered, as had Smith, with some minor shortening of his leg.[35]

Other observers were less blindly loyal to the profession. One, identified only as "R. C.," criticized Goodyear and Hyde in an 1841 issue of the *Medical Examiner*. He commented that, though it was proper that amputation was considered, he was "acquainted with no experienced surgeon in this section of the country who would have ventured to perform it in the then existing state of the constitution." He believed that Shipman's treatment was correct and would have "expected with some confidence to see the necessity of wearing a high-heeled shoe, the worst ultimate consequence of the avoidance of amputation" in this type of case. Though the writer held that "a difference of opinion on this subject would not be just ground for a charge of ignorance or even censure," he believed that there were "more formidable questions" about the case. He wondered why the bone was allowed to become displaced after it had been adjusted following the accident and why the wound was not dressed and cleaned. He did not condemn Goodyear and Hyde; instead, he asked probing questions and made it clear that he opposed amputation.[36]

After reading the whitewashed account of the case that had appeared in the *Boston Medical and Surgical Journal*, "R. C." of the *Medical Examiner*, composed a follow-up to his original commentary. He believed that his first report a week earlier had been written "in a spirit, perhaps, of too great mildness." While he could "sympathise" with the *Boston Medical and Surgical Journal* author's "leaning toward the profession," he could not "forget that the first professional duty is toward the patient." He said that though "malignity and sordid calculation are no infrequent instigators of prosecutions for mal-practice, it is quite possible for medical men, in these days of easy graduation and multiplied professorships, to be guilty of culpable neglect or—in the existing condition of many medical schools—scarcely blamable ignorance." On reviewing the evidence, the author concluded that "had we been the prosecuting party,—not only should we have avoided requesting the withdrawal of the case, but we would have not permitted it." Shipman's pamphlet, the writer concluded, "as painful as it must be to lovers of professional concord . . . will have the effect of 'placing surgeons on their guard', as to the necessity of keeping pace with the advance of science." [37]

This writer's response underlined physicians' and medical societies' dilemma in dealing with local quarrels and public malpractice controversies. By courageously supporting the best medical practices and condemning incompetent physicians, the author helped to publicize what constituted good practice, but he damaged professional solidarity and the profession's public image. Individual physicians, such as Shipman, retained their reputations, but the profession was exposed as a factious, sometimes dishonest, group of practitioners possessing an uneven amount of skill and knowledge.

Early in 1842 George W. Norris lamented in the *American Journal of Medical Science* that commenting

upon the doctrines and practice of members of our profession where malpractice has occurred, is one of the most unpleasant duties of the medical journalist, and would in the present instance be avoided, did we not hold it to be a duty both to our readers and the cause of truth, to raise our voice in support of sound surgical principles.

Norris stated frankly that Goodyear and Hyde's treatment had been poor. Moreover, he defended Shipman's refusal to accede to an amputation. "Is it the custom of the gentlemen, who recommended and approved such a course [amputation], to doom to amputation every limb affected with fracture and issue of the bone, which is found to be irreducible, without first resorting to other means of relief?" Norris asked. He reminded his readers that amputation was a dangerous operation and that "sound surgical principles, humanity and daily experience teach" that it should never be resorted to until other means had failed. Norris included accounts of several cases similar to Smith's dating as early as 1815 in which amputation was avoided and the patient survived with only a shortening of the leg.[38]

Despite these articles defending proper treatment in the face of blind professional loyalty, physicians in Cortland, New York, still supported Goodyear and Hyde. At their January 1842 meeting the Cortland County Medical Society, of which Shipman was still president, discussed a new bylaw. The rule would have required that before "any member shall instigate a prosecution against another member of this Society," he must submit the question to the annual meeting of the society and obtain a two-thirds vote of confidence before proceeding. In addition, he must give the accused physician thirty days notice of the charge or be expelled from the society. It was clear that "there would have been an almost unanimous vote in favor of the resolution." But no vote occurred. Shipman, president of the society, refused to put the question to a vote when it was moved and seconded and refused to leave the chair when requested to do so. Though the society tabled the bylaw, its members removed Shipman from the presidency and replaced him with Goodyear. The society then passed a resolution stating "[t]hat on review of the facts in relation to the prosecution by Wm. Smith against Drs. Goodyear and Hyde, for mal-practice, we have yet to see nothing [sic] to diminish our confidence in their skill as practical Surgeons." The society published a report of the proceedings in the *Cortland Democrat* and relayed this vote of confidence to the Philadelphia and Boston medical journals.[39]

After hearing of the activities of the Cortland Medical Society, a writer for the *Medical Examiner* noted that "although it seems a clique of his [Shipman's] professional brethren in the neighborhood are weak enough to put him down for doing his duty," Shipman deserved "great praise" for his "manly and successful efforts to save the limb." The medical society's resolutions, the commentator noted, "besides endorsing bad surgery, have another obvious ill tendency":

They create among the public an impression that physicians are disposed to screen each other from the just consequences of ignorance and incapacity, that they regard their duty to their patients as secondary, and that, as in the present instance, they deem the preservation of limb and life as of little weight in the balance with the observance of a false code of professional etiquette.[40]

The Aftermath. This editorial offered a remarkably clear perspective on the case, in which three arms of the profession—a medical journal, an expert witness, and a local medical society—had attempted to close ranks and express solidarity. In doing so, they refused to condone good practice and condemn obsolete procedures. The public, as the author noted, could believe only that members of the profession were "disposed to screen each other from the just consequences of ignorance and incapacity." However, the physicians who had attacked Goodyear and Hyde and supported modern techniques damaged the profession in other ways. When malpractice debates exposed professional discord and therapeutic uncertainty, physicians' status and legitimacy suffered. The public distrust born of these debates aggravated patients' suspicions and encouraged additional suits.

The Goodyear and Hyde case also demonstrated how malpractice litigation and the profession's reaction to it could discourage medical advancement. Amputation was considered the standard treatment for compound fractures until the 1820s. By 1835, in cases of compound fractures of the tibia and fibula near the ankle joint, the injury suffered by Smith, Astley Cooper, the leading expert on orthopedic injuries, eschewed amputation and recommended removing the broken and jagged pieces of bone with a saw.[41] Goodyear and Hyde were sued in part for refusing to do so and for advocating amputation instead. When Shipman took over the case and followed the most current authorities on fractures, Goodyear and Hyde's supporters attacked him at the trial and later in newspapers. Similarly, the members of the Cortland county medical society, two expert witnesses, local physicians, and a few medical commentators, spurned the evidence of almost a decade, condemned Shipman, and defended Goodyear and Hyde.

By ignoring these advancements in orthopedics, Goodyear and Hyde's supporters impeded the acceptance of improved forms of treatment and encouraged the discredited alternative of amputation. Indiscriminate amputation also conflicted with the general trend toward "conservative medicine" and placing a greater trust in the healing powers of nature.[42] For example, one of Shipman's supporters, a writer for a medical journal, claimed that "nature" had pointed out the correct treatment. The same observer could not find a single reason to support amputation and suggested, as had some of the witnesses, that "[i]n the absence of every other motive, one might almost suppose that amputation was desired to get rid of a troublesome case, and the more effectively to conceal a bad piece of surgery."[43] The author's suggestion was not so farfetched. The vagaries of malpractice litigation could have affected treatment decisions by making it more attractive to condone amputation than to follow the safer and more effective procedure of saving limbs.

The professional and personal animosity aggravated by Goodyear and Hyde's prosecution persisted. In the spring of 1842 Henry Brockway fractured his leg and dislocated his ankle when he jumped from a buggy pulled by a runaway horse. Shipman treated the injury until August 1842. Brockway then went to work as a millwright and told Shipman that he was pleased with the results of the treatment. Early in 1844 Brockway visited several local physicians who told him that his ankle was dislocated and advised him to sue Shipman for malpractice. The editors of the *Boston Medical and Surgical Journal* received an anonymous letter informing them of the suit and "rejoicing" over Shipman's prosecution.[44] The editors refused to print the report but warned that western New York was rife with accusations of malpractice. The writer noted that Shipman had been a witness for the prosecution in a malpractice case three years previously and acknowledged that the suit had probably been instigated by another physician with a private grudge. The following week the journal reported that a Cortland County jury voted eleven to one to dismiss the charges against Shipman.[45]

Surprisingly, these public battles did not drive Goodyear, Hyde, and Shipman out of Cortland or into professional obscurity, In 1845 Goodyear and Hyde opened a private school of anatomy and surgery. Later, in 1855, Hyde filled the chair of surgery at Geneva Medical College, in 1865 he was elected president of the state medical society, and, when Geneva Medical College joined with Syracuse University in the 1870s, Hyde became the dean of the new faculty. Shipman eventually served as a professor of surgery at Indiana University.[46]

Although the three physicians survived the ordeal, the profession suffered significant damage from the public conflict. In an 1846 article F. Campbell Stewart tried to warn New York physicians that self-aggrandizement often amounted to professional suicide. Stewart claimed that "many of our body fall into the gross error of considering that their individual success depends on decrying their professional rivals and indirectly leading patients to conclude that they alone, of all others are able and capable of rendering effectual assistance." He insisted that this "course [was] calculated both to impair the credit of the general body and lessen the estimation in which it should be held by the public at large" and advised that "all of our faults and our errors should be kept within our own bounds."[47] Despite Stewart's initial insight, malpractice litigation rendered his advice inappropriate and useless.

Local medical societies and codes of ethics failed to contain completely individual ambition in disputes over patients, education, therapy, and malpractice incidents. Some doctors were willing to use malpractice accusations as competitive tools. Their no-holds-barred, free-market competition was a significant cause and an aggravating factor in the crisis. Once a physician was accused of malpractice, the charge disrupted professional relations in a variety of ways, all of which damaged the profession.

The spectacle of one physician testifying against another itself shattered the thin veneer of professional solidarity that Stewart and other writers recommended. However, when physicians defended obviously ignorant, incompetent, or careless colleagues, suspicious lay observers could rightly accuse them of protecting quacks. As *Smith* v. *Goodyear and Hyde* demonstrated, malpractice litigation could be antagonistic to medical advancement. The medical profession's fear of the malpractice epidemic and the desperate efforts to establish a united front sometimes encouraged physicians to accept substandard performances from their colleagues and implicitly support outdated and dangerous treatments. And, especially in the case of amputations and fractures, the best treatment for the patient was not necessarily the safest treatment for the physician.

Local medical societies and medical journals that were founded in part to unify the profession sometimes served instead as public forums for personal disputes. These institutions failed to devise an objective means of responding to the flood of malpractice suits that did not harm the profession they were intending to promote and protect. The societies and journals damaged the profession by either exposing an incompetent surgeon, implying that there must be other doctors who could not be trusted, or helping to perpetuate poor or outdated treatment and confirming the claims of their many critics by sheltering substandard practitioners. Finally, malpractice suits in the 1830s and 1840s were a self-perpetuating phenomenon. Some cases, like Goodyear and Hyde's, generated retaliatory suits against physicians who testified for the prosecution. Almost all malpractice cases in the period, however, contributed to the public distrust and resentment, and the professional competitiveness and divisiveness that helped cause the suits initially.

CHAPTER 7

The Road Not Taken: Medical Malpractice and the Path of the Common Law

In 1956 a North Carolina state supreme court judge declared that a physician agreeing to accept a person as a patient "does not create a contract in the sense that the term is ordinarily used." In medical malpractice cases, the judge observed, "it is apt and perhaps more exact to say it [the doctor-patient relationship] creates a status or relation rather than a contract."[1] This observation is consistent with the modern tendency to view medical malpractice as a tort of negligence rather than a breach of contract. Twentieth-century legal theorists define *torts* broadly as private civil wrongs that violate certain duties or responsibilities within a social context that condones certain behaviors and condemns others. The modern law of *contract*, by contrast, holds that the duty owed by the respective parties is theoretically agreed upon by the individuals involved in the contract.[2]

One hundred and fifty years ago the picture was less clear. Judges and legal theorists had not yet molded the notions of tort and contract into discrete categories, and there was no need or basis upon which to classify malpractice under one abstract heading or the other. The prevailing writ system designated specific legal actions and procedures for various civil wrongs and obviated much of the need for overarching doctrinal theory.[3] When lawyers brought a suit before a court, they selected the appropriate action and cited pertinent case-law precedent.

The earliest American malpractice cases relied heavily on English common law procedures and assumptions about the nature of the doctor-patient relationship.

The political, social, and economic changes of the first half of the nineteenth century, however, transformed the American public view of the physician's role in society and threatened to alter fundamentally the grounds of the physician's personal and legal responsibility. By the 1830s a significant number of Americans were willing to treat medical practice as if it were a purely commercial enterprise. Malpractice law reflected this trend, and some judges and physicians tentatively incorporated aspects of contractual language into medical liability doctrines. Although this deviation was not directly related to the sudden increase in litigation, the two phenomena shared political and social origins. If the midcentury flirtation of malpractice law with contractual doctrine had matured, the nature of a doctor's liability would have been profoundly different. Ultimately, however, subjective feelings about medical practice, the medical community's self-image, and the inappropriate matching of commercial doctrines to the doctor-patient relationship doomed the marriage of malpractice and contract and relegated medical liability to the province of tort.

Common Law Origins

Blackstone categorized malpractice under neither contract or mercantile law, but under private wrongs. He defined *mala practice* as an injury or damage to a person's "vigor or constitution" sustained as a result of "the neglect or unskillful management of [a] physician, surgeon, or apothecary." Blackstone declared that malpractice was an offense because "it breaks the trust which the party placed in his physician." The injured patient possessed a remedy for damages with the special legal action, or writ, of "trespass on the case."[4]

According to eighteenth-century lawyers, when a defendant was charged with a civil offense, the court required the plaintiff to designate the specific writ or action that entitled him or her to recover damages. There were ten basic writs or actions, and, if the purported offense did not fall under one of the ten, then the plaintiff did not have a legal remedy.[5] The *writ of trespass* was the legal remedy for damages resulting from direct force to a person or his or her property. Broken contracts were prosecuted under the *writ of assumpsit*.[6]

When the writ system was established in the late fourteenth century, it did not initially include the action of trespass on the case, the writ Blackstone designated to prosecute malpractice cases. Since the trespass writ applied exclusively to a direct and unauthorized interference with an individual's person or property, a plaintiff could not use the trespass writ if he or she had voluntarily submitted to a physician's care. The writ was also useless in cases where injury or damage was the result of an indirect or careless action by the defendant. With no remedy available for an entire class of cases, English courts slowly accepted the notion that injured plaintiffs were entitled to remuneration even where there was no breach of contract (assumpsit) or injury by force (trespass).

In two cases in the 1370s English courts allowed a special trespass writ (which would become known as *trespass on the case*) to apply against veterinary surgeons who injured horses instead of curing them. Through the fifteenth century courts accumulated a significant body of precedents in which they allowed the application of the special trespass writ.[7] In 1553 in his *Natura Brevium* Anthony Fitzherbert declared that individuals were liable for injuries caused by negligent conduct even when there was no breach of contract or actual trespass. This new writ, which had been evolving for one and a half centuries, was called *trespass on the case*, or *action on the case*. Fitzherbert asserted that if a [black]smith prick my horse with a nail, I shall have an action upon the case against him [even] without any warranty by the smith to do it well. . . . For it is the duty of every artificer to exercise his art rightly and truly as he ought."[8] Fitzherbert's remarks were the modern foundation for action on the case. Later writers argued that his statement applied not only to smiths, but also to innkeepers, ferrymen, carpenters, barbers, and physicians.[9]

Sixty years later Edward Coke, the great English jurist, explicitly used the trespass on the case writ for damages arising out of the doctor-patient relationship. In *Everard v. Hopkins*, a man employed a physician who promised to cure his injured servant's leg,[10] but who instead prescribed harmful medicines and delayed the servant's recovery by a year. Coke declared that the master could sue using the writ of assumpsit because the physician had failed to fulfill his part of the contract to cure the servant. If the physician had not promised a cure, then the master could not have recovered under the writ of assumpsit. More significantly for modern malpractice law, however, Coke held that the servant, even though he had not made a contract with the physician, could bring charges against the doctor under the writ of trespass on the case. This holding was important because it supported the notion that the physician's liability and responsibility for his patient emanated not from a commercial contractual agreement but from the affirmative act of entering into the doctor-patient relationship.[11]

Writing in the late eighteenth century, Blackstone drew from this long evolution. Judges adopted this variant of the trespass writ to fill in situations where there had been no remedy. Blackstone explained that the malpractice prosecution allowed a plaintiff "to bring a special action on his own case, by a writ formed according to the particular circumstances of his own particular grievance." The plaintiff's official form of action would be trespass on the case but the whole "cause of complaint [is] set forth at length in the original writ."[12]

In 1767 the case of *Slater* v. *Baker and Stapleton* involved a man who sued a physician and an apothecary, claiming that they had rebroken his partially healed leg and caused it to heal poorly. In addition, the physician had used an experimental steel device with gears to stretch the limb. Employing a special trespass on the case action, Slater declared that he had hired the physician and his assistant to treat his broken leg but that they, "not regarding their promise and undertaking, and the duty of their business and employment, so ignorantly and unskillfully treated" him that his leg was permanently injured. Several other physicians testified that injured limbs should be rebroken only in cases of extreme deformity and that they had neither seen, nor heard of the experimental device. The court agreed with Slater and ruled that the physician had acted "ignorantly and unskillfully contrary to the known rule and usage of surgeons."[13]

The decision in *Slater* made it clear that a physician would be held liable for unskillful and negligent conduct even if the damage to the patient was unintentional. The accused physician's medical treatment would be measured against the therapeutic conventions or standards of the profession. *Slater* granted juries the important role of determining "questions of fact" such as what constituted carelessness and what were standards and practices of the medical profession at large.

Early American lawyers and trial court judges used *Slater* as a guide for the presentation of malpractice pleas in the trial courts, and appellate judges cited the case regularly in the first half of the nineteenth century. Other English cases also shaped early malpractice pleas.[14] In *Seare* v. *Prentice* (1807) Lord Ellenborough, the chief justice of the King's Bench, declared that a physician could be held responsible for either negligence or unskillfulness. Ellenborough stated:

an ordinary degree of skill is necessary for a surgeon who undertakes to perform surgical operations . . . in the same manner as it is necessary for every other man to have . . . common skill at least in his business, and that is implied in his undertaking.[15]

Ellenborough's ruling confirms that physicians and members of other occupations had special duties that arose out of their calling or role in society. The judge implicitly warned these men that their status as innkeepers, ferrymen, barbers, blacksmiths, lawyers, and physicians implied that they possessed the "ordinary degree of skill" essential for the fulfillment of their respective tasks.

Until the civil procedure reforms of the late 1840s and 1850s the trespass on the case writ remained the appropriate remedy for American malpractice prosecutions. In his plea to the court, the prosecuting attorney adopted the language of Blackstone, *Slater*, and *Seare* to justify the charge. For example, a Connecticut appellate court in *Landon* v. *Humphrey* used these precedents when it ruled that anyone who undertakes "any office, employment, duty, or trust" must "perform it with integrity, diligence and skill." If an individual was injured as a result of the want of any of these qualities, then the courts would accept an action on the case.[16] Prosecuting attorneys used this language in their initial pleas, judges incorporated it into their charges to juries, and appellate jurists measured lower court proceedings against it.

While the basic action of trespass on the case did not change, its underlying principles and the wording of the justification evolved as more appropriate precedents surfaced. *Lamphier and Wife* v. *Phipos* (1838) was the last English decision to contribute influential statements of principle to American malpractice law.[17] As a result of physician

Phipos's failure to diagnose correctly Mrs. Lamphier's broken wrist, she lost the use of her hand. In charging the jury, Judge Tyndall explained that every person who entered into "a learned profession undertakes to bring a fair, reasonable, and competent degree of skill to his endeavor." Attorneys did not "undertake" to win every case; surgeons did not "undertake" consistently to cure. Because some practitioners would always have "higher educations and greater advantages" than others, no physician was required to use the profession's highest degree of skill or care.[18]

Tyndall's charge did not alter earlier precedents, but it did provide the clearest and most enduring elaboration of the principles of malpractice. Trial and appellate court use of Tyndall's language made it the standard charge in nineteenth-century malpractice charges.[19] The formula, like the prescriptions of Blackstone, *Slater*, and *Seare*, was consistent with the notion that medical men were accountable for their actions because of the public nature of their calling. It did not suggest that physicians incurred responsibilities because they had entered into commercial associations with their patients. By measuring accused physicians' skill and care against the "ordinary" standard set by the rest of the profession, judges demonstrated that doctor's duties arose out of their general status as medical men rather than from their particular one-on-one "contracts" with their patients. These rulings supported the idea that the medical profession could represent an independent "community of the competent" wherein a member's actions were judged against the standards of peers. The responsibility, both moral and legal, of medical professionals emanated from membership in that community. It could not be abrogated or altered by agreements with persons outside that body.[20]

American Innovations

While American courts accepted the wording of these malpractice principles, they did not completely adopt the traditional conception of professional relationships. According to English common law, the services of lawyers and physicians were considered gratuitous. Blackstone had declared that lawyers could not sue for fees, and, since medicine was an "honorary employment," a physician could not recover compensation for his practice but had to take what was voluntarily given him.[21] This doctrine originated in Roman civil law in an era when physicians did not practice medicine as their sole livelihood, and the legal relation of doctor to patient was referred to as a *mandate*, an implicit agreement to provide service for no fee.[22] English common law gradually dropped the idea of a strict mandate, but it retained the assumption that medical and legal services were intrinsically gratuitous and that doctors had a legal right only to an honorarium.

American courts never accepted the concept of honorariums. As the nineteenth-century judge and treatise writer Gulian Verplank explained, the growing demand for the services of full-time lawyers and physicians "pointed out the injustice, as well as the absurdity, of leaving them, as a class remediless for the value of such services as they may render to the public."[23] His views reflected the growing belief that physicians did not occupy a special social or legal status in American society. He contended that it was "wholly inconsistent with all our ideas of equality to suppose that" medicine or law, businesses or professions "by which one earns the daily bread of himself or his family, [are] so much more honorable than the business of other members of the community."[24] Significantly, Verplank's major contribution to general American law was his *Essay on the Doctrine of Contracts* (1825), where he attempted to "modernize" contract law and bring it in line with the demands of a free-market economy.[25]

John Ordronaux, who had both legal and medical training, argued that repudiating the conception of the doctor-patient relationship as an intrinsically gratuitous service "reduce[d] professions to the status of artisanship" and placed them on a par with manual laborers. The unrestricted right of professionals to sue for fees in America brought the legal relationships and liabilities "directly within the pale of consensual agreements based upon sufficient consideration."[26] Therefore, in suits for fees the legal relationship of doctor to patient shifted from *status-based* responsibilities growing out of a physician's role as a public servant to *contract-based* responsibilities emanating from bilateral agreements.

In his pioneering *Ancient Law* (1884) Henry Maine contended that in "progressive societies" legal relationships tend to evolve from status-determined duties to contract-determined duties; legal rights, duties, and liabilities derived more from explicit, conscious agreements than from a person's role, position, or status in society.[27] More recent writers have portrayed the specific development of contract law in a similar vein.[28] They argue that in earlier times legal obligations, including those originating in private agreements between two parties, were often judged by the community's standards of fairness instead of the contracting parties' agreement. Implied obligations often went beyond the responsibilities the parties themselves had chosen to undertake. During the eighteenth and especially the nineteenth centuries these arrangements were replaced by the belief that legal obligations seldom went beyond what the individual parties had specifically agreed to in a contract. The specific agreement represented a so-called "meeting of the minds." The swing away from community determined standards and the acceptance of the idea that masters, employers, and vendors owed no special duty beyond the cash-based commercial agreements with their apprentices, employees, and customers, reached its apex by the mid–nineteenth century.[29]

Americans' repudiation of the notion of honorariums for physicians and lawyers and the recognition of commercial relationships in allowing suits-for-fees illustrated the evolution of status-based to contract-based liabilities. The move from status to contract in malpractice law, however, was subtle, complex, slow, and ultimately incomplete. Initially Americans accepted English malpractice precedents and the technicalities involved in the common law system of writ pleading.[30] The rationale for the writ system was that through it a simple, specific, well-defined issue could be presented whereby plaintiffs could offer only appropriate evidence for their claim and defendants could respond with suitable rejoinders. In theory juries would decide a clear, simple issue of fact. The system was intricate and technically unforgiving. Judges dismissed charges, for example, when a plaintiff's lawyer failed to state the full name of a party to the suit, misspelled the town or county where the defendant resided, or did not properly state the occupation of both the plaintiff and the defendant. Procedural rules required the plaintiff to choose the correct writ (action) under which he or she was bringing suit. If a plaintiff sued using a writ of debt when he or she should have used a writ of ejectment, the judge would dismiss the case and the plaintiff would have to start over and repeat the entire, costly, complicated pretrial process. The selection of the correct writ or charge was not simple and required extensive legal training.[31]

Popular and professional discontent with the intricate writ system led to a gradual abandonment of the technical pleading. Opponents of the system complained that the strict procedural rules often interfered with substantive justice, that specific forms of action, such as trespass and assumpsit, had outgrown their usefulness, and that the rules that defined their applicability did not fit new social circumstances. In the late eighteenth century American judges began to ignore many common law pleading technicalities. Judges became less interested in technical exactitude and more concerned with providing substantive justice.[32] Specific pleas as answers to specific writs were less important than the underlying nature of the cause of action.[33]

The writ system, in its strict form, had served as a substitute for doctrinal classification. Judges and lawyers did not have to think in terms of contract and tort because there were specific writs for specific wrongs. When pleading became more concerned with substance and less with form, the distinction among writs such as debt, covenant, and assumpsit became blurred, and judges allowed them to be applied to a broader array of breach of contract offenses. By the early 1800s lawyers and judges began to segregate informally the wrongs previously covered by specific writs into the categories of tort and contract and searched for general principles that characterized the two areas of law.[34] Many ancient writs fell readily into one category or the other. Covenant, debt, and assumpsit could be combined under the rubric of contract violations; trespass was a tort violation.

Malpractice and its common law remedy, the writ of trespass on the case, did not fall naturally into these abstract categories. Blackstone explained that when a litigant sued for damages because of a debt or a breach of personal duty, the suit belonged to the broad theoretical class of contract. When plaintiffs sued complaining of injuries to their persons or property, however, Blackstone classified the claim as a tort.[35] Malpractice exhibited characteristics of both categories. It was a breach of duty, and it resulted in personal injury. This doctrinal ambiguity probably caused few problems in ordinary law practice as

long as strict adherence to the writ system made theoretical classification irrelevant. In addition, the language of English malpractice precedents demonstrated that a physician's liability emanated from his status as a public servant and not from his contractual, commercial
relationship with his patient.[36] As formal pleading rules were more
frequently ignored and eventually abandoned, and as American society's attitude toward the medical profession changed, malpractice law
felt the strong pull of contract.

Early nineteenth-century legal handbooks reflected the blurred distinctions among specific writs. The 1812 American edition of Joseph
Chitty's *Practical Treatise on Pleading* informed lawyers that they could
sue physicians for malpractice using either a writ of assumpsit, which
provided for the recovery of damages for the nonperformance of a
simple contract, or they could use trespass on the case, which offered
a remedy for injuries resulting from a breach of duty.[37] Other legal
handbooks published before the civil procedure reforms of the late
1840s and early 1850s echoed Chitty's guidelines. In *Law of Pleading
and Evidence* (1844) John Saunders advised that physicians were "liable
in assumpsit or [trespass on the] case, for ignorance or unskillfulness,
and for negligence in the exercise of [their] profession." Citing *Slater*
and *Seare*, Saunders explained that the law implied a "duty" on the
part of the physician to exercise "due and reasonable skill." To win a
case, the plaintiff had to "prove that the defendant was a surgeon or
apothecary by profession, *or* that he was retained and paid as such by
the plaintiff, *or* that he especially engaged to cure the plaintiff for
reward" (emphasis added). The patient/plaintiff was required to present "persons of skill and experience" as expert witnesses who would
offer testimony on the suitability of the defendant's treatment. The
patient would have to prove that the physician's treatment had been
unskillful and improper and that he caused a "wound or complaint, or
increased [the] wound or complaint of the plaintiff."[38]

The malpractice references in these early nineteenth-century hand
books suggested that the law was beginning to reflect the contractual
aspects of the doctor-patient relationship as well as the traditional legal
duties associated with a common calling. Both Chitty and Saunders
declared that malpractice charges could be initiated under the writ of
assumpsit (simple contract) or under trespass on the case. None of the

eighteenth-century English precedents mentioned the use of assumpsit as a remedy for malpractice; they uniformly used trespass on the case.[39] The incorporation of assumpsit into the malpractice lawyer's armory is an example of the informal loosening of technical requirements. Under Saunders' criteria, a doctor's legal responsibility arose from his status as a medical man, or his financial contract with a particular patient, or his explicit promise to cure an illness or injury.

Drifting toward Contract

The commercial aspect of a physician's liability was consistent with American judges' abandonment of the notion of honorariums and their acceptance of physicians' suits-for-fees. The early nineteenth-century doctor-patient relationship seemed to drift equivocally between the legal categories of contract and tort, which remained vague and unqualified until at least the middle of the century.[40] As the notion of contract gained more acceptance in society and law, it played a more important role in defining the doctor-patient relationship and in influencing malpractice litigation.

The process was slow because state supreme court judges erected barriers against this growing tendency. For example, in the Connecticut supreme court case of *Grannis* v. *Branden* (1812) a man claimed that he had paid a physician "reasonable compensation" to deliver his wife's child. The infant died during delivery, and, while removing the dead fetus, the physician severely cut and injured the mother. The husband's charge implied that a physician's liability originated in the economic relationship that was established when the fee was paid. A jury found the physician guilty of malpractice. When the state supreme court reviewed the case, it let the conviction stand but emphasized that "the only point in issue between the parties, was whether the defendant had neglected to perform his professional duty." The judges ignored the service-for-pay claim of the husband.[41]

In another Connecticut case in order to meet the requirements of a new state law requiring vaccinations, the board of health of Salisbury, Connecticut, hired Dr. Asabel Humphrey and three other physicians to vaccinate all the town's uninoculated citizens against smallpox.[42]

Humphrey and his colleagues contracted to carry out their task "in a faithful manner" and "according to our best skill and judgment." The Salisbury board of health agreed to pay the four physicians together $50 for the treatment. The doctors divided the town into four districts and assigned each physician one section as his personal responsibility. The fee, split among the four physicians, averaged about $.04 for each person vaccinated in the town.[43]

Dr. Humphrey, who was ill, hired Rollin Sprague, a young medical student, to vaccinate the residents of his district. The procedure required Sprague to make a small, shallow incision on the upper part of the patient's arm and insert a quill containing the vaccine virus. Sprague apparently vaccinated several residents successfully before he visited twenty-year-old Harriet Landon. "[F]rom real or affected modesty," she refused to raise her sleeve, and Sprague made two punctures in her upper arm just above her elbow but about one inch lower than standard practice. According to witnesses, she immediately experienced great pain and was unable to use her arm for several weeks.[44]

Landon brought an action on the case against Humphrey for malpractice. The plea to the court, to justify the writ, consisted of two separate counts. Landon first claimed that Humphrey had held "himself out to the world as a skillful practitioner [and] was employed by the plaintiff . . . to inoculate her with kine pox." Humphrey had been paid, but he "unskillfully" and "unfaithfully" treated the patient and "cut a tendon, cord, ligament, and nerve of the patient's arm." Because he vaccinated Landon in "an improper, unusual, and dangerous place," she had been "deprived of the use of her arm, [and] prevented from pursuing her necessary business."[45]

Landon's complaint was noteworthy because it accepted without comment that Sprague was Humphrey's direct agent and presumed that a duty-filled relationship existed between Humphrey and Landon even though the two had never met. Humphrey, by virtue of his status as a physician and his acceptance of the responsibility of inoculating the residents of his district, entered into a relationship with Landon that rendered him liable if he did not act according to certain standards.[46] In a second count, to support the action on the case writ, Landon argued that the board of health had employed Humphrey to vaccinate the inhabitants of the town in "a skillful and safe manner."

Instead, Humphrey had acted with a "negligence and unskillfulness" that resulted in an injury to Landon. In other words, Humphrey, through his agent, failed to act with the skill and care that his status as a physician demanded.[47]

Thomas Hubbard, a professor of surgery at Yale, testified that Landon's affliction could have been caused by damage to the nerve suffered if the medical assistant made the puncture too deep. Several other physicians confirmed that the punctures were in a very unusual place. The physicians who testified for Humphrey agreed that the incisions were not in the place usually selected, but argued that it was perfectly safe to inoculate that portion of the arm and that they had not heard of a single case where this type of injury had occurred after a vaccination.[48]

The trial court judge instructed the jury that anyone who undertook "any office, employment, duty, or trust *contracts* to perform it with integrity, diligence and skill" (emphasis added). If a physician lacked any of these qualities and injured a patient, the judge continued, the injured party could claim damages by a special action on the case. The judge also charged the jury that a physician who vaccinated patients was "liable for all the consequences if he neglects the usual precautions, or fails to insert the virus in that part of the arm *usually selected* for the purpose" (original emphasis). The jury ruled in favor of Landon and awarded her $500 and costs. The total judgment against Humphrey amounted to $1,000.[49]

Humphrey appealed the verdict to the Connecticut supreme court of errors. He argued that he did not have a contract with Landon and that the written agreement to vaccinate the citizens of Salisbury should not have been accepted into evidence. He maintained that he had contracted with the board of health and that Harriet Landon "had nothing to do with it personally." Humphrey asserted that physicians should be liable for "nothing short of gross ignorance or gross negligence." Because there was "nothing like mechanical perfection in the healing art," he pleaded, "some little failure might sweep from [a physician] the whole earning of a life of toil and drudgery." According to Humphrey, even skilled physicians would not be able to avoid prosecution and fewer men would enter the profession.[50]

The language of both the trial court judge and the physician reflected the influence of contract ideas. The judge told the jury that a physician "contracts" to perform his duty with "integrity, diligence and skill." In addition, he ruled that a physician was required to vaccinate patients in the place "usually selected for the purpose" even if there were more suitable locations. He illustrated this principle by explaining that a man transporting property would be liable for all consequences if he departed from the usual route. Portraying the physician not as a healer with a special status, but as a technician for hire who had to perform in the manner expected of him, the trial judge reinforced the notion that physicians carried contractual responsibilities; as did the physician when he argued that the "contract" was with the board of health and Landon "had nothing to do with it personally."

The Connecticut supreme court refused to grant the physician a new trial. The majority opinion explained that the written contract between Humphrey and the board of health was not an important part of the evidence against the physician and that its inclusion as evidence was, at worst, unnecessary. The court ruled that there was sufficient evidence without the contract to prove that Humphrey had accepted the responsibility of inoculating the residents of his district. The contract was merely additional proof that he had undertaken the role of physician in the community. Including superfluous evidence could not be grounds for a new trial.[51]

The supreme court's comments and lack of interest in the written contract demonstrated that the origin of Humphrey's liabilities and duties was his status as a medical man and his informal relationship with his patient rather than an explicit agreement. Humphrey had argued that Landon took no part in the agreement, so the contract could not be used against him. The supreme court, however, was concerned only with establishing Humphrey's status in the community as a physician and his relationship to the patient. Explicit, contractual arrangements were irrelevant.

Although the state supreme court eschewed the notion that a physician's liability arose out of a bilateral, exchanged-based relationship, the contentions of Dr. Humphrey and the lower court judge suggested that contractual ideas had made significant inroads into American legal thought. The roots of these attitudes were intertwined with the country's political, social, and economic history. A Lockean version of the social contract had helped justify the colonists' break from the mother country and explained their subsequent reliance on a written constitution to create a new government.[52] The unforeseen social leveling effect of the new environment, the revolutionary rhetoric of equality, and the failure to translate old-world institutions in America combined to undermine traditional relationships of status. For example, apprenticeship relationships had been governed by a set of unwritten, mutual responsibilities that were shared and sanctioned by the entire community. The apprentice owed the master work and respect; the master owed his apprentice such things as room, board, training, and religious instruction. In America this status-based relationship broke down, and each party owed the other only what they had mutually agreed to exchange.[53]

Similarly, the guild system never took hold in the colonies, and access to crafts and professions was generally open.[54] In the late eighteenth century elite American physicians attempted to replicate English institutions that gave professional men a special legal and social status. However, the medical schools, professional societies, and licensure laws failed to elevate the physician's image. Professional monopolies were inconsistent with the republican rhetoric of the post-Revolution years. The schools, designed to enhance the physician's status, instead contributed to a backlash against professionalism by producing undertrained and ignorant practitioners. Licensure regulations were weak and ignored.

Laissez-faire sentiment toward medical licensure developed at the same time as reliance on status in other legal relationships declined. From his travels in early nineteenth-century America de Tocqueville concluded that democratic revolutions are followed by an attack on symbols of social aristocracy and an increase in individualism. He observed, "[E]ach citizen of an aristocratic society has his fixed station, one above another, so that there is always someone above him whose protection he needs and someone below him whose help he may require."[55] In short, many rights and duties were a result of social or professional status. During the first half of the nineteenth century this system disintegrated in America. A society filled with people who praised equality and individualism took its place. Especially between 1800 and 1860 localism was broken up by economic development, transportation improvements, and massive migration, and these forces in turn contributed to the antiprivilege, antimonopoly, antiprofessional philosophy of the Jacksonian period.

Free trade, laissez-faire ideas, individualism, and the breakdown of status relationships all served as the underpinnings of the so-called "golden age of contract." The *will theory of contract* was a model that suggested that legal responsibilities were the consequence of a "meeting of the minds" of two presumably equal bargainers. According to one writer, the "will theory of contracts carried the republican impulse to the smallest unit of society—two individuals, who in concert formed a microlegislature and made law."[56] Under this concept, which gained prominence between 1750 and 1850, the law more frequently disregarded traditional community standards of fairness and protected only the explicit expectations of the bargaining parties as expressed in their private agreements.[57] This notion of contract seeped into many areas of law and altered traditional liability.

Employers abandoned their status-based, paternalistic, hierarchical relationships with their employees and customers and relied on written agreements to define respective rights and liabilities. Just price and fair wage standards were out; caveat emptor ("let the buyer beware") was in. Employers' traditional liability for the actions of their employees under *respondeat superior* was diminished. Common carriers such as trains and steamboats frequently asked their customers to sign contractual waivers and relinquish their rights to sue for damages in case of accidents. Virtually every area of law felt the impact of this movement.[58]

The rise of contract mentality in the 1830s, 1840s, and 1850s contributed to the already declining professional status of the physician. Medical sectarians who claimed to embody free-market Jacksonian sentiment called for an end to restrictive licensing and praised open competition. By 1850 only two states retained licensure statutes, and the medical world became characterized by "free trade in doctoring." Physicians' changing legal and social status and the rise of contract mentality in other areas of law spilled over into malpractice prosecutions. Although the technical legal forms did not change, the language and implications of many malpractice cases reflected the growing predilection to treat physicians like ordinary businessmen. In *Grannis* v.

Branden (1812), *Landon* v. *Humphrey* (1832), and other cases, doctors, patients, or trial lawyers attempted to define physicians' liabilities in contractual terms. The appellate court judges, however, had refused to refer to the doctor-patient relationship as contractual. Instead, state supreme court judges, drawing on the guidance of English precedents, usually agreed that physicians' professional responsibilities emanated from their status as members of a common calling. In the 1840s and 1850s, physicians, lawyers, and judges more frequently referred to the relationship as contractual and began to apply general legal doctrines, drawn from the growing category of contract law, in malpractice cases. Malpractice law was drifting from status to contract.

The Iowa case *Bowman* v. *Woods* (1848) exhibited the impact of contract doctrine on malpractice liability. Bowman, a Thomsonian, or botanic, doctor, delivered Woods's child, but failed to remove the afterbirth. Thomsonians believed that the placenta should remain in the uterus until expelled by nature. Although Mrs. Woods survived, her husband sued Bowman for malpractice. A jury agreed and awarded Woods $50.[59]

The Iowa supreme court overturned the conviction. The majority decision explained that since Iowa had no licensure laws, no particular system of medicine was legally supported or prohibited. While the appellate court judges clearly preferred regular practitioners to medical sectarians, such as homeopaths or Thomsonians, they ruled that the standards of regular physicians were not the exclusive standard or test by which the other systems were to be judged. "A person professing to follow one system of medical treatment, cannot be expected by his *employer* to practice any other," the court noted (emphasis added). Although the law required physicians to use an "ordinary degree of care and skill," it did not require a man "to accomplish more than he undert[ook], nor in a manner different from what he profess[ed]." The wording of the majority decision implied that this doctor-patient relationship resembled a contract. There had been a "meeting of the minds" between Bowman and Woods. Bowman had been hired as a Thomsonian, so he only needed to perform as a Thomsonian.[60]

Since physicians possessed no special status in law or society, the idea of contractual responsibilities became more important. The *Bowman* v. *Woods* decision constructed a clear analogy between the doctor-patient relationship and the commercial marketplace. "If a person will knowingly employ a common mat maker to weave or embroider a fine carpet, he may impute the bad workmanship to his own folly." Therefore, the court reasoned, if a patient chose the wrong type of physician to treat him, "in all such cases, the employer ought properly to attribute loss or injury to his own negligence and mismanagement." The court recognized that the country was filled with quacks, "novices," and "empirics," but lamented that "these are evils which courts of justice possess no adequate power to remedy."[61]

According to *Bowman* v. *Woods*, the medical world was a free market where physicians and patients met to bargain. The watchword was *caveat emptor*. If patients were careless when hiring physicians, then the courts would not protect them. This doctrine could have easily been used to diminish physicians' liability, especially in a country where the elimination of licensing had denied physicians official status and eliminated official standards. Though judges in the 1840s and 1850s did not abandon basic legal forms or the common law prescription that physicians had to perform with "ordinary skill and care," the growing reliance on doctrines associated with contract signaled a significant shift in judicial emphasis.

Although many courts at the trial and appellate levels began to view the doctor-patient relationship in at least quasicontractual terms, they still recognized that much of a physician's liability arose from his status as a member of a common calling.[62] After witnessing a malpractice trial in 1860, a physician noted that "our Judiciary look upon the relation of Physician and Patient as that of a CONTRACT" (original emphasis). At the same time, however, he explained that the contract required physicians to act with the "ordinary amount of skill, care, and attention that pertains to the profession of which he is a member."[63] A quasicontractual view did not automatically alter a physician's liability.[64] But if local and appellate courts allowed defense attorneys to apply contractual doctrines such as caveat emptor and contractual waivers of liability to medical relationships, then physicians' traditional liability would be modified. The decision in *Leighton* v. *Sargent* (1853) provides one of the most frank examples of contractual language in malpractice cases and demonstrates the practical ramifications of this doctrinal drift.

Leighton v. Sargent

In September 1850 Joseph Leighton injured his ankle and leg when he lost his balance and fell from a moving carriage in Strafford, New Hampshire. Friends of Leighton sent for Dr. Sargent who lived in Barnstead six miles away. After examining the injury, Sargent discovered that Leighton had dislocated his ankle and fractured and partially shattered his lower leg. Sargent wrapped Leighton's inflamed and swollen limb in a starched bandage and immobilized the entire leg in a homemade fracture box.[65] Leighton's injury, a compound fracture, was profound. The starch dressings irritated Leighton's leg, and his foot became "greatly inflamed" and covered with a "mass of gathering putrid sores." During his long convalescence, Leighton suffered "feverish excitement" and coughs and "had to resort to stimulation to withstand the prostrating effects of the disease"—that is, he resorted to brandy, port, or some other alcoholic beverage. Sargent attended Leighton from September 1, 1850, until January 12, 1851. During this time, he visited and treated Leighton sixty-two times, or an average of once every two days.[66]

Though Sargent did not see his patient after January 1851, Leighton continued to suffer from his injury. Pus-filled sores periodically formed on his ankle, and slivers of bone occasionally oozed from the ulcerations. By the spring of 1852 Leighton's foot had healed, but his ankle joint was frozen in an unusual position so that the toes of his foot were permanently pointed downward and three to five inches lower than his heel. Leighton was unable to work and could not walk without the use of a cane or crutches.[67]

Leighton charged Sargent with malpractice, complaining that the physician's starch wrapping and the setting of his leg had resulted in a "greatly inflamed, virulent, corrupt and festering . . . mass of gathering and putrid sores" which caused him great bodily pain and caused the ankle to heal in a deformed position.[68] Medical witnesses from both sides immediately undermined Leighton's case. They testified that the swelling, inflammation, and sores that plagued Leighton for so many months were a "necessary and unavoidable consequence of the severe injury" he had received and would "accompany even the best possible surgical and medical treatment." Since Leighton had linked the inflammation to the fixed joint, his claim lost its credibility.[69]

Seeing his case destroyed by his own expert witnesses, Leighton changed his complaint in the middle of the trial. Ignoring the objections of Sargent's lawyer, the trial court judge allowed Leighton to enter his new claim. He now argued that he had "employed [Sargent] for a reasonable reward" to treat, set, and cure his right ankle and foot, but that Sargent had instead behaved "negligently, carelessly, and unskillfully" and allowed the foot to become deformed and useless. Leighton produced a new parade of witnesses who testified that the deformed position of his foot was identical to its position when Sargent first placed it in the fracture-box. They recalled that they had brought the unnatural position of the foot to the physician's attention on many occasions, but that Sargent had answered that the angle of the joint was correct and that the toes should be dropped "to get the spring of the foot."[70]

Only two medical men testified for the prosecution. They declared that, though Leighton's injury was severe, there was no difficulty in fixing the foot in any position desired and that they had "never seen an instance where it could not be maintained in that [the correct] position."[71] Twenty witnesses for Sargent testified that they frequently saw a three-quarter–inch book behind the footboard of the fracture box. Defense lawyers claimed that the book would have positioned the foot at nearly a right angle with the leg. They argued therefore that Leighton's foot had become deformed for some other reason than its position in the fracture-box. Other medical witnesses told the jury that compound dislocations were very severe injuries and often resulted in amputations. "The best treatment," one testified, "cannot make a good limb . . . and the patient and doctor should be glad to get off with any foot that will do to walk on."[72] In his instructions to the Strafford County jury, the trial judge stated that a physician must possess "a reasonable degree of skill, such as is ordinarily possessed by his profession," and he must "exercise that skill with reasonable care and diligence." Although the "legal gentlemen of the Strafford bar" believed that the jury would exonerate Sargent, the jury declared that the physician was guilty and awarded Leighton $1,500.

Sargent appealed the verdict to the New Hampshire supreme court in 1853. The court ruled that the trial court judge should not have allowed Leighton to change his charge in the middle of the trial, overturned the jury's decision, and granted the physician a new trial. Judge Bell, who wrote the opinion for the New Hampshire supreme court, noted, however, that the principles of malpractice were of "great consequence to all classes of professional men" and should be "settled and well understood." "At the present moment," he observed, "it is to be feared there is a tendency to impose some perilous obligations beyond the requirements of the law on some professional men."[73] Bell declared that while doctors did not implicitly guarantee the results of their work, they were required to possess a "reasonable, fair, and competent degree of skill" and exercise this skill with "ordinary care and diligence." Judge Bell's definition of professional responsibility was no different in substance from the trial court judge's charge to the jury or the common law precedents articulated in previous appellate decisions. Bell's description of the legal relationship between doctor and patient, however, while it resembled the ruling in *Bowman* v. *Woods*, did vary significantly from the opinions of his early nineteenth-century counterparts.

Bell stated that when a physician "offers his services to the community generally, or to any individual, for employment in any professional capacity, [he] *contracts* with his employer. (emphasis added)"[74] Judge Bell's use of the term *contract* in his decision was not a harmless and meaningless abstraction. The judge was concerned that medical men were suffering under "some perilous obligations," and he was going to give them a judicial remedy. Bell ruled that while physicians must exercise "ordinary good judgement," the risk from "mere errors and mistakes is upon the employer [patient] alone." The judge continued: "He [the patient] too has judgement to exercise in the selection of the physician or the lawyer whom he will employ, and if he makes a bad selection, if he fails to choose a man of the best judgement, the result is fairly attributed to his own mistake."[75]

Judge Bell's decision, like the majority ruling in *Bowman* v. *Woods*, viewed the doctor-patient relationship through the lens of contract. Two years later in *Cater* v. *Fernald* a New Hampshire trial court judge used this medical version of caveat emptor to charge a jury in a malpractice case. He reminded them that the "employer has to exercise judgment too in the employment of a professional man."[76]

The Connecticut supreme court judge in the 1832 *Landon v. Humphrey* ruling had dismissed the importance of a contract in adjudicating malpractice cases. In the *Bowman*, *Leighton*, and *Cater* decisions, however, the judges specifically referred to the doctor and his patient as *employee* and *employer*. The decisions assumed that the medical world was merely an analogue of the commercial marketplace and should operate by many of the same rules. The judges embraced contract doctrines and provided physicians with a defensive legal weapon by constructing a medical malpractice version of caveat emptor. Treating malpractice as a type of contract could affect potential financial awards to injured patients in other ways. If malpractice were considered purely under the rubric of tort law, as it eventually was, pain and suffering, as well as damages, could be used as grounds for remuneration. If malpractice was treated as a contract case, the law generally provided only that plaintiffs be placed in the same position they would be in if the contracts had been properly performed.[77]

Contractual Waivers of Liability

If the doctor-patient relationship was truly a "meeting of the minds," the doctor should have also been able to contract for less liability. Despite the efforts of some corporations, state courts of the 1830s and 1840s had refused to allow common carriers to "contract away" their common law liability. But the abstract notion of freedom of contract and a desire by state court judges to encourage economic expansion broke down old barriers. In 1850 New York judges allowed common carriers to restrict their liability by special agreement with their customers. By 1853 corporations could limit lawsuits even for gross negligence. Despite these decisions, treatise writers remained tentative in their support of contractual protection from lawsuits.[78]

Physicians began to seek the same right. They attempted to force their patients to accept liability waivers. Many doctors asked prospective patients to sign a bond agreement that stipulated a monetary penalty in event of a malpractice charge. Patients could still sue for malpractice, but they would presumably lose more than they would gain.

As early as 1847 an editorialist advised Ohio physicians to use bonds to slow the "endless vexations and pecuniary losses" of malpractice suits.[79] By the early 1850s the practice had become common. In 1851 the *Medical Examiner* advised that "[i]t would perhaps be the course of prudence for surgeons among us to keep blank bonds on hand."[80] A New York physician reported that he refused to treat the fractures and dislocations of working-class patients, perceived as the group most likely to sue, without first receiving an indemnity bond. He warned his colleagues, "Surgeons! Take an indemnity bond or never treat a poor patient."[81] In 1854 a writer for the *Boston Medical and Surgical Journal* lamented:

It is almost a wonder that any surgeon, now-a-days, can be found . . . to remedy a deformity, or treat a case of injury, without a bond from the patient or his legal guardian that he shall not be subjected to a suit for damages in case he should fail to make the patient as whole and perfect as he was when he came from the hands of the creator.[82]

The injuries generally convinced patients to sign bonds, and the penalties were usually high enough to discourage them from violating the agreements. Horace Nelson, a New York physician, recounted his use of bonds. In December 1855, when Louisa Bovee brought the physician her two-year-old child, who had fractured and dislocated his right arm, Nelson informed the woman that he would not treat the child unless she signed a bond agreement guaranteeing not to sue for malpractice. Bovee declined, and the physician refused to treat the child. After conferring with her friends, the woman returned and signed the bond agreeing to pay the physician $2,000 if she attempted to sue him for malpractice. In Nelson's words, "We are now safe, let the result be what it may."[83] Nelson published a copy of the bond as a model and promised that it was good in any state of the Union.

STATE OF NEW YORK
Clinton County

KNOW all men by these presents, that I, Louisa Bovee, the wife of Orrey Bovee, am held and firmly bound to Doctor Horace Nelson, practicing surgeon, of the town of Plattsburg, in the county of Clinton, in the sum of two thousand dollars, lawful money in the United States, to be paid to the said Doctor Horace

Nelson, his executors, administrators, or assigns; for which payment, well and truly to be made bind myself and each of my
heirs, executors, and administrators, jointly and severally firmly
be these presents. Sealed with my seal. Dated this 28th day of
December, 1855.

Whereas the above bounden has this day applied to, and
requested the said Horace Nelson, surgeon aforesaid, to set and
reduce a fracture and dislocation of the right elbow joint of
Charles Leonard Perry, an infant, and now child by adoption of
the above bounden, the wife of Orrey Bovee, of Plattsburg.

Now therefore, the condition of this obligation is such, that if
the above bounden Louisa Bovee, shall well and truly keep and
bear harmless, and indemnify the said Horace Nelson, surgeon
aforesaid, his executors, administrators and assigns, and every
other person or persons aiding and assisting him in the premises,
of and from all harm, let, trouble, damages, costs, suits, actions,
judgments, and executions that shall be brought against them, or
any of them, as well for the setting of said arm, as for the
inconvenience and damage arising therefrom. Then this obligation to be void, else to remain in full force and virtue.

Louisa Bovee [L.S.]

Sealed and delivered in presence of F.L.C.
Sailly, Justice of the Peace[84]

The careful, legalistic exactness of Nelson's bond mocked Blackstone's notion that medical men held a position of public trust or that
they were honored public servants with a special legal and social
status. Instead, the written pretreatment agreement resembled, more
than anything else, a carefully framed labor or commercial contract.
Moreover, the bonds reinforced the Jacksonian contention that physicians were no different from mechanics or merchants, a contention
that ran counter to the elite physicians' claims that medicine was a
profession and not a trade.

The use of bonds was probably the surest method of discouraging
litigation by contract. Physicians also experimented with contracts that
completely immunized them from lawsuits. These agreements were

identical to the court-supported liability waivers of common carriers. Some physicians attempted to mimic the corporations, in the shadow of the 1850s rulings, and to contract away their liability with a waiver. The legal status of these arrangements, however, was ambiguous. Apparently absolute waivers of liability were used only infrequently. .

In 1861 an Ohio man caught his leg in the flywheel of a sawmill. Physician G. W. Butler examined the injured leg and discovered a compound fracture and crushed bone. The doctor warned the patient that the injury was severe and dangerous and declared, "I will not treat your case at all unless you clear me of all responsibility for results." According to witnesses, the injured man replied: "I will clear you of all responsibility. Go on and treat my case. I would rather have you than anyone else." Butler placed the leg in a bandage and splint but after eight days, the leg required amputation.[85]

The patient sued for malpractice, claiming that the physician cut off the circulation by bandaging the limb too tightly. The defense attorney argued that the physician had made a "special contract" with the patient absolving him of all liability. The patient's attorney

quoted legal decisions to show that Dr. Butler could not make a special contract with the patient, by the terms of which he obligated himself to render to the patient anything less than the ordinary amount of "skill, care and attention," [and] that such a rule would do away with all standards of comparison and prove positively injurious to the interests of society.[86]

Ignoring the arguments of the defense attorney, the trial court judge accepted the validity of the pretreatment agreement. "This contract," the judge ruled, "the defendant had the right to make." If the jury believed that an agreement existed, then Butler was not liable for the loss of the leg. The jury retired and after a "short absence" decided in favor of the physician. A jubilant editorialist declared that if other physicians and courts used contractual immunity, "damages in favor of the plaintiff could not in one case in a hundred be obtained."[87]

Despite this isolated case, there was no simple solution to the malpractice problem. The use of agreements to contract away liability was rare. No specific case ruling on special contracts and malpractice existed. However, the near consensus of both legal and medical writers suggested that absolute abrogation of medical liability never completely took hold and was in any case discredited by the 1860s. Similarly, judges' use of contractual language in defining the origin of physicians' malpractice liability declined in the late 1850s.

The Road Not Taken

Doctors generally resisted the notion of contractual relationships with patients because it conflicted with the image of the physician as a public servant with a distinct social status. Most physicians maintained this position even though some contractual doctrines, such as waivers and caveat emptor, could have mitigated verdicts in malpractice cases. Worthington Hooker warned the profession: "The relation of a physician to his employers is not shut up within the narrow limits of mere pecuniary considerations. There is a sacredness in it, which should forbid its being subjected to the changes incident to the common relations of trade and commerce among men."[88] Valentine Mott, an eminent surgeon, enjoined physicians, "Condemn with relentless severity the slightest deviation from professional honor. Find no excuse for anyone who is induced to lower our noble art to the condition of a trade."[89]

A Massachusetts medical society committee on malpractice agreed that the doctor-patient relationship was different from purely economic arrangements. "[T]he peculiar relations always existing between physician and patient and the fact of one of the parties always being more or less incapacitated by his condition, have put out of sight the idea of a bargain, as in other engagements between man and man."[90] The committee concluded, "It cannot be conducive to the interests of the patient that his relation with his physician should be reduced to a mere business transaction, to be judged as a contract, to which the employer strictly holds the employed."[91]

Medical and legal writers also attacked the use of bonds and contractual waivers. Constitutional commentator Joel Parker, at one time a Massachusetts supreme court judge and professor of medical jurisprudence at Dartmouth, deflated the hopes of those physicians who believed that bonds and contracts could protect them from malpractice suits. In an 1855 lecture he explained that while there was no specific ruling on the issue, there was "very grave doubt whether it [contractual waivers of liability] could have any legal operation to exempt the physician from any responsibility." Since waivers from liability remained a controversial practice in other areas of law, Parker felt that the best a physician could hope for was that the agreement, despite its feeble legitimacy, might discourage the disgruntled patient from instituting a suit.[92] Physicians undoubtedly recognized the legal weakness of contractual waivers, but most opposed it on other grounds.

One physician argued that while some of his colleagues required bonds or contracts before treatment, he objected on the grounds that "in the first course, such refusals would be considered *inhuman;* and in the second, it is *undignified* for a well qualified profession to resort to such expedients" (original emphasis).[93] Both John Elwell, in his *Medico-Legal Treatise on Malpractice* (1860), and John Ordronaux, in *The Jurisprudence of Medicine* (1869), agreed that physicians could not use special contracts to protect themselves. According to Ordronaux, "With or without such a bond he may still be prosecuted for malpractice. And certainly, it is a derogation of his dignity, and an attempt on his part to pervert the equitable streams of jurisprudence."[94]

Ordronaux, a physician and a lawyer, was one of the leading nineteenth-century experts on medical jurisprudence. He declared unequivocally that "the duty of professing skill and exhibiting correctness in prescribing is not created by contract, but by law." Drawing on the status of physicians in Roman law, Ordronaux explained that "the very nature of the relation between patron and client raised it [the doctor-patient relationship] above all taint of a mercenary character." Professional responsibility had its origins in "the character publicly assumed by him who undertakes to render such services."[95] Liability flowed not from the financial arrangement between doctor and patient, but from the practitioner's public assertion that he was a physician. According to Ordronaux doctor-patient associations could never be considered "purely commercial" relations. He argued that they are "far higher in their nature and consequences than any transactions relating merely to tangible materialities and have always been regarded among civilized nations as not amenable to any similar standards of value." He held that physicians owed their patients duties and responsibilities that could never be enumerated in or bound by a contract.[96]

Ordronaux shared the assumptions of the majority of judges in the late 1850s and 1860s. Although some earlier courts had referred to the doctor-patient relationship as contractual, most judges objected. A Massachusetts judge observed that medical relationships were fundamentally different from purely commercial contracts. He noted, "In ordinary cases the employer governs or directs the employed; but in surgery the case is reversed. The surgeon controls the patient."[97] In an 1854 case the plaintiff's attorney declared that the physician had agreed to treat his client "for a reasonable reward and compensation." The trial court judge, in his charge to the jury, however, stressed that this

> is not an action on a contract, although the declaration alleges what the law would make a contract . . . still the action is not for a breach of contract, it is not for the defendant's not doing what he agreed to do, but for doing what he did agree to do in a careless, unskillful and negligent manner as to injure the patient.[98]

In the void left by the decaying and abandoned writ system, lawyers and judges yearned for rationalized, general legal principles on which to base legal duties. Midcentury treatise writers segregated legal duties into the broad categories of tort and contract. Traditional, status based responsibilities were generally classified as torts.[99] Francis Hillard wrote the first American treatise on torts in 1859, dividing all legal actions into contracts, torts, and crimes. *Contracts* were based on "agreements, express or implied"; *torts* were "injuries of omission or commission, done to individuals"; and *crimes* were "injuries done to the public or the state."[100] Hillard included malpractice actions under the heading of tort because the offense was a breach of public duty.[101] Amasa Redfield and Thomas Sherman's important 1870 treatise on negligence also reflected the noncommercial basis of physicians' liability. Redfield noted: "The peculiar nature of the services which a medical man undertakes to render, often makes it his duty to continue them long after he would gladly cease to do so . . . Even if his services are gratuitous, he must continue them until reasonable time has been given to procure other attendance."[102]

Appellate court judges in the 1850s and 1860s reinforced the notion that a physician's responsibility emanated from his status as a professional instead of from the relationship created by a contract. They resurrected the contractual language of *Bowman, Leighton,* and *Cater* only when the suit involved a conflict over fees or an explicit promise to cure.[103]

In *Smith* v. *Overby* the Georgia supreme court sanctioned a jury charge that explained that "the profession of physician is one of the learned professions . . . as in all professions in which learning and skill are required, the rule of law is, that every person who enters into a learned profession undertakes to bring to the exercise of his profession, a reasonable degree of care and skill."[104] The Illinois supreme court in *Ritchey* v. *West* affirmed that "when a person assumes the profession of a surgeon, he must in its exercise, be held to employ a reasonable amount of care and skill."[105] Finally, the majority in *McNevins* v. *Lowe* ruled:

> If a person holds himself out to the public as a physician he must be held to ordinary care and skill in every case of which he assumes the charge, whether in the particular case he has received fees or not. But if he does not profess to be a physician nor practice as such, and is merely asked his advice as a friend or neighbor, he does not incur any professional responsibility.[106]

Overby, *Ritchey*, and *McNevins* were characteristic enunciations of malpractice case law in the mid 1860s. In contrast to some of the rulings of the late 1840s and early 1850s, they banished contractual language from the doctrine of physicians' liability. A doctor was liable for his actions not because he treated a patient for pay, but because he held a special status in society: that of the public servant, the professional.

The midcentury flirtation of malpractice law with contractual language and doctrine and the eventual abandonment of the notion reflected the paradoxical legal and social position of the American medical profession. The English precedents that informed early malpractice law were based on the assumption that physicians' liability arose from their special status as public servants. English common law prohibitions on suits for fees reinforced the noncommercial nature of the doctor-patient relationship. American courts never accepted the idea of honorarium pay for physicians, but they did initially follow the malpractice rulings that implied status-based responsibility.

But by the late 1840s the contractual view of society was strong enough in America to threaten the status-based foundations of malpractice law. The Lockean, contractual character of a written constitution and the ideals of individualism and free trade in the Jacksonian era provided a fertile environment for contractual interpretations. Jacksonian commentators condemned traditional professional groups as antidemocratic and aristocratic. Other status-based relationships were being undermined as well: master-servant doctrine, aspects of family law, and the responsibility of common carriers all increasingly reflected the influence of contract mentality. In suits for fees, the legal relationship of doctor and patient had already evolved from status-based responsibility to contract-based liability. Since Jacksonian Americans refused to grant physicians either legal status through licensure or social status through respect, it is not surprising that some judges, attorneys, and physicians began to integrate market-oriented principles into malpractice law.

Ultimately, judges and treatise writers turned away from contractual views of the doctor-patient relationship because the medical world was not analogous to the commercial world. Physicians retained remnants of the idea of the doctor as public servant and sought to raise the profession morally above the position of a mere wage earner. The contractual model of two presumably equal bargainers engaging in a "meeting of the minds" does not accurately describe medical relationships. Patients who have injuries cannot freely consent to treatment in the same way a merchant freely decides to purchase commercial goods. Lay people approach the doctor-patient relationship with less knowledge about their illness, their probability of recovery, and the various treatments and medical alternatives than the physicians with whom they deal. Therefore, notions such as caveat emptor are not appropriate or effective safeguards on the "medical market."[107] Open self-interest from both parties is an acknowledged component of contractual theory. This doctrine is inconsistent with the majority of the medical community's self-image as a benevolent profession.[108]

The banishment of the will theory of contract from mainstream malpractice law had ethical and practical consequences. It was an implicit recognition that physicians filled an extraordinary role in society that severed the doctor-patient relationship legally, ethically, and economically from the principles that usually governed the exchange of goods and services in a laissez-faire economy. In the late twentieth century medical practice, institutions, and organization have increasingly taken on the appearance of commercial enterprises.[109] A growing segment of the population and the profession have again begun to view physicians as mere businessmen, and medical ethicists debate the viability of contract as a source of professional responsibility. In addition patients and scholars have attacked paternalistic features of the medical relationship and argued in favor of a greater role for the patient in the decision-making process. Emphasis on individual rights in many areas of American life and law since the 1950s has nourished this trend and elevated the value of patient autonomy. Consequently, contract is again discussed as a potential source of professional liability.[110] Medical commentators debate the sufficiency of contract as a guide for acceptable and ethical behavior, and some of the debates surrounding twentieth-century malpractice reform have suggested the use of contract as a basis for defining physicians' liability.[111] Society, the courts, and the profession may have to decide again the way in which the doctor-patient relationship is different from a commercial contract.

CHAPTER 8

The More Things Change . . . : Medical Malpractice, 1865–1900

Medical malpractice suits continued to plague physicians through the last third of the nineteenth century. Although the suits and professional responses to them changed in several important respects, the trends and patterns that surfaced between 1835 and 1865 endured. The rate of suits and size of the awards climbed steadily but undramatically. The evolution of medical practice and organization generated new suits and new issues. Ceaseless development of medical innovations inspired new litigation in the same way that the improvement in fracture treatment engendered suits in the first half of the century. Physicians blamed many of the same factors they had earlier for the litigation, but changes in the legal and medical professions altered the ways in which they interpreted and dealt with the suits. Appellate courts modified traditional legal doctrines, but the central tenets of malpractice law remained unchanged. While physicians' experience with malpractice between 1865 and 1900 followed a course set earlier in the century, the suits, responses, and the law reacted to the evolving medical environment and represented a prelude to the twentieth century.

"The Malpractice Fad Is upon Us"

Physicians were relieved when malpractice rates apparently abated somewhat during the tumultuous 1860s. Editorials and reports of cases appeared less frequently in medical journals. One observer at the end of the decade remarked that the problem was "not so urgent as it was a dozen years ago, when the number of actions for malpractice brought against respectable practitioners caused a good deal of excitement in the medical profession."[1]

The respite, if it did indeed occur, did not last long. By the early 1870s, patients were suing physicians with renewed vigor. In 1872 William Wey, the president of a New York medical society, commented that while suits were "rarely found" in previous years, "of late they have become frequent. At nearly every sitting of the court one or two of such cases are on the calendar."[2] A writer in 1875 remembered that "suits were prominent between 1833 and 1861 in New York and also in the Eastern and Western states." He lamented that "[l]atterly the danger to the profession has been revived."[3] Another physician echoed that writer's concern the following year and reported that "the increase in the number of suits for malpractice has again become a topic of remark in medical circles."[4]

After suffering two suits in the 1870s, Eugene Sanger, a prominent physician in Maine, produced a detailed report of malpractice litigation in the state. Sanger's study, published in 1879, surveyed approximately six hundred regular physicians practicing in Maine and yielded the most evocative picture of the phenomenon in the nineteenth century.[5] Of the 114 doctors who responded to Sanger's query, only 58 had escaped prosecutions, threats of suits, or "the payment of smart money." The remaining 56 physicians had been threatened with legal action 55 times and actually charged with malpractice a total of 70 times. In 6 of those cases prospective defendants paid amounts ranging from $100 to $350 rather than allow a trial to commence.[6] Sanger argued that the true number of suits for the state was undoubtedly higher since many physicians "from modesty and disinclination to advertise their contributions to the patients and attorneys, who follow us as the shark does the emigrant ship, have failed to report."[7]

Through the remainder of the century physicians and other observers claimed that doctors were subjected to an ever-increasing burden of litigation. Not only did malpractice accusations continue without relief, but most writers believed that each decade was more litigious than the last. The problem was evident enough for an editorialist in

Popular Science Monthly (then a serious effort to popularize science) to complain in 1880 that "[s]o jealously does the law guard the lives and persons of the people, that every time the physician writes a prescription, or the surgeon makes an incision, he takes his purse, his liberty, or, perhaps, his life in his hand."[8] A physician in 1882 warned that "[t]he increasing frequency of the allegations of malpractice in surgery makes the subject one of great interest to nearly every physician."[9] In a paper read before the Chicago Medical Society in 1886 a local doctor declared that "[i]t is undoubtedly a fact that such suits against physicians are on the increase. The New York *Medical Record* has reported a large number in the course of the past year, and a glance over the Court-record in this city will prove the correctness of my assertion, as far as Chicago is concerned."[10] In 1889 a San Francisco physician reported that "the majority of physicians who have attained prominence and a reputation for ability to pay, have been obligated to defend suits of this character."[11] The following year, a Michigan physician informed the state medical society that "[t]here is scarcely a surgeon of any great experience in this State who has not either been prosecuted or many times threatened."[12] By the turn of the century the *Colorado Medical Journal* reported that "[t]he malpractice fad is upon us."[13]

Although appellate decisions are an uncertain measure of trial court litigation rates, they tend to confirm physicians' impressions that malpractice suits were a growing problem. State appellate courts handled a gradual but clearly increasing stream of cases as the decades passed: 1860–1870—25; 1870–1880—45; 1880–1890—47; 1890–1900—77; 1900–1910—116.[14] While figures on the absolute number of cases remain elusive, appellate rates and contemporary commentary demonstrate that frequent malpractice suits were a persistent phenomenon from the late 1830s through 1900. Malpractice rates in the last third of the century were a natural continuation of the course and patterns set in antebellum America.

Awards

While immense monetary penalties did not become popular until much later, damage awards slowly climbed between 1865 and 1900. Before

1865 the typical malpractice judgment was between $200 and $800, with a few isolated verdicts reaching $1,000 to $3,000.[15] In contrast, 38 sample malpractice awards between 1870 and 1900 averaged $2,492 (see appendix B). Of those judgments 19 were over $2,000, and only 13 were $1,000 or lower.[16] Some of the larger awards included: $3,000 to a woman who lost her nose, allegedly to cancer treatment, in 1876; $4,000 for a fracture case in 1872; $4,000 in 1882 for a man who lost the use of his legs; $7,000 for a fracture case in 1885; $12,000 for a fracture case in 1894; and $5,000 for a destroyed penis in 1895.[17] Other studies suggest a similar range in the judgments, most awards falling between $1,000 and $5,000.[18] Physicians' average income in this period probably ranged from about $1,000 to $1,500 per year when the average annual income for all nonfarm occupations averaged about $500.[19]

Appellate courts refused to overturn or reduce the gradually increasing malpractice judgments as excessive. While it is true that most malpractice defendants escaped paying any penalty, the awards, when compared to the income of physicians, were substantial. If the sample judgments averaging over $2,000 are a reliable gauge, they represent a larger portion of physicians' income than the typical award of the late twentieth century. For example, in 1971, at a time when the median income of physicians hovered around $100,000 a year, 59.9 percent of all malpractice awards were under $3,000.[20] Late nineteenth-century appellate courts deferred to the damages awarded at the trial level and generally stepped in only if the jury had "acted under some bias, prejudice, or improper influence, or [had] made some mistake of fact or law."[21] In 1882 the Indiana supreme court affirmed a judgment against a physician for rendering a patients' legs useless. The court compared the $4,000 award to other personal injury judgments against railroads, corporations, and municipalities and ruled that it was not excessive.[22] Similarly, when a physician was penalized $5,000 for carelessly tying off a newborn infant's penis instead of its umbilical cord, the Texas supreme court upheld the judgment.[23] The increases are significant but not dramatic and underscore the continuity with the first two-thirds of the century.

"Impecunious Clients of Desperate Lawyers"

Medical spokesmen reiterated many prewar assumptions. In the early 1870s and 1880s physicians continued to blame their colleagues for many of the suits. Writers complained of "traitorous" and careless physicians. In 1872 Stephen Smith declared that "the origin of nearly every trial for alleged malpractice may be traced to the reckless criticisms which rival practitioners pass upon the works of one another."[24] But as the profession became less contentious and more solidified, both socially and organizationally, there were progressively fewer charges of physician complicity in malpractice suits. By 1900 editorials rarely cited intraprofessional competition as a major source of the suits. The development of professional solidarity and the threat of suits encouraged physicians to close ranks.

While doctors ceased blaming their fellow physicians for their malpractice woes, the profession remained convinced that the poor and laboring classes were their chief tormentors.[25] The contention that base greed, and status and class resentment generated suits remained central in malpractice editorials. In the 1840s New York physicians lived in fear of malpractice juries filled with "anti-rent communists" and antiprofessional Jacksonian Democrats.[26] In the 1870s physicians still claimed that suits and convictions were generated by "an ill-feeling toward the 'class to which the defendants belong.' " This prejudice, a physician explained in 1872,

is simply the same idea which led to the robberies and murders of the [1871] Paris Commune, and which is subversive of justice everywhere. For it represents simply the jealousy and hate which unsuccessful and poor men bear those who have been, through greater industry and care, more fortunate than they in amassing wealth . . . What is it but robbery to adjudge against all evidence, the equalization of property between the doctor and his patient.[27]

The Paris Commune had ballooned anxieties of American elites, and was widely considered a symbol of the evils of out-of-control democracy. The antebellum upper and professional classes feared egalitarian farmers and workers. In the late nineteenth century, this anxiety metamorphized into elite alarm over social unrest, labor agitation, and Granger, Alliance, and Populist political organization. Frightened social and political elites in the late 1800s decried the common man's supposed perversion of democracy and declining respect for property and authority.[28] Physicians in the 1840s had believed that excessive democracy engendered antipathy toward regular practitioners and helped incite malpractice suits. By the 1890s doctors were even more convinced that their malpractice problems originated in one class of patients and jurors. As one writer explained, "the evil is in the imperfection and prejudices of the twelve specimens of human nature, in the jury box."[29]

Although class resentment existed against physicians, theirs was a profession whose average income still placed most of its members in the middle class. Much of the public antipathy toward doctors emanated from the physicians' quest and demands for the social status and prestige of learned professionals. Jacksonians had been repelled by the quasiaristocratic, gentlemanly ideals espoused by early nineteenth-century physicians. Many later patients also resented what they saw as the unjustified pretension and affected dignity of physicians.

Indeed, much as it had attempted to do earlier in the century, late nineteenth-century professional advice literature counseled physicians to maintain a social distance from their patients to inspire respect. D. W. Cathell, who published *The Physician Himself* in 1881, cautioned that intimacy and familiarity between doctor and patient has a "levelling effect and divests the physician of his proper prestige." Dressing or acting poorly in public, according to his professional etiquette guide, would "show weakness, diminish your prestige, detract from your dignity, and lessen public esteem, by forcing on everybody the conclusion that you are, after all, but an ordinary person."[30] Many Americans, even in this period of growing but grudging respect for experts, deeply resented the notion that one segment of society merited special deference.

But the impulse behind the hostility of some segments of the population to the profession had clearly begun to shift. In the early nineteenth century, antagonism was status-based and had arisen from antiaristocratic, democratic sentiments. Physicians had hoped to translate enhanced status into both honor and gold, but progress was slow. By the late nineteenth century, however, physicians' income had begun to rise. Status-based antagonism remained and probably continues to inspire negative feelings toward doctors to the present. But hostile attitudes toward physicians, where they existed, increasingly merged with class-based resentment. As medical incomes slowly increased, segments of the population took offense at physicians both for making more money than the average American and for believing that they were better than common people. Late nineteenth-century doctors contended that these feelings were more prevalent in working class and lower income families.

Observers continued to maintain, as they had before the Civil War, that "[p]hysicians and corporations are too often regarded as fair game by the impecunious clients of desperate lawyers." The young physician, they argued, soon had "his ardor dampened, his interest cooled, [and] his humanity chilled by the hardness of the material with which he comes in contact . . . he is gradually brought to regard a certain class of his patients as seeking to enrich themselves."[31] Sanger's study of malpractice in Maine seemed to confirm the profession's informal profile of the typical plaintiff. Out of the 70 malpractice charges he investigated, only 8 plaintiffs were able to pay the costs of the trials and allegedly "very many of them were drunken and shiftless persons."[32] Most physicians agreed that "nine times out of ten the plaintiff is a pauper who has received the gratuitous service of the man who [sic] he prosecutes."[33] Sanger warned that physicians would have to give up surgery entirely, select among reliable patients cases that promised favorable results, or "leave the afflicted poor, as barbaric tribes do, to perish by the wayside." In disgust and anger, he drafted a proposal to the Maine Medical Association: "Resolved, that with the existing laws on civil malpractice, it is unsafe to practice surgery among the poor." The medical society approved the resolution.[34]

Physicians felt that working class juries were particularly susceptible to the lawyer who "alluded to the poor laboring man and [the] rich doctor."[35] Sanger's 1878 report warned of "the dangers from jealous rivals, tricky lawyers, [and] impecunious and ignorant patients."[36] In the first half of the century physicians seldom accused lawyers of fomenting or aggravating malpractice suits. They considered lawyers a sometimes ill-informed but "noble sister profession."[37] Physicians and lawyers in the early nineteenth century were often drawn from the same social class, and both groups suffered under the antiprofessional Jacksonian sentiment of the 1830s and 1840s.[38] This social and political common ground may have bred sympathy between the professions.

But beginning in the 1870s physicians began to revile lawyers for their alliances with working-class plaintiffs. By the 1880s the composition of the bar was more socially diverse, more lawyers came from the working classes, and the two professions lost some of their natural social affinity.[39] It also appeared to many observers that lawyers were relinquishing their traditional role as protectors of social order. James Bryce, an English visitor, was one of the most perceptive commentators on American culture and public life in the late nineteenth century. He confirmed in 1889 that American lawyers had "it in their power to promote or to restrain vexatious litigation, to become accomplices in chicane, or to check the abuse of legal rights in cases where morality may require men to abstain from exacting all that the letter of the law requires."

It was evident to Bryce, however, that lawyers no longer fulfilled the function they had in the age of Jackson and de Tocqueville. Bryce reported that "taking a general survey of the facts of to-day, as compared with those of sixty years ago, it is clear that the Bar counts for less as a guiding and restraining power, tempering the crudity or haste of democracy by its attachment to rule and precedent, than it did then."[40] While law remained an essentially conservative discipline, the social attitudes of its membership had become less monolithic, and an increasing number of individual attorneys were willing to serve nonelite interests and clients.

In addition, the number of lawyers in the country increased in the last half of the century, from about 22,000 in 1850, to 60,000 in 1880, to 114,000 in 1900. Per capita estimates increased from 1 lawyer to 947 inhabitants in 1870 to 1 lawyer for every 662 inhabitants in 1990.[41] This increase put financial and competitive pressures on American lawyers and may have driven some to create business in previously objectionable ways.[42] In 1877 a physician exclaimed, "A surplus of cheap and briefless lawyers fosters the spirit of litigation, which is too common among certain classes of all large cities."[43] Another complained, "Every large city is overrun with petty lawyers, who have little or nothing to do, and are always willing to undertake any suit whether there is the least prospect of getting something out of the defendant."[44]

The abusive language physicians hurled at plaintiffs' attorneys reflected the depth of the medical profession's new fears. Physicians called malpractice lawyers "human vampires," "sharks," "jackals," "legal adventurers," "pettifogging attorneys," and "shysters."[45] An Illinois physician in 1882 claimed that unethical lawyers played the central role in inciting unwarranted suits. He warned his colleagues to beware of the "wily machinations of that most despicable of creatures (excepting only the quack doctors)—the shyster lawyer like the vulture hovering near his prey, he quietly watches for his opportunity to pounce upon the purse of the unwary surgeon."[46] Theoretically, the common law offenses of *barratry* and *maintenance* prohibited lawyers from inciting suits. Many states, however, required a succession of abuses before charges could be filed, and the remedies were rarely invoked.[47]

Yet while lawyers were an important component in the prosecution of malpractice cases, they did not constitute the chief cause of increased litigation. Lawyers were, at most, a match to a fuse, taking advantage of a situation that already existed, another immediate, aggravating cause of the late century suits. The fundamental explanation remains the social and cultural factors behind the patients' proclivity to sue.

Physicians also denounced the increased use of contingency fees by lawyers representing poor patients. The no award–no fee arrangements were not unknown in the first half of the century. Contingency arrangements were probably a more informal and less visible aspect of legal practice. Antebellum physicians rarely mentioned contingency arrangements in conjunction with malpractice suits. In the last third of the century they became a common, if incompletely accepted, legal practice. Lawyers who employed them charged no initial fee and generally received 50 percent of the damage award if victorious. Defendants could not benefit from the contingency fee's new popularity, and defendant physicians felt that they were at an immediate disadvantage. Physician/defendants had to pay for their legal help and expert witnesses whether they won or not. In addition, doctors believed that contingency fees, by giving the attorney an interest in the case, tended to increase the amount of damage awards. William Wey, president of the New York State Medical Society, argued that attorneys who encouraged suits and then represented patients under contingency fee arrangements were "mischief makers" and "professional pirates" who were themselves guilty of the "most flagrant malpractice."[48] The *Medical Times* editorialized "that respectable members of the legal profession do not usually accept contingent fees from poor people."[49]

The author's comment expressed the profession's persistent belief that malpractice suits were a subtle form of class and status conflict. It also strengthened the overt and underlying connections between physicians and other personal injury defendants, especially corporations. Like physicians, railroads and other corporations became the frequent object of damage claims beginning in the late 1830s. And, like physicians, railroads and other corporations suffered an intensified rate of personal injury litigation as the century progressed.[50]

As in malpractice suits, a growing number of plaintiff's attorneys accepted contingency fees when attacking corporate defendants. Although the United States Supreme Court upheld the legitimacy of contingency arrangements, elite members of the legal profession condemned them.[51] Supreme Court Justice Joseph Bradley declared that the fee "degrad[ed]" the profession and encouraged "stale or doubtful claims, which would have never been put in suit." Bradley argued that "the peace of society is disturbed by litigation fomented by those who are not concerned with it."[52] Thomas McIntyre Cooley, one of the most influential constitutional theorists of the century, claimed that the fees produced "a feeling of antagonism between aggregated capital on the one side and the community in general on the other."[53]

Observers like Bradley and Cooley feared the social unrest and class disquiet of the late nineteenth century and believed that contingency fees gave poor, resentful plaintiffs the means to attack possibly innocent targets. According to these writers, Granger and Populist groups harassed propertied interests in state legislatures while individuals sued corporations for personal injuries. Some poor patients were able and willing to sue physicians who represented status, privilege, and gradually increasing income.

Although conservative critics overstated the threats of supposedly irresponsible democracy, it is easy to see how physicians believed that corporations and doctors were the working class' common victims. As a physician complained in 1890, "Suits against corporations, lumber companies, railroad companies, and against physicians are pursued to an alarming extent."[54] During the Jacksonian period popular feeling ran against banks and physicians. By the 1870s railroads had replaced financial corporations as the focus of popular resentment, but physicians remained villains through both periods.

Remedies

Physicians in the late nineteenth century proposed a variety of remedies and strategies to discourage malpractice suits. Antebellum doctors were concerned with the problem, but their proposed solutions were fewer, less sophisticated, and generally useless. One writer mocked an 1853 Massachusetts Medical Society pamphlet on the causes and prevention of malpractice. "After reading the ten pages, we defy anyone to determine from the directions therein contained, how to stop a lawsuit." The commentator maintained that the only sensible solution was to refuse to treat certain classes of patients and injuries.[55] Indeed, physicians at midcentury had regularly threatened to shun complex fracture cases if the danger of lawsuits did not diminish, but apparently only a few actually resorted to this tactic. Most doctors probably felt that turning away injured patients would violate the humanitarian foundation of medical practice. The large number of regular and irregular practitioners in Jacksonian America also undermined the effectiveness of this remedy. If one physician abandoned fracture treatment, a competitor was always waiting to take his business. Finally, avoiding dangerous cases was an inappropriate response to the malpractice "crisis" because only a small minority of patients sued their physicians. By refusing to treat a whole class of cases, a physician turned his back on many deserving patients and their fees.

Medical observers in the 1840s and 1850s had believed that raising educational standards and reinstituting licensure would raise the profession's status and contain the malpractice threat. By 1900 the profession was well on its way to accomplishing these goals. Almost all the states that had abandoned licensure before the 1850s had reestablished it by the turn of the century. The early reenactments, coming in the 1870s, were weak and did little to control access to practice or raise standards. But by 1880 half the states enacted licensure laws, and by 1901 every state imposed punishment for unlicensed practice. The various state legislatures created boards to administer the statutes. Some jurisdictions required an examination as well as a medical diploma for certification. Other states established curriculum and content requirements for the medical schools from which license applicants would be accepted. These reforms eventually reached and surpassed the goals of antebellum medical leaders who wished to elevate the practice of medicine.[56]

Antebellum observers also felt that improved medical education would slow malpractice rates by producing better physicians and by raising the public perception of the medical community. In the last third of the century physicians could point to a virtual revolution in medical training. Beginning in the 1870s schools such as Harvard, Pennsylvania, Michigan, and Johns Hopkins pioneered a new model of medical education. While proprietary institutions and absurdly low standards remained prevalent, the outlines of the modern medical school were becoming clear. Leading schools lengthened the course of study from one to as many as four years. Basic science was integrated into the curriculum and pace-setting schools employed full-time, salaried professors. Administrators initiated higher entrance qualifications and more demanding requirements for graduation. Aspiring physicians at these select schools were required to study an expanded range of subjects including chemistry, physiology, and the young science of bacteriology. Equally important, schools such as Harvard symbolized a fundamentally different approach to medical training. Under the inspiration of university president Charles Eliot, it abandoned its slavish reliance on the traditional lecture method and dramatically expanded the role of "hands on" laboratory training and research. Led by Johns Hopkins, elite medical schools also introduced extensive programs in clinical clerkships in which students could work directly with patients in hospital wards. These reforms, originating in only a handful of institutions, had inspired imitation by less prestigious schools by the 1880s and 1890s. By the time Abraham Flexner published his 1910 report condemning the state of medical education, the scandalous schools of the antebellum years were rapidly closing their doors and were clearly destined for extinction.[57]

While the public distrust reserved for learned experts had aggravated the antebellum malpractice problem, and while physicians felt that they were popular targets often merely because they claimed expertise, by the late nineteenth century the Jacksonian hatred of the expert and the professional had virtually passed. Americans began to accept and value the role and judgment of the expert on a variety of subjects. Engineers, geologists, scientists, and agricultural specialists proliferated. Social scientists influenced all levels of government. Academics and intellectuals were expected to play a central role in shaping late-century progressive reforms. The status and influence of the expert/professional grew as an increasingly complex industrial society posed new questions and demanded innovative responses.[58]

Physicians had believed that inadequate education, the lack of effective licensure, and antiprofessional bias helped generate litigation in the first half of the century. These conditions dissipated in the 1880s and 1890s, but suits continued to thrive seemingly unabated. Universal licensure, educational reforms, and the rise of the expert appear to have had very little impact on patients' propensity to sue in the latter part of the century. These factors had indeed helped multiply the number of suits in the 1840s, but they did not constitute a fundamental cause of the litigation. They merely incited and aggravated litigation in a specific historical period. Therefore, when they weakened late in the nineteenth century and virtually disappeared in the twentieth, suits did not automatically cease. Instead, other aggravating factors arose, and the cultural presuppositions that nurtured and encouraged the phenomenon remained.

The medical community was pleased with the progress it had made in education, licensure, and status, but it searched for effective tactics to combat the continuing law suits. While it is difficult to determine how much late nineteenth-century proposals influenced litigation rates, physicians developed additional and more comprehensive remedies than their midcentury counterparts. Most solutions were designed to stem the tide of suits without undermining the profession's dignity or blunting its boldness in practice. In a bizarre 1871 anecdote a fracture patient told his physician that he was going to sue for his badly healed leg. The physician asked the man in to his office and offered to operate on the limb and repair the deformity. When the patient refused, the doctor knocked him down, chloroformed him, and operated on the unconscious man's leg. The patient recovered and dropped all charges against the physician. A medical journal praised the physician for having "the courage that many surgeons lack, to take the responsibility to act, and look up the law afterward."[59] Of course, such approaches to the malpractice problem were rare.

Some physicians believed that charging fees to all patients would discourage litigation. D. W. Cathell continued the refrain that poor patients were not to be trusted. He counseled his colleagues that "you should not induce people to let you involve yourself for their benefit without being paid for your risk and responsibility." Cathell believed that physicians should "send [their] bill promptly to dissatisfied patients who are threatening to sue for malpractice." "[S]ending your bill," he reasoned, "gives you a better position before the public, and raises an issue that checkmates theirs. *Do not fail to charge the full amount in all such cases*" (original emphasis).[60] A writer for the *New York Medical Journal* also believed that immediate payment of fees was "the best possible safeguard" against suits for malpractice.[61] Such commentators reasoned that, having paid for services, patients would be less tempted to escape the charges by a claim of malpractice. Moreover, they hoped that a paid fee implied satisfaction and would be a good defensive weapon in court. Despite the internal logic of this tactic, the realities of medical practice rendered it unfeasible. As part of their self-image and public posture, physicians were expected to perform a certain amount of charity practice and could never completely eliminate non-paying patients.

Late nineteenth-century physicians seldom blamed their colleagues for instituting suits because strengthened professional organizations were able to soften the competitive medical market of the 1840s.[62] Local and state medical societies with enhanced moral and professional authority discouraged physician complicity in malpractice suits. Stephen Smith advised that the class of physicians who incited litigation "should be stricken from the membership of every medical organization."[63] During the late 1870s medical societies condemned "ill advised" remarks against "brother practitioners" and ostracized members who willingly supported unjustified suits. The Baltimore Medical and Surgical Society encouraged its members to "be on the safe side by actively discouraging all such suits."[64]

The medical community's campaign proved increasingly successful and effective. In 1879 a medical journal celebrated that a malpractice plaintiff had been "unable to produce a single medical witness to controvert the testimony" of the defendant.[65] By 1890 attorneys and the public believed that members of the medical profession invariably supported the malpractice defendant. Physicians, however, responded that "[t]his is as it should be because we can always give the benefit of the doubt to the right side."[66]

William Mayo, patriarch of the famous Rochester, Minnesota, surgical clinic, typified the new jurisprudential posture of many American physicians. By the 1880s malpractice suits were common in Minnesota. Leaders of the state medical society pointed out that doctors' performances as expert witnesses often made physicians accomplices in the prosecutions. They warned that doctors should learn to defend their colleagues in court if they hoped to reduce the overall risk of malpractice charges. Mayo followed the society's advice. Ironically, he testified at the trial of a long time personal and professional enemy, Edwin Cross. A patient claimed that the physician had bandaged his arm too tightly, cutting off the circulation and leading to an unwarranted amputation. Mayo not only testified in behalf of Cross, but also devised the substance of the defense attorney's position. He argued that the vital arteries of the arm may have been damaged as a result of the fracture itself and not from the treatment. The jury found Cross innocent of wrongdoing. When a Rochester man asked Mayo why he so fervently defended a despised enemy, the physician responded: "I did it for the profession, not for him, damn him."[67] This variant of professional solidarity was not nearly as common in the first half of the century.

As frequent malpractice prosecutions became a permanent feature of American medical practice, advice literature became more prevalent. "It would seem," a speaker told the Medico-Legal Society of New York in 1876, "that the most efficient means of prevention (and consequently self-protection) is enlightenment—the knowledge of medical men of their legal duties and liabilities, the knowledge among courts of law and the general public of the possibilities of surgical skill."[68] Medical jurisprudence was not a standard part of medical school curricula in the 1870s, and interested physicians had to rely on handbooks and professional journals for practical guidance.[69] John Elwell's 1860 treatise on malpractice was reprinted three times before 1881, John Ordronaux published his erudite *Jurisprudence of Medicine* in 1869, and Milo McClelland added a huge compendium, *Civil Malpractice: A Treatise on Surgical Jurisprudence*, in 1877. McClelland reprinted extensive samples of Frank Hamilton's fracture tables and representative court decisions that "are inaccessible to medical and legal practitioners."[70] His commentary explained the various legal dangers of medical practice.

Physicians turned to professional periodical literature for more practical advice and strategies. One article counseled that the prospective defendant, "instead of spending the best of his time in vehement vituperation against 'ungrateful patients,' [and] 'rascally lawyers' . . . should select one or more *good* lawyers, and go to work, for a malpractice suit means business." The defendants should coach their attorneys on the medical and anatomical aspects of the case. They should also interview their expert witnesses, with their attorneys, before the trial. Juries, according to the article, "are partial to print [so] it is better to have six recorded cases similar to the one under trial, than the testimony of six experts."[71] Medical journals also instructed defendant physicians in finer points of trial tactics. Writers warned doctors to avoid continuations of trials from one term to another because valuable evidence could be lost. They also cautioned physicians "not [to] reveal to the outside world what you propose to use as evidence." Plaintiffs' depositions, a potential source of defense evidence, should be taken as early as possible.[72]

Some writers suggested that physicians could best avoid and defend suits by practicing more "ethical" medicine. According to McClelland,

To avoid the annoyance of such suits, surgeons should above all be *honest* with their patients, apprising them of the difficulties of the case and the uncertainties of perfect results . . . They should be candid in regard to their deficiencies, claiming no more than they can perform, no more knowledge than they possess.[73]

Other advisors admonished physicians to drink moderately or not at all and to "[b]e careful in profession deportment" and diligent in their studies, keeping up with every advance. Cautious physicians warned patients to be aware of "all the possible contingencies which may result from the operation—be they ever so remote." One writer claimed that the reputation of a good, safe physician "will make imputations of malpractice too improbable to be feared."[74]

Most observers doubted that ethical and careful medical practice alone could immunize physicians against malpractice charges. Physicians claimed that most suits and threats of suits were only "blackmail" ruses to extort money from reputation-conscious doctors. They argued that the majority of plaintiffs and lawyers did not intend for their cases to reach the courtroom but hoped to settle out of court. The generally low quality of the plaintiff's expert witnesses and evidence and estimates of high acquittal rates lent credibility to physicians' claims. Eugene Sanger's study of 70 prosecutions revealed that only 9 plaintiffs won judgments.[75] Estimates of acquittal sometimes reached 9 out of 10. Many physicians, according to one journal, would have been "unwilling to face the annoyance and publicity which a trial necessarily entail[s]." When John Reese, an expert on medical jurisprudence, faced a malpractice case, he "might have easily avoided [it] by listening to the base proposals of the plaintiff's counsel to pay blackmail." Instead, he decided, in his words, "fearlessly [to] meet this lawsuit."[76] Lewis Sayer and Samuel Gross, two renowned surgeons, were also sued in the early 1870s, and, when the plaintiffs' attorneys attempted to settle the cases out of court, both men declined. Gross "scornfully refused . . . deeming it but just to himself and to the profession to defy the threats of the plaintiff."[77] When Reese, Sayer, and Gross decided to face public trials, their prosecutors were left with embarrassingly weak cases and lost.[78] After the trials, the *Medical Record* entreated, "Let us hope that the manly conduct of Professors Gross and Reese . . . as well as the results of the suits . . . has convinced the most unscrupulous among the legal fraternity that members of our profession, one and all, intend to resist all attempts to levy black-mail upon them."[79]

The message was clear. Most charges were unwarranted and indefensible. The strategy and best hope of lawyers representing patients was to coerce the payment of "smart money." When the physician refused, he won his case and was congratulated in the pages of medical journals. In 1889 a Chicago attorney agreed with the medical profession's impression of the typical case. After discussing the issue with some of his colleagues, the lawyer reported that "nine-tenths of the malpractice suits were blackmailing suits."[80] Wealthy surgeons, especially, preferred to pay off plaintiffs, but editorialists argued that this was a "mistaken policy, and has a tendency to propagate an evil which in the end reacts with terrible force upon the poorer surgeon."[81] In his commentary on malpractice McClelland sternly declared that "[u]nder no circumstances should suits be compromised." After performing their duty, surgeons "owe it to their professional brethren to let the matter be tried by the letter of the law."[82]

Mutual Protection

Physicians slowly realized that profound problems were involved in fighting every case in court. Not only did they risk their reputations, but legal fees and court costs were often prohibitive. One doctor, a defendant in two trials in the 1870s, reported that he paid $1,100 to lawyers and witnesses and for other court costs.[83] Sanger's study suggested that legal expenses, even in successful cases, averaged between $800 and $1,000.

The threat of suits, financial realities, and the commitment to fight all charges of malpractice inspired the innovation of group defense organizations. Although mutual insurance groups had been suggested earlier in the century, the notion was opposed or ignored until the 1880s.[84] In 1886 a speaker before the Chicago Medical Society proposed the creation of an association of local physicians. Each physician, after screening by the society, would contribute five dollars a year to the legal defense fund. The association would hire a prominent law firm to defend any suit arising against a member physician. According to the speaker,

Let it be known that the individual physician is backed by the financial and moral support of a few hundred of the best physicians, and aided by the best legal talent available, and he will be let severely alone by the dregs of society who constitute, almost without exception, the blackmailing element in our professional life.[85]

Although some critics believed that a mutual defense association would "prejudice the jury against the defendant, just as corporations do," the notion gained many converts in the 1880s. In 1887 a writer for the *Boston Medical and Surgical Journal* agreed that physicians should combine to protect themselves from the "ever impending risk of actions for malpractice." Because the lawsuits were expensive in time, money, and anxiety, "there are few [physicians] who can afford to engage in defending a suit[;] an easy and honorable way of avoiding it is afforded."[86] By the first decade of the twentieth century legal defense associations sponsored by medical societies had become popular in many areas including Massachusetts, New York, Chicago, Cleveland, and Detroit. Local medical societies embraced the innovation with enthusiastic, but ultimately unfounded, optimism. In 1902 the *New York State Journal of Medicine* predicted that "through the publicity given to a suit or two, the blackmailing variety of malpractice suits will cease. This class constitutes 97% of all such suits brought."[87]

The medical defense leagues were closely linked with the rejuvenated professional organizations of the late nineteenth and twentieth centuries. Physicians became increasingly confident that they could slow malpractice rates by group concert. Although malpractice insurance from private companies did not become available until after 1900, group defense associations could promote medical malpractice insurance, and societies could castigate or even expel members who instigated or participated in suits. As medical societies gained control over licensure, access to hospital practice, and referrals, they could increasingly dictate individual physicians' behavior.[88]

Organized physicians were also becoming a more potent political force, and many medical societies began to investigate legislative remedies to malpractice suits. Sanger had argued that "[s]urgery is indispensable to the welfare and existence of the human race, and by saving life and utilizing labor it is a productive industry which needs the protection of general law." He reasoned that there were laws protecting other public service entities, such as towns, and contended that physicians too deserved a shield so that they could practice their "hazardous" but essential calling.[89] Similarly, a writer declared in 1882 that the "medical profession surely is entitled to, and I believe possesses, sufficient influence if we would exert it, to have framed and passed by our legislative bodies such laws as we are justly entitled to for our protection."[90] Medical societies drafted prospective legislation that would retain the jury trial but institute a system by which the court, and not the parties to the suit, would select the expert witnesses who would be paid by the county.

Sponsors believed that this provision would decrease contradictory and interested testimony and protect defendants.[91] Other proposals included recommendations that prospective plaintiffs be forced to post bonds to cover the costs of the trials. Physicians designed this alteration with the litigious poor patient in mind, but they held little hope of getting it passed in state legislatures because it clearly prevented legitimate claims from being brought by destitute patients.[92] Some proposals merely asked for the legitimation of contractual waivers, while others petitioned for the complete abolition of the jury trial. The Ohio Medical Association, for example, sent a draft to the legislature to introduce trial by arbitrators to the state. The three-man board would consist of physicians: one chosen by the plaintiff, one by the defendant, and the third by the other two arbitrators.[93] The spate of proposals in the last two decades of the century was not fruitful. State legislatures did not tamper significantly with the malpractice trial procedure, and the process remained essentially unchanged.

The Law of Malpractice

Despite the significant leap in appellate decisions between 1865 and 1900, the basic requirement that physicians "must possess and exercise that degree of skill ordinarily possessed by members of the profession" proved durable, and the doctrine governing malpractice law stable.[94] Courts reaffirmed the antebellum doctrine that physicians did not automatically guarantee cures, but were responsible only for failures if they specifically promised success. Most of the many appellate cases in the late nineteenth century dealt with important, but mechanical, procedural, pleading, or administrative issues or questions of fact relating only to individual cases.[95] State appellate judges also ruled on the proper role of expert testimony. Witnesses could offer or comment on hypothetical examples to illustrate a case, but they could not draw conclusions on the facts of the case. When witnesses crossed this indistinct line, appellate judges usually overturned the lower court decision.[96]

Appellate courts also reversed decisions in which the verdict seemed to be unjustified by the evidence. For example, in 1875 a jury ignored the overwhelming evidence that a physician had properly set a plaintiff's broken arm and awarded $4,000. The Minnesota supreme court reversed the decision and granted a new trial because "the jury did not accept and weigh as they should have done, the testimony of the experts, but must have acted independently of it."[97] Appellate judges also overturned decisions when trial judges made inappropriate conclusions on the facts when defining the legal issues for the jury.[98]

These rulings were important and occasionally significant as precedents, but they did not set a basic common law doctrine of malpractice. Courts were frequently asked to rule on the different instructions on the "ordinary standard of skill and care" requirement offered by trial judges. Appellate courts overturned convictions in cases in which trial judges required the skill of a "thoroughly educated physician." State supreme court judges also rejected trial definitions that demanded that the physician possess and exercise "full skill" or be liable for "any want of skill." These definitions set too high a standard for medical practitioners.[99] When a trial court announced that a physician must take advantage of the "most accredited sources of knowledge," the Iowa supreme court overturned the judgment because it demanded too high a standard of education.[100] An Illinois appellate court reversed a decision in which the trial judge instructed the jury that if the physician "could have learned the nature of the injury, and applied the proper remedy, and failed, he is liable."[101] And in 1873 the Indiana supreme court overturned a conviction in which the judge stated that a physician is "required to exercise care and skill proportionate to the character of the injury he treats."[102] Courts rarely held that the degree of care and skill set by the trial court was too low.

Although rulings varied slightly from state to state, courts in the late nineteenth century accepted a variety of substitutes for the term *ordinary* in the description of the physician's responsibilities. Appellate judges generally agreed that terms such as *average skill*, *fair knowledge and skill*, *adequate care*, and *reasonable skill* were legitimate synonyms for *ordinary.*[103] These modifications did not materially alter the doctrine, and judges continued to use midcentury precedents to frame the basic charge to malpractice juries. Late nineteenth-century treatises on malpractice and tort reflected this continuity. Elwell's work on malpractice remained essentially unchanged through four editions. Thomas Cooley's 1906 *Law of Torts* held that a physician must "possess ordinary skill, [and] that he will use ordinary care."[104]

The organizational structure of medical practice changed considerably between 1865 and 1900. These developments led to new forms of malpractice litigation that required adaptation to but no significant alteration of the common law. The absolute dominance of the solo practitioner began to wane, and physicians joined with other physicians, clinics, and hospitals. The increasing importance of technology and access to new techniques encouraged hospital practice.[105] As hospitals became increasingly important in the delivery of medical care, they also became targets of malpractice charges.

In the first two-thirds of the century most hospitals were charity institutions. The legal doctrine concerning charity hospitals was clear and unequivocal. Although physicians who practiced at the institutions were liable for their conduct under the standard rules of law, the hospital was virtually immune from prosecution. If the charity hospital had "exercised due care in the selection of its agents, it [was] not liable for injury to a patient caused by their negligence."[106] Group practices, like the Mayo Clinic, and for-profit hospitals also proliferated. When malpractice plaintiffs sued such an institution, judges held it responsible only for exercising the same "due diligence in securing skillful and careful medical men for the treatment of its patients."[107] Railroad companies occasionally organized hospitals or clinics to provide free care for their employees. Courts generally gave the railroad company medical facilities the benefit of the doctrine that applied to other medical institutions.[108]

The *Medical Record* applauded these rulings, rejoicing that "[f]or the first time, therefore, in our history, hospitals are protected from suits of this kind, for it is not to be conceived that any respectable hospital will not exercise due diligence in securing careful medical officers."[109] For once, medical optimism regarding a facet of malpractice was well founded. Institutional plaintiffs in the late nineteenth century appeared easily to convince courts and juries that they had carefully selected their staff physicians. Judges had effectively eliminated the doctrine of *respondeat superior* from hospital malpractice law, which held that employers were liable for the actions of their employees. This generous move allowed most medical institutions to escape payment of damages in the nineteenth century.

The last third of the century brought other notable changes to the law of malpractice. In antebellum America the physician could not be held liable for malpractice if a patient contributed in any way to his or her injury. The doctrine irregularly influenced verdicts in the first half of the century, perhaps because it was a complete defense and entirely absolved the defendant/physicians.[110] Some jurisdictions continued to accept a strict interpretation of contributory negligence in malpractice cases through the end of the century. In 1883 the Indiana supreme court ruled that "a party seeking to recover for an injury must not have contributed to it in any degree, either by his negligence or the disregard of a duty imposed upon him by his physician."[111]

Some appellate judges, however, fashioned exceptions to the strict doctrine of contributory negligence. In *Carpenter* v. *Blake* (1878) a physician's attorney asked a trial judge to instruct the jury that if the patient had contributed in any degree to his injuries, then the physician was not responsible even if he too was negligent. The judge refused, and the jury found the physician guilty of malpractice. The physician claimed that he had not received the full benefit of the contributory negligence defense. The highest court in New York, however, ruled that once the physician had negligently caused an injury, "The most that could be claimed on account of any subsequent negligence would be that it should mitigate damages."[112] Therefore, it was possible to hold a physician responsible for damages even if the patient aggravated the injury.

An *Albany Law Journal* writer explained in 1881 that while irresponsibility and complicity of patients usually absolved the physician from all liability, the doctrine could have limits if the respective responsibilities could be "separated."[113] This version of contributory negligence was especially important in cases in which patients refused to follow the instructions of their physicians. In *Dubois* v. *Decker* (1891) a physician failed to leave enough tissue to cover the protruding bone on the stump of a patient's amputated leg. Consequently, the leg took an inordinately long time to heal, and the patient was left with protruding bone. The physician argued that the patient had refused to leave the leg in the prescribed position, declined to take medicine, and eventually left the physician's care without permission. The jury found the physician guilty of malpractice, and he appealed the decision to the New York high court. Citing *Carpenter* v. *Blake*, the court ruled that even though the patient's actions may have aggravated his injury, the physician was clearly liable for the initial malpractice. Therefore, the patient's actions could only mitigate and not preclude the damage award he would receive from the physician.[114]

This modification of the contributory negligence doctrine worked against physicians/defendants, but its effect was not clear cut in malpractice cases. Each state developed variant patterns and bodies of case law, but a clear bending of the doctrine occurred in most jurisdictions. In the first half of the century, when the doctrine was in its strictest form, judges and juries may have avoided its use in malpractice cases because it completely indemnified physicians from liability. Though the softened version of contributory negligence threatened physicians because it abandoned absolute immunity, it may have indirectly helped some defendants by forcing juries and judges to reduce damage awards.[115]

Locality Rule

Another late innovation in malpractice law bestowed unambiguous advantage to the defendant/physician. Through the first two-thirds of the century physicians and scattered trial court judges contended that malpractice defendants should be measured against the "ordinary" practitioners in the locality in which they practiced. These physicians and jurists argued that because physicians' skill, education, and experience differed greatly in various geographic locations and social surroundings, it was unrealistic and unfair for a jury to require the same degree of skill from a small-town rural practitioner as from a hospital-based physician with a thriving urban practice. Notwithstanding these arguments, trial judges only irregularly instructed juries to calculate medical competence by community standards, and appellate courts never made the notion part of malpractice doctrine.[116]

Despite appellate judges' midcentury indifference toward the locality rule, physicians and treatise writers campaigned for its inclusion into case law. Although Hillard's treatise on torts did not mention the doctrine, Elwell supported community standards in 1860, as did Ordronaux in 1869 and McClelland in 1873.[117] In his important 1870 treatise on negligence Redfield cited no precedential support, but asserted that "the standard of skill may vary according to circumstances, and may be different even in the same state or country." He explained that in "country towns, and in unsettled portions of the country remote from cities, physicians, though well informed in theory, are but seldom called upon to perform difficult operations in surgery, and do not enjoy the greater opportunities of daily observation and practice which large cities afford." Therefore, he declared, it would be unreasonable to expect the same degree of skill from both classes of physicians.[118]

In the wake of these writings the idea became more widely cited both in trial and appellate courts. William Wey called for the universal use of the locality rule in 1872. He noted that "[t]his estimate of skill has undoubtedly been considered by courts in holding physicians to account for alleged malpractice, and in this way we are enabled to reconcile the otherwise conflicting character of the principles of law by which such cases have been governed."[119] Appellate judges began to discuss the community standard rule in their judicial opinions. The Kansas supreme court quoted Elwell in *Teft* v. *Wilcox* (1870) and stated that "[t]he opportunities by reason of locality, or other circumstances, of one portion [of the profession], may be many times more favorable than those of another; and the responsibilities resting upon them would be correspondingly greater."[120] The court, however, reversed the physician's conviction on other grounds. Therefore, the comments were probably obiter dictum and did not have the precedential legitimacy of an explicit ruling on the issue.

In *Smothers* v. *Hanks* (1872) the locality rule gained further ground. The Iowa supreme court overturned a malpractice conviction because the trial judge's instructions to the jury required that the defendant be a "thoroughly educated" physician. The majority opinion, citing

Redfield, noted that "[i]t is also doubtless true that the standard of ordinary skill may vary even in the same state, according to the greater or lesser opportunities afforded the locality for observation and practice."[121] Like *Teft* v. *Wilcox*, the discussion of the community standard in *Smothers* was superfluous to the central issue of the appeal, and its comments were probably not binding as precedent.

The locality rule did not yet command universal approbation. A dissenting judge in *Smothers* argued against the locality rule because "In this age [1872] of books, professional periodicals, and mails . . . [w]e may safely say that no respectable surgeon, wherever he may be, is uninformed of the progress and discoveries in his profession."[122] In 1876 the Vermont supreme court accepted a trial court charge to a jury that incorporated the rule without comment. But the following year the Indiana supreme court refused to overturn a conviction on the grounds that the trial judges did not invoke the community standard.[123]

The Massachusetts supreme court provided the definitive precedent in support of the locality rule in the 1880 case of *Small* v. *Howard*. A man living in a small country town of about 2,500 residents severely cut the inside of his wrist with a piece of glass, severing vital arteries and tendons. The local physician, a common general practitioner, possessed no extraordinary surgical skill to treat complicated and unusual injuries. When the injury healed imperfectly, the patient sued. Over the objection of the patient, the trial judge instructed the jury that the physician was "bound to possess that skill only which physicians and surgeons of ordinary ability and skill, practicing in similar localities . . . ordinarily possess." The jury found for the physician, and the patient appealed the case to the state supreme court, claiming that the community standard rule lowered the standard of care required of a physician. In *Small* v. *Howard* the Massachusetts appellate court ruled that it was a matter of common knowledge that physicians in small country towns and villages could not possess the same degree of skill as their big city counterparts, who had more opportunities to observe practice. The Massachusetts court made this decision despite the fact that an eminent physician, who could have treated or advised on the case, lived only four miles from the patient's community.[124]

The decision in *Small* v. *Howard* ushered in an almost universal, one-hundred year acceptance of the locality rule. The doctrine was a powerful defensive weapon for defendants. It explicitly lowered the standard of skill courts required of some physicians. In its strictest form, it limited the pool of expert witnesses to those physicians who practiced in the same community as the defendant. While it is not certain why appellate courts included the locality rule in the common law definition of malpractice, several reasons are possible. The burgeoning number of appellate cases allowed judges to fine-tune aspects of the law that had been previously ignored. Judges may have sympathized with the plight of the medical profession and wished to provide physicians with a defensive strategy. But the doctrine was not pure judicial creation. The locality test had been invoked by scattered trial court judges throughout the century and other areas of law recognized the relevance of local custom. Perhaps most importantly, appellate judges in the last third of the century became increasingly receptive to ideas promulgated by treatise writers who argued that a physician's standard of skill should be judged by local circumstances.

As professional opposition to malpractice suits solidified, local medical societies gained coercive power over their members. Some societies threatened prospective medical witnesses with expulsion if they gratuitously testified against other practitioners. It was sometimes difficult for plaintiffs to secure qualified expert testimony. Physicians who were the sole practitioners in their communities could likewise escape prosecution by asserting that they set the standard of care for their location or by claiming that there existed no legitimate expert witnesses to participate in the trial. Judges soon recognized the difficulties of narrow applications of the locality rule and modified the doctrine.[125] Appellate courts ruled that physicians should not be protected merely because they were the only practitioners in a particular community. They altered the locality rule so that physicians were required to exercise the skill and care of doctors in "similar" or "like" surroundings.[126] This adjustment in the doctrine made it easier to prosecute isolated practitioners and to secure expert testimony in communities where physicians had established a united front against malpractice prosecutions.

In *Pike* v. *Honsinger* (1898) the New York high court relied on traditional precedent, incorporated the changes of the previous twenty years, and articulated the precepts that would guide malpractice litigation through much of the twentieth century. The case began when George Pike, a middle-aged farmer, was kicked in the knee by his horse. Pike drove his wagon to the medical office of Willis T. Honsinger. Honsinger was absent, but his physician son set Pike's leg with adhesive plasters and splints. Pike returned home but sent for the elder physician a week later. Honsinger examined the man's badly swollen leg and told him that he had ruptured a ligament. The injury resisted the physician's treatment over the next two months, but he allowed Pike to continue working the fields. Pike repeatedly complained that the leg was not set correctly. The following spring Pike consulted another physician and learned that he had broken his kneecap. Honsinger admitted that he had initially misdiagnosed the injury, but told Pike that "the leg was not worth a damn and he would have to go into something besides farming." Pike reported that he could lift only half as much as he could before the accident and that he was unable to walk on plowed ground.

Pike sued Honsinger for malpractice. The physicians who testified at the trial contended that Honsinger had not only erred in diagnosing the injury, but also should have watched the patient more carefully and kept him in splints and out of work for at least a year. The trial court judge did not allow the jury to decide the case, but directed a verdict in favor of Honsinger. Pike appealed, and in 1898 the New York appellate court agreed that he deserved a new trial and that the judge should have allowed the jury to decide the case.[127]

The appellate judges also restated the "well-settled" tenets of American malpractice in "simple language." The court explained that a physician was required to possess "that reasonable degree of learning and skill that is ordinarily possessed by physicians in the locality where he practices." In addition, every physician must "keep abreast of his times." If the physician departed from "approved methods, in general use" and injured a patient, he would be liable for damages. Once physicians began treatment, they were required to exercise their "best judgment" and "use reasonable care and diligence."[128] Although *Pike* did not represent a significant departure from previous decisions, it served as a key precedent because it clearly delineated the physician's legal responsibilities.[129] The *ordinary* standard of care remained unchallenged as the central tenet of American malpractice law until the last third of the twentieth century. Then, important rulings suggested that in some instances advanced technological procedures could be required, even if accepted ordinary practice did not customarily make use of the technology.[130]

New Treatments, New Suits

Treatment for fractures and dislocations continued to generate the vast majority of malpractice suits through the beginning of the twentieth century. In 1884 a writer estimated that nine-tenths of all suits were the result of orthopedic treatment.[131] This figure was undoubtedly inflated. Fracture and dislocation cases probably constituted between two-thirds and three-quarters of the litigation.[132] Some physicians claimed that fracture cases remained common because those injuries plagued manual laborers, "the poorer and more ignorant classes . . . precisely the class to be influenced, by their necessities, to be open to the golden dreams of plenty which a crafty and unscrupulous lawyer knows how to awaken."[133] The explanation is somewhat more complicated. The first rise in suits had been fueled in part by the rapid advances in fracture treatment between 1820 and 1850 and the accompanying exaggerated expectations.[134] Frank Hamilton and his supporters had believed that his 1850s fracture tables would reduce suits for this class of treatment. They reasoned that statistical demonstrations of standard treatments and standard results would lower the expectations of both physician and patient and provide evidence of what constituted competent practice.

Despite their popularity and wide dissemination, Hamilton's tables and other similar strategies could not suppress suits. The device was ultimately ineffectual because it could not take account of perpetual and rapid medical technological advancement. For instance, the profound advances of antebellum fracture treatment had been rapidly superseded. In the 1870s plaster of Paris dressings for fractures became "the rage, and, he who neglected to employ it was an 'old fogy' or was not up in progress." The initial reports of plaster of Paris recalled the early responses to the advances of the prewar years. Enthusiasts claimed

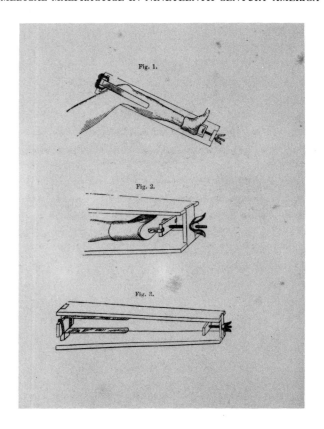

Fracture box with adjustable footboard. From Frank Hastings Hamilton, "Report on Deformities after Fractures," TAMA *10 (1857): 239–453. (Courtesy of the Historical Research Center, Houston Academy of Medicine, Texas Medical Center Library, Houston, Texas.)*

perfect cures with no shortening or deformity. The innovation brought about a "revolution" in fracture treatment. Older methods were "thrown out as relic[s] of barbarianism." Results, however, did not always meet expectations, and less proficient physicians did not always achieve optimum results. Consequently, the "revolution" of plaster of Paris gave rise to suits, just as the advancements of the first half of the century had.[135]

In fractures as well as other areas of medical treatment innovation often ran through the cycle of advancement, inflated expectations, limited successes, and lawsuits. By the 1890s fracture treatment had undergone yet another "revolution," provoked in part by the advances in aseptic surgery, and physicians predicted total cures. In 1893 one writer reported, "So great and rapid have been the advances in the treatment of compound fracture within the last two decades that, when properly managed, now many lives and limbs are spared which were formerly sacrificed, distortions obviated, inflammation, necrosis, tetanus, and mortification prevented." Recent advances had brought "the treatment of compound fractures to well-nigh a state of perfection."[136] Despite the steady therapeutic advancement, suits for fractures continued.

Although fracture cases dominated malpractice litigation, new classes of suits arose out of new and improved practice. After the invention of the ophthalmaloscope (a device that allowed physicians to view the structure of the retina) in 1851, ophthalmology made rapid and dramatic advancements in the last half of the century. Accompanying this progress, suits against physicians for eye damage became more common between 1880 and 1900.[137] Obstetric and gynecological surgery also flourished in these years. Surgeons performed a variety of new and sometimes unjustified operations on women's reproductive organs, from clitoridectomies to hysterectomies.[138] Ovariotomies were especially popular. These treatments contributed to the rising and increasingly diverse body of suits. Beginning in the 1880s, women sued physicians for removing their ovaries unnecessarily or without their consent. They also accused physicians of malpractice for complications following obstetrical surgery.[139]

Malpractice suits for general surgery proliferated more slowly than those for ophthalmology, obstetrics, and gynecology. Surgical procedures were neither rational nor predictable. Few physicians attempted major operations, and patients rarely expected positive results. The specters of infection, hemorrhage, and incompletely understood shock haunted operating theaters and blocked physicians' paths into the abdomen, chest, and head. As late as 1876 Samuel Gross reported that "enlightened" American surgeons "scrupulously refrained from the employment of the knife whenever it was possible." According to

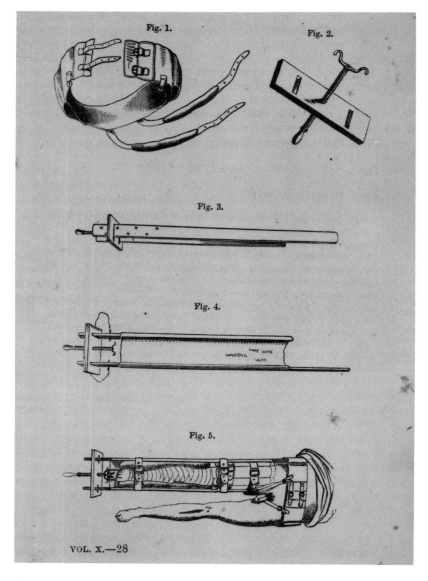

Flagg's apparatus for thigh fractures with straps and adjustable footboard. From Frank Hastings Hamilton, "Report on Deformities after Fractures," TAMA 10 (1857): 239–453. (Courtesy of the Historical Research Center, Houston Academy of Medicine, Texas Medical Center Library, Houston, Texas.)

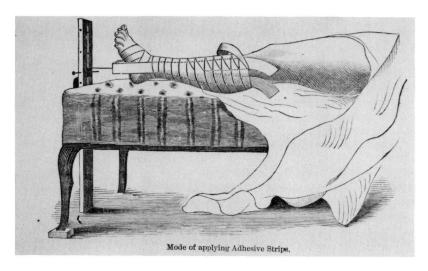

Mode of applying Adhesive Strips.

Adhesive strip with counterweight method of setting leg fractures. From Frank Hastings Hamilton, Principles and Practice of Surgery *(1886). (Courtesy of the Historical Research Center, Houston Academy of Medicine, Texas Medical Center Library, Houston, Texas.)*

Gross, surgeons limited themselves to "the great family of external diseases and accidents."[140]

Rampant postoperative infections, especially in hospitals, had severely restricted the range and frequency of surgical procedures. Joseph Lister began to popularize his theories on antiseptic surgery in the late 1860s. Using the findings of microbiologist Louis Pasteur, Lister recognized that microorganisms in the air could produce infections in compound fractures, wounds, and surgical incisions. But his ideas were not perfected, accepted, or practiced on a wide scale in America until the late 1880s. Lister had devised a cleansing system by which the wound, the instruments, and even the air in the operating room would be sprayed with a carbolic acid solution. Although the procedure had its merits, it was not always effective, and sometimes it was even harmful. In addition, many surgeons failed to appreciate the importance of the scrupulous disinfection ritual. They dropped instruments and continued surgery without resterilization. Some probed wounds with their bare hands after wiping their brows or noses. Other surgeons regularly wore operating smocks imbued with the gore of previous operations. Moreover, American physicians only gradually accepted the value of developing sterile surgery and opposed the notion of the germ theory in general. The retarded development and proliferation of sterile operating practices slowed surgical progress. With few surgical procedures attempted and muted optimism, malpractice charges were seldom associated with general surgery before the 1880s.

Eventually, however, physicians accepted the essentials of Lister's findings and developed more effective devices and procedures, such as steam and dry heat sterilization. In addition, in the late 1880s and 1890s surgeons and their staffs adopted sterile caps, gowns, masks, and rubber gloves. Medical inventors developed more efficient and sanitary stainless steel instruments. Physicians discovered that the use of finer needles and silk thread led to better results and developed new techniques and devices to control surgical bleeding. Finally, more sophisticated analgesics and anesthetics made surgery easier and safer.[141]

Consequently, by 1890, with the advent of sterile practice, innovative procedures, and new instruments, body cavity surgery slowly became a viable and attractive frontier for physicians.[142] Physicians were quicker to perform nonemergency appendectomies. Hernia operations and simple surgery on the stomach, intestines, liver, and kidneys became more feasible.[143]

These accomplishments raised the general status of physicians, but paradoxically also increased their vulnerability to dissatisfied patients. By the first decade of the twentieth century patients were suing their physicians for surgically related offenses such as leaving sponges, broken needles, or drainage tubes in closed incisions. Ignorance of deadly surgical shock, as well as other mysteries, however, blunted surgical daring and progress. Therefore, the frequency of surgical procedures and the certainty of regular success remained low. General surgery cases would not surpass orthopedics as the most common source of malpractice suits until the 1940s.[144] By then, physicians had solved some of the problems associated with operative shock and infection, advanced surgery further, and helped create the impression that many procedures were routine.

The speed of medical innovation created opportunities, dilemmas, and dangers for physicians. Advancements increased the medical community's status, but they also intensified expectations and demands. Doctors who attempted new, nonstandard procedures did so at their own peril. A physician who practiced in the late nineteenth century noted in his memoirs that "[t]he surgeon who is advancing his profession with new work stands at all times over the muzzle of a loaded gun hoping that no lawyer will come along to pull the trigger."[145] In the early 1880s one woman sued a physician after an operation, claiming that the carbolic acid solution, intended as a sterilizing agent, had complicated her injury.[146] The physician, who had apparently attempted to keep pace with enlightened practice, instead found himself in court.

At the same time new procedures surfaced and were accepted faster than many physicians could assimilate them. In 1886 a physician used chloroform to sedate a young girl on whom he was performing eye surgery. During the operation, the patient flinched, and the surgeon's knife blinded her. The girl's parents sued, claiming that standard practice demanded the use of cocaine as a local anesthetic in similar operations. The physician had consulted an 1880 treatise on eye surgery that prescribed chloroform; in 1884, however, a German surgeon, for the first time, had successfully employed cocaine anesthetic in the same procedure. By 1886, when the surgery took place, cocaine had already superseded general anesthetic as the accepted analgesic in such operations.[147] Physicians could be penalized for adopting a new practice too soon, but they were also under immense pressure, intellectually, professionally, and legally, to keep pace with rapidly evolving medical technology.

Willhelm Röentgen, a German researcher discovered the power of x-rays in November 1895. The inexpensive and simple construction of the device put it in the hands of many American physicians within weeks. Physicians as well as the public not only appreciated the invention's intrinsic interest but also immediately realized its diagnostic and jurisprudential potential.[148] One optimistic writer declared that "[t]he courts can show endless histories of grave errors committed, to the detriment of poor patients and not the less of poor practitioners; but the discovery of William Conrad Röentgen has come to do away with all of this." Another observer predicted in early 1896 that x-rays would play a leading role in "cases where surgeons are charged with having

overlooked a fracture, or dislocation, where no such injury is present."
Many writers, as early as 1897, recommended its use in every orthopedic case.[149] They were partially correct. Radiological evidence
often convinced juries that physicians had acted properly.

X-ray technology, however, proved a mixed blessing for malpractice defendants. By 1896, less than a year after the discovery, patients
were suing physicians for failing to take x-rays before fracture treatment.[150] In 1897 a writer for the *American X-Ray Journal* realized, "If it
increases our diagnostic ability it also increases our responsibilities,
and we are more exposed to suits for malpractice in fractures, particularly if deformity exits and we have not used it as a means of diagnosis." Other patients and their attorneys secured x-rays as evidence of a
physician's incompetence. Novelty x-ray studios, which pandered to
public curiosity, often provided the photographs for dissatisfied patients and their lawyers. One physician claimed in 1899, "Ever since
its discovery, especially in the last year, every malicious person who
can scrape up enough money for a shadow-graph [x-ray] is having one
taken for the purpose of bringing a damage suit for personal injuries or
malpractice."[151] The first x-rays introduced into a Maine court were
supplied by the plaintiff in a malpractice case. A music teacher in
Bangor claimed that her physician had failed to treat a backward
dislocation of her forearm properly. After examining an x-ray, three
expert witnesses agreed that the injury had not been properly treated.
The jury found the physician guilty and charged him $500.[152]

X-ray results, especially from the early equipment, were often distorted, inconclusive, and vulnerable to subjective interpretation by
"innovative attorneys." The reliability and objectivity of x-ray evidence depended on the angle of the photograph, the thickness of the
flesh surrounding the bone, the quality of the plate, and the length of
the exposure. Fractures could exist without x-rays' revealing evidence
of the injury. Conversely, enterprising lawyers soon discovered that
merely flexing one's muscles could severely distort results and simulate
injuries.[153]

Primitive machines, rudimentary knowledge, and inexperienced op-
erators led to burned patients and provided another source of malpractice suits. Burns could be induced by excessive electric current or
duration of exposure, frequent repetition, or individual differences of

sensitivity. In October 1897 a patient sued a physician after an x-ray machine produced "a severe dermatitis." The physician was attempting to locate a foreign object lodged in the patient's body. The patient's attorney claimed that the physician had been careless and that the technology was insufficiently developed to use for this purpose.[154] In less than five years after its discovery x-ray technology evolved from a promising medical and legal tool, to a source of suits when physicians failed to use it, to a cause of suits when it injured patients. X-rays and other more sophisticated technology would play a much larger role in malpractice litigation in the twentieth century.

Malpractice suits between 1865 and 1900 invoked the same legal doctrine, followed the same patterns, and provoked many of the same responses as they had in the prewar years. Appellate judges fine-tuned traditional common law doctrine to create a standard that would last into the next century. Technological advancement and professional relations had begun to change the character of the phenomenon. Physicians still blamed poor, resentful patients for their woes, but they discovered a new villain: the lawyer. More tightly organized medical societies, with the newly ratified locality rule, were able to limit the use of malpractice litigation as an intraprofessional, competitive weapon. By 1900 American medicine was on the eve of therapeutic and social respectability. As the scope of medical practice widened, the type of suits changed, hinted at the future, and provided a preview of the twentieth century.

CHAPTER 9

Conclusion

Malpractice suits became a prominent and permanent feature of American medical life in the 1840s. A combination of immediate, short-term causes and underlying, long-term developments explain the first dramatic increase in the litigation. Although the short-term, inciting factors disappeared, new technological, social, professional, and legal factors arose to take their place in generating suits. Moreover, the long-term cultural preconditions for the suits matured, allowing and even encouraging a broader segment of society to sue for a wider range of misfortunes.

Physicians' declining status in the first half of the century provided the context for the initial malpractice "crisis." Poor, uneven, and disorganized medical education left physicians ill prepared to deal with the complexities of the human body. The notoriously low quality of medical training aggravated the profession's declining status. Ironically, segments of the public in Jacksonian America distrusted physicians both for their poor education and for possessing any education at all. The prevailing spirit of the period glorified the virtues of native intelligence and common sense and derided formal education and the authority of experts. These sentiments formed the basis for the antiprofessional feeling that pervaded the age. In the socially and politically increasingly egalitarian country, the public resented any quasi-aristocratic trappings of economic or social privilege. Physicians who had hoped to rely on licensure to improve the state of the profession antagonized large segments of the population who believed in the merits and morality of free and open competition.

Competition among regular physicians also played a central role in the initial increase in litigation. The weak and ultimately nonexistent medical licensure laws of the Jacksonian period swelled the ranks of physicians. Dozens of medical schools with low educational standards graduated thousands of practitioners to compete for patients and fees. Intraprofessional competition engendered suits in two ways. Individual physicians were willing to denigrate the therapeutic practices of their medical competitors to improve their own position. Open criticism sometimes encouraged patients to sue their physicians.

When physicians appeared as expert witnesses in malpractice trials, they often exaggerated their own abilities and results of their treatments while implicitly demeaning the defendant's performance. Other physicians used malpractice suits as a competitive weapon against potential competitors. They explicitly encouraged patients to sue rivals. Occasionally these attacks generated retaliatory suits. When rival practitioners testified as expert witnesses, they were in a particularly strategic position to attack their competitors. Although local, state, and national medical societies existed at midcentury, they did not have sufficient influence or coercive power to limit physician complicity effectively in malpractice prosecutions.

Dramatic technological advances also contributed to the rise in malpractice litigation. At the beginning of the nineteenth century amputation served as the standard treatment for severe fractures and dislocations. These cases generated few malpractice suits in the first third of the century. By 1840 physicians had learned to save seriously injured limbs that would have previously been amputated. These improvements inspired inflated expectations in both physicians and patients. Many professionals and laypeople characterized orthopedic practice as a mechanical task with predictable, standard results. However, badly injured limbs, though saved, seldom healed perfectly. These cases constituted the bulk of the malpractice suits in the nineteenth century.

While antiprofessional sentiment, low educational standards, intraprofessional rivalry, and technological development were central components in the increase of suits in the Jacksonian period, the mere existence of these factors would not have generated suits without the accompanying appearance of three interrelated cultural preconditions. First, although community life had been evolving for at least a century, traditional community customs inhibiting litigation weakened in many parts of the country. This change occurred in different parts of the country at different rates, but by the mid–nineteenth century it allowed a larger number of individuals to resort to courts for redress of personal injuries.

Second, Americans began to change their attitudes toward divine providence and misfortune. While many individuals retained the notion of God working through history, they abandoned the idea of special or direct providence. Progressively fewer individuals believed that God willed every event that occurred on earth. An absolute belief that God ordained every occurrence precluded a search for earthly causes and earthly culprits. By the 1840s a large number of Americans had shifted their beliefs and were free to look for remedies in reforms and in courts. General secularizing trends, perfectionist impulses of northern evangelicals, and advancements in industry, transportation, and science combined to give society a new faith in the possibility and probability of progress. Finally, an increasingly mechanistic, interventionist view of the world, along with various social changes, introduced a new view of the body. Individuals from a wide spectrum of society became conscious of their bodies as "things" and grew progressively more concerned with pursuing physical well-being. Consequently, as optimism and expectations grew, patient intolerance for imperfect results increased, and patients began to sue physicians far more frequently for less severe injuries.

Transformed attitudes toward the body, providence, and the community were the result of long-term, continuous developments and are the preconditions of modern medical malpractice. These factors allowed more frequent litigation, but they did not directly cause its dramatic increase in the early 1840s. If the immediate causes of antiprofessional sentiment, low educational standards, and intraprofessional competition had not existed in Jacksonian America, malpractice suits would have increased slowly as a result of the underlying cultural developments. The immediate causes were a match to a fuse. They account for the dramatic jump in rates, but not for the widespread acceptability of suing for personal injuries. In areas of the country such as the antebellum South, where the immediate factors existed but the cultural preconditions did not, suits remained rare.

In the last half of the century and beyond, many of the inciting agents present in the Jacksonian period disappeared. Medical education slowly improved, state legislatures reinstituted licensure, and medical societies were able to blunt the malevolent effects of intraprofessional competition. But suits continued. New aggravating factors arose to provoke litigation. As Americans lost some of their antipathy toward professionals, a class-based resentment toward physicians gradually merged with the status-based resentment that had characterized attitudes of the first half of the century. A slowly increasing population of lawyers and more frequent use of contingency fee arrangements gave a greater number of dissatisfied patients access to legal remedies.

Rapidly advancing medical technology routinized more treatments, raised expectations and demands, and provided the basis for more suits. Beginning in the early twentieth century, newly introduced medical discoveries yielded continual practical improvements in treatments. Bacteriological science contributed both preventative and curative remedies for a parade of dread diseases, including diphtheria, cholera, malaria, gonorrhea, and influenza. Nutritional advances, especially the identification of vitamins, destroyed the endemic threat of disorders such as scurvy, rickets, beri-beri, and pellegra. The field of pharmacy blossomed, and in the 1930s and 1940s scientists produced the "miracle" sulfonamide drugs and penicillin. Surgery, which was only beginning to show promise in the 1890s, became common in the first half of the twentieth century with the control of shock, hemorrhage, and greater weapons against wound infection. Since the 1940s discoveries in immunology, heredity, molecular biology, and chemistry as well as the development of a pantheon of diagnostic and therapeutic technologies have profoundly increased the capabilities of modern medicine.[1]

The tremendous advances in medical science and practice have had a paradoxical impact on the origins of malpractice suits. Therapeutic progress as well as steady improvement of the medical education system have inspired deep public respect for physicians, and their status has risen dramatically.[2] Consequently, one of the inciting causes of suits in the antebellum era—low public esteem—has been virtually eliminated. Suits, however, have continued because low status was only a secondary, aggravating cause of the litigation in a specific historical period. Other sources of resentment toward physicians have remained. Moreover, the highly visible successes of twentieth-century medicine have created higher expectations in both physicians and the public, much in the same way that improvements in antebellum fracture treatment produced inflated predictions of regular, complete cures. Higher expectations have bred higher demands and greater dissatisfaction when treatments fail.

The cultural developments that had made suits more acceptable in the Jacksonian period neither disappeared nor remained static. Instead they ripened. There is evidence that relatively homogeneous, stable, community environments continued to slow the use of law to settle conflicts, especially for personal injuries, well into the twentieth century.[3] But shared communal values and the power of public opinion over individual action only decreased as the decades passed.

It is impossible and unnecessary to identify any one period as the fundamental break with communal life. The movement from insular communities to individualism and pluralism has been a long process. This transformation has occurred in different regions at different rates. In most areas, however, a variety of factors has overwhelmed the insular community. The rise of the national corporation has tied the fates of individual communities with the outside world. Continuing developments in transportation and communication have made both people and ideas more mobile, and immigration from other countries has diversified the composition of cities and towns. Finally, increased urbanization and the growth of urban populations have made American life progressively more anonymous. As historian David Potter puts it, by the mid–twentieth century "the solidarity of communities was fractured, their cohesion was diluted, and their power over individuals was but a shadow of what it had been."[4] As a result, most cities and towns have gradually lost the consensus and structures that slowed suits in the eighteenth and early nineteenth centuries.

Similarly, American attitudes toward the role of God in the world have continued to evolve. By the late nineteenth century more Americans were replacing their acceptance of "providence" with a faith in "progress."[5] Scientific and material advancements from late in the century to the present have given Americans good reason to expect ongoing improvement both socially and personally. While the notion of providence still plays a role in the lives of many individuals, its nature has been altered and its potency profoundly diluted. People are much more likely to depend on government agencies, reformers, or scientists to cure the ills of the world than they are to expect divine rescue. Southern culture continued to espouse traditional Christian notions regarding God's actions on earth, but there too the idea has weakened.

Americans have also continued to become more materialistic and increasingly concerned with physical well-being. An attorney discussing malpractice litigation in 1889 suggested that some of the blame for the suits should be attributed to "the materialistic tendency of modern days."[6] His comment reflected the heightened late nineteenth-century preoccupation with health and the body. The 1890s brought an enthusiasm for physical culture that surpassed that of the pre–Civil War period. Even more individuals viewed the human form as a mechanical entity susceptible to manipulation and alteration. This attitude was expressed in the late-century expansion and institutionalization of exercise and sports and the new popularity of outdoor activities, bicycling, and body building.[7] Health reformers built on mechanistic antebellum conceptions of the body and worked for and promised physical soundness.

Since the late nineteenth century a variety of popular movements progressively elevating the importance of health and physical appearance in the American mind has surfaced.[8] These trends, especially in the twentieth century, have been given added impetus by the values generated by modern advertising and the abundance of consumer culture.[9] Religious transformations, scientific and material progress, and the comforts of a growing consumer society have led to what one author describes as a "therapeutic ethos—the fretful preoccupation with preserving secular well-being."[10] While most eighteenth- and early nineteenth-century Americans worried first about the soundness of their soul, a growing segment of the population has put a higher premium on physical and psychic health and pleasure. Indeed, in the twentieth century Americans' pursuit of comfort, pleasure, and physical well-being is often characterized by a quasireligious dedication. Ironically, this transformed attitude does not always inspire greater care of the body; but it has made some individuals more confident that something can be done to cure their ills and less patient when failure occurs.

One historian has argued that Americans in the twentieth century have come to expect something akin to a system of "total justice" in many areas of the law. In some respects general tort law moved from a notion of no liability without a demonstration of fault early in the nineteenth century, to a form of absolute liability represented by workers' compensation laws by 1900. A similar movement is suggested by the history of contributory negligence. The doctrine was slowly undercut by the introduction of comparative negligence, which allowed individuals to gain awards even if they were partially responsible for their own injuries. In numerous other fields, from civil rights and constitutional law to government regulation and the creation of the welfare state, legal doctrine and practice have moved toward a posture of greater access to wider remedies for personal and social misfortune and wrongs. This tendency in policy and practice has helped provide fair treatment where there used to be discrimination and relief where there used to be suffering. Like the profound advances in material culture, it has also given rise to higher expectations and greater anticipation of social success and personal health.[11]

The continuation and intensification of the cultural trends first clearly visible in the years before the Civil War help explain the persistent expansion in the range and number of malpractice suits in late nineteenth- and twentieth-century America. In addition, a legal system that provides access and availability to virtually every inhabitant and a medical system that constantly promises grander achievements and better health have influenced twentieth-century malpractice rates. While Americans may devise methods to slow or discourage suits, it is unlikely that they wish to stifle the medical advancement or legal traditions that have contributed to malpractice litigation. And no reform, no matter how ingenious, can reverse the long-term cultural trends that underlie the suits.

Abbreviations

ABFRJ	*American Bar Foundation Research Journal*
AHR	*American Historical Review*
AJLH	*American Journal of Legal History*
AJMS	*American Journal of Medical Science*
AJPH	*American Journal of Public Health*
AJS	*American Journal of Sociology*
ALJ	*Albany Law Journal*
AMM	*American Medical Monthly*
AP	*American Practitioner*
AtlM	*Atlantic Monthly*
BHM	*Bulletin of the History of Medicine*
BMSJ	*Boston Medical and Surgical Journal*
BufMJMR	*Buffalo Medical Journal and Monthly Review*
BufMSJ	*Buffalo Medical and Surgical Journal*
CH	*Church History*
CM	*Connecticut Medicine*
CS	*Christian Spectator*
DPLR	*DePaul Law Review*
DTMJ	*Daniel's Texas Medical Journal*
For	*Fortune*
Gym	*Gymnasium*
Har	*Harper's*
HCR	*Hastings Center Report*
HTR	*Harvard Theological Review*
IMH	*Indiana Magazine of History*
JAAR	*Journal of American Academy of Religion*
JAH	*Journal of American History*
JAMA	*Journal of the American Medical Society*
JHMAS	*Journal of the History of Medicine and Allied Sciences*

JISHS	*Journal of the Illinois State Historical Society*
JLH	*Journal of Legal History*
JLM	*Journal of Legal Medicine*
JLP	*Journal of Legal Pluralism*
JMCS	*Journal of Medicine and Collateral Sciences*
JPH	*Journal of Presbyterian History*
JSH	*Journal of Sports History*
JSocH	*Journal of Social History*
JSJ	*Justice System Journal*
LHR	*Law and History Review*
LSR	*Law and Society Review*
MassR	*Massachusetts Review*
MA	*Mid-America*
MCMMS	*Medical Communications of the Massachusetts Medical Society*
ME	*Medical Examiner*
MLR	*Modern Law Review*
MNL	*Medical News and Library*
MRep	*Medical Reporter*
MSR	*Medical and Surgical Reporter*
MT	*Medical Times*
MVHR	*Mississippi Valley Historical Review*
NEJM	*New England Journal of Medicine*
NEQ	*New England Quarterly*
NHJM	*New Hampshire Journal of Medicine*
NMSJ	*Northwestern Medical and Surgical Journal*
NOMSJ	*New Orleans Medical and Surgical Journal*
NYH	*New York History*
NYJM	*New York Journal of Medicine*
NYJMCS	*New York Journal of Medicine and Collateral Sciences*
NYMPJ	*New York Medical and Physical Journal*
NYSJM	*New York State Journal of Medicine*
OMSJ	*Ohio Medical and Surgical Journal*
PAAS	*Proceedings of the American Antiquarian Society*
PBM	*Perspectives in Biology and Medicine*
PSI	*Physician's and Surgeon's Investigator*
PSM	*Popular Science Monthly*
RAH	*Reviews in American History*
SA	*Scientific American*
Scal	*Scalpel*
SCLR	*South Carolina Law Review*
SLR	*Stanford Law Review*
SR	*Sewanee Review*
StLMSJ	*St. Louis Medical and Surgical Journal*
TAMA	*Transactions of the American Medical Society*

TLQ	*Temple Law Quarterly*
TM	*Texas Medicine*
TOMS	*Transactions of the Ohio Medical Society*
TRBM	*Texas Reports on Biology and Medicine*
TSMSNY	*Transactions of the State Medical Society of New York*
VLR	*Virginia Law Review*
VMHB	*Virginia Magazine of History and Biography*
WJMPS	*Western Journal of Medical and Physical Science*
WJMS	*Western Journal of Medicine and Surgery*
WL	*Western Lancet*
WMSJ	*Western Medical and Surgical Journal*

Representative Malpractice Awards, 1835–1865

Source	Awards
"Excision of Tonsils," *BMSJ* 28 (15 February 1843):29–33	$100
"Trial for Malpractice," *BMSJ* 31 (22 January 1845):43–45	$275
"Case of False Aneurism—Action for Malpractice," *BMSJ* 35 (12 August 1846):43–45	$275
Dan Brainard, "Another Prosecution for Malpractice," *JMCS* 3 (November 1846):406–7	$300
Howard v. Grover 28 Me. 97 (1847)	$2,025
Alden March, "Prosecutions for Mal-Practice," *ME* 10 (1847):502–5	$450
"Surgical Malpractice," *BMSJ* 36 (5 May 1847):283–85	$2,500
"Prosecutions for Mal-Practice in the State of N. York," *BMSJ* 36 (14 July 1847):477–80	$450
"Trial for Mal-Practice in Pennsylvania," *BMSJ* 37 (15 September 1847):141–42	$30
"Trial for Malpractice. *Francis Bugard* v. *George Gross*," *BMSJ* 37 (22 September 1847):162–64	$1,000

The figures represent the damage awards. Losing defendants were generally also charged for court costs. Some of these awards may have been increased, reduced, or overturned on retrial or on appeal. Where available, the subsequent award is included parenthetically.

"Trial for Malpractice, and One Thousand Dollars Damages," *BufMJMR* 3 (1847–1848):145–48	$1,000
Walter K. Manning, "Prosecutions for Malpractice," *BMSJ* 40 (23 May 1849):318–19	$362.50
"Suit for Malpractice," *NWMSJ* 6 (1849–1850):227–30	$200
"Trial for Mal-Practice," *BMSJ* 41 (17 October 1849):216–19	$500
"Trial for Malpractice in Surgery," *BMSJ* 2 (January 1850): 213–22	$200
William M. Wood, "A Statement of two Suits for Malpractice, tried in November and December, 1850, in the Court of Erie County, Pa.," *AJMS* 22 (July 1851):43–50	$1,400; $500
McCandless v. McWha 22 Penn. 261 (1853)	$850 ($500)
"Prosecution for Mal-Practice," *BMSJ* 48 (4 May 1853):281–83	$1,675
Leighton v. Sargent 7 Foster 460 (N.H. 1853)	$1500
Twombly v. Leach 6 Mass. 397 (1853)	$300
"Trial for Malpractice—Dr. Crosby's Acquittal," *BMSJ* 50 (21 June 1854):424–25	$900
"A Surgical Case of Mal-Practice," *BMSJ* 51 (8 November 1854):289–97	$1,500 ($525)
"The Greenpoint Malpractice Case," *Scal* 8 (April 1856):311–25	$2,500 ($3,000)
"Report on the Difficulties Growing Out of alleged Mal-Practice in the Treatment of Fractures," *TOMS* 11 (1856):53–66.	$150; $100; $300; $1,200
"Case of a Trial for Malpractice," *BMSJ* 61 (19 March 1857):148	$1,000
"Alleged Malpractice," *BMSJ* 62 (31 May 1860):364–65	$120
Woodward v. Hancock 1 *Quarterly Law Review* 385 (1860–1)	$500
"Malpractice," *BMSJ* 66 (24 July 1862):524	$300

Representative Malpractice Awards, 1865–1900

Source	Awards
Teft v. Wilcox 6 Kan. 460 (1870)	$2,900
John J. Reese, "Case of Alleged Malpractice," *MT* 1 (1 December 1870):73–74	$1,359.70
W. F. Hutchinson, "A Recent suit for Malpractice," *BufMSJ* 12 (1872–1873):290–99	$4,000
Smothers v. Hanks 34 Iowa 287 (1872)	$2,000
Almond v. Nugent 34 Iowa 300 (1872)	$2,000
Kendall v. Brown 74 Ill. 232 (1874)	$1,375.17
Getchell v. Hill 21 Minn. 464 (1875)	$4,000
Weger v. Calder 78 Ill. 275 (1875)	$1,500
Musser v. Chase 29 Ohio 577 (1876)	$3,000
McKehoe v. Hall (pre-1877), McClelland, *Civil Malpractice*, 261–69	$800
Young v. Fullerton (pre-1877), McClelland, *Civil Malpractice*, 253–56	$1,000

The figures represent the damage awards. Losing defendants were generally also charged for court costs. Some of these awards may have been increased, reduced, or overturned on retrial or appeal.

Means v. Hallam & Barns (pre-1877), McClelland, *Civil Malpractice*, 176–80 — $1,000

"An Outrageous Suit for Malpractice," *BMSJ* 99 (28 November 1878):700–704 — $4,916.67

Brooke v. Clarke 57 Tx. 1905 (1882) — $5,000

Kelsey v. Hey 84 Ind. 189 (1882) — $4,000

"Some Recent Malpractice Suits," *MR* 28 (19 December 1885):690–91 — $7,000

Quinn v. Higgins 63 Wisc. 664 (1885) — $1,600

Hyrne v. Erwin 23 S.C. 226 (1885) — $1,000

E. J. Doering, "Mutual Protection against Blackmail," *JAMA* 6 (1886):114–17 — $4,480

Gates v. Fleisher 67 Wisc. 504 (1886) — $350

Holtzman v. Hoy 118 Ill. 534 (1886) — $2,500

Reber v. Herring 115 Penn. 599 (1887) — $900

Graves v. Santway 6 N.Y. Supp. 892 (1889) — $500

Sanderson v. Holland 39 Mo. App. 233 (1889) — $1,000

F. J. Groner, "The Causes and the Remedies for Suits for Malpractice," *MR* 37 (9 August 1890):143–44 — $1,000

Langford v. Jones 18 Ore. 307 (1890) — $1,000

Stevenson v. Gelsthorpe 10 Mont. 563 (1891) — $500

Link v. Sheldon 136 N.Y. App. 1 (1892) — $4,000

Lewis v. Dwinell 84 Me. 497 (1892) — $450

Peck v. Hutchinson 88 Iowa 321 (1893) — $2,500

Carpenter v. McDavitt 53 Mo. App. 393 (1893) — $2,000

Cayford v. Wilbur 86 Me. 414 (1894) — $2,075

"Confidential Communications and Suits for Malpractice," *NYMJ* 60 (3 November 1894):576 — $1,500

Jackson v. Burnham 20 Colo. 533 (1895) — $5,000

"Verdict Against a Physician," *MR* 47 (12 January 1895):64 — $12,000

Hedin v. Minneapolis Medical & Surgical Inst. 62 Minn. 146 (1895) — $500

Eighmy v. Union Pacific Railway Co. 93 Iowa 538 (1895) — $1,500

Gores v. Graff 77 Wisc. 174 (1896) — $2,500

ℛotes

Preface

1. J. R. Weist, "Civil Malpractice Suits: How Can the Physician Protect Himself against Them?" *AP* 30 (1884):161.

2. Hubert Winston Smith, "Legal Responsibility for Medical Malpractice," *JAMA* 116 (1941):942–47, 2149–59, 2670–79, and *JAMA* 117 (1941):23–33.

3. Andrew Sandor, "The History of Professional Liability Suits in the United States," *JAMA* 163 (9 February 1957):459–66; Earl F. Rose, "Major Court Decisions that Have Influenced the Practice of Medicine," *TM* 72 (October 1976):90–96; Victor Gordon, "The Origin, Basis, and Nature of Medical Malpractice Liability," *CM* 35 (February 1971):73–77; Joseph C. Stetler, "The History of Reported Medical Professional Liability Cases," *TLQ* 30 (1957):366–83; E. A. Reed, "Understanding Tort Law: The Historical Basis of Medical Liability," *JLM* 5 (1977):50–53.

4. Louis B. Harrison, Melvin H. Worth, Jr., and Michael A. Carlucci, "The Development of the Principles of Medical Malpractice in the United States," *PBM* 29 (1985):41–72; Edward J. Larson, "Medicine, Physicians and Malpractice Law," Paper delivered to the American Association for the History of Medicine, Rochester, New York, 30 April–3 May 1986; and Joseph F. Sandusk, "Analysis of Professional Factors in Medical Malpractice Claims," *JAMA* 161 (2 June 1956):442–47, discuss malpractice in the twentieth century.

5. Chester Burns, "Malpractice Suits in American Medicine Before the Civil War," *BHM* 43 (1969):41–56; and Burns, "Medical Malpractice Law and the Public's Health in the United States During the Nineteenth Century," *Actes Proceedings, XXVIIIᶜ Congrès International d'Histoire de la Médecine* 1 (1982):75–77.

6. William Rothstein, *American Physicians in the Nineteenth Century* (Baltimore: Johns Hopkins University Press, 1972), 324.

7. Burns, "Malpractice Suits," 42.

8. See Gerald N. Grob, "The Social History of Medicine and Disease: Problems and Possibilities," *JSocH* 10 (1977):393–405; and Ronald L. Numbers, "The History of American Medicine: A Field in Ferment," *RAH* 10 (1982):245–52.

1. Before the Flood, 1790–1835

1. Landon v. Humphrey 9 Day 209 (Conn. 1832); "Alleged Mal-Practice," *BMSJ* 6 (21 March 1832):98–99. For an extended discussion of this case, see chapter 7.

2. Lawrence M. Friedman, *A History of American Law* (New York: Simon and Schuster, 1973), 282–83.

3. Hubert Winston Smith, "Legal Responsibility for Medical Malpractice," *JAMA* 116 (14 June 1941):2671; and Andrew A. Sandor, "The History of Professional Liability Suits in the United States," *JAMA* 163 (9 February 1957):465.

4. Even an incomplete search of antebellum medical journals uncovers a large percentage of the 243 expected suits using the 9:1 ratio and there were clearly many cases that journals did not report. See Bibliography.

5. "Prosecutions for Mal-Practice," *OMSJ* 13 (January 1861):253–60; Bliss v. Long 1 Wright 351 (Ohio 1833) and Grindle v. Rush 7 Ohio 123 (1836).

6. Drawn from Smith, "Legal Responsibility," 2672–73. A decade-by-decade tally: 1790–1800, 1 case; 1800–1810, 0 cases; 1810–1820, 1 case; 1820–1830, 0 cases; 1830–1840, 5 cases; 1840–1850, 3 cases; 1850–1860, 13 cases; 1860–1870, 25 cases; 1870–1880, 45 cases; 1880–1890, 47 cases; 1890–1900, 77 cases. For another useful pioneering study, see Chester R. Burns, "Malpractice Suits in American Medicine Before the Civil War," *BHM* 43 (1969):41–56.

7. Francis A. Walker, *A Compendium of The Ninth Census* (Washington, D.C.: GPO, 1872), 8–9, and *Abstract of the Eleventh Census: 1890* (Washington, D.C.: GPO, 1894), 3. The number of appellate decisions was calculated from Smith, "Legal Responsibility," 2672–73.

8. Figures drawn from Smith, "Legal Responsibility," 2672–73 (1790–1920 case counts); Sandor, "History of Professional Liability Suits," 461–63 (1920–1950 case counts); and Walker, *Compendium of The Ninth Census*, 8–9, for population statistics.

9. "Mal-Praxis in Midwifery," *BMSJ* 2 (9 June 1829):270 (France); "Malpraxis in Midwifery," *BMSJ* 3 (3 March 1830):50 (England); "Alleged Malpractice," *BMSJ* 6 (21 March 1832):98–9 (United States).

10. See Bibliography for citations

11. Sandra Cirincione, "The History of Medical Malpractice in New York State: A Perspective from the Publications of the Medical Society of New York," *NYSJM* 86 (July 1986):361–62.

12. While an increase in the number of medical journals may account for some of the increase in reported cases, as many as 74 journals had been founded by 1840. See James H. Cassedy, *Medicine and American Growth, 1800–1860* (Madison: University of Wisconsin Press, 1986), 66–67; and Henry Burnell Shafer, *The American Medical Profession, 1783–1850* (New York: AMS Press, 1968), 181–99, for a discussion of early nineteenth-century medical journals.

13. See Chester R. Burns, "Medical Ethics and Jurisprudence," in *The Education of American Physicians*, edited by Ronald L. Numbers (Berkeley: University of California Press, 1980), 273–89.

14. Theodoric R. Beck, *Elements of Medical Jurisprudence* (Albany: Webster and Skinner, 1823); and Joseph Chitty, *A Practical Treatise on Medical Jurisprudence* (London: Butterworth, 1834).

15. Chester R. Burns, "Medical Ethics in the United States Before the Civil War," Ph. D. dissertation (Johns Hopkins University, 1969), 140, 143. For more on antebellum writers and their neglect of the medical jurisprudence of malpractice, see the glowing testimonials to the first book-length treatise on the topic: John Elwell, *A Medico-Legal Treatise on Medical Malpractice and Medical Evidence* (New York: John S. Voorhis, 1860). The comments are printed before the preface in the first edition.

16. Timothy Walker, *Introduction to American Law, Designed as a First Book for Students* (Philadelphia: P. H. Nicklin and T. Johnson, 1837; reprint DACAPO Press, 1972), 467, 472.

17. Friedman, *History of American Law*, 88–89, 282–91. See also Charles Warren, *A History of the American Bar* (Boston: Little, Brown, 1911), 19–39, 325–41.

18. Friedman, *History of American Law*, 280.

19. William Blackstone, *Commentaries*, St. George Tucker's ed. (Philadelphia: William Birch Young and Abraham, 1803), 122–23.

20. For an extended and more detailed discussion of the legal aspects and development of malpractice law as well as its English origins, see chapter 7.

21. This quotation is from Landon v. Humphrey 9 Day 209 (Conn. 1832).

22. There was nothing unique in the jury's power to determine "questions of fact" in malpractice cases. This role was routine in other areas of Anglo-American law.

23. Burns, "Medical Ethics in the United States," 91–92.

24. Cross v. Guthery 1 Amer. Dec. 61 (Conn. 1794).

25. Idem.

26. "*Michael O'Neil v. Gerard Bancker*," *NYMPJ* 6 (1827):145–52. This case is discussed at length in chapter 5.

27. Bliss v. Long Wright 351 (Ohio 1833). A *nonsuit* results when a judge dismisses the charges after ruling that the plaintiff had no grounds for prosecution.

28. The words *guilt, conviction, defendant, plaintiff,* and *prosecutor* are now

the language of criminal law. In the nineteenth century they were also accept-able and commonly used terms in civil cases. I will use the nineteenth-century terminology throughout this work.

29. Grannis v. Branden 5 Day 260 at 261, 267 (Conn. 1812).

30. Bemus v. Howard 3 Watts 255–58 (Penn. 1834). See Grindle v. Rush 7 Ohio 123 (1836) for another pre-1835 amputation malpractice case.

31. Landon v. Humphrey 9 Day 209 (Conn. 1832).

32. Sumner v. Utley 7 Conn. 256 at 260 (1828). This was a slander case where a patient accused a physician of malpractice but did not file a formal charge.

33. James H. Cassedy, *American Medicine and Statistical Thinking, 1800–1860* (Cambridge: Harvard University Press, 1984), 9–10.

34. See chapter 4.

35. Charles Lowell, *An Authentic Report of a Trial before the Supreme Judicial Court of Maine for the county of Washington, June Term 1824, Charles Lowell v. John Faxon & Micajah Hawks Surgeons and Physicians In an Action of Trespass on the Case for Ignorant and Negligent Treatment with Observations on the Prejudices and Conduct of [Unreadable] in Regard to This Case* (Portland: Printed for the Author, 1826), 4, 9.

36. Ibid., 9–10.

37. Ibid., 4.

38. Ibid., 5, 18; James Adams, Jr., comp., *Report of a Trial of an Action, Charles Lowell Against John Faxon and Micajah Hawks Doctors of Medicine, Defendants for Malpractice in the Capacity of Physicians and Surgeons at the Superior Judicial Court of Maine Held at Machias for the County of Washington June, 1824 before the Hon. Nathan Weston* (Portland: Printed for James Adams, Jr., by David and Seth Paine, 1825), 7; John Collins Warren, *A Letter to the Hon. Isaac Parker, Chief Justice of the Supreme Court of Massachusetts, Containing Remarks on the Dislocation of the Hip Joint* (Cambridge: Hillard and Metcalf, 1826), 1, 6. For biographical information on Warren, see Howard Kelly, *A Cyclopedia of American Medical Biography: Comprising the Lives of Eminent Deceased Physicians and Surgeons, 1610–1900* (Philadelphia: W. B. Saunders, 1912), 2:478; and Henry K. Beecher and Mark D. Altschule, *Medicine at Harvard: The First Three Hundred Years* (Hanover: University Press of New England, 1977), 35–39.

39. Warren, *A Letter*, 7–9.

40. Ibid.

41. Lowell, *Authentic Report*, 5, 18; and Adams, *Report of a Trial*, 7.

42. Lowell, *Authentic Report*, 6–7; Adams, *Report of a Trial*, 5.

43. Adams, *Report of a Trial*, 10–30. For Warren's testimony, see ibid., 12–13, 15, 23–25.

44. Kelly, *American Medical Biography*, 388–89; Lowell, *Authentic Report*, 15; Adams, *Report of a Trial*, 33–36.

45. Lowell, *Authentic Report*, 18, 20; Adams, *Report of a Trial*, 110.

46. Adams, *Report of a Trial*, 49–50, 52–53, 71.

47. Ibid., 48, 74, 99.

48. Ibid., 97.

49. Ibid., 86–95, 100–101.

50. Ibid., 112–22.

51. Lowell, *Authentic Report*, 29 pp.; Adams, *Report of a Trial*, 117 pp.; and Warren, *A Letter*, 142 pp.

52. Lowell, *Authentic Report*, 7, 18.

53. Eugene F. Sanger, "Report on Malpractice," *BMSJ* 100 (9 January 1879):41–50.

54. The newspaper article is excerpted in Warren, *A Letter*, 138.

55. Ibid., 15, 58.

56. Ibid., 1, 11, 12, 16.

57. Rowland Berthoff, *An Unsettled People: Social Order and Disorder in American History* (New York: Harper and Row, 1971), 177–295. The impact of this social transformation on law and litigation is analyzed in chapters 5 and 7.

58. Most legal writers trace the origins of the locality rule to the 1870s and 1880s, but it is clear that the doctrine was employed much earlier. For comments on the locality rule and medical malpractice, see Jon R. Waltz, "The Rise and Gradual Fall of the Locality Rule in Medical Malpractice Litigation," *DPLR* 17 (1969):408–21; David D. Armstrong, "Medical Malpractice—The 'Locality Rule' and the 'Conspiracy of Silence,' " *SCLR* 22 (1970):811–21; Carleton Chapman, *Physicians, Ethics, and the Law* (New York: New York University Press, 1984), 96. See chapters 2 and 8 for more on the locality rule.

59. Adams, *Report of a Trial*, 51.

60. Stephen Smith, "[Review of John Elwell's *A Medico-Legal Treatise on Malpractice and Medical Evidence* 1860]," *AJMS* 40 (July 1860):158–59.

61. Adams, *Report of a Trial*, 100.

62. Lowell, *Authentic Report*, 6, 7.

63. The increased supply of physicians and their impact on malpractice is discussed in chapter 3.

64. Lowell, *Authentic Report*, 18.

65. For a discussion of the transformation of attitudes toward providence and its role in the malpractice epidemic, see chapter 5.

66. Adams, *Report of a Trial*, 52.

67. James Thomas Flexner, *Doctors on Horseback: Pioneers of American Medicine* (New York: Dover, 1969), 115–18.

2. *The Deluge, 1835–1865*

1. "Accusation of Mal-Practice," *BMSJ* 31 (11 September 1844):123–24.

2. "Reviews," *WJMPS* 28 (1853):309.

3. Frank H. Hamilton, "Suits for Malpractice in Surgery: Their Causes and Their Remedies," *Papers Read before the Medico-Legal Society of New York, 1875–1878* (New York: Medico-Legal Society of New York, 1886), 98.

4. John Elwell, *A Medico-Legal Treatise on Malpractice and Medical Evidence* (New York: John S. Voorhis, 1860), 83.

5. See chapter 1.

6. [Alden March], "Case of Alledged *[sic]* Malpractice in Surgery," *BMSJ* 37 (4 August 1847):9–14.

7. "Prosecution for Malpractice," *ME* 14 (November 1851):728–29.

8. Worthington Hooker, *Physician and Patient: or, A Practical View of the Mutual Duties, Relations, and Interests of the Medical Profession and the Community* (New York: Baker and Scribner, 1849; facsimile reprint Arno Press, 1972), 277.

9. "Surgical Malpractice," *BMSJ* 36 (5 May 1847):283–84.

10. Hamilton quoted in Chester Burns, "Medical Ethics in the United States Before the Civil War," Ph.D. dissertation (Johns Hopkins University, 1969), 143.

11. "Accusation of Mal-Practice," *BMSJ* 31 (11 September 1844):123–24. The case, *Smith* v. *Goodyear & Hyde*, is the subject of the study in chapter 6.

12. "Report of Trial for Mal-Practice. *William Tims* v. *James P. White.* Supreme Court Erie County Circuit, June 26th, 1848," *BufMJMR* 4 (August 1848):135.

13. "Trial for Malpractice," *BufMJMR* 10 (1854–1855):569–70.

14. "Bibliographic Notices," *NYJM* (September 1853):272–75.

15. For examples of other New York cases from this period see: "Excision of the Tonsils," *BMSJ* 28 (15 February 1843):29–32; "Prosecutions for Mal-Practice in the State of New York," *ME* 10 (August 1847):502–5; "Trial for Malpractice, and One Thousand Dollars Damages," *BufMJMR* 3 (1847–1848):145–48; "Trial for Malpractice," *BufMJMR* 10 (1854–1855):568–70; "The Greenpoint Malpractice Case," *Scal* 8 (April 1856):311–15; and "Alleged Malpractice," *BMSJ* 62 (31 May 1860):364–65.

16. See chapters 3–5 for an exposition of these social and professional conditions.

17. For example, see *Gallaher* v. *Thompson* (1833) in Elwell, *Treatise on Malpractice*, 115–17; Bliss v. Long 1 Wright 351 (Ohio 1833); and Grindle v. Rush 7 Ohio 123 (1836).

18. S. P. Hildreth, "Trial for Mal-Practice in Surgery," *OMSJ* 2 (January 1850):213–22; and Arthur Merrill, "Mal-Practice in Surgery," *WL* 11 (1850):763–68.

19. "Report on Difficulties Growing Out of Alleged Mal-Practice in the Treatment of Fractures," *TOMS* 11 (1856):54. For examples of other Ohio cases in this period, see Theodore Nichols, "Trial for Mal-Practice," *OMSJ* 2 (September 1849):6–10; "Suit for Malpractice," *OMSJ* 2 (November 1849):161–63; Elwell, *Treatise on Malpractice* (four Ohio cases from the 1850s), 81–82,

146–62, 163–68; "Suit for Alleged Mal-Practice," *OMSJ* 10 (September 1857):13–24; "Important Case of Alleged Mal-Practice," *Scal* 9 (April 1857):54–57; "Suit for Alleged Mal-Practice," *OMSJ* 10 (May 1858):447–51; "*Terrence Mc Queeney v. W. W. Jones*. A Prosecution for Alledged [sic] Mal-Practice," *OMSJ* 12 (September 1859):22–24; "*Mary Ann Decrow, et al., v. H. H. Little*. A Prosecution for Alleged Mal-Practice," *OMSJ* 12 (January 1860):194–98; and John Dawson, "Suit for Damages in a Case of Fracture of the Leg," *OMSJ* 14 (July 1862):283–90.

20. "Prosecutions for Mal-Practice," *OMSJ* 13 (January 1861):253–60.

21. William M. Wood, "Thoughts on Suits for Malpractice, Suggested by Certain Judicial Proceedings in Erie County, Pennsylvania," *AJMS* 18 (October 1849):398; and Wood, "A Statement of Two Suits for Malpractice, Tried in November and December 1850, in the Court of Erie County, Pa.," *AJMS* 22 (July 1851):43–50.

22. "Extracts from the Report of the Committee on the Prevalence of Suits for Mal-Practice," *MNL* 8 (March 1850):17–20. For examples of other Pennsylvania cases from this period, see Mertz v. Detweiler 8 Watts 376–8 (1845); "Trial for Mal-Practice in Pennsylvania," *BMSJ* 37 (15 September 1847):141–42; Fowler v. Sargent 1 Grant's Cases 355 (1856); Isaac Lefever, "Report of a Trial for Malpractice in the Court of Common Pleas of Perry County, Pennsylvania," *AJMS* 48 (July 1864):72–86; "Trial for Mal-Practice," *AJMS* 12 (1865):555–58, 569–73; and Stephen Smith, *Doctor in Medicine and Other Papers on Professional Subjects* (New York: William Wood, 1872), 277–82.

23. "Prosecution of Mal-Practice," *BMSJ* 50 (21 June 1854):424–25. For examples of cases from New Hampshire and Vermont in this period, see "[Suit for malpractice]," *WMSJ* 28 (1853):346–47 (N.H.); "Suit for Mal-Practice," *BMSJ* 51 (8 November 1854):289–97 (N.H.); "Trial for Mal-Practice," *BMSJ* 51 (22 November 1854):345 (N.H.); "A Case of Alleged Mal-Practice," *BMSJ* 54 (24 April 1856):229–42 (N.H.); "Prosecution for Malpractice," *MRep* 8 (November 1855):522–29 (N.H.); "Trial for Mal-Practice," *BMSJ* 41 (17 October 1849):216–19 (Vt.): "Trial for Mal-Practice," *BMSJ* 41 (23 January 1850):500–502 (Vt.); "Suit for Mal-Practice in Vermont," *BMSJ* 44 (11 June 1851):377–88 (Vt.); "Trial for Mal-Practice," *BMSJ* 54 (20 March 1856), 129–38, *BMSJ* 54 (27 March 1856):149–56 (Vt.); "Malpractice," *BMSJ* 66 (24 July 1862):524 (Vt.); and Wilmot v. Howard 39 Vt. 447 (1863).

24. "Prosecution for Malpractice," *BMSJ* 30 (29 May 1844):344–45.

25. "Surgical Malpractice," *BMSJ* 36 (5 May 1847):283–84.

26. "Prosecution for Malpractice," *BMSJ* 48 (11 May 1853):304.

27. "Mal-practice," *BMSJ* 49 (26 October 1853):270.

28. "Case of Malpractice," *BMSJ* 54 (13 March 1856):109–12. For examples of other cases from Massachusetts in this period, see McClallen v. Allen 19 Pick. 333 (Mass. 1837); Worthington Hooker, *Physician and Patient*, 160–64; Walter K. Manning, "Prosecution for Mal-Practice," *BMSJ* 40 (23 May 1849):318–19; Walter K. Manning, "Trial for Mal-Practice," *BMSJ* 42 (27

February 1850):79–80; "Prosecution for Mal-Practice," *ME* 14 (November 1851):728–29; Moody v. Sabin 63 Mass. 505 (1852); Twombly v. Leach 65 Mass. 397–406 (1853); "Prosecution for Mal-Practice," *BMSJ* 48 (4 May 1853): 281–83; "Suit for Mal-Practice," *BMSJ* 50 (19 April 1854):246; "The 'Suit for Malpractice,' " *BMSJ* 50 (3 May 1854):287; "Prosecutions for Mal-Practice," *BMSJ* 51 (8 November 1854):305; "Another Suit for Mal-Practice," *BMSJ* 51 (17 January 1855):504; "Case of Mal-Practice," *BMSJ* 54 (13 March 1856):109–13; "Trial for Malpractice," *BMSJ* 55 (22 January 1857):515; and "Trial for Malpractice," *BMSJ* 56 (5 February 1857):9–26.

29. Hamilton, "Suits for Malpractice in Surgery," 98. Chapter 5, below, contains a short comment on the absence of widespread litigation in the nineteenth-century South.

30. "A Report of the Facts and Circumstances Relating to a Case of Compound Fracture, and Prosecution for Mal-Practice . . . ," *AJMS* 3 (January 1842):181–84.

31. [Frank] Hamilton, "Prosecution for Alledged [*sic*] Mal-Practice," *BufMJMR* 4 (1848–1849):274–77.

32. "Prosecution for Mal-Practice," *BMSJ* 48 (20 July 1853):503–4.

33. See chapter 4.

34. Elwell, *Treatise on Malpractice*, 55.

35. Steven Smith, "[Review of John Elwell's *Treatise on Malpractice*]," *AJMS* 40 (July 1860):162. Unfortunately, Smith did not provide the total number of cases used in his study. However, he noted that 142 cases represented a "little over two-thirds" of his total. Therefore, his study was drawn from approximately 213 cases. I have used this total in calculating these percentages.

36. These issues will be discussed further, and more fully, in chapter 4.

37. John Ordronaux, *The Jurisprudence of Medicine* (Philadelphia: T. and J. W. Johnson, 1869), 101.

38. Ibid., 101.

39. "Heroic Surgery: Extirpation of a Malignant Tumor from the Arm, Death the Next Day," *Scal* 2 (1850):121–22.

40. "Shocking Outrage on Professional Humanity," *Scal* 7 (January 1856):253–55.

41. "Gross Malpractice," *MSR* 22 (5 February 1870):121–22.

42. One physician, whose patient died after he had dosed her with cayenne pepper, wrapped her in kerosene-soaked blankets, and put her in a steam bath for three days, was acquitted under the Thomson doctrine. The Thomson case and its legacy is chronicled in Milo A. McClelland, *Civil Malpractice: A Treatise on Surgical Jurisprudence* (New York: Hurd and Houghton, 1877), 384–92.

43. Baker v. Bolton 1 Camp. 493 (1808); Wex Malone, *Essays on Torts* (Baton Rouge: Paul M. Herbert Law Center, Louisiana State University Press, 1986), 75–117; Richard Morris, *Studies in the History of American Law* (Philadelphia: J. M. Mitchell, 1959), 247–48; and Leonard Levy, *The Law of the Com-*

monwealth and Chief Justice Shaw (Cambridge: Harvard University Press, 1957), 156.

44. For example, in the 1793 Connecticut case Cross v. Guthery 1 Amer. Dec. 61 (Conn. 1793), a woman died after an inept breast amputation. Despite the English precedents and the objections of the defendant, the Connecticut superior court awarded the husband £40.

45. Wex Malone, "The Genesis of Wrongful Death," *SLR* 17 (July 1956):1043–76.

46. Shaw's key decisions included *Farwell* v. *Boston and Worcester R.R. Corp.* (1842) and *Brown* v. *Kendall* (1850). See, Levy, *Law of the Commonwealth*, 166–82; Lawrence M. Friedman and Jack Ladinsky, "Social Change and the Law of Industrial Accidents," *Columbia Law Review* 67 (1967):151–82.

47. Carey v. Berkshire R.R. 55 Mass. 475 (1848); Levy, *Law of the Commonwealth*, 155–65; and Malone, *Essays on Torts*, 79–91.

48. "Braunberger v. Cleis," in McClellend, *Civil Malpractice*, 127–45; and "Trial for Malpractice," *MSR* 12 (1865):555–59, 569–73.

49. McClelland, *Civil Malpractice*, 139–40, 145.

50. Hyatt v. Adams 16 Mich. 179 (1867).

51. Peter Davis, "Michigan's First Malpractice Case: Its Lessons Linger," *Journal of Legal Medicine* (June 1977):49–52. Although this is a good account of the details of the case, it is not the first malpractice case in Michigan as the title suggests, but only the first case appealed to the state supreme court.

52. Ibid., 51.

53. Hyatt v. Adams, 182.

54. Idem, 174.

55. Idem, 192.

56. Idem, 198.

57. "Report on the Difficulties Growing Out of Alleged Mal-Practice in the Treatment of Fractures," *TOMS*, 11 (1856):57–58.

58. "Suit for Alleged Malpractice," *OMSJ* 10 (1857–1858):13–24. The physician eventually won the case.

59. Alden March, "Prosecutions for Mal-Practice in the State of N. York," *BMSJ* 36 (14 July 1847):477–80.

60. A. B. Shipman, *A Report of the Facts and Circumstances Relating to a Case of Compound Fracture and Prosecution for Mal-Practice* (Cortlandville, N.Y.: Cortland Democrat, 1841).

61. See two cases described in "Report on the Difficulties Growing Out of Alleged Mal-Practice in the Treatment of Fractures," *TOMS*, 11 (1856):53–66.

62. Under strict application of the eighteenth-century writ system, prospective litigants would be forced to file an entirely separate action for malpractice. For discussion of the writ system see chapter 7.

63. Piper v. Menifee 51 Ky. 465 (1851).

64. Graham v. Gautier 21 Tex. 111 (1858). For examples of other malpractice suits that originated out of suit-for-fees, see Bellinger v. Craigue 31

Barbour 534 (N.Y. 1860); Akin v. Green (N.Y. circa 1850s), in Elwell, *Treatise on Malpractice*, 102–3; and *McClallen v. Adams* 19 Pick. 33 (Mass. 1837).

65. Alden March, "Case of Alleged Mal-Practice in Surgery," *BMSJ* 37 (4 August 1847):13.

66. Eugene Sanger, "Report on Malpractice," *BMSJ* 100 (2 January 1879):14–23; and Sanger, "Report on Malpractice," *BMSJ* 100 (9 January 1879):41–50. Sanger did not provide dates but noted that the suits and threats occurred within the "remembrance of the present generation."

67. Smith, "[Review of Elwell]," 153–66.

68. "Correction," *WMSJ* 32 (1855):50.

69. Ibid.

70. "Trial for Mal-Practice," *BMSJ* 54 (27 March 1856):156.

71. Samuel Parkman, "On the Relations of the Medical Witness with the Law and the Lawyer," *AJMS* 23 (January 1852):132.

72. "Report on the Difficulties Growing Out of Alleged Mal-Practice in the Treatment of Fractures," *TOMS*, 11 (1856):56.

73. "Alleged Malpractice," *BMSJ* 62 (31 May 1860):364–65.

74. Elwell, *Treatise on Malpractice*, 2.

75. "Trial for Malpractice," *BMSJ* 56 (5 February 1857):9–23; "Trial for Malpractice," *BMSJ* 55 (22 January 1857):515.

76. T. J. W. Pray, "Suits for Mal-Practice," *BMSJ* 51 (8 November 1854):297.

77. Alexis de Tocqueville, *Democracy in America*, translated by George Lawrence, edited by J. P. Mayer (Garden City, N.Y.: Doubleday, 1969), 263, 268.

78. See, for example, Perry Miller, ed., *The Legal Mind in America: From Independence to the Civil War* (Garden City, N.Y.: Doubleday, 1962), 238–84.

79. Elwell, *Treatise on Malpractice*, 44.

80. Competition's role in generating malpractice suits will be discussed in greater length in chapter 3.

81. In one Michigan case in the late 1840s a jury had granted the plaintiff $300 in damages for injuries that supposedly resulted when a physician failed to diagnose a dislocated arm immediately. A state appellate court judge granted the physician a new trial, but removed the case from the court and referred the complaint to two physician-arbitrators. The arbitrators reported to the chief justice of the state supreme court. They decided that although the dislocation was not discovered, it was a rare injury and in many cases was untreatable even if diagnosed. They recommended no award with both parties paying their own costs. The judge accepted their recommendation. See Dan Brainard, "Another Suit for Malpractice," *JMCS* 3 (November 1846):406. For another case of the anomalous use of referees, see "Trial for Mal-Practice," *BMSJ* 51 (November 1854):345.

82. See chapters 1 and 7 for discussion of common law writs.

83. For some history and impact of the civil procedure reforms, see Joseph H. Koffler and Alison Reppy, *Handbook of Common Law Pleading* (St. Paul:

West Publishing, 1969), 15, 22–29; Robert Wyness Millar, *Civil Procedure of the Trial Court in Historical Perspective* (New York: Law Center for New York University, 1952), 52–54; Edson R. Sunderland, *Cases on Procedure Annotated, Code Pleading* (Philadelphia: Callaghan, 1913), 1–23. Compare pleading requirements for malpractice before and after reforms, see Joseph Chitty, *A Practical Treatise on Pleading* (New York: C. Wiley, 1812), 92, 137–38; John Simcoe Saunders, *The Law of Pleading and Evidence in Civil Actions* (Philadelphia: Robert Small, 1844), 89–90, 109; and Conway Robinson, *The Practice of Courts of Justice* (Richmond: A. Morris, 1855), 394–95, 398–99.

84. See chapter 7 for a discussion of legal theory and the source of malpractice liability.

85. *Bliss v. Long* 1 Wright 351 at 352.

86. *Grindle v. Rush* 7 Ohio (Charles Hammond Reports 7) part 2, 123–25.

87. Mc Candless v. Mc Wha 22 Penn. 261 (1853) at 263–64, 267. Reynold v. Graves 3 Wisc. 416 (1853) is another of the rare examples in which a trial judge allowed a defendant/physician to be held responsible for an implied contract to cure. The decision against the physician, as with all similar cases, was overturned.

88. Landon v. Humhrey 9 Day 209, 216 (Conn. 1832).

89. Howard v. Grover 28 Me. 97, 101 (1848).

90. Ritchey v. West 23 Ill. 329, 330 (1860).

91. Francis Hillard, *The Law of Torts or Private Wrongs* (Boston: Little, Brown, 1859), 1:238–40; and Thomas G. Shearman and Amasa A. Redfield, *A Treatise on the Law of Negligence* (New York: Baker, Voorhis, 1870), 504–13.

92. Chapter 7 contains a discussion of state courts' use of English precedents.

93. Elwell, "Experts—Professional Opinions," in *Treatise on Malpractice*, 273; and John Ordronaux, *The Jurisprudence of Medicine in its relations to the Law of Contracts, Torts, and Evidence* (Philadelphia: T. and J. Johnson, 1869), 8–9, 27; Simon Greenleaf, *A Treatise on the Law of Evidence* (Boston: Charles C. Little and James Brown, 1842; reprint Arno Press, 1972), 153, 376, 488–91.

94. Bowman v. Woods 1 Iowa 441.

95. Idem, 442–43. Also see Patten v. Wiggin 51 Me. 594 (1862) for a ruling that held that physicians were to be judged by the standards of their school of practice only.

96. A preliminary paper prepared by James B. Speer suggests that irregular practitioners and physicians on the outside fringes of respectability were the most common victims of malpractice charges. Speer, "Malpractice: The Historical Viewpoint," in *Proceedings of the Malpractice Conference: The Interaction of Medicine and Justice Through Public Policy*, edited by Donnie J. Self (Eastern Virginia Medical School, Old Dominion University, 1976), 1–10. But my evidence, and nineteenth-century commentary, confirms the claim that irregulars were relatively immune to charges.

97. Wood, "Thoughts on Suits," 399.

98. Chapter 3 contains more discussion on the issue of intraprofessional rivalry.

99. Elwell, *Treatise on Malpractice*, 81, 146–62.

100. Ibid., 37. See also Elisha Bartlett, *An Inquiry into the Degree of Certainty in Medicine; and into the Nature and Extent of Its Power over Disease* (Philadelphia: Lea and Blanchard, 1848), excerpted and reprinted in Gert H. Brieger, ed., *Medical America in the Nineteenth Century: Readings from the Literature* (Baltimore: Johns Hopkins University Press, 1972), 115–27; Erwin H. Ackerknect, "Elisha Bartlett and the Philosophy of the Paris Clinical School," *BHM* 24 (January–February 1950):43–60; and Worthington Hooker, "Uncertainty of Medicine," in Hooker, *Physician and Patient*, 25–49.

101. See chapter 4 for discussion of fracture treatment.

102. Isaac Lefever, "Report on a Trial for Malpractice in the Court of Common Pleas of Perry County, Pennsylvania," *AJMS* 48 (July 1864):72–86.

103. [Justice], "The Late Suit for Mal-Practice in Delaware Co., N.Y.," *BMSJ* 37 (11 August 1847):35–37.

104. "Trial for Malpractice," *BufMJMR* 10 (1854–1855):570.

105. See chapter 1.

106. Smith, "[Review of Elwell]," 159.

107. Wood, "Thoughts on Suits," 400.

108. Elwell, *Treatise on Malpractice*, 22.

109. Ibid., 162.

110. Walter K. Manning, "Prosecution for Mal-Practice," *BMSJ* 40 (23 May 1849):318–19; "Trial for Malpractice," *BMSJ* 41 (10 October 1849):206; W. K. Manning, "Trial for Mal-Practice," *BMSJ* 42 (27 February 1850):79–80.

111. Henry Steele Commager, "The Nationalism of Joseph Story," in *The Bacon Lectures on the Constitution of the United States* (Boston: Boston University Press, 1953), 33–94; and R. Kent Newmyer, *Supreme Court Justice Joseph Story: Statesman of the Old Republic* (Chapel Hill: University of North Carolina Press, 1985), 154–235.

112. Gibbons v. Ogden 9 Wheaton 1 (1824); Wilson v. Blackbird Creek Marsh Co. 2 Peters 245 (1829); and Genessee Chief v. Fitzhugh 12 Howard 443 (1851).

113. Swift v. Tyson 16 Peters 1 (1842).

114. Morton J. Horwitz, *The Transformation of American Law, 1788–1860* (Cambridge: Harvard University Press, 1977), 160–211. See also chapter 7.

115. Story quoted in Horwitz, *Transformation*, 196–97.

116. The locality rule did not surface as a defensive tool for physicians until 1880, when state appellate courts began to rule that the doctrine set limits on the skill required of doctors. Small v. Howard 128 Mass. 131 (1880) is usually cited as the first appellate decision requiring the use of the locality rule. The acceptance of the locality rule by appellate courts is discussed in chapter 8.

117. "Trial for Malpractice," *BufMJMR* 10 (1854–1855):570.

118. "Correction," *WMSJ* 32 (July 1855):50.

119. "Legal Liabilities of Physicians and Surgeons," *BufMSJ* 5 (1865–1866):353–56.

120. "Mal-Practice," *OMSJ* 12 (November 1859):166–67.

121. Andrew A. Sandor, "The History of Professional Liability Suits in the United States," *JAMA* 163 (9 February 1957):459–66.

122. The only study of cases and convictions prepared in the nineteenth century was Eugene F. Sanger's review of physicians and malpractice in Maine. Sanger, "Report on Malpractice," *BMSJ* 100 (2 January 1879):14–23 and *BMSJ* 100 (9 January 1879):41–50.

123. Elwell, *Treatise on Malpractice*, 8.

124. "Prosecution for Mal-Practice," *BMSJ* 48 (20 July 1853):503–4; "Prosecution of Mal-Practice," *BMSJ* 50 (21 June 1854):424–25; and Dixi Crosby, comp., *Report of a Trial for Malpractice* [85 pp.] (Woodstock: Printed by Lewis Pratt, Jr., 1854).

125. T. J. W. Pray, "A Surgical Case of Malpractice," *BMSJ* 51 (8 November 1854):289–97; Leighton v. Sargent 7 Foster 460 (N.H. 1853); and Leighton v. Sargent 31 N.H. 39 (1855). There is a discussion of this case in another context in chapter 7.

126. "Case of Malpractice," *BMSJ* 54 (13 March 1856):109–12.

127. See appendix A.

128. Howard v. Grover 28 Me. 97 at 101 (1848).

129. "Trial for Mal-Practice in Pennsylvania," *BMSJ* 37 (15 September 1847):141–2.

130. Henry Burnell Shafer, *The American Medical Profession, 1783 to 1850* (New York: AMS Press, 1968), 166–68; and Paul Starr, "Medicine, Economy, and Society in Nineteenth-Century America," *JSocH* 10 (Summer 1977):602.

131. See Sandra Cirincione, "The History of Medical Malpractice in New York State: A Perspective from the Publications of the Medical Society of the State of New York," *NYSJM* 86 (July 1986):363–68 for comments on early group defense and insurance plans after 1900.

132. Theodore Nichols, "Trial for Mal-Practice," *OMSJ* 2 (September 1849):10.

133. "Prosecution for Mal-Practice," *OMSJ* 13 (January 1861): 253.

134. Ibid.

3. Schools for Scandal

1. "Extracts from the Report of the Committee on the Prevalence of Suits for Mal-Practice," *MNL* 8 (March 1850):17–20; "[Proceedings of the Kentucky Medical Society, October 1854]," *WJMS* 30 (November 1854):365–67; [S]amuel Parkman and Calvin P. Fiske, "Report on the Causes and Prevention of Suits

for Mal-Practice," *MCMMS* 8 (1853):appendix, 123–32; and "Report on Difficulties Growing Out of Alleged Mal-Practice in the Treatment of Fractures," *TOMS* 11 (1856):53–66.

2. "[The Status of Physicians]," *MSR* 11 (Jan. 1858):60–63.

3. Ibid., 62.

4. Alexander Y. P. Garnett, "Professional Standing; Its Decadence; the Cause; How to Be Remedied; Radicalism; Young America," *MSR* 7 (March 1854):99–100. For other comments on the declining status of physicians in the first half of the nineteenth century, see "The Status of Our Profession," *MSR* 11 (February 1858):133–36; "The Status of Our Profession," *MSR* 11 (March 1858):194–96; and O. H. Taylor, "On the Obvious Decline in the Respect of the Public for the Medical Profession in New Jersey with an Inquiry into Some of Its Causes," *MSR* 11 (July 1858):460–69.

5. Paul Starr, *The Social Transformation of American Medicine* (New York: Basic Books, 1982), 30–32.

6. Ibid., 32–37; and Joseph Kett, *The Formation of the American Medical Profession, 1780–1860* (New Haven: Yale University Press, 1968), 30–31; James H. Cassedy, "Why Self-Help? Americans Alone with their Diseases, 1800–1850," in *Medicine Without Doctors: Home Health Care in American History*, edited by Guenter B. Risse, Ronald L. Numbers, and Judith Walzer Leavitt (New York: Science History Publications, 1977), 31–47.

7. Cassedy, "Why Self-Help?" 31–47; Charles E. Rosenberg, "Medical Text and Social Context: Explaining William Buchan's *Domestic Medicine*," *BHM* 57 (1983):22–42; John Blake, "From Buchan to Fishbein: The Literature of Domestic Medicine," in *Medicine without Doctors*, 11–48; and John Harvey Young, *The Toadstool Millionaires: A Social History of Patent Medicines in America before Federal Regulation* (Princeton: Princeton University Press, 1961), 3–43.

8. Richard Harrison Shryock, *Medicine and Society in America: 1660–1860* (Ithaca: Cornell University Press, 1960), 67–72; and James H. Cassedy, *American Medicine and Statistical Thinking, 1800–1860* (Cambridge: Harvard University Press, 1984), 50–54.

9. Quoted in Martin Kaufman, *Homeopathy in America: The Rise and Fall of a Medical Heresy* (Baltimore: Johns Hopkins University Press, 1971), 2–3.

10. George J. Monroe, quoted in William G. Rothstein, *American Physicians in the Nineteenth Century* (Baltimore: Johns Hopkins University Press, 1972), 49.

11. Quoted in Kaufman, *Homeopathy in America*, 12.

12. Ibid., 1–14; and Sarah Stage, *Female Complaints: Lydia Pinkham and the Business of Women's Medicine* (New York: Norton, 1971) provide useful sketches of heroic practice.

13. Quoted in Rothstein, *American Physicians*, 127.

14. Charles Rosenberg, "The American Medical Profession: Mid–Nineteenth Century," *MA* 44 (1962):166; Rosenberg, "The Therapeutic Revolution: Medicine, Meaning, and Social Change in Nineteenth-Century America,"

in *The Therapeutic Revolution: Medicine Meaning and Change in 19th Century America*, edited by Morris J. Vogel and Charles E. Rosenberg (Philadelphia: University of Pennsylvania Press, 1979), 3–25. John S. Haller surveys nineteenth-century *materia medica* in *American Medicine in Transition, 1840–1910* (Urbana: University of Illinois Press, 1981), 67–99.

15. Rothstein, *American Physicians*, 54; Gert H. Brieger, "Therapeutic Conflicts and the American Medical Profession in the 1860s," *BHM* 41 (1967):215–22.

16. Shryock, *Medicine and Society*, 130–32; Erwin Ackernecht, "Elisha Bartlett and the Philosophy of the Paris Clinical School," *BHM* 24 (1950):49–60; and Cassedy, *American Medicine*, passim.

17. Worthington Hooker, *Physician and Patient* (New York: Baker and Scribner, 1849; reprint, Arno Press, 1972), 25–49; Elisha Bartlett, *An Inquiry into the Degree of Certainty in Medicine; and into the Nature and Extent of Its Power over Disease* (Philadelphia: Lea and Blanchard, 1848), excerpted in *Medical America in the Nineteenth Century: Readings from the Literature*, edited by Gert H. Brieger (Baltimore: Johns Hopkins University Press, 1972), 115–27; Jacob Bigelow, "On Self-Limiting Diseases," *MCMMS* 5 (1836):319–58, excerpted in ibid., 98–106; and Austin Flint, "Conservative Medicine," *AMM* 18 (1862):1–24, reprinted in ibid., 115–26.

18. John Harley Warner, however, demonstrates that the drift away from heroic theory was slow and subtle. See *The Therapeutic Perspective: Medical Practice, Knowledge, and Professional Identity in America, 1820–1885* (Cambridge: Harvard University Press, 1986).

19. See ibid., 58–80.

20. "[Proceedings of the Kentucky Medical Society, October 1854]," 366.

21. Linden F. Edwards, "Resurrection Riots During the Heroic Age of Anatomy in America," *BHM* 25 (1951):178–84; and John B. Blake, "Anatomy," in *The Education of American Physicians*, edited by Ronald L. Numbers (Berkeley: University of California Press, 1980), 34–38.

22. Quoted in Edwards, "Resurrection Riots," 178.

23. Blake, "Anatomy," 37.

24. "Another Prosecution for Malpractice," *JMCS* 3 (November 1846):406.

25. James Sheldon, "Report of Trial for Malpractice. *William Tims v. James P. White*," *BufMJMR* 4 (August 1848):135.

26. John Elwell, *A Medico-Legal Treatise on Medical Malpractice and Medical Evidence* (New York: John S. Voorhis, 1860), 53–54.

27. Blake, "Anatomy," 37–38.

28. Eric H. Christianson, "Medicine in New England," in *Medicine in the New World*, edited by Ronald L. Numbers (Knoxville: University of Tennessee Press, 1987), 117–26.

29. Ibid., 103–6.

30. Ibid.; and Starr, *Transformation*, 37–40.

31. Shryock, *Medicine*, 3–5.

32. Christianson, "Medicine," 112–15, 119–20.

33. Starr, *Transformation*, 40–47.

34. See below for more on licensure in America.

35. Shryock, *Medicine*, 7.

36. In comparison, France had three medical schools in 1850. James H. Cassedy, *Medicine and American Growth, 1800–1860* (Madison: University of Wisconsin Press, 1986), 68.

37. Ludmerer, *Learning*, 11, 47–48; and Martin Kaufman, "American Medical Education," in *Education of American Physicians*, 10–12.

38. [Alfred Stillé and R. M. Huston], "Medical Reform," *MNL* 5 (May 1847):49.

39. [R.C.], "A Report of the Facts and Circumstance Relating to a Case of Compound Fracture and Prosecution for Malpractice," *ME* 4 (1841):712–14.

40. Alden March, "Case of Alleged Mal-Practice in Surgery," *BMSJ* 37 (4 August 1847):13.

41. Peter Dobkin Hall discusses this idea in "The Social Foundations of Professional Credibility: Linking the Medical Profession to Higher Education in Connecticut and Massachusetts," in *The Authority of Experts: Studies in History and Theory*, edited by Thomas L. Haskell (Bloomington: Indiana University Press, 1984), 107–41. However, Hall does not provide a detailed picture of the profound difficulties faced by these early professionals.

42. Richard Hofstadter, *Anti-Intellectualism in American Life* (New York: Vintage, 1962), 154–59; and John William Ward, *Andrew Jackson: Symbol for an Age* (New York: Oxford University Press, 1953), 46–78.

43. Hooker, *Physician and Patient*, 223–24.

44. William M. Wood, "Thoughts on Suits for Malpractice, suggested by certain Judicial Proceedings in Erie County, Pennsylvania," *AJMS* 18 (October 1849):400.

45. [Stillé and Huston], "Medical Reform," 49.

46. Ibid., 49.

47. "To What Causes Are We to Attribute the Diminishing Respectability of the Medical Profession in the Estimation of the American Public?" *MSR* 1 n.s. (1858):141–43.

48. Cassedy, *Medicine and American Growth*, 67–68.

49. These figures include any practitioner, educated or not, who called himself a *physician*.

50. These statistics were drawn from Cassedy, *Medicine and American Growth*, 66–68, 232–33.

51. Samual Jackson, "Critical Analysis," *NYMJ* 8 (March 1847):218–22.

52. Ibid., 232–33. See also Rothstein, *American Physicians*, 344–45 for a discussion of the perceived surplus of physicians.

53. Cassedy, *Medicine and American Growth*, 70.

54. "To What Causes?" 141–43.

55. Stewart, "The Actual Condition of the Medical Profession in This

Country; with a Brief Account of Some of the Causes which Tend to Impede Its Progress, and Interfere with Its Honors and Interests," *NYJM* 6 (1846):151–71, excerpted in *Medical America*, 64.

56. James Adams, Jr., comp., *Report of a Trial of an Action, Charles Lowell against John Faxon and Micajah Hawks Doctors of Medicine, Defendants for Malpractice in the Capacity of Physicians and Surgeons at the Superior Court of Maine Held at Machias for the County of Washington, June 1824 before the Hon. Nathan Weston* (Portland: Printed for James Adams, Jr., by David and Seth Paine, 1825), 7.

57. See chapter 1 for a fuller discussion of this case.

58. Morton J. Horwitz, "The Emergence of an Instrumental Conception of American Law, 1780–1820," in *Law in American History*, edited by Donald Fleming and Bernard Bailyn (Boston: Little, Brown, 1971), 287–326. See also Horwitz, *The Transformation of American Law, 1780–1860* (Cambridge: Harvard University Press, 1977), passim.

59. The standard work on the subject is George Rosen, *Fees and Fee Bills: Some Economic Aspects of Medical Practice in Nineteenth-Century America*, supplement to the *Bulletin of the History of Medicine*, no. 6 (Baltimore: Johns Hopkins University Press, 1946).

60. Daniel H. Calhoun, *Professional Lives in America: Structure and Aspiration, 1750–1850* (Cambridge: Harvard University Press, 1965), 20–58.

61. Stewart, "The Actual Condition," passim and 69, 71. For other comments on the effect of professional quarrels on professional status, see "Review: Medical Ethics," *AJMS* 23 (January 1852):151.

62. "Code of Medical Ethics Adopted by the National Medical Convention in Philadelphia, June 1847," article VI § 1, printed in Hooker, *Physician and Patient*, appendix, 440–53. See Chester R. Burns, "Medical Ethics in the United States Before the Civil War," Ph.D. dissertation (Johns Hopkins University, 1969), 91–125, for a discussion of how other ethical codes were used to blunt the conflict among physicians.

63. Quoted in Starr, *Social Transformation*, 64.

64. S. W. Butler, "Physician's League," *MSR* 7 (March 1854):97.

65. James Harvey Young, *Toadstool Millionaires*, 44–57; Joseph Kett, *Formation of the American Medical Profession*, 96–127.

66. Martin Kaufman, *Homeopathy in America*, 23–47; Kett, *Formation of the American Medical Profession*, 132–64; and James H. Cassedy, *American Medicine and Statistical Thinking*, 124–39.

67. For example, see Wood, "Thoughts on Suits for Malpractice," 395–400.

68. Alden March, "Prosecutions for Malpractice," *BMSJ* 36 (14 July 1847):477–80.

69. Parkman and Fiske, "Report on the Causes and Prevention of Suits for Mal-Practice," 128–29.

70. "S.", "Suits for Mal-Practice," *BMSJ* 51 (13 December 1854):402–3.

71. Stephen Smith, "[Review of John Elwell's Treatise on Malpractice],"

AJMS 40 (July 1860):156. For other claims that suits were instigated by rival practitioners, see William M. Wood, "A Statement of Two Suits for Malpractice, Tried in November and December 1850, in the Court of Erie County, Pa.," *AJMS* 22 (July 1851):43–53.

72. Samuel Parkman, "On the Relations of the Medical Witness with the Law and the Lawyer," *AJMS* 23 (January 1852):128.

73. The jury could not agree on a verdict, and the patient withdrew the charges. Both parties paid their own legal fees and court costs. March, "Case of Alleged Mal-Practice," 9–10.

74. "Critical Analysis," *NYMJ* 3 (March 1847):218–22.

75. Lewis Bauer, "Surgical Contributions," *MSR* 13 (1865):270–72.

76. T. J. W. Pray, "A Surgical Case of Malpractice," *BMSJ* 51 (8 November 1854):289–97. This case is discussed in chapter 7.

77. "Trial for Mal-Practice," *BMSJ* 41 (17 October 1849):216–19.

78. "Trial for Mal-Practice," *BMSJ* 41 (23 January 1849):500–502; "Suit for Mal-Practice in Vermont," *BMSJ* 44 (11 June 1851):377–78.

79. "Prosecution for Mal-practice," *BMSJ* 48 (20 July 1853):503–4.

80. William M. Wood, "Thoughts on Suits," 395–96; Wood, "A Statement of Two Suits," 43–50.

81. Flexner, *Doctors on Horseback: Pioneers of American Medicine* (New York: Dover, 1968), 217–64.

82. "Suit for Mal-Practice," *JMCS* 3 (November 1846):407–8; and "Suit for Malpraxis," *StLMSJ* 3 (May 1846):553–54.

83. [Justice], "The Late Suit for Mal-Practice in Delaware Co., N.Y.," *BMSJ* 37 (11 August 1847):35.

84. T. J. Pray, "A Case of Alleged Mal-Practice," *BMSJ* 54 (24 April 1856):242. For another writer who counseled physicians to be circumspect in judging the work of their peers, see March, "Case of Alleged Malpractice," 9–14.

85. "Suits for Mal-Practice," *BMSJ* 51 (13 December 1854):402–3.

86. Richard Harrison Shryock, *Medical Licensing in America, 1650–1965* (Baltimore: Johns Hopkins University Press, 1967), 3–23.

87. Starr, *Transformation*, 44–45; and Charles E. Rosenberg, *The Cholera Years: The United States in 1832, 1849, and 1866* (Chicago: University of Chicago Press, 1962), 70.

88. See specifically, Alexis de Tocqueville, *Democracy in America*, edited by J. P. Mayer, translated by George Lawrence (Garden City, N.Y.: Doubleday, 1969), 506–13.

89. Arthur M. Schlesinger, Jr., *The Age of Jackson* (Boston: Little, Brown, 1945), 306–21; Marvin Meyers, *The Jacksonian Persuasion* (New York: Vintage, 1960), 185–205; and Rush Welter, *The Mind of America, 1820–1860* (New York: Columbia University Press, 1975), 72–104.

90. Rosenberg, *Cholera Years*, 151–72, quotation at 161.

91. Shryock, *Medical Licensing*, 30–31.

92. Garnett, "Professional Standing," 99–100.

93. Wood, "Thoughts on Suits for Malpractice," 395–96.

94. Smith, "[Review of Elwell]," 154.

95. [Stillé and Huston], "Medical Reform," 50.

96. Lawrence M. Friedman, *A History of American Law* (New York: Simon and Schuster, 1973), 165.

97. Schlesinger, *Age of Jackson*, 329–31.

98. "Extracts from the Report of the Committee," 17, 19. See Kett, *Formation*, 107–21, for a discussion of political rhetoric of the medical sectarians.

99. "Prosecutions of Medical Men," *WJMS* 28 (1853):346–47.

100. March, "Case of Alleged Malpractice," 13.

101. Wood, "Thoughts on Suits," 395–96.

102. [Frank] Hamilton, "Prosecution for Alledged *[sic]* Mal-Practice," *BufMJMR* 4 (1848–1849):275.

103. A "farmer," quoted in "The Greenpoint Malpractice Case," 312–13.

104. Ibid., 313.

105. Ibid.

106. Parkman and Fisk, "Report on the Causes and Prevention of Suits," 129–30.

107. Christopher L. Tomlins, "A Mysterious Power: Industrial Accidents and the Legal Construction of Employee Relations in Massachusetts, 1800–1850," *Law and History Review* 6 (Fall 1988):386, 395.

108. Kenneth Ludmerer, *Learning to Heal: The Development of American Medical Education* (New York: Basic Books, 1985), passim; and Starr, *Transformation*, 123–27.

109. Rothstein, *American Physicians*, 249–81; and Starr, *Transformation*, 102–7.

110. Rothstein, *American Physicians*, 305–10; and Thomas Haskell, *The Emergence of Professional Social Science* (Urbana: University of Illinois Press, 1977).

111. See chapter 5 for a discussion of the rarity of malpractice suits in the South.

4. *"The Expression of a Wellmade Man"*

1. Walt Whitman, *Leaves of Grass: The First (1855) Edition*, edited with an introduction by Malcolm Cowley (New York: Viking Press, 1960), 116.

2. See chapter 2; and Charles J. Weigel II, "Medical Malpractice in America's Middle Years," *TRBM* 32 (Spring 1974):193–94.

3. "Suit for Mal-Practice," *OMSJ* 10 (1857–1858):21.

4. See, for example, Charles E. Rosenberg, *The Care of Strangers: The Rise of*

America's Hospital System (New York: Basic Books, 1987), 101; and James H. Cassedy, *American Medicine and Statistical Thinking, 1800–1860* (Cambridge: Harvard University Press, 1984), 85.

5. William G. Rothstein, *American Physicians in the Nineteenth Century: From Sects to Science* (Baltimore: Johns Hopkins University Press, 1972), 27.

6. For example, see Judith Walzer Leavitt, *Brought to Bed: Childbearing in America, 1750–1950* (New York: Oxford University Press, 1986), 36–63 and passim; and Cassedy, *American Medicine and Statistical Thinking*, 80–81.

7. Sumner v. Utley 7 Conn. 257, 260 (1827). Also quoted and discussed in chapter 1. Practitioners in America, unlike many of their counterparts in Britain, performed both surgical and medical procedures, so the judge was drawing a distinction between *surgical* practice and *medical* practice even though both were usually embodied in one practitioner. See Richard Harrison Shryock, *Medicine and Society in America, 1660–1860* (Ithaca: Cornell University Press, 1960), 59–60.

8. Bell quoted in William J. Walker, "On the Treatment of Compound and Complicated Fractures," *MCMMS*, 7 (1842–1848):209.

9. Percival Pott, *Treatise on Compound Fractures* (Philadelphia, 1819), 1:266.

10. Samuel Cooper, *A Dictionary of Practical Surgery* (London, 1813), 420. It is important to note that, as early as 1776, John Jones called perfunctory amputation in compound fractures into question. Jones's position, however, was not accepted. John Jones, *Plain Concise Practical Remarks on the Treatment of Wounds and Fractures* (Philadelphia: Robert Bell, 1776; reprint Arno Press, 1971), 45–46.

11. The issue of *wrongful death* actions is complicated. While there was apparently a common law action for wrongful death, many judges in the early nineteenth century held that there was not. Husbands could, however, sue for loss of consortium. In the early nineteenth century *consortium* was the husband's conjugal rights to his wife's labor and companionship. Women could not sue for loss of consortium until much later in the century. Wex Malone sheds some light on the topic in "The Genesis of Wrongful Death," *SLR* 17 (July 1965):1043–76.

12. Astley Cooper, *The Lectures of Sir Astley*, 4th American ed. (Philadelphia: E. L. Carey and A. Hart, 1835), 616; and Cooper, *A Treatise on Dislocations and on Fractures of the Joints*, 1st American ed., 3rd London ed. (Boston: Wells and Lilly, 1825), 193.

13. For example, see several dozen healed cases reported in Walker, "On the Treatments of Compound and Complicated Fractures," i–lvi; *ME* 3 (1841):207; and *ME* 5 (1843):1555.

14. See note 8, above.

15. Martin S. Pernick, *A Calculus of Suffering: Pain, Professionalism, and Anesthesia in Nineteenth-Century America* (New York: Columbia University Press, 1985), 30, 82–83.

16. Cassedy, *American Medicine and Statistical Thinking*, 85–87.

17. George W. Norris, "Statistical Account of the Cases of Amputation Performed at the Pennsylvania Hospital from Jan. 1, 1831, to Jan. 1, 1838," *AJMS* 22 (1838):356–65. See also Norris, "Statistical Account of the Cases of Amputation Performed at the Pennsylvania Hospital from Jan. 1, 1838, to Jan. 1, 1840," *AJMS* 26 (1840):35–36; Henry W. Buel, "Statistics of Amputation in the New York Hospital from Jan. 1, 1839, to Jan. 1, 1848," *AJMS* 16 (1848):33–43.

18. Austin Flint, "Conservative Medicine," *AMM* 18 (1862):1–24, reprinted in *Medical America in the Nineteenth-Century: Readings from the Literature*, edited by Gert H. Brieger (Baltimore: Johns Hopkins University Press, 1972), 135.

19. Walker, "On the Treatments of Complicated and Compound Fractures," 181.

20. John Elwell, *A Medico-Legal Treatise on Medical Malpractice and Medical Evidence* (New York: John S. Voorhis, 1860), 56, 54–58, and passim.

21. "A Surgical Case of Mal-Practice," *BMSJ* 51 (8 November 1854):292.

22. "Legal Robbery of a Physician," *MN* 14 (April 1856):61–62.

23. Harry E. Pratt, "The Famous 'Chicken Bone' Case," *JISHS* 45 (Summer 1952):166; and Clark Heath, "How Abraham Lincoln Dealt with a Malpractice Suit," *NEJM* 295:735–36.

24. "Anesthesia and Its Influence on Surgery," *MN* 9 (1851):21–22.

25. "A Report of the Facts and Circumstances relating to a case of Compound Fracture and Prosecution for Malpractice . . . ," *WMSJ* 5 (1842):145.

26. Robert T. J. Fox, "The Natural Bonesetters, with Special Reference to the Sweet Family of Rhode Island," *BHM* 28 (1954):416–41.

27. Worthington Hooker, *Physician and Patient: or, A Practical View of the Mutual Duties, Relations, and Interests of the Medical Profession and the Community* (New York: Baker and Scribner, 1849; facsimile reprint Arno Press, 1972), 156, 154–70, and passim.

28. Ibid., 160.

29. Ibid., 161; emphasis added.

30. "Report on Difficulties Growing Out of Alleged Mal-Practice in the Treatment of Fractures," *TOMS* 11 (1856):64–65.

31. S. P. Hildreth, "Trial for Malpractice in Surgery," *OMSJ* 2 (January 1850):220.

32. Quoted in Charles Rosenberg, *The Cholera Years: The United States in 1832, 1849, and 1866* (Chicago, University of Chicago Press, 1962), 157.

33. James Sheldon, "Report of [a] Trial for Mal-practice. *William Times v. James P. White,*" *BufMJMR* 4 (August 1848):132.

34. "Prosecutions for Mal-Practice," *NHJM* 4 (January 1854):20–23.

35. James H. Cassedy, *American Medicine and Statistical Thinking*, 87–88.

36. "Reviews," *WJMPS* 28 (1853):309–12.

37. For example, see Hamilton, "Report on Deformities after Fractures," *TAMA* 8 (1855):347–93, *TAMA* 9 (1856):69–233, *TAMA* 10 (1857):239–453;

and Hamilton, *A Practical Treatise on Fractures and Dislocations* (Philadelphia: Blanchard and Lea, 1860).

38. "Legal Liability of Physicians and Surgeons," *BuffMSJ* 5 (1865–1866):353–56.

39. "Suit for Alleged Mal-Practice," *OMSJ* 10 (1857–1858):13–24. There was also strong evidence that the patient himself had contributed to the bad result. See above, this chapter.

40. "*Steele* v. *Newton*, Superior Court, Cincinnati; Nov. Term, 1856," Reprinted in Milo Adams McClelland, *Civil Malpractice: A Treatise on Surgical Jurisprudence* (New York: Hurd and Houghton, 1877), 50; "Suit for Alleged Mal-Practice," *OMSJ* 10 (May 1858): 447–51; and "*Mary Ann Decrow, et. al, v. H. H. Little:* A Prosecution for Malpractice," *OMSJ* 12 (January 1860):194–98.

41. "Reviews [Review of Frank Hamilton's work]," *AJMS* 39 (April 1860):422.

42. "Jarvis' Adjuster," *WJMPS* 22 (1851):272–73.

43. "A Case of Alleged Mal-Practice," *BMSJ* 54 (24 April 1856):234.

44. "Extracts from the Report of the Committee on the Prevalence of Suits for Malpractice," *MNL* 8 (March 1850):17, 19.

45. Thomas C. Cochran and William Miller, *The Age of Enterprise: A Social History of Industrial America* (New York: Harper and Row, 1961), 1–59.

46. Hugo A. Meier, "Technology and Democracy, 1800–1860," *MVHR* 43 (1956–1957):632; and Arthur Alphonse Ekirch, *The Idea of Progress in America, 1815–1860* (New York: Peter Smith, 1951), 72–143.

47. Meir, "Technology and Democracy," 624–25. Specifically, see Alexis de Tocqueville, "Why the Americans are More Concerned with the Applications than with the Theory of Science," *Democracy in America*, edited by J. P. Mayer, translated by George Lawrence (Garden City, N.Y.: Doubleday, 1969), 459–65.

48. Leo Marx, *The Machine in the Garden: Technology and the Pastoral Ideal in America* (New York: Oxford University Press, 1973), 160–61, 194–97, quotation at 197.

49. James C. Whorton, *Crusaders for Fitness: The History of American Health Reformers* (Princeton: Princeton University Press, 1982), 17–18. For background see Richard S. Westfall, *The Construction of Modern Science Mechanisms and Mechanics* (New York: John Wiley, 1971), 82–104; Siegfried Gideion, *Mechanization Takes Command: A Contribution to Anonymous History* (New York: Norton, 1978), 16–37; and Jan Broekhoff, "Physical Education and the Reification of the Human Body," *Gym* 9 (1972):4–11.

50. Thomas Carlyle, "Signs of the Times" (1829) in *Critical and Miscellaneous Essays* (London: Chapman and Hall, 1899), 2:63, 67.

51. de Tocqueville, *Democracy*, 530, 540.

52. Ibid., 462.

53. Bruce Halley, *The Healthy Body and Victorian Culture* (Cambridge: Harvard University Press, 1978), 21–22.

54. Ailene S. Lockhart and Betty Spears, eds., *Chronicle of American Physi-*

cal Education: Selected Readings, 1855–1930 (Dubuque, Iowa: William C. Brown, 1972), 3–43. See also John R. Betts, "Mind and Body in Early American Thought," *JAH* 54 (March 1968):787–805.

55. Quoted in Harvey Green, *Fit for America: Health, Fitness, Sport and American Society* (New York: Pantheon, 1986), 14.

56. Channing and Emerson quoted in Roberta J. Park, "The Attitudes of Leading New England Transcendentalists Toward Healthful Exercise, Active Recreations, and Proper Care of the Body, 1830–1860," *JSH* 4 (1977):39–41 and 46. See also Roberta J. Park, "Embodied Selves: The Rise and Development of Concern for Physical Education, Active Games and Recreation for American Women, 1776–1865," *JSH* 5 (1978):5–41.

57. Thomas Wentworth Higginson, "Saints and Their Bodies," *AtlM* 1 (March 1858):582–86.

58. Whitman, *Leaves of Grass*, 122–23.

59. Betts, "Mind and Body," 788; Broekhoff, "Physical Education and the Reification of the Human Body," 4–11; and Charles W. Griffin, "Physical Fitness," in *Concise Histories of American Popular Culture*, edited by M. Thomas Inge (Westport, Conn.: Greenwood Press, 1982), 262–70.

60. The best discussion of these changes is in Martha H. Verbrugge, *Able-Bodied Womanhood: Personal Health and Social Change in Nineteenth-Century Boston* (New York: Oxford University Press, 1988), esp. 3–10. Anita Clair Fellman and Michael Fellman, *Making Sense of Self: Medical Advice Literature in Late Nineteenth Century America* (Philadelphia: University of Pennsylvania Press, 1981), 5–6; and Green, *Fit for America*, 11–14, are also excellent.

61. Ronald G. Walters, *American Reformers, 1815–1860* (New York: Hill and Wang, 1978), 145–57, quotation at 145.

62. T. J. Jackson Lears, "From Salvation to Self-Realization: Advertising and the Therapeutic Roots of Consumer Culture," in *The Culture of Consumption: Critical Essays in American History, 1880–1980*, edited by Richard Wightman Fox and T. J. Jackson Lears (New York: Pantheon, 1983), 3–38; and Philip Rieff, *The Triumph of the Therapeutic* (New York: Harper and Row, 1966).

5. Community, Providence, and the Social Construction of Legal Action

1. James Adams, Jr., *Report of an Action, Charles Lowell against John Faxon and Micajah Hawks, Doctors of Medicine, Defendants* (Portland: Printed for James Adams, Jr., by David and Seth Paine, 1825), 52. See also chapter 1.

2. Carol J. Greenhouse, "Nature is to Culture as Praying is to Suing: Legal Pluralism in an American Suburb," *JLP* 20 (1982):17.

3. Sally Engle Merry and Susan S. Sibley, "What Do Plaintiffs Want? Reexamining the Concept of Dispute," *JSJ* 9 (1984):151–78; David M. Engel,

"The Oven Bird's Song: Insiders, Outsiders, and Personal Injuries in an American Community," *LSR* 18 (1984):551–61; and Greenhouse, "Nature is to Culture," are enormously helpful in understanding the relationship between community and certain types of litigiousness.

4. Debate concerning the notion of *community* is one of the most contentious and treacherous in contemporary historiography. For the best overview of the complex issues, see Thomas Bender, *Community and Social Change in America* (New Brunswick: Rutgers University Press, 1979).

5. The term and characterization is from Kenneth A. Lockridge, *A New England Town: The First Hundred Years* (New York: Norton, 1970), 16.

6. Ibid., passim.

7. Greenhouse, "Nature is to Culture," 18.

8. Lockridge, *New England Town*, 13–14, 159–60; and Jerold S. Auerbach, *Justice Without Law?* (New York: Oxford University Press, 1983), 19–46.

9. James A. Henretta, *The Evolution of American Society, 1700–1815: An Interdisciplinary Analysis* (Lexington, Mass.: D. C. Heath, 1973), 112–16. Michael Zuckerman, *Peaceable Kingdoms: New England Towns in the Eighteenth Century* (New York: Random House, 1970), argues for the retention of community consensus through 1776 but probably makes his point too strongly.

10. See Richard Bushman, *From Puritan to Yankee: Character and the Social Order in Connecticut, 1690–1765* (Cambridge: Harvard University Press, 1967), 183–95, 258–88.

11. William E. Nelson, *Dispute and Conflict Resolution in Plymouth County, Massachusetts, 1725–1825* (Chapel Hill: University of North Carolina Press, 1981). For a vigorous critique of Nelson's position, see Robert Gordon, "Accounting for Legal Change in American Legal History," in *Law in the American Revolution and the Revolution in the Law*, edited by Hedrick Hartog (New York: New York University Press, 1981), 93–112. For a more general attack on the notion that America has become more litigious, see Marc Galanter, "Reading the Landscape of Disputes: What We Know and Don't Know (and Think We Know) about Our Allegedly Contentious and Litigious Society," *UCLA Law Review* 31 (1983):4–71.

12. Michael H. Frisch, *Town into City: Springfield, Massachusetts, and the Meaning of Community, 1840–1880* (Cambridge: Harvard University Press, 1972), 32–49, quotation at 35.

13. Rowland Berthoff, *An Unsettled People: Social Order and Disorder in American History* (New York: Harper and Row, 1971), 177–234; Richard Brown, "Modernization and the Modern Personality in Early America, 1600–1865: A Sketch of a Synthesis," *Journal of Interdisciplinary History* 11 (Winter 1972):221–22; Robert N. Bellah, et al., *Habits of the Heart: Individualism and Commitment in American Life* (Berkeley: UCLA Press, 1985), vii, viii, 37–38, 222.

14. Engel, "Oven Bird's Song," 559. I have relied heavily on Engel for this argument.

15. These suits were common in early communities. See John Demos, *A*

Little Commonwealth: Family Life in Plymouth Colony (New York: Oxford Press, 1982), 49, 112, 138, 153.

16. Engel, "Oven Bird's Song," 558.

17. Henry F. May, "The Decline of Providence?" in *Ideas, Faiths, and Feelings: Essays on American Intellectual and Religious History, 1952–1982* (New York: Oxford University Press, 1983), 136 and passim.

18. Perry Miller provides an excellent discussion of early American attitudes toward divine providence in *The New England Mind: From Colony to Province* (Cambridge: Harvard University Press, 1953).

19. Perry Miller, *The New England Mind: The Seventeenth Century* (Cambridge: Harvard University Press, 1939), 14–17.

20. See, for example, Charles Edwin Clark, "Science, Reason, and an Angry God: The Literature of an Earthquake," *NEQ* 38 (1965): 340–62; Eleanor M. Tilton, "Lightning Rods and the Earthquake of 1755," *NEQ* 13 (March 1940):85–97; and Miller, *From Colony to Province*, 345–66.

21. John Winthrop, *Winthrop's Journal: History of New England, 1630–1649*, edited by James Kendall Hosmer (New York: Charles Scribner's Sons, 1908), 1:114–9, 226, 270, 291; 2: 138, 141, 153–54, 209–10, 220, 354–55.

22. Lewis O. Saum, "Providence in the Popular Mind of Pre–Civil War America," *IMH* 72 (1976):341–42.

23. Miller, *The Seventeenth Century*, 30; and Richard Brown, *Modernization: The Transformation of American Life, 1600–1865* (New York: Hill and Wang, 1976), 111.

24. Charles D. Cashdollar, "Social Implications of the Doctrine of Divine Providence: A Nineteenth-Century Debate in American Theology," *HTR* 71 (1978):268.

25. Religious, "The Doctrine of Providence Vindicated," *CS* 5 (1823):173–74.

26. "The Doctrine of a Particular Providence," *CS* 8 (1836):2.

27. Religious, "The Doctrine of Providence," 175; Cashdollar, *Social Implications*, 277–78.

28. Cashdollar, *Social Implications*, 268, 275, 279, 280–82. For a description of how Americans in the Jacksonian period came to see God's hand in broad national and historical trends, see Lewis O. Saum, *The Popular Mind of Pre–Civil War America* (Westport, Conn.: Greenwood Press, 1980), 3–26; and John William Ward, *Andrew Jackson — Symbol for an Age* (New York: Oxford University Press, 1953), 101–49.

29. "*Michael O'Neil* v. *Gerard Bancker*," *NYMPJ* 6 (1827):145–52.

30. Ibid.

31. Ibid., 150–51.

32. Charles Lowell, *An Authentic Report of a Trial before the Supreme Judicial Court of Maine for the County of Washington, June Term 1824, Charles Lowell v. Jon Faxon & Micajah Hawks Surgeons . . .* (Portland: Printed for the author, 1826).

33. Ibid., 8. See chapter 1 for an extended narrative on this case.

34. See Grindle, etc. v. Leo Rush et al. 7 Ohio 123–25 (1836).

35. "Extracts from the Report of the Committee on the Prevalence of Suits for Malpractice," *MNL* 8 (March 1850):18–19.

36. Cashdollar, *Social Impliations*, 280; Donald Caton, "The Secularization of Pain," *Anesthesiology* 62 (April 1985):493–501; Ronald L. Numbers and Ronald C. Sawyer, "Medicine and Christianity in the Modern World," in *Health/Medicine and the Faith Traditions: An Inquiry into Religion and Medicine*, edited by Martin E. Marty and Kenneth Vaux (Philadelphia: Fortress Press, 1982), 133–60; Miller, *The Seventeenth Century*, passim; and Albert Post, *Popular Freethought in America, 1825–1850* (New York: Columbia University Press, 1943).

37. Charles Cashdollar, "European Positivism and the American Unitarianism," *CH* 45 (1976):490–92.

38. Cashdollar, *Social Implications*, 283; and Robert Bremner, *From the Depths: The Discovery of Poverty in the United States.* (New York: New York University Press, 1956), 16–45.

39. John L. Thomas, "Romantic Reform in America, 1815–1865," *American Quarterly* 17 (Winter 1965):656–81.

40. The literature on the history of reform is both rich and vast. A small sample includes: James Turner, *Reckoning with the Beast: Animals, Pain, and Humanity in the Victorian Mind* (Baltimore: Johns Hopkins University Press, 1980); Robert Bremner, *American Philanthropy* (Chicago: University of Chicago Press, 1960), ch. 1 and 2; Arthur M. Schlesinger, *The American as Reformer* (Cambridge: Harvard University Press, 1950); and Ronald G. Walters, *American Reformers, 1815–1860* (New York: Hill and Wang, 1978).

41. Cashdollar, *Social Implications*, 280; Caton, "Secularization of Pain," 497.

42. James H. Cassedy, *American Medicine and Statistical Thinking, 1800–1860* (Cambridge: Harvard University Press, 1984); and in general Thomas M. Porter, *The Rise of Statistical Thinking, 1820–1900* (Princeton: Princeton University Press, 1986).

43. Numbers and Sawyer, "Medicine and Christianity," passim.

44. Irving H. Bartlett, *The American Mind in the Mid–Nineteenth Century* (New York: Thomas Y. Crowell Company, 1967), 5–18; and Martin E. Marty, *Righteous Empire: The Protestant Experience in America* (New York: Dial Press, 1970), 83–88.

45. William G. McLoughlin, "Introduction to Charles G. Finney, *Lectures on Revivals of Religion*," in *Essays on Jacksonian America*, edited by Frank Otto Gatell (New York: Holt, Rinehart and Winston, 1970), 242.

46. Ibid., passim. Also, for an insightful commentary on these issues, see Major L. Wilson, "Paradox Lost: Order in Evangelical Thought in Mid–Nineteenth-Century America," *CH* 44 (September 1975):352–66.

47. Walters, *American Reformers*, 145–46, 171, and 145–72 generally.

48. McLoughlin, "Introduction," 252–53; and Paul E. Johnson, *A Shopkeeper's Millennium: Society and Revivals in Rochester, New York, 1815–1837* (New York: Hill and Wang, 1978), 3–14.

49. McLoughlin, "Introduction," 252; see also Whitney R. Cross, *The Burned-Over District: The Social and Intellectual History of Enthusiastic Religion in Western New York, 1800–1850* (New York: Harper and Row, 1965).

50. Johnson, *Shopkeeper's Millennium*, 5, 109.

51. John Duffy, *Epidemics in Colonial America* (Baton Rouge: Louisiana State University, 1953); J. H. Powell, *Bring Out Your Dead* (Philadelphia: University of Pennsylvania Press, 1949).

52. Quoted in William Gribbin, "Divine Province or Miasma? The Yellow Fever Epidemic of 1822," *NYH* 53 (July 1972):287, 289.

53. Ibid., 294–97.

54. Ibid., 298.

55. Rosenberg, *The Cholera Years: The United States in 1832, 1849, and 1866* (Chicago: University of Chicago Press, 1962), 43.

56. Ibid., 40–54. See also Numbers and Sawyer, "Medicine and Christianity," 137–40.

57. Quoted in Rosenberg, *Cholera Years*, 128, 130.

58. "Causes and Prevention of Epidemics," *Har* 15 (1857):194–203.

59. Rosenberg, *Cholera Years*, 193–96.

60. See for example Cassedy, *American Medicine and Statistical Thinking*, 222–27.

61. Numbers and Sawyer, "Medicine and Christianity," 139; Rosenberg, *Cholera Years*, 5. For a helpful interpretation of the origins of this transformation see Thomas, *Religion*, 647–68.

62. For example, Keith Thomas offers a discussion of the use of supernatural explanations to ease acceptance of misfortune, *Religion and the Decline of Magic: Studies in Popular Beliefs in the Sixteenth and Seventeenth Centuries in England* (London: Weidenfeld, 1971), 5–7, 651–63. See also Ivan Illich, *Medical Nemesis: The Expropriation of Health* (New York: Pantheon, 1976), 133–54.

63. See Walter Kaufman, "Suffering and the Bible," in *The Faith of a Heretic* (Garden City, N.Y.: Doubleday, 1961), 137–69; and H. B. Gibson, *Pain and Its Conquest* (Boston: Peter Owen, 1982), 22.

64. Caton, "Secularization of Pain," 493.

65. Although he makes a slightly different argument, Daniel De Moulin, "A Historical-Phenomenological Study of Bodily Pain in Western Man," *BHM* 48 (Winter 1974):540–71, surveys some of the literature. See also Caton, "Secularization of Pain," passim.

66. Nathan P. Rice, *Trials of a Public Benefactor* (New York: Pudney and Russell, 1859), 124.

67. Ibid., 125.

68. Ibid., 126.

69. Two of the most learned discussions of these general issues are: Boyd Hilton, *The Age of Atonement: The Influence of Evangelicalism on Social and Economic Thought, 1795–1865* (Oxford: Clarendon Press, 1988); and Charles D. Cashdollar, *The Transformation of Theology, 1830–1890: Positivism and Protestant Thought in Britain and America* (Princeton: Princeton University Press, 1989).

Martin Pernick provides the most important discussion of the interrelationship of pain, anesthesia, and religious beliefs in *A Calculus of Suffering: Pain, Professionalism and Anesthesia in Nineteenth Century America* (New York: Columbia University Press, 1985), 49–57 and passim.

70. Caton, "Secularization of Pain," 496. For samples of Bentham's and Mill's comments on pain see *Utilitarianism and Other Essays*, edited by Alan Ryan (New York: Penguin, 1987), 93–97, 278–79.

71. Caton, "Secularization of Pain," 497.

72. See Turner, *Reckoning with the Beast.*

73. Pernick, *A Calculus of Suffering*, 49–57; and John Duffy, "Anglo-American Reaction to Obstetrical Anesthesia," *BHM* 38 (January–February 1964):32–44.

74. North Carolina; Alabama; Arkansas; Florida; Georgia; Louisiana; South Carolina; Mississippi; Tennessee; Texas; and Virginia — calculated from Hubert Winston Smith, "Legal Responsibility for Medical Malpractice," *JAMA* 116 (1941):2672–73; and Chester R. Burns, "Malpractice Suits in America before the Civil War," *BHM* 43 (1969):41–56.

75. "Case of a Trial for Malpractice," *BMSJ* 57 (March 19, 1857):148.

76. Hamilton, "Suits for Malpractice in Surgery," in *Papers Read Before the Medico-Legal Society of New York, 1875–1878* (New York: Medico-Legal Society of New York, 1886), 98–99.

77. "Report of the Section of Surgery and Anatomy," *TAMA* (1873):226–29.

78. For example, see John Harley Warner, "Southern Medical Reform: The Meaning of the Antebellum Argument for Southern Medical Education," *BHM* 57 (Fall 1983):367; James O. Breeden, "Thomsonianism in Virginia," *VMHB* 82 (1974):150–80; John Duffy, ed., *History of Medicine in Louisiana* (Baton Rouge: Louisiana State University Press, 1962), 2:32–42; and Alex Berman, "The Thomsonian Movement and its Relation to American Pharmacy and Medicine," *BHM* 25 (September–October 1951):407.

79. James O. Breeden, "Body Snatchers and Anatomy Professors: Medical Education in Nineteenth-Century Virginia," *VMHB* 83 (1975):321–45; and Todd L. Savitt, "The Use of Blacks for Medical Experimentation and Demonstration in the Old South," *Journal of Southern History* 48 (1982):331–48.

80. John Duffy, "American Perceptions of the Medical, Legal, and Theological Professions," *BHM* 58 (1984):7.

81. John Harley Warner, *The Therapeutic Perspective: Medical Practice, Knowledge, and Professional Identity in America, 1820–1885* (Cambridge: Harvard University Press, 1986), 71–72; Martin Kaufman, *Homeopathy in America: The Rise and Fall of a Medical Heresy* (Baltimore: Johns Hopkins University Press, 1971), 10–11; John Duffy ed., *History of Medicine in Louisiana* (Baton Rouge: Louisiana State University Press, 1950), 1:69–80; Duffy, *Medicine in Louisiana*, 2:3–42; J. Marion Sims, *The Story of My Life* (New York: Da Capo Press, 1968), 171–72, for comments on heroic practice in the antebellum South.

82. Elliot J. Gorn, " 'Gouge and Bite, Pull Hair and Scratch': The Social Significance of Fighting in the Southern Backcountry," *AHR* 90 (February, 1985):27, 29, 40. See also Bertram Wyatt-Brown, *Southern Honor: Ethics and Behavior in the Old South* (New York: Oxford University Press, 1982), passim; and Edward L. Ayers, *Vengeance and Justice, Crime and Punishment in the Nine-teenth-Century American South* (New York: Oxford University Press, 1984).

83. See Brown, *Modernization*, 114, 129, 152–53, for comments on the South's retention of traditional communal structures.

84. John B. Boles, "Evangelical Protestantism in the Old South: From Religious Dissent to Cultural Dominance," in *Religion in the Old South*, edited by Charles Reagan Wilson (Jackson: University Press of Mississippi, 1985), 13–34.

85. Elizabeth Fox-Genovese and Eugene D. Genovese, "The Divine Sanction of Social Order: Religious Foundations of the Southern Slaveholders' World View," *JAAR* 55 (Summer 1987):211–33; and Anne Loveland, *Southern Evangelicals and the Social Order, 1800–1860* (Baton Rouge: Louisiana State University Press, 1980).

86. Clement Eaton, *The Mind of the Old South* (Baton Rouge: Louisiana State University Press, 1964), 159–61, 174–80; Eaton, *The Freedom of Thought Struggle in the Old South* (New York: Harper and Row, 1964), 300–305; Frank Lawrence Owsley, *Plain Folk of the Old South* (Baton Rouge: Louisiana State University Press, 1949), 96; and R. M. Weaver, "The Older Religiousness in the South," *SR* 51 (1943):237–49.

87. C. Vann Woodward, *The Burden of Southern History* (Baton Rouge: Louisiana State University Press, 1968), 21; and Winfred B. Moore, Jr., Joseph F. Tripp, and Lyon G. Tyler, Jr., eds., *Developing Dixie: Modernization in a Traditional Society* (Westport, Conn.: Greenwood Press, 1988), xvii–xxiii.

88. John B. Boles, *The Great Revival, 1787–1805* (Lexington: University Press of Kentucky, 1972), 183–203; and Tommy W. Rogers, "Dr. Fredrick Ross and the Presbyterian Defense of Slavery," *JPH* 45 (March 1967):112–24, esp. 118–19, 122–24.

89. Caton, "Secularization of Pain," 498–99.

90. For example, see Wyatt-Brown, *Southern Honor*, 165–66, 340, 341, 344–46.

91. Samuel D. Gross, *Autobiography of Samuel D. Gross* (Philadelphia: George Barrie, Publisher, 1887; reprint Arno Press, 1972), 2:44, 202–3.

92. Edward Warren, *A Doctor's Experiences in Three Continents* (Baltimore: Cushings and Bailey, 1885), 31.

93. Quotation from Gorn, "Gouge and Bite," 40. Also see W. J. Cash, *The Mind of the South* (New York: Random House, 1941), 56–57, 83–84; and Wyatt-Brown, *Southern Honor*, 25–30.

94. Carol Greenhouse, *Praying for Justice: Faith, Order, and Community in an American Town* (Ithaca: Cornell University Press, 1986); Greenhouse, "Interpreting American Litigiousness," paper presented at the Wenner-Gren Foun-

dation for Anthropological Research, Bellagio, Italy, 10–18 August 1985; and "Nature is to Culture as Praying is to Suing: Legal Pluralism in an American Suburb," *JLP* 20 (1982):17–35.

95. Residents relied on such biblical invocations as: "Pray for them which despitefully use you" (Matthew 5:44); "Be not overcome by evil, but overcome evil with good." (Romans 13:21); and "Dearly beloved, avenge not yourself" (Romans 12:19). See Greenhouse, *Praying*, 80–81.

96. Ibid., 43, 79, 107, 115, 118, 182.

97. See, for example, Martin E. Marty," "From Providence to Progress," in *Righteous Empire*, 188–98.

6. *"Dangerous Ground for a Surgeon"*

1. "Accusation of Mal-Practice," *BMSJ* 31 (11 September 1844):123–24.

2. Frank H. Hamilton, "Suits for Malpractice in Surgery," *Papers Read Before the Medico-Legal Society of New York, 1875–1878* (New York: Medico-Legal Society of New York, 1886), 99, 100.

3. "Prosecutions for Mal-Practice," *NHJM* 4 (January 1854):20–23.

4. "Medical Science in New York," *BMSJ* 15 (16 November 1836):241–42.

5. Alex Berman, "The Thomsonian Movement and Its Relation to American Pharmacy and Medicine," *BHM* 25 (September–October 1951):405–8.

6. Marvin Meyers, *The Jacksonian Persuasion: Politics and Beliefs* (New York: Vintage, 1957), 235–36.

7. Walter Hugins, *Jacksonian Democracy and the Working Class: A Study of the New York Workingman's Movement, 1829–1837* (Stanford: University of Stanford Press, 1960), 166–71; William Trimble, "The Social Philosophy of the Loco-Foco Democracy," *AJS*, 31 (May 1921):710–15; Meyers, *Jacksonian Persuasion*, 183–205.

8. Stewart, "The Actual Condition of the Medical Profession in This Country . . . ," *NYJM* 6 (1846):151–71, reprinted in Gert H. Brieger, ed., *Medical America in the Nineteenth Century: Readings from the Literature* (Baltimore: Johns Hopkins University Press, 1972), 69–70.

9. These observations on the New York medical profession before 1850 were drawn mostly from Daniel Calhoun's study of the physicians in that state. See chapter 2 of his *Professional Lives in America: Structure and Aspiration, 1750–1850* (Cambridge: Harvard University Press, 1965), especially 24–27, 34–37, 46–58.

10. See chapter 2.

11. "Surgical Malpractice," *BMSJ* 36 (5 May 1847):283–84.

12. "A Report of the Facts and Circumstances Relating to a Case of Compound Fracture, and Prosecution for Malpractice," *AJMS* 3 n.s. (January 1842):181–84; some accounts reported that the scaffolding collapsed beneath Smith.

13. D. W., "Shipman, Azariah B. (1803–1868)," *A Cyclopedia of American Medical Biography: Comprising the Lives of Eminent Deceased Physicians and Surgeons, 1610–1900*, edited by Howard Kelly (Philadelphia: W. B. Saunders, 1912), 2:366–67.

14. "A Report of the Facts," *AJMS* 3 n.s. (January 1842):181; also "A Report of the Facts and Circumstances Relating to a Case of Compound Fracture and Prosecution for Malpractice," *WMSJ* 5 (1842):141–48.

15. Howard A. Kelly and Walter L. Burrage, *Dictionary of American Medical Biography* (New York: D. Appleton, 1928), 626–27; "Hyde, Fredrick," *A Biographical Dictionary of Contemporary American Physicians and Surgeons*, 2d ed., edited by William Biddle Atkinson, (Philadelphia: Brinton, 1879), 208.

16. *Courtland Republic and Eagle*, 17 May 1836, 5.

17. Ibid.

18. A. B. Shipman, *A Report of the Facts and Circumstances Relating to a Case of Compound Fracture and Prosecution for Malpractice, in which William Smith Was Plaintiff, and Drs. Goodyear and Hyde Defendants, at Cortland Village, Cortland County, N. Y., March 1841: Comprising Statements of the Case by Several Medical Gentlemen, Together with Notes and Comments on the Testimony* (Cortlandville: Printed at the office of the *Cortland Democrat*, 1841), 8, 13, 16.

19. "A Report of the facts," *AJMS* 3 n.s. (January 1842):181–83; Shipman, *A Report of the Facts*, 4.

20. "A Report of the Facts," *AJMS* 3 n.s. (January 1842):181–84; "A Report of the Facts," *WMSJ* 5 (1842):141–48.

21. Shipman, *A Report of the Facts*, 17.

22. "A Report of the Facts," *AJMS* 3 n.s. (January 1842):181–84; "A Report of the Facts," *WMSJ* 5 (1842):141–48.

23. Shipman, *A Report of the Facts*, 7.

24. Hamilton published his famous fracture tables between 1849 and 1860. Though his study appeared too late to influence this case, his work was often cited by defense attorneys in later malpractice cases. See chapter 4.

25. "A Report of the Facts," *AJMS* 3 n.s. (January 1842):181–82. For excerpts of Webster's and Hamilton's testimony, also see "A Report of the Facts," *Western Journal of Medical and Physician Surgery* 5 (1842):145–48.

26. Shipman, *A Report of the Facts*, 16.

27. *Cortland Democrat*, 4 May 1841, 2. Reproductions of the *Cortland County Whig* for the 1840s are not existant, but the debate may be followed with some success in the *Democrat*, which reprinted several of the letters that appeared initially in the *Whig*.

28. Ibid.

29. Ibid.

30. "A Report of the Facts," *AJMS* 3 n.s. (January 1842):182.

31. Shipman, *A Report of the Facts*, 3.

32. See n. 17 above.

33. "Trial for Malpractice," *BMSJ* 25 (8 September 1841):73–75.

34. See chapter 4.

35. "Cases of Compound Fracture of the Leg," *BMSJ* 25 (8 September 1841):73–75.

36. R. C., "A Report of the Facts and Circumstance Relating to a Case of Compound Fracture and Prosecution for Malpractice," *ME* 4 (1841):712–14.

37. R. C., "The Cortlandville Trial for Malpractice," *ME* 4 (1841):766–67.

38. G. W. N. [George W. Norris], "Bibliographic Notices," *AJMS* 3 n.s. (January 1842):181–84.

39. *Cortland Democrat*, 2 February 1842, 2–3; "The Cortland Case of Malpractice," *ME* 5 (5 March 1842):149–51.

40. "The Cortland Case," *ME* 5 (5 March 1842):149–51.

41. Cooper, *The Lectures of Sir Astley Cooper*, 4th American ed. (Philadelphia: E. L. Carey and A. Hart, 1835), 628–30.

42. See chapters 3 and 4.

43. "A Report of the Facts," *WJMS*, 5 (1842):145.

44. "Trial of Dr. Shipman for Mal-Practice," *BMSJ* 31 (18 September 1844):140–42.

45. "Accusation of Mal-Practice," *BMSJ* 31 (11 September 1844):123–24; "Trial of Dr. Shipman for Mal-Practice," *BMSJ* 31 (18 September 1844):140–42.

46. Kelly and Burrage, *American Medical Biography*, 626–27; and Atkinson, *Dictionary of Contemporary American Physicians*, 208.

47. Stewart, "Actual Condition of the Medical Profession," 70–71.

7. The Road Not Taken: Medical Malpractice and the Path of the Common Law

1. Kennedy v. Parrott 243 N.C. 355 (1956), quoted in Louis B. Harrison, Melvin H. Worth, Jr., and Michael A. Carlucci, "The Development of the Principles of Medical Malpractice in the United States," *PBM*, 29 (Autumn 1985):46.

2. Harrison, Worth, and Carlucci, "Principles of Medical Malpractice," 42.

3. G. Edward White, *Tort Law in America: An Intellectual History* (New York: Oxford University Press, 1980), 8–10. See also Percy H. Winfield, *The Province of The Law of Tort* (Cambridge: Cambridge University Press, 1931), 27–28; and Richard B. Morris, "Responsibility for Tortious Acts in Early American Law," in *Studies in the History of American Law* (Philadelphia: J. M. Mitchell, 1959), 207.

4. William Blackstone, *Commentaries*, St. George Tucker's ed. Vol. 3 (Philadelphia: William Birch Young and Abraham, 1803), 122, 123.

5. The ten actions included: trespass; debt; covenant; account; assumpsit; detinue; trespass on the case; trover; ejectment; and replevin. For a short and clear description of early American pleading see Mitchell G. Williams, "Plead-

ing Reform in Nineteenth-Century America: The Joinder of Actions at Common Law under the Codes," *JLH* 6 (1985):299–335; and William Nelson, *The Americanization of the Common Law: The Impact of Legal Change on Massachusetts Society, 1760–1830* (Cambridge: Harvard University Press, 1975), 21–23, 71–87.

6. C. H. S. Fifoot, *History and Sources of the Common Law* (New York: Greenwood Press, 1970), 67–78.

7. Ibid., 75–77, 156–58. Research is underway which challenges the standard historiography on the origins and development of the modern writ system. See Robert Palmer, "In Plague and Oppression: The Foundations of Anglo-American Law, 1348–1381," presented as the Harold and Margaret Rorschach Lecture in Legal History, Rice University, 15 February 1989.

8. Quoted in Hubert Winston Smith, "Legal Responsibility for Medical Malpractice," *JAMA* 116 (31 May 1941):2490.

9. Fifoot, *History and Sources*, 157.

10. Everard v. Hopkins 2 Bulst. 332; 80 E. R. 1164; quoted in Smith, "Legal Responsibility," 2491.

11. Smith, ibid., makes a similar point at 2492.

12. Blackstone, *Commentaries*, 3:123.

13. Slater v. Baker and Stapleton 2 Wils 359.

14. *Slater* is noted, for example, in Landon v. Humphrey 9 Day 209 (Conn. 1832); Howard v. Grover 15 Me. 97 (1848); and Mc Candless v. Mc Wha 22 Penn. 261 (1857).

15. Seare v. Prentice 8 East's Term Rep. 347 (1807).

16. Landon 9 Day 216.

17. Lamphier v. Phipos 8 Carr & Payne 475 (1838).

18. Decision reprinted in Martin J. Wade, *A Selection of Cases on Malpractice of Physicians, Surgeons, and Dentists* (St. Louis: Medico-Legal Pub. Co., 1909), 21–23.

19. For examples of American judges who incorporated Tyndall's language, see Patten v. Wiggin 51 Me. 549; Leighton v. Sargent 7 N. H. 460 (1853); Reynolds v. Graves 3 Wisc. 416 (1854); Graham v. Gautier 21 Tx. 111 (1858); and Richey v. West 23 Ill. 385 (1860).

20. I am indebted to Thomas L. Haskell, *The Emergence of Professional Social Science: The American Social Science Association and the Nineteenth-Century Crisis of Authority* (Urbana: University of Illinois Press, 1977), 65–75, for introducing me to these ideas.

21. Blackstone, *Commentaries*, 3:28; John Ordronaux, *The Jurisprudence of Medicine* (Philadelphia: T. and J. W. Johnson, 1869), 34–35.

22. Ordronaux, *Jurisprudence of Medicine*, 10–11.

23. Ibid., 37.

24. Adams v. Stevens & Cagger 26 Wendell 448 at 455 (N.Y. 1841).

25. Morton Horwitz, *The Transformation of American Law, 1780–1860* (Cambridge: Harvard University Press, 1977), 181–83.

26. Ordronaux, *Jurisprudence of Medicine*, 14.

27. Henry Maine, *Ancient Law* (New York: Henry Holt, 1884), 164–65. See also Bernard Schwartz, *Law in America* (New York: McGraw Hill, 1974), 117–18. This explanatory theory can easily be carried too far. For a sober analysis of its utility, see R. H. Graveson, "The Movement from Status to Contract," 4 *MLR* (April 1941):261–67.

28. Grant Gilmore, *The Death of Contract* (Columbus: Ohio State University Press, 1974); Horwitz, *Transformation*, 160–210; Lawrence Friedman, *Contract Law in America: A Social and Economic Case Study* (Madison: University of Wisconsin Press, 1965); and P. S Atiyah, *The Rise and Fall of Freedom of Contract* (Oxford: Clarendon Press, 1979), esp. 167–68.

29. Horwitz, *Transformation*, 160–201.

30. Nelson, *Americanization*, deals with early American practice in detail. Also, though some of the conclusions are questionable, Herbert A. Johnson, "Civil Procedure in John Jay's New York," *AJLH* 11 (January 1967):69–80, discusses early legal practice.

31. Nelson, *Americanization*, 21–23, 71–76; Joseph H. Koffler and Alison Reppy, *Handbook of Common Law Pleading* (St. Paul: West Publishing, 1969), 10–17, 37–45.

32. Edson R. Sunderland, *Cases on Procedure Code Pleading* (Chicago: Callaghan and Company, 1923), 6; Nelson, *Americanization*, 77.

33. Nelson, *Americanization*, 83.

34. White, *Tort Law in America*, 9–12; Nelson, *Americanization*, 81; and Percy H. Winfield, *The Province of the Law of Tort*, 27–30, for the imprecise distinction between the various categories of law in the late eighteenth and early nineteenth centuries.

35. Koffler and Reppy, *Common Law Pleading*, 47.

36. See chapter 1.

37. Joseph Chitty, *A Practical Treatise on Pleading and on Parties to Actions and Forms of Actions* (New York: C. Wiley, 1812), 1:92, 134, 137.

38. John Simcoe Saunders, *The Law of Pleading and Evidence in Civil Actions* (Philadelphia: Robert H. Small, 1844), 1:90.

39. See above, chapter 1.

40. White, *Tort Law in America*, chs. 1 and 2.

41. Grannis et ux v. Branden 5 Conn. 260 at 269.

42. Charles Lee, "Medical Jurisprudence," *NYJMCS* 1 (November 1843):352.

43. For more on the case, see Landon v. Humphrey 5 Conn. 209 (1832); and "Alleged Malpractice," *BMSJ* 6 (21 March 1832):98–99.

44. Lee, "Medical Jurisprudence," 354–56.

45 Landon v. Humphrey 5 Conn. 209, 210 (1832).

46. The prosecution was allowed as many counts of wrongdoing as they wished, but all the counts had to support the one writ. In this first count, Landon's attorney accused Humphrey of what amounted to misfeasance. *Misfeasance* was grounds for an action on the case and was the doing of an act in an injurious manner, or the improper performance of an act that might other-

wise have been lawfully done. In this instance, Humphrey, acting through his agent, had improperly performed the otherwise legal act of vaccination.

47. In this count Humphrey was being accused of nonfeasance. *Nonfeasance* occurred when a person failed to perform a duty that was required of him.

48. Lee, "Medical Jurisprudence," 354–59.

49. Ibid., 360–61; Landon v. Humphrey 5 Conn. 209, 212–13 (1832).

50. Landon v. Humphrey 5 Conn. 209, 213–14 (1832).

51. Idem, 209.

52. Gordon Wood, *The Creation of the American Republic, 1776–1787* (New York: Norton, 1969), 295–305; and Carl L. Becker, *The Declaration of Independence: A Study in the History of Political Ideas* (New York: Random House, 1921), 30–36, 68–75.

53. Bernard Bailyn, *Education in the Forming of American Society* (New York: Vintage, 1960), 29–36.

54. Magali Sarfatti Larson, *The Rise of Professionalism: A Sociological Analysis* (Berkeley: University of California Press, 1977), 105, 110.

55. Alexis de Tocqueville, *Democracy in America*, edited by J. P. Mayer, translated by George Lawrence (Garden City, N.Y.: Anchor, 1969), 507.

56. George Dargo, *Law in the New Republic: Private Law and the Public Estate* (New York: Alfred A. Knopf, 1983), 40.

57. Horwitz, *Transformation*, 173–210. Horwitz's thesis is not universally applicable and has come under considerable attack. For example, see A. W. B. Simpson, *Legal Theory and Legal History: Essays on the Common Law* (London: Hambledon Press, 1987). While much of the criticism of Horwitz is justified, he does illuminate an important trend in early nineteenth-century law and errs mostly from overstatement.

58. Horwitz, *Transformation*, 201–10.

59. Bowman v. Woods 1 G. Greene 441 at 442 (Iowa). See chapter 2 for a discussion of another aspect of this case.

60. Idem, at 442–43.

61. Idem, at 443–44.

62. For cases that exhibited similar contractual language, see Piper v. Menifee 51 Ky. 465 (1851); Alder v. Buckley 1 Swan 69 (Tenn. 1851); Moody v. Sabin 63 Mass. 505 (1852).

63. John Dawson, "Suit for Damages in a Case of Fracture of the Leg, Followed by Mortification and Amputation," *OMSJ* 14 (1 July 1862):284.

64. Ordronaux, *Jurisprudence of Medicine*, in fact refers to the doctor-patient relationship as quasicontractual.

65. T. J. W. Pray, "A Surgical Case of Malpractice," *BMSJ* 51 (8 November 1854):289–90.

66. Ibid.

67. Ibid., 289–91.

68. Leighton's lawyer used a "trespass on the case writ."

69. Leighton v. Sargent 7 Foster 460 at 460–63, 465 (N.H. 1853); *BMSJ*

51 (1854):290; Chester Burns presented a short discussion of this case in his "Medical Ethics in the United States Before the Civil War," Ph.D. dissertation (Johns Hopkins University, 1969), 147–48.

70. Leighton v. Sargent 7 Foster 460 at 465; (N.H. 1853); *BMSJ* 51:290.

71. Pray, "A Surgical Case," 290.

72. Ibid., 291.

73. Leighton v. Sargent 7 Foster 460 at 464–66 (N.H. 1853).

74. Idem, at 468, 469, 471, 472.

75. Idem, 460 at 472. After losing his award in the state supreme court, Leighton again charged Dr. Sargent with malpractice in the Strafford county court. The jury again sided with Leighton and fined Sargent $525 plus the cost of both trials. Sargent appealed to the state supreme court in 1855, claiming that three jurors at the second trial had shared a "gill" of brandy the night before they agreed on the guilty verdict. On these grounds, the supreme court set aside the verdict and called for a third trial. Finally, after five years of litigation, Leighton and Sargent agreed to an undisclosed, out-of-court settlement. Leighton v. Sargent 11 Foster 119, 130, 138 (N.H. 1855); and Milo McClelland, *Civil Malpractice* (New York: Hurd and Houghton 1877), 210.

76. "Case of Alleged Malpractice," *BMSJ* 54 (24 April 1856):239.

77. Harrison, Worth, and Carlucci, "Development of the Principles of Medical Malpractice," 42, 44, 45.

78. Horwitz, *Transformation*, 206.

79. "Surgical Malpractice," *BMSJ* 36 (5 May 1847):283–84.

80. "Prosecution for Malpractice," *ME* 14 (n.s. 8) (1851):728–29.

81. "Important Case of Alleged Malpractice," *Scal* 9 (April 1857): 56.

82. "Suit for Malpractice," *BMSJ* 50 (19 April 1854):246. For other references to the use of bonds to stifle suits, see "Prosecutions for Malpractice," *BMSJ* 51 (8 November 1854):305; "Prosecutions of Medical Men," *WMSJ* 28 (1853):346–47; "Prosecutions for Malpractice," *BMSJ* 48 (11 May 1853):304.

83. "The Greenpoint Malpractice Case," *Scal* 8 (April 1856):311–15.

84. Ibid., 315.

85. John Dawson, "Suit for Damages in a Case of Fracture of the Leg, Followed by Mortification and Amputation," *OMSJ* 14 (1 July 1862):283–84.

86. Ibid., 284–85.

87. Ibid., 287–88. For more discussion of contracting away, see Joel Parker, "Extract from a Lecture on the Rights and Liabilities of the Physician and Surgeon," *WMSJ* 31 (March 1855):217–19.

88. Worthington Hooker, *Physician and Patient*, 410.

89. "Valentine Mott on Medical Ethics; He Throws a Medical Boomerang," *Scal* 9 (July 1857):125–26.

90. Samuel Parkman and Calvin P. Fiske, "Report on the Causes and Prevention of Suits for Mal-Practice," *MCMMS* 8 (1853): appendix, 124.

91. Parkman and Fiske, "Report on the Causes and Prevention," 130.

92. Joel Parker, "Extract from a Lecture," 218.

93. "Case of Mal-Practice," *BMSJ* 54 (13 March 1856):112. See also "Trial for Malpractice—Dr. Crosby's Acquittal," *BMSJ* 50 (21 June 1854):424–25, for more medical opposition to contracting away.

94. Ordronaux, *The Jurisprudence of Medicine*, 104; and Elwell, *A Medico-Legal Treatise on Malpractice and Medical Evidence* (New York: John Voorhis, 1860). Courts accepted special contracts from common carriers until 1873, when the United States Supreme Court, in N.Y. Central R.R. v. Lockwood 84 U.S. 357, ruled against them.

95. Ordronaux, *Jurisprudence of Medicine*, 11, 71, 73, and 96.

96. Ibid., 2.

97. "Trial for Alleged Malpractice," *BMSJ* 50 (8 March 1854):120–21.

98. Dixi Crosby, comp., *Report of a Trial for Alleged Malpractice Against Dixi Crosby* (Woodstock, N.H.: Printed by Lewis Pratt, Jr., 1854) 5, 79.

99. White, *Tort Law in America*, 10–12, 40.

100. Francis Hillard, *The Law of Torts or Private Wrongs* (Boston: Little, Brown, 1859), 1–2.

101. Ibid., 238–40.

102. Thomas G. Sherman and Amasa A. Redfield, *A Treatise on the Law of Negligence* (New York: Baker, Voorhis, Publishers, 1870), 511.

103. See for example Piper v. Menifee 51 Ky. 465 (1851); and Alden v. Buckley 1 Swann R. 69 (Tenn. 1851).

104. Smith v. Overby 30 Ga. 241 (1860).

105. Ritchey v. West 23 Ill. 329, 330 (1860).

106. McNevins v. Lowe 40 Ill. 209, 210 (1866).

107. There are rich philosophical and ethical discussions of contract and the nature of the doctor-patient relationship. See Roger Masters, "Is Contract an Adequate Basis for Medical Ethics?" *HCR* 5 (December 1975):24–28; William May, *The Physician's Covenant: Images of the Healer in Medical Ethics* (Philadelphia: Westminister Press, 1983), 42–45, 116–27; and May, "Adversarialism in America and the Professions," in *Community in America: the Challenge of Habits of the Heart*, edited by Charles H. Reynolds and Ralph V. Norman (Berkeley: University of California Press, 1988), 185–201.

108. Elizabeth Heitman "Caring for the Silent Stranger: Ethical Hospital Care for Non-English Speaking Patients," Ph.D. dissertation (Rice University, 1988), 11.

109. Starr, *Transformation*, 421–49; Donald W. Light, "Corporate Medicine for Profit," *SA* 255 (December 1986):38–45; and Gwen Kinkead, "Humana's Hard-Sell Hospitals," *For* (17 November 1980):68–81.

110. There is a synthetic overview of the debate over contract, ethics, and the doctor-patient relationship in Heitman, "Caring for the Silent Stranger," 1–32.

111. Richard A. Epstein, "Medical Malpractice: The Case for Contract," *ABFRJ* (1976):87–149; and Epstein, "Market and Regulatory Approaches to

Medical Malpractice: The Virginia Obstetrical No-Fault Statute," *VLR* 74 (1988):1451–74.

8. The More Things Change . . . : Medical Malpractice, 1865–1900

1. Alexander Young, "The Law of Malpractice," *BMSJ* 5 (9 June 1870):443.
2. H. F. Montgomery, "Suits for Malpractice," *BufMSJ* 11 (July 1872):445.
3. "On the Avoidance of Causeless Suits for Malpractice," *MSR* 33 (25 September 1875):255–56.
4. "The Liability of Physicians," *MSJ* 34 (15 April 1876):315–16. See also John J. Reese, "Case of Alleged Malpractice," *MT* 1 (1 December 1870):73–74; and George M. Blake, "Suits Against Surgeons," *BufMSJ* 18 (1879–1880):309–16, for comments on renewed malpractice suits.
5. Sanger's study included suits brought against respondent physicians at any time (including the first half of the century) up to the time of the survey. Eugene F. Sanger, "Report on Malpractice," *BMSJ* 100 (2 January 1879):14–23; and Sanger, "Report on Malpractice," *BMSJ* 100 (9 January 1879):41–50. Sanger first read his report in 1878 before the Maine Medical Association.
6. Sanger, "Report on Malpractice," *BMSJ* 100 (2 January 1879):19–20.
7. Sanger quoted in "Medical Notes," *BMSJ* 100 (9 January 1878):91.
8. O. E. Lyman, "Some Notes on a Doctor's Liability," *PSM* 18 (1880–1881):770.
9. A. M. Powell, "Surgical Malpractice," *StLMSJ* 42 (March 1882):231.
10. E. J. Doering, "Mutual Protection Against Blackmail," *JAMA* 6 (1886):114.
11. "Malpractice Suits," *MSR* 61 (21 September 1889):326.
12. F. J. Groner, "The Causes and the Remedies for Suits for Malpractice," *MR* 37 (9 August 1890):143.
13. Quoted in Robert H. Shikes, *Rocky Mountain Medicine: Doctors, Drugs, and Disease in Early Colorado* (Boulder, Colo.: Johnson Books, 1986), 118–19. See also J. R. Weist, "Civil Malpractice Suits: How Can the Physician Protect Himself Against Them?" *AP* 30 (1884):160–74; and "Medical Malpractice," *MSR* 47 (23 December 1882):716–17, for more on the increase of suits.
14. Hubert Winston Smith, "Legal Responsibility for Medical Malpractice," *JAMA* 116 (14 June 1941):2672–73; and Charles J. Weigel II, "Medical Malpractice in America's Middle Years," *TRBM* 32 (Spring 1974):203.
15. See chapter 2.
16. See appendix B.
17. Musser v. Chase 29 Ohio 577 (1876) (lost nose $3,000); W. F. Hutchinson, "A Recent Suit for Malpractice," *BufMSJ* 12 (1872–1873):290–91 ($4,000, fracture); Kelsey v. Hey 84 Indiana 189 (1882) ($4,000, damage to legs); "Some Recent Malpractice Suits," *MR* 28 (19 December 1885):690–91 ($7,000, frac-

ture); "Verdict Against Physician," *MR* 47 (12 January 1895):64 ($12,000, fracture); and Jackson v. Burnham 20 Col. 533 (1895) ($5,000, lost penis). Some of these awards, as well as the judgments rendered in the 38 sample cases, were reduced on retrial.

18. Weigel's study, based on appellate decisions between 1860 and 1915, uncovered awards in 34 cases: 5 awards were less than $100; 4 awards were less than $500; 22 awards were between $1,000 and $5,000; and 3 awards were between $6,000 and $10,000. Weigel, "Medical Malpractice," 194, 195. The awards cited in Eugene Sanger's 1878 study averaged only $584, but he drew many of his cases from the first half of the century, so I did not include them in my averages. Sanger, "Report on Malpractice," *BMSJ* 100 (2 January 1879): 20.

19. Paul Starr, *The Social Transformation of American Medicine* (New York: Basic Books, 1984), 84–85.

20. Awards average from Department of Health, Education, and Welfare report quoted in David Ghitelman, "Medical Malpractice in the Last Thirty Years," *MD Magazine* (April 1987):62–73. Physician mean, real income (in 1983 dollars) from H. E. French III, ed., *Health Care in America: The Political Economy of Hospitals and Health* (San Francisco: Pacific Research Institute for Public Policy, 1988), 311.

21. Cayford v. Wilbur 86 Me. 414 (1894).

22. Kelsey v. Hay 84 Ind. 189 (1882).

23. Brooke v. Clarke 57 Tx. 1905 (1882).

24. William C. Wey, "Medical Responsibilty for Malpractice. Anniversary Address delivered before the Medical Society of the State of New York," *TSMSNY* (1872):84; and Steven Smith, *Doctor in Medicine* (New York: William Wood, 1872; reprint, Arno Press, 1972), 286.

25. See chapter 3 for a discussion of the working class and the role of the poor in malpractice litigation.

26. Wey, "Medical Responsibility," 87.

27. W. F. Hutchinson, "A Recent Suit for Malpractice," *BufMSJ* 12 (1872–1873):297.

28. See Harold M. Hyman, *A More Perfect Union: the Impact of the Civil War and Reconstruction on the Constitution* (New York: Alfred A. Knopf, 1973), 360, 347–49, 359–61, and passim; and Samuel Bernstein, "The Impact of the Paris Commune in the United States," *MassR* 12 (1971):435–45.

29. Blake, "Suits against Surgeons," 316.

30. Starr, *Transformation*, 85–88. D. W. Cathell, *Physician Himself* (1890), quoted in ibid.

31. "Civil Malpractice," *BMSJ* 96 (19 April 1877):470.

32. Sanger quoted in "Medical Notes " (summary of Sanger's study), *BMSJ* 99 (18 July 1878):91.

33. "The Animus of Suits for Malpractice," *MSR* 34 (September 1878):218.

34. Sanger, "Report on Malpractice," *BMSJ* 100 (9 January 1879):43, 50.

35. "Medico-Legal Notes," *BMSJ* 100 (1879):390.

36. Sanger, "Report on Malpractice," *BMSJ* 100 (2 January 1879):18.

37. See chapter 2. John J. Elwell, *A Medico-Legal Treatise on Malpractice and Medical Evidence* (New York: John Voorhis, 1860), 44.

38. Daniel H. Calhoun, *Professional Lives in America: Structure and Aspiration, 1750–1850* (Cambridge: Harvard University Press, 1965), 2–7; and John Duffy, "American Perceptions of the Medical, Legal, and Theological Professions," *BHM* 58 (1984):8, discuss Jacksonian attitudes towards the professions.

39. For comments on the composition of the early bar, see Kermit Hall, *The Magic Mirror* (New York: Oxford University Press, 1989), 216–18.

40. James Bryce, *American Commonwealth* (London: Macmillan, 1889), 2:490–91.

41. Lawrence Friedman, *A History of American Law* (New York: Simon and Schuster, 1973), 549; and Joseph Gordon Hylton, Jr., "The Virginia Lawyer from Reconstruction to the Great Depression," Ph.D. dissertation (Harvard University, 1986), 139.

42. See Hylton, "Virginia Lawyer," 99–145 passim. The issue and significance of the "overcrowding" of the lawyers are much-debated and unresolved. See, for example, J. Willard Hurst, *The Growth of American Law: The Law Makers* (Boston: Little, Brown, 1950), 313–19; Terrance C. Halliday, "Six Score and Ten: Demographic Transitions in the American Legal Profession," *LSR* 20 (1986):53–77.

43. "Civil Malpractice," *BMSJ* 96 (19 April 1877):471.

44. Doering, "Mutual Protection," 114.

45. For example, see *"Fisher v. Gross,"* *MR* 6 (15 May 1871):133–34; J. K. Stockwell, "Suits for Malpractice," *MR* 17 (7 February 1880):161–62; "The Animus of Suits for Malpractice," *MSR* 34 (September 1878):218; and "The Proper Steps for Physicians in Suits for Malpractice," *MSR* 27 (7 December 1872):496–97.

46. Powell, "Surgical Malpractice," 232.

47. Weist, "Civil Malpractice," 165.

48. Wey, "Medical Responsibility," 83; Simon Greenleaf, *A Treatise on the Law of Evidence* (Boston: Little, Brown, 1853), 3:63–64.

49. "The Suit Against Professor Gross," *MT* 1 (1 May 1871):281. For other attacks on contingency fees from physicians, see Weist, "Civil Malpractice Suits," 164; *"Fisher v. Gross,"* 133; Stockwell, "Suits for Malpractice," 161; and "A Suit for Malpractice", *MR* 52 (1898):925–26.

50. Lawrence M. Friedman, *Total Justice* (Boston: Beacon Press, 1985), 25.

51. Stanton v. Embrey 93 U.S. 548 (1877). For a history of the attacks from the bar on the use of the contingency fees, see Jerold S. Auerbach, *Unequal Justice: Lawyers and Social Change in Modern America* (New York: Oxford University Press, 1976), 45–49; and F. B. MacKinnon, *Contingent Fees for Legal Services* (Chicago: Aldine, 1964), 8–15.

52. "The Contingency Fee Business," *ALJ* 24 (1881):24–25.

53. Cooley quoted in Lawrence M. Friedman, *A History of American Law*, 422–23.

54. F. J. Groner, "The Causes and the Remedies for Suits for Malpractice," *MR* 37 (9 August 1890):143–44.

55. "Causes and Prevention of Suits for Mal-Practice," *BMSJ* 48 (27 July 1853):525; the writer was referring to Samuel Parkman and Calvin P. Fiske, "Report on the Causes and Prevention of Suits for Mal-Practice," *MCMMS* appendix 8 (1853):124–32.

56. Samuel L. Baker, "Physician Licensure Laws in the United States, 1865–1915," *JHMAS* 39 (April 1984):173–97; and Richard Harrison Shyrock, *Medical Licensing in America, 1650–1965* (Baltimore: Johns Hopkins University Press, 1967), 48.

57. Kenneth Ludmerer, *Learning to Heal: The Development of American Medical Education* (New York: Basic Books, 1985), 47–101.

58. Richard Hofstadter, *Anti-Intellectualism in American Life* (New York: Vintage, 1962), 197–213; and Robert H. Wiebe, *The Search for Order, 1877–1920* (New York: Hill and Wang, 1967), 112–23.

59. W. L. Appley, "How Rip Van Winkle, Jr., M.D. Disposed of a Case of Malpractice," *MSR* 25 (25 October 1871):381–82.

60. D. W. Cathell, *The Physician Himself and What He Should Add to His Scientific Acquirements* (Baltimore: Cushings and Bailey, 1882; reprint, Arno Press, 1972), 49.

61. "Remarks on Suits for Malpractice," *NYJM* 65 (15 May 1897):676–8 at 678.

62. See Starr, *Transformation*, 99–127.

63. Smith, *Doctor in Medicine*, 156.

64. "Suits for Malpractice," *MR* 16 (20 December 1879):591; and "Suit for Malpractice," *MR* 16 (20 December 1879):599.

65. "Malpractice," *MR* 15 (24 May 1879):492.

66. "Concerning Suits for Malpractice," *MR* 36 (5 October 1889):375.

67. Quoted in Helen Clapesattle, *The Doctors Mayo* (New York: Simon and Schuster, 1970), 63–64.

68. James J. O'Dea, "Medico-Legal Science: A Sketch of its Progress, Especially in the United States," *Papers Read Before the Medico-Legal Society of New York*, 3rd series, 1875–1878 (New York: Medico-Legal Society, 1886), 305.

69. Chester R. Burns, "Medical Ethics and Medical Jurisprudence," in *The Education of American Physicians*, edited by Ronald L. Numbers (Berkeley: University of California Press, 1980), 273–89.

70. Elwell, *Treatise on Malpractice* (1860, 1866, 1871, 1881); John Ordronaux, *The Jurisprudence of Medicine* (Philadelphia: T. and J. W. Johnson, 1869; reprint, Arno Press, 1973); and Milo A. McClelland, *Civil Malpractice: A Treatise on Surgical Jurisprudence* (New York: Hurd and Houghton, 1877), v.

71. Brewer Mattocks, "Malpractice," *NMSJ* 3 (August 1872):51–52.

72. "Actions for Malpractice," *NYMJ* 68 (24 December 1898):940.

73. McClelland, *Civil Malpractice*, 528.

74. "Effect of Malpractice Charges and How to Avoid Them," *MR* 44 (30 December 1893):847–48; and Mattocks, "Malpractice," 46.

75. Sanger, "Report on Malpractice," *BMSJ* 100 (2 January 1879):20.

76. John J. Reese, "A Case of Alleged Malpractice," *MT* 1 (1 December 1870):73–74. For comments on success rates of suits, see Mordecai Price, "Remarks on Suits for Malpractice," *NYMJ* 65 (15 May 1897):676–78.

77. "*Fisher* v. *Gross*," *MR* 6 (15 May 1871):133–34.

78. "A Case of Alleged Malpractice," *MR* 5 (16 January 1871):517–18; "A Case of Alleged Malpractice," *NYMJ* 13 (January 1871):124–28; "Judge Thayer's Charge in the Case of *Haire* v. *Reese*," *MT* 1 (15 December 1870):99–101; and "[Suit against Dr. Sayer]," *MR* 5 (1 November 1870):398–99.

79. "The Suit against Professor Gross," *MT* 1 (May 1871):281.

80. Lucius Weinschenk, "Malpractice," *DTMJ* 5 (1889):219.

81. "Blackmailing of Surgeons and Malpractice Suits," *MR* 13 (20 April 1878):315–16. See also "The Proper Steps in Suits for Malpractice," *MSJ* 27 (7 December 1872):496–97.

82. McClelland, *Civil Malpractice*, 528.

83. E. J. Doering, "Mutual Protection Against Blackmail," *JAMA* 6 (1886):116; and Sanger, "Report on Malpractice," *BMSJ* 100 (2 January 1879):21 and passim.

84. See Parkman and Fiske, "Report on the Causes and Prevention of Suits for Mal-Practice," 131.

85. Doering, "Mutual Protection," 114.

86. "*Stogdale* v. *Baker*," *BMSJ* 117 (1887):610.

87. "Organized Medical Defence," *JAMA* 38 (4 January 1902):37; "Organized Medical Defence," *JAMA* 38 (4 January 1902):43; "The Varied Functions Possible in the County Medical Society," *JAMA* 44 (18 March 1905):881–82; Starr, *Transformation*, 111; and Sandra Cirincione, "The History of Medical Malpractice in New York State: A Perspective from the Publications of the Medical Society of New York," *NYSJM* 86 (July 1986):363–64.

88. Starr, *Transformation*, 111–12; William G. Rothstein, *American Physicians in the Nineteenth Century* (Baltimore: Johns Hopkins University Press, 1972), 324–25. See, Cirincione, "History of Medical Malpractice," 364–65.

89. Sanger, "Report on Malpractice," *BMSJ* 100 (9 January 1879):46.

90. Powell, "Surgical Malpractice," 236.

91. Weist, "Civil Malpractice Suits," 173; and "Medical Expert Testimony," *BMSJ* 116 (31 February 1887):119–20.

92. Weist, "Civil Malpractice Suits," 169; "On Suits for Malpractice," *NYMJ* 49 (9 February 1889):158; and "Malpractice Suits and their Prevention," *MR* 29 (13 February 1886):188.

93. "Malpractice—Proposed Law," *MR* 9 (1 October 1874):527; and "Law of Malpractice," *MSR* 30 (28 February 1874):2.

94. Ritchey v. West 23 Ill. 329 (1860).

95. Weigel, "Medical Malpractice in America's Middle Years," 198.

96. Hoener v. Koch 84 Ill. 408 (1877); and Weigel, "Medical Malpractice," 199.

97. Gerchell v. Hill 21 Minn. 464 (1875). See also Fisher v. Niccolls 2 Ill. App. 484 (1877); Gores v. Graff 77 Wisc. 174 (1890); Stevenson v. Gelsthorpe 10 Mont. 563 (1891); Feeney v. Spalding 89 Me. 111 (1896); and Richards v. Willard 176 Penn. 181 (1896) for samples of cases overturned for verdicts rendered against the weight of the evidence.

98. Spalding v. Bliss 83 Mich. 31 (1890).

99. Weigel, "Medical Malpractice," 195–96; McNevins v. Lowe 40 Ill. 209 (1866); and Smothers v. Hanks 34 Iowa 286 (1872).

100. Almond v. Nugent 34 Iowa 300 (1872).

101. Quinn v. Donovan 85 Ill. 194 (1877).

102. Utley v. Burns 700 Ill. 162 (1873).

103. Kendall v. Brown 74 Ill. 232 (1874); Jones v. Angell 95 Ind. 376 (1883); and Carpenter v. Blake 60 N.Y. 12 (1878). See also David McAdam, *Malpractice with Reference to the Legal and Medical Professions* (1893), 13.

104. Thomas M. Cooley, *A Treatise on the Law of Torts*, 3rd ed., (Chicago: Callaghan, 1906), 2:1391. For another example of the essential stability of basic malpractice doctrine, see Marshall D. Ewell, *A Manual of Medical Jurisprudence for the Use of Students at Law and of Medicine* (Boston: Little, Brown, 1887), 282–83.

105. In general, see Charles E. Rosenberg, *The Care of Strangers: The Rise of America's Hospital System* (New York: Basic Books, 1987); Stanley Joel Reiser, *Medicine and the Reign of Technology* (New York: Cambridge University Press, 1978), 153–56; and Starr, *Transformation*, 209–15.

106. McDonald v. Massachusetts General Hospital 120 Mass 432 (1876). See also Downes v. Harper Hospital 101 Mich. 555 (1894); and Hearns v. Waterbury Hospital 66 Conn. 93 (1895).

107. "Malpractice," *MR* 15 (24 May 1879):492. See also "Noteworthy Malpractice Decisions," *NYMJ* 33 (April 1881):731; "Malpractice," *MR* 15 (17 May 1879):468–69; "Malpractice Suits Against Hospital Surgeons," *NYMJ* 54 (26 December 1891):718; Hedin v. Minneapolis Medical & Surgical Institute 62 Minn. 146 (1895); and Beck v. German Klinik 78 Iowa 696 (1889).

108. Union Pacific Ry Co. v. Artist 60 Fed. Rep. 365 (1894); and Eighmy v. Union Pacific Railway Co. 93 Iowa 538 (1895).

109. "Malpractice," *MR* 15 (24 May 1879):492.

110. See chapter 2.

111. Jones v. Angell 95 Ind. 376 (1883). See also Hibbard v. Thomson 109 Mass. 286 (1872); and Potter v. Warner 91 Penn. 362 (1879).

112. Carpenter v. Blake 75 N.Y. 12 (1878). For the medical profession's view of the softening of the contributory negligence doctrine, see T. C. Becker, "*Carpenter v. Blake*: An Important Decision by the Highest Court of

New York State for an Action for Malpractice," *PSI* 1 (1880):119–25, 142–44, 174–76.

113. "Contributory Negligence in Malpractice," *ALJ* 24 (1881):403–6.

114. Dubois v. Decker 130 N.Y. 331 (1891). For a similar example, see Sanderson v. Holland 39 Mo. App. 233 (1889).

115. The full history of the doctrine and application of contributory negligence has yet to be written. The best introduction is Wex S. Malone, "The Formative Era of Contributory Negligence," in *Essays on Torts* (Baton Rouge: Paul M. Herbert, 1986), 116–45. After the turn of the century, various state legislatures played a role in limiting contributory negligence by statute. G. Edward White, *Tort Law in America: An Intellectual History* (New York: Oxford University Press, 1980), 164–68.

116. See chapter 2.

117. Elwell, *Treatise on Malpractice*, 22; and McClelland, *Civil Malpractice*, 17–18.

118. Amasa A. Redfield and Thomas G. Shearman, *A Treatise on the Law of Negligence* (New York: Baker, Voorhis, 1870), 508.

119. Wey, "Medical Responsibility," 72, 73.

120. Teft v. Wilcox 6 Kan. 46 (1870), at 63, 64.

121. Smothers v. Hanks 34 Iowa 286 (1872).

122. Dissent quoted in David D. Armstrong, "Medical Malpractice—The 'Locality Rule' and the 'Conspiracy of Silence,' " *SCLR* 22 (1970):812.

123. Hawthorn v. Richmond 48 Vt. 557 (1876); and Gramm v. Boener 56 Ind. 497 (1877).

124. Small v. Howard 128 Mass. 131 at 131, 136 (1880); and "Measure of Skill Required by the Law," *NYMJ* 33 (April 1881):731–32.

125. Starr, *Transformation*, 111; Armstrong, *Medical Malpractice*, 813; and John R. Waitz, "The Rise and Gradual Fall of the Locality Rule," *DPLR* 18 (1969):410–11.

126. Pelky v. Palmer 109 Mich. 561 (1896); and Whitesell v. Hill 101 Iowa 630 (1897). Progressively more exceptions were made to the locality rule until 1968, when states began to eliminate it outright. See, Waitz, "The Rise and Gradual Fall," passim.

127. Pike v. Honsinger 151 N.Y. 201 at 204–8 (1898).

128. Idem, 209–10.

129. Louis B. Harrison, Melvin H. Worth, Jr., and Michael A. Carlucci, "The Development of the Principles of Medical Malpractice in the United States," *Perspectives in Biology and Medicine* 29 (Autumn 1985):41–72, discusses *Pike* and the fundamentals of twentieth-century malpractice law.

130. See, for example, William J. Curren, "The Unwanted Suitor: Law and the Use of Health Care Technology," in *Machine at the Bedside: Strategies for Using Technology in Patient Care*, edited by Stanley Joel Reiser and Michael Anbar (New York: Cambridge University Press, 1984), 119–33.

131. E. F. Hodges, "Malpractice," *AP* 3 (1884):152.

132. Weigel, "Medical Malpractice," 193.

133. Hodges, "Malpractice," 155.

134. See chapter 4.

135. Thomas Manley, "The Medico-Legal Aspects of Fractures of the Bones of the Extremities, and Others," *NYMJ* 58 (9 September 1893):288–89; and "Heavy Damages in a Malpractice Suit," *MR* 41 (30 January 1892):131.

136. Manley, "Medico-Legal Aspects," 290.

137. Fielding H. Garrision, *An Introduction to the History of Medicine* (Philadelphia: W. B. Saunders, 1914), 548–55. For examples of suits, see "Malpractice," *MR* 15 (17 May 1879):468–69; Pettigrew v. Willard 46 Kan. 79 (1891); Jones v. Vroom 8 Col. 143 (1896); "Some Recent Malpractice Suits," *MR* 28 (19 December 1885):690–91; Feeney v. Spalding 89 Me. 111 (1896); and Peck v. Hutchinson 88 Iowa 320 (1893). If a physician portrayed himself as a "specialist," such as an ophthalmologist, the ordinary skill and care test was modified to "the degree of skill and diligence which other physicians in the same general neighborhood and in the same general line of practice ordinarily have and practice." See Force v. Gregory 63 Conn. 167 (1893).

138. Rothstein, *American Physicians*, 251–59; Laurence D. Longo, "The Rise and Fall of Batty's Operation: A Fashion in Surgery," *BHM* 53 (1979):244–67; and G. J. Barker-Benfield, *Horrors of a Half Known Life* (New York: Harper and Row, 1976), 120–32.

139. "Some Recent Malpractice Suits," *MR* 28 (19 December 1885):690–91; Langford v. Jones 18 Ore. 307 (1890); Kansas v. Reynolds 42 Kan. 320 (1889); and Lewis v. Dwinell 84 Me. 497 (1892).

140. Samuel D. Gross, "A Century of American Medicine, 1776–1876," *AJMS* 71 (1876):484; and Gross, quoted in Peter C. English, *Shock, Physiological Surgery, and George Washington Crile: Medical Innovation in the Progressive Era* (Westport, Conn.: Greenwood Press, 1980), 25.

141. For a survey of developments leading to improvement of surgery, see Rothstein, *American Physicians*, 249–56; and Gert H. Brieger, "American Surgery and the Germ Theory of Disease," *BHM* 40 (1966):135–45.

142. Rothstein, *American Physicians*, 249–56; and English, *Shock, Physiological Surgery*, 20–29.

143. For a good survey of surgical milestones in the late nineteenth century, see Morris J. Fogelman and Elinor Reinmiller, "1880–1890: A Creative Decade in World Surgery," *American Journal of Surgery* 115 (1968):812–24; and English, *Shock, Physiological Surgery*, 30–33.

144. Andrew A. Sandor, "The History of Professional Liability Suits in the United States," *JAMA* 163 (9 February 1957):464.

145. Robert T. Morris, *Fifty Years a Surgeon* (New York: E. P. Dutton, 1935), 66.

146. "Judge Aldrich's Decision in a Suit for Malpractice," *BMSJ* 106 (4 May 1882):425–26.

147. Peck v. Hutchinson 88 Iowa 320 (1893); and Fogelman and Reinmiller, "A Creative Decade," 819.

148. Reiser, *Medicine and the Reign of Technology*, 58–67.

149. "Report of the Committee of the American Surgical Association on the Medico-Legal Relation of the X-Rays," *AJMS* 120 n.s. (1900):13, 32; and physician quoted in David Walsh, *The Röentgen Rays in Medical Work* (New York: William Wood, 1898), 125–26.

150. Shikes, *Rocky Mountain Medicine*, 118–19; and "Report of the Committee on X-Rays," passim.

151. Quoted in "Report of the Committee on X-Rays" 8, 16, 32.

152. Ibid., 12.

153. Ibid., 21, 25, 26.

154. F. Boyd, "X-Ray Dermatitis; Suit for Damages," *JAMA* 30 (12 February 1898):381; and Ruth and Edward Brecher, *The Rays: A History of Radiology in America* (Baltimore: William and Wilkens, 1969), 106.

9. Conclusion

1. Leighton E. Cluff, "America's Romance with Medicine and Medical Science," *Daedalus* 115 (Spring 1986):137–59.

2. John Duffy, "American Perceptions of the Medical, Legal, and Theological Professions," *BHM* 58 (1984):1–15.

3. David Engel, "Oven Bird's Song: Insiders, Outsiders, and Personal Injuries in an American Community," *LSR* 18 (1984):551–61; and Carol Greenhouse, *Praying for Justice: Faith, Order and Community in an American Town* (Ithaca: Cornell University Press, 1986).

4. David M. Potter, "Social Cohesion and the Crisis of Law," in *American Law and the Constitutional Order, Historical Perspectives*, edited by Lawrence M. Friedman and Harry M. Scheiber (Cambridge: Harvard University Press, 1978), 432; and Robert H. Wiebe, *The Search for Order, 1877–1920* (New York: Hill and Wang, 1967), 1–10, 44–75.

5. Martin Marty, "From Providence to Progress: A New Theology," in *The Righteous Empire: The Protestant Experience in America* (New York: Dial Press, 1970), 188–89.

6. Lucius Weinschenk, "Malpractice," *DTMJ* 5 (1889):208.

7. John Higham, "The Reorientation of American Culture in the 1890s," in *Writing American History: Essays in Modern Scholarship* (Bloomington: Indiana University Press, 1970), 73–102; and Donald J. Mrozek, "Toward a New Image of the Body," in *Sport and the American Mentality, 1880–1910* (Knoxville: University of Tennessee Press, 1983), 189–222.

8. John C. Burnham, "Change in Popularization of Health in the United States," *BHM* 58 (1984):185–97.

9. Mike Featherstone, "The Body in Consumer Culture," *Theory, Culture, and Society* 1 (1982):18–33.

10. T. J. Jackson Lears, "From Salvation to Self-Realization: Advertising and the Therapeutic Roots of Consumer Culture, 1880–1930" in *The Culture of*

Consumption: Essays in American History, 1880–1980, edited by Richard Wightman Fox and T. J. Jackson Lears (New York: Pantheon, 1983), 4; Lears, *No Place of Grace: Antimodernism and the Transformation of American Culture 1880–1920* (New York: Pantheon, 1981), 54–56, 221–22, 296–97, 303–5; and Philip Rieff, *The Triumph of the Therapeutic* (New York: Harper and Row, 1966).

11. This is Lawrence M. Friedman's thesis. See his *Total Justice* (Boston: Beacon Press, 1985), 43–51, 63–67, 147. See also Charles O. Gregory, "Tresspass to Negligence to Absolute Liability," *Virginia Law Review* 37 (April 1951):359–97.

Bibliography

Primary Sources

JOURNAL ARTICLES AND BOOKS

These articles do not constitute all the accounts of malpractice prosecutions and editorials on the topic published in the nineteenth century. Instead they are the sources that I cited and consulted in preparation of this essay. Elwell, McClelland, and Wade (see below) contain dozens of accounts not noted in the bibliography. A fuller survey of nineteenth-century medical journals would undoubtedly yield a considerable number of additional cases.

A list of unattributed articles precedes works whose authors are given.

"The Accountability of Medical Men. *Commonwealth* v. *Franklin Pierce*." *BMSJ* 3 (1884):545–46.
"Accusation of Mal-Practice." *BMSJ* 31 (11 September 1844):123–24
"Action for Mal-Treatment in a Case of Dislocation." *BMSJ* 32 (28 May 1845):346–47.
"Action for Malpractice." *MSR* 20 (20 January 1868):18–19.
"Actions for Malpractice." *NYMJ* 68 (24 December 1898):940.
"Alleged Mal-Practice." *BMSJ* 6 (21 March 1832):98–99.
"Alleged Malpractice." *BMSJ* 62 (31 May 1860):364–65.
"Alleged Malpractice." *MT* 1(1 June 1871):327–28.
"Alleged Malpractice—Case of *Russel* v. *Warden*." *MSR* 24 (1871):410–11.
"American Intelligence [suit]." *MNL* 6 (May 1848):60.
"Anesthesia and Its Influence on Surgery." *MN* 9 (1851):21–22.

"Animus of Suits for Malpractice." *MSR* 34 (September 1878):218.

"Another Malpractice Suit." *NOMSJ* 10 (1882):470–71.

"Another Prosecution for Malpractice." *JMCS* 3 (November 1846):406.

"Another Suit for Mal-Practice." *BMSJ* 51 (17 January 1855):504.

"A Bar to an Action for Malpractice." *NYMJ* 37 (3 February 1883):139.

"A Bar to Malpractice Suits." *MSR* 50 (31 May 1884):703.

"Bibliographic Notices." *NYJM* (September 1853):272–75.

"Bibliographic Notices." *BMSJ* 89 (24 July 1873):85–86.

"Blackmailing of Surgeons and Malpractice Suits." *MR* 13 (20 April 1878): 315–16.

"Case of Alleged Mal-Practice." *BMSJ* 54 (24 April 1856):229–42.

"A Case of Alleged Malpractice." *NYMJ* 13 (January 1871):124–28.

"A Case of Alleged Malpractice." *MR* 5 (16 January 1871):517–18.

"A Case of Alleged Malpractice." *NYMJ* 38 (25 August 1883):212–13.

"Case of False Anneurism—Action for Malpractice." *BMSJ* 35 (12 August 1846):43–45.

"Case of Mal-Practice." *BMSJ* 34 (8 July 1846):449–51.

"Case of Mal-Practice." *BMSJ* 54 (13 March 1856):109–13.

"A Case of Malpractice." *BMSJ* 9 (28 March 1872):201.

"A Case of Malpractice." *MR* 45 (23 June 1894):793–94.

"Case of Trial for Malpractice." *BMSJ* 56 (19 March 1857):148.

"Cases of Compound Fracture of the Leg." *BMSJ* 25 (8 September 1841): 73–75.

"Causes and Prevention of Epidemics." *Har* 15 (1857):194–203.

"Causes and Prevention of Suits for Mal-Practice." *BMSJ* 48 (27 July 1853):525.

"Civil Malpractice." *BMSJ* 84 (24 July 1873):85–86.

"Civil Malpractice." *BMSJ* 96 (19 April 1877):470–73.

"Concerning Suits for Malpractice." 36 *MR* (5 October 1889):375–76.

"Confidential Communications and Suits for Malpractice." *NYMJ* 60 (3 November 1894):576.

"Contributory Negligence in Malpractice." *ALJ* 24 (1881):403–6.

"Correction." *WMSJ* 32 (July 1855):49–50.

"The Cortland Case of Malpractice." *ME* 5 (5 March 1842):149–51.

"The Cortlandville Trial for Malpractice." *ME* 4 (1841):766–67.

"Critical Analysis" (address of Samuel Jackson to the medical class of University of Pennsylvania, 1846). *NYMJ* 8 (March 1847):218–22.

"A Curious Malpractice Suit." *NYMJ* 67 (12 March 1898):373.

"Damages for Fracture." *BMSJ* 101 (11 September 1879):390.

"Death by Supposed Mal-Practice." *BMSJ* 44 (28 May 1851):345.

"Discouragement of Suits for Malpractice." *MSR* 42 n.s.(1880):37.

"The Doctrine of Particular Providence." *CS* 8 (1836):1–12.

"The Doctrine of Providence Vindicated." *CS* 5 (1823):169–75.

"Dr. Riggs of Cortland County." *MSR* 6 (July 1861):81.

"Effect of Malpractice Charges and How to Avoid Them." *MR* 44 (30 December 1893):847–48.

"The End of a Curious Malpractice suit." *MR* 31 (8 January 1887):54.

"The End of a Malpractice Suit." *MR* 42 (2 July 1892):16.

"Estimation of Damages in Actions for Malpractice." *NYMJ* 72 (18 August 1900):308.

"Excision of Tonsils." *BMSJ* 28 (15 February 1843):29–33.

"Extracts from the Report of the Committee on the Prevalence of Suits for Mal-Practice." *MNL* 8 (March 1850):17–20.

"*Fisher* v. *Gross.*" *MR* 6 (15 May 1871):133–34.

"Fracture of the Thigh Bone—The Late Suit Against Dr. Colby." *BMSJ* 30 (31 July 1844):509–14.

"The Greenpoint Malpractice Case." *Scal* 8 (April 1856):311–15.

"*George Chase* v. *Calvin Sweeny.*" *MSR* 19 (28 May 1868):449.

"Gross Malpractice." *MSR* 22 (5 February 1870):121–22.

"Heavy Damages in a Malpractice Suit." *MR* 41 (30 January 1892):131.

"Heroic Malpractice." *MT* 1 (1 October 1870):16.

"Heroic Surgery: Extirpation of a Malignant Tumor from the Arm, Death the Next Day." *Scal* 2 (1850):121–22.

"Important Case of Alleged Mal-Practice." *Scal* 9 (April 1857):54–57.

"An Interesting Malpractice Suit." *MR* 32 (16 July 1887):81.

"An Interesting Question in a Charge of Malpractice." *MR* 25 (16 February 1884):186.

"Jarvis' Adjuster." *WJMPS* 22 (1851):272–73.

"Judge Aldrich's Decision in a Suit for Malpractice." *BMSJ* 106 (4 May 1882):425–26.

"Judge Thayer's Charge in the Case of *Haire* v. *Reese.*" *MT* 1 (15 December 1870):99–101.

"The Late Suit for Mal-Practice in Delaware Co., N.Y.." *BMSJ* 37 (11 August 1847):35–37.

"Law of Malpractice." *MSR* 30 (28 February 1874):2.

"Legal Liabilities of Physicians and Surgeons." *BufMSJ* 5 (1865–1866):353–56.

"The Legal Responsibilities of Physicians." *MSR* 46 n.s. (1882):298–99.

"Legal Responsibility." *BMSJ* 54 (24 April 1856):228.

"Legal Robbery of a Physician." *MN* 14 (April 1856):61–62.

"Legal Robbery of a Surgeon." *MSR* 10 (April 1857):217.

"Liability of Physicians." *MSR* 34 (15 April 1876):315–16.

"Mal-practice." *BMSJ* 49 (26 October 1853):270.

"Malpractice." *OMSJ* 6 (November 1853):182.

"Mal-practice." *OMSJ* 12 (November 1859):166–67.

"Malpractice." *BMSJ* 66 (24 July 1862):524.

"Malpractice." *MR* 15 (17 May 1879):468–69.

"Malpractice." *MR* 15 (24 May 1879):492.

"The Malpractice Case in Brooklyn." *MR* 12 (27 October 1877):688.

"Malpractice Case Settled." *MSR* 24 (20 May 1871):428.

"Malpractice Decisions." *NYMJ* 33 (April 1881):731.

"Malpractice in a Case of Midwifery." *BMSJ* 32 (30 April 1845):266.

"Malpractice in a Case of Midwifery." *BMSJ* 32 (28 May 1845):346.

"Malpractice in Its Legal Relations." *MSR* 15 n.s. (1866):444–45.

"Malpractice Insurance." *MR* 44 (1892):401.

"Mal-Practice in Midwifery." *BMSJ* 2 (3 March 1830):50.

"Malpractice in Surgery." *BMSJ* 25 (26 January 1842):404.

"Malpractice—Proposed Law." *MR* 9 (1 October 1874):527.

"A Malpractice Suit Triumphantly Defended." *MR* 17 (17 January 1880): 67–68.

"Malpractice Suits." *MR* 14 (6 July 1878):13.

"Malpractice Suits." *MSR* 61 (21 September 1889):326.

"Malpractice Suits against Hospital Surgeons." *NYMJ* 54 (26 December 1891):718.

"Malpractice Suits and Their Prevention." *MR* 29 (13 February 1886):188.

"Malpractice, with Reference to the Legal and Medical Professions." *MR* 45 (3 February 1894):145.

"Malpraxis." *BMSJ* (3 July 1873):22.

"Malpraxis in Midwifery." *BMSJ* 2 (9 June 1829):270.

"*Mary Ann Decrow, et al. v. H. H. Little:* A Prosecution for Alleged Malpractice." *OMSJ* 12 (January 1860):194–98.

"Measure of Skill Required By the Law." *NYMJ* 33 (April 1881):731–32.

"Medical Expert Testimony." *BMSJ* 116 (3 February 1887):119–20.

"Medical Malpractice." *MSR* 47 n.s. (23 December 1882):716–17.

"Medical Notes" (comments on Eugene Sanger's malpractice study). *BMSJ* 99 (18 July 1878):91.

"Medical Reform." *MNL* 5 (May 1847):49–54.

"Medical Science in New York." *BMSJ* 15 (16 November 1836):241–42.

"Medical Testimony in Malpractice Cases." *MSR* 28 (1 February 1873): 122–23.

"*Michael O'Neil v. Gerard Bancker.*" *NYMPJ* 6 (1827):145–52.

"New York Supreme Court Decision of Justice Laurence in the Case of Mary Ann Proctor against the Manhattan Eye and Ear Hospital." *MR* 15 (1879):599.

"Noteworthy Malpractice." *NYMJ* 33 (April 1881):731–32.

"The Old Excuse for Cheating the Doctor." *MR* 45 (6 January 1894):19.

"On the Avoidance of Causeless Suits for Malpractice." *MSR* 33 (25 September 1875):255–56.

"On Suits for Malpractice." *NYMJ* 49 (9 February 1889):158.

"Outrageous Suit for Malpractice." *BMSJ* 99 (28 November 1878):700–704.

"Organized Medical Defence." *JAMA* 38 (4 January 1902):37.

"Organized Medical Defence." *JAMA* 38 (4 January 1902):43.

"A Physician Sued for Malpractice and Acquitted." *MSJ* 27 (2 November 1872):415.

"Plans for Restraining Groundless Suits for Malpractice." *MSR* 34 (24 August 1878):171–72.

"[Proceedings of the Kentucky Medical Society, October 1854, discussed malpractice]." *WJMS* 30 (November 1854):365–67.

"Proper Steps for Physicians in Suits for Malpractice." *MSR* 27 (7 December 1872):496–97.

"Prosecution for Alledged Mal-Practice." *BufMJMR* 4 (1848–1849):274–77.

"Prosecution for Malpractice." *BMSJ* 30 (29 May 1844):344–45.

"Prosecution for Malpractice." *BMSJ* 32 (2 April 1845):185.

"Prosecution for Mal-Practice." *BMSJ* 48 (4 May 1853):281–83.

"Prosecution for Mal-Practice." *BMSJ* 48 (11 May 1853):304.

"Prosecution for Mal-Practice." *BMSJ* 48 (20 July 1853):503–4.

"Prosecutions for Mal-Practice." *ME* 14 (November 1851):728–29.

"Prosecutions for Mal-Practice." *NHJM* 4 (January 1854):20–23.

"Prosecutions for Mal-Practice." *BMSJ* 51 (8 November 1854):305.

"Prosecutions for Mal-Practice." *OMSJ* 13 (January 1861):253–60.

"Prosecutions of Medical Men." *WMSJ* 28 (1853):346–47.

"The Recent Malpractice Suit." *MR* 19 (4 June 1881):630–31.

"Report of the Committee of the American Surgical Association on the Medico-Legal Relations of the X-Rays." *AJMS* 120 n.s. (1900):7–35.

"Report of the Facts and Circumstances Relating to a Case of Compound Fracture and Prosecution for Malpractice . . ." *ME* 4 (1841):712–14.

"Report of the Facts and Circumstances Relating to a Case of Compound Fracture, and Prosecution for Malpractice . . ." *AJMS* 3 n.s. (January 1842):181–84.

"Report of the Facts and Circumstances Relating to a Case of Compound Fracture, and Prosecution for Malpractice . . ." *WMSJ* 5 (1842):141–48.

"Report on Difficulties Growing Out of Alleged Mal-Practice in the Treatment of Fractures." *TOMS* 11 (1856):53–66.

"Review: Medical Ethics." *AJMS* 23 (January 1852):149–178.

"Reviews" (review of Frank H. Hamilton's 1853 *Fracture Tables*). *WJMPS* 28 (1853):309–12.

"Reviews" (review of Frank Hamilton's 1860 work). *AJMS* 39 (April 1860):419–39.

"Shocking Outrage on Professional Humanity." *Scal* 7 (January 1856):253–55.

"Singular Suit for Spiritualistic Surgery Malpractice." *MSR* 28 (15 April 1873):290.

"Some Recent Malpractice Suits." *MR* 28 (19 December 1885):690–91.

"Status of Our Profession." *MSR* 11 (February 1858):133–36.

"Status of Our Profession." *MSR* 11 (March 1858):194–96.

"[The Status of Physicians]." *MSR* 11 (January 1858):60–63.

"*Stogdale* v. *Baker*." *BMSJ* 117 (1887):610.

"*Stogdale* v. *Baker*." *Annals of Gynaecology* 1 (1887–1888):150–51.

"Stover-Catlin: The Malpractice Suit." *MR* 17 (1880):573–74.

"Strictures on Professor Parker's Surgical Evidence in the Suit for Malpractice at Green Point: The Value of Title and Consultations." *Scal* 5 (August 1853):230–36.

"Suit against a Physician for Neglect of Vaccination." *MSR* 28 (1 March 1873):202.

"The Suit against Professor Gross." *MT* 1 (1 May 1871):280–81.

"Suit for Alleged Mal-Practice." *OMSJ* 10 (1857–1858):13–24.

"Suit for Alleged Malpractice." *OMSJ* 10 (May 1858):447–51.

"A Suit for Alleged Malpractice. *Gallagher* v. *Herrick*," *CMG* 2 (1886–1887):117–32.

"Suit for Damages . . ." *BMSJ* 66 (31 July 1862):544.

"Suit for Mal-Practice." *JMCS* 3 (November 1846):407–8.

"Suit for Malpractice." *OMSJ* 2 (November 1849):161–63.

"Suit for Mal-Practice." *BMSJ* 50 (19 April 1854):246.

"The 'Suit for Malpractice.' " *BMSJ* 50 (3 May 1854):287.

"Suit for Malpractice." *NMSJ* 6 (1849–1850):227–30.

"Suit for Mal-Practice." *BMSJ* 66 (27 February 1862):95.

"[Suit for Malpractice]." *BMSJ* 6 n.s. (27 October 1870):276.

"[Suit for Malpractice]." *MR* 5 (1 November 1870):398–99.

"Suit for Malpractice." *MSR* 32 (22 May 1875):419.

"Suit for Malpractice." *MR* 19 (28 May 1881):616.

"A Suit for Malpractice." *NYMJ* 46 (24 December 1887):718.

"Suit for Malpractice." *MR* 44 (18 November 1893):658.

"A Suit for Malpractice Decided against the Surgeon." *MR* 39 (14 March 1891): 322.

"A Suit for Malpractice." *MR* 52 (18 June 1898):925–26.

"Suit for Malpractice: Prof. Spencer on Mercury in Dysentery." *WJMPS* 24 (1851):168–70.

"Suit for Malpractice Decided." *MSR* 7 (1 March 1862):525–26.

"Suit for Malpractice Withdrawn." *MSR* (6 January 1866):19.

"Suits for Mal-Practice." *BMSJ* 51 (13 December 1854):402–3.

"Suits for Malpractice." *MR* 16 (20 December 1879):599.

"Suits for Malpractice." *MSR* 40 n.s. (1879):197.

"Suits for Malpractice." *MR* 17 (7 February 1880):161–62.

"Suits for Malpractice." *BMSJ* 96 (17 May 1887):598–99.

"Suits of Malpractice." *MR* 16 (20 December 1879):591.

"A Surgical Case of Mal-Practice." *BMSJ* 51 (8 November 1854):289–97.

"Surgical Malpractice." *BMSJ* 36 (5 May 1847):283–84.

"To What Causes Are We To Attribute the Diminishing Respectability of the Medical Profession in the Estimation of the American Public?" *MSR* 1 (1858):141–43.

"*Travers* v. *Boardman*: An Action of Tort, and What It Teaches." *BMSJ* 104 (17 February 1881):160–61.

"Trial for Alleged Malpractice." *BMSJ* 50 (8 March 1854):120–21.

"Trial for Mal-Practice." *BMSJ* 25 (10 November 1841):226–27.

"Trial for Malpractice." *BMSJ* 37 (22 September 1847):162–64.

"Trial for Malpractice." *NMSJ* 5 (1848–1849):536–46.

"Trial for Malpractice." *BMSJ* 41 (10 October 1849):206.

"Trial for Malpractice." *BMSJ* 51 (22 November 1854):345.

"Trial for Malpractice." *BufMJMR* 10 (1854–1855):568–70.
"Trial for Mal-Practice." *BMSJ* 54 (20 March 1856):129–38.
"Trial for Mal-Practice." *BMSJ* 54 (27 March 1856):149–56.
"Trial for Malpractice." *BMSJ* 55 (22 January 1857):515.
"Trial for Malpractice." *BMSJ* 56 (5 February 1857):9–23.
"Trial for Malpractice." *BMSJ* 56 (5 February 1857):25–26.
"Trial for Mal-Practice." *MSR* 12 (1865):555–58.
"Trial for Mal-Practice." *MSR* 12 (1865):569–73.
"Trial for Malpractice." *MSR* 28 (24 May 1873):399–401.
"Trial for Malpractice, and One Thousand Dollars Damages." *BufMJMR* 3 (1847–1848):145–48.
"Trial for Malpractice—Dr. Crosby's Acquittal." *BMSJ* 50 (21 June 1854):424–25.
"Trial for Mal-Practice in Pennsylvania." *BMSJ* 37 (15 September 1847):141–42.
"Trial for Malpraxis." *StLMSJ* 3 (May 1846):529–62.
"Trial of Dr. Shipman for Mal-Practice." *BMSJ* 31 (18 September 1844):140–42.
"Trial of Dr. Spencer for Mal-Practice." *BMSJ* 44 (11 June 1851):384.
"An Undefended Suit for Malpractice." *NYMJ* 69 (29 April 1899):616.
"An Unfounded Charge of Malpractice." *NYMJ* 38 (22 September 1883):324.
"An Unsuccessful Malpractice Suit." *MR* 47 (25 May 1895):669.
"Valentine Mott on Medical Ethics." *Scal* 9 (July 1857):125–26.
"The Varied Functions Possible in the County Medical Society." *JAMA* 44 (18 March 1905):881–82.
"Verdict Against a Physician." *MR* 47 (12 January 1895):64.
"The Whitney Case Again." *OMSJ* 12 (November 1859):167.
"X-Ray Dermatitis. Suit for Damages." *BMSJ* 38 (17 February 1898):166; and *JAMA* 30 (1898):397.
Adams, James, Jr. *Report of an Action, Charles Lowell against John Faxon and Micajah Hawks, Doctors of Medicine, Defendants*. Portland: Printed for James Adams, Jr., by David and Seth Paine, 1825.
Appley, W. L. "How Rip Van Winkle, Jr., M.D. Disposed of a Case of Malpractice." *MSR* 25 (28 October 1871):381–82.
Barnett, Clement B. "Trial for Malpractice." *BMSJ* 30 (19 June 1844):405–6.
Bauer, Lewis, "Surgical Contributions." *MSR* 13 (1865):270–72.
Beck, Theodoric R. *Elements of Medical Jurisprudence*. Albany: Webster and Skinner, 1823.
Becker, T. C. "*Carpenter* v. *Blake*: An Important Decision by the Highest Court of New York State for an Action for Malpractice." *PSI* 1 (1880):119–25, 144–47, 174–76.
Bentham, Jeremy, and John Stuart Mill. *Utilitarianism and Other Essays*. Edited by Alan Ryan. New York: Penguin, 1987.
Blackstone, William. *Commentaries*. St. George Tucker's edition. Philadelphia:

William Birch Young and Abraham, 1803; reprint, Augustus M. Kelly, Publishers, 1969.

Blake, G. M. "Suits Against Surgeons." *BufMSJ* 18 (1879–1880):309–16.

Brainard, D. "Trial for Malpractice." *BMSJ* 31 (22 January 1845):501–2.

Brown, William A. "*Mary Ann Decrow et al.*, v. *H. H. Little*: A Prosecution for Alleged Mal-Practice." *OMSJ* 12 (January 1860):194–98.

Bryce, James. *The American Commonwealth*. London and New York: Macmillan, 1889.

Buel, Henry W. "Statistics of Amputation in the New York Hospital from Jan. 1, 1839, to Jan. 1, 1848." *AJMS* 16 (1848):33–43.

Burnham, Walter. "The Dangers and Responsibilities of a Surgeon." *BMSJ* 5 (3 February 1870):77–78.

Carlyle, Thomas. "Signs of the Times" (1829). In *Critical and Miscellaneous Essays*, vol. 2. London: Chapman and Hall, 1899.

Cathell, D. W. *The Physician Himself and What He Should Add to His Scientific Acquirements*. Baltimore: Cushings and Bailey, 1882; reprint, Arno Press, 1972.

Chitty, Joseph. *A Practical Treatise on Medical Jurisprudence*. London: Butterworth, 1834.

Clinton, G. W. "Malpractice." *BufMSJ* 19 (1879–1880):229–40.

Cooley, Thomas M. *A Treatise on the Law of Torts*. Chicago: Callaghan, 1880, 1906.

Cooper, Astley. *A Treatise on Dislocations and on Fractures of the Joints*. 1st American ed., 3rd London ed. Boston: Wells and Lilly, 1825.

———. *The Lectures of Sir Astley Cooper*. 4th American ed. Philadelphia: E. L. Carey and A. Hart, 1835.

Cooper, Samuel. *A Dictionary of Practical Surgery*. London, 1813.

Crosby, Dixi, comp. *Report of a Trial for Alleged Mal-Practice*. Woodstock: Printed by Lewis Pratt, Jr., 1854.

Cunningham, H. S. "Fracture with Treatment and Suit for Malpraxis." *MSR* 54 (8 May 1886):579–80.

D. W. C. "Suits for Malpractice." *BMSJ* 40 (2 May 1869):287.

———. "Civil Malpractice." *BMSJ* 96 (19 April 1877):470–73.

Dawson, John. "Suit for Damages in a Case of Fracture of the Leg, Followed by Mortification and Amputation." *OMSJ* 14 (1 July 1862):283–90.

de Tocqueville, Alexis. *Democracy in America*. Translated by George Lawrence. Edited by J. P. Mayer. Garden City, N.Y.: Doubleday, 1969.

Detwiler, B. H. "Malpractice Suits and Their Remedy." *Pennsylvania Medical Journal* 1 (1897):295–98.

Doering, E. J. "Mutual Protection against Blackmail." *JAMA* 6 (30 January 1886):114–17.

Elwell, John. *A Medico-Legal Treatise on Medical Malpractice and Medical Evidence*. New York: John S. Voorhis, 1860.

Ewell, Marshall D. *A Manual of Medical Jurisprudence for the Use of Students at Law and of Medicine*. Boston: Little, Brown, 1887.

Garnett, Alexander Y. P. "Professional Standing; Its Decadence; the Cause; How to Be Remedied; Radicalism; Young America." *MSR* 7 (March 1854): 98–103.

Greenleaf, Simon. *A Treatise on the Law of Evidence*. Boston: Charles C. Little and James Brown, 1853; reprint, Arno Press, 1972.

Groner, F. J. "The Causes and the Remedies for Suits for Malpractice." *MR* 37 (1890):143–46.

Gross, Samuel D. "A Century of American Medicine, 1776–1876." *AJMS* 71 (1876):431–84.

———. *Autobiography of Samuel D. Gross*, vol. 2. Philadelphia: George Barrie, 1887; reprint, Arno Press, 1972.

Hadden, A. "Ohio Statutes and Decisions Relating to Malpractice." *Cleveland Medical Gazette* 13 (1897–1898):687–700.

Hamilton, Frank H. *Fracture Tables*. Buffalo: Jewett, Thomas, 1853.

———. "Deformities after Fractures." *TAMA* 8 (1855):349–54.

———. "Report on Deformities after Fractures." *TAMA* 8 (1855):347–93; *TAMA* 9 (1856):69–233; and *TAMA* 10 (1857):239–453.

———. *A Practical Treatise on Fractures and Dislocations*. Philadelphia: Lea and Blanchard, 1860.

———. "Suits for Malpractice in Surgery: Their Cause and Their Remedies." In *Papers Read before the Medico-Legal Society of New York*. 3rd Ser. New York: Medico-Legal Society of New York, 1886.

Hildreth, S. P. "Trial for Mal-Practice in Surgery." *OMSJ* 2 (January 1850): 213–22.

Hillard, Francis. *The Law of Torts or Private Wrongs*. 2 vols. Boston: Little, Brown, 1859.

Higginson, Thomas Wentworth. "Saints and Their Bodies." *AtlM* 1 (March 1858):582–95.

Hodges, E. F. "Malpractice." *AP* 30 (1884):152–60; *Transactions of the Indiana Medical Society* 34 (1884):147–58; and *Fort Wayne Journal of Medical Science* 4 (1884–1885):146–54.

Holt, A. F. "Medical Expert Testimony, as Given in the Courts at Present," *BMSJ* 105 (25 November 1886):493–96.

Hooker, Worthington. *Physician and Patient: or, A Practical View of the Mutual Duties, Relations and Interests of the Medical Profession and the Community*. New York: Baker and Scribner, 1849; facsimile reprint, Arno Press, 1972.

Hunt, W. "Inequality in Length of the Lower Limbs, with a Report of an Important Suit for Malpractice, and also a Claim for Priority." *AJMS* 77 (1879):102–7.

Hutchinson, W. F. "A Recent Suit for Malpractice." *BufMSJ* 12 (1872–1873):290–98.

Jones, John. *Plain Concise Practical Remarks on the Treatment of Wounds and Fractures*. Philadelphia: Robert Bell, 1776; reprint, Arno Press, 1971.

[Jones, W. W.] *"Terrence Mc Queeney v. W. W. Jones." OMSJ* 12 (September 1859):22–24.

Ledergeber, Fred. "Suggestions in Relation to Questions of Law that May Be of Service to the Medical Practitioner." *StLMSJ* 43 (1882):494–504.

Lee, Charles A. "Medical Jurisprudence, — Being Notes of a Trial for Mal-Practice." *NYJMCS* 1 (November 1843):352–62.

Lefever, Isaac. "Report of a Trial for Malpractice in the Court of Common Pleas of Perry County, Pennsylvania." *AJMS* 48 (July 1864):72–86.

Lowell, Charles. *Authentic Report of a Trial before the Supreme Judicial Court of Maine for the County of Washington, June Term 1824.* Portland: Printed for the Author, 1826.

Lyman, Oliver E. "Some Notes on a Doctor's Liability." *PSM* 18 (1880–1881):769–76.

McAdam, David. *Malpractice with Reference to the Legal and Medical Professions.* 1893.

McClelland, Milo. *Civil Malpractice.* New York: Hurd and Houghton, 1877.

Manley, T. H. "The Medico-Legal Aspects of Fractures of the Extremities, and Others, from a Consideration of Their Aetiology, Diagnosis, Prognosis, and Treatment." *NYMJ* 58 (1893):281–90.

Manning, Walter K. "Prosecution for Mal-Practice." *BMSJ* 40 (23 May 1849):318–19.

———. "Trial for Mal-Practice." *BMSJ* 42 (27 February 1850):79–80.

March, Alden. "Prosecutions for Malpractice in the State of N. York." *BMSJ* 36 (14 July 1847):477–80.

———. "Prosecutions for Mal-Practice in the State of New York." *ME* 10 (August 1847):502–5.

———. "Case of Alleged Mal-Practice in Surgery." *BMSJ* 37 (4 August 1847): 9–14.

Mattocks, B. "Malpractice." *NMSJ* 3 (1872–1873):45–52.

Medora, E. "*White* v. *Hiram L. Chase.*" *BMSJ* 99 (1878):700–704.

Merrill, Arthur. "Court of Common Pleas, Meigs County, Ohio, September Term, 1850: Hon. A. G. Brown, Presiding. *Holt* v. *Rathburn.* Mal-Practice in Surgery." *WL* 11 (1850):763–68.

Miller, Perry, ed. *The Legal Mind in America: From Independence to the Civil War.* Garden City, N.Y.: Doubleday, 1962.

Montgomery, H. F. "Suits for Malpractice." *BufMSJ* 11 (1871–1872):445–60.

Moore, A. "Prosecution for Malpractice, in a Case of Imperfect Recovery from a Dislocation of the Elbow." *MR* 8 (November 1855):552–59.

Morris, Robert T. "Circumstances Alter Malpractice Case." *MR* 38 (20 December 1890):718.

———. *Fifty Years a Surgeon.* New York: E. P. Dutton, 1935.

Nichols, Theodore. "Trial for Mal-Practice." *OMSJ* 2 (September 1849): 6–10.

[Norris, George W.] "Bibliographic Notices." *AJMS* 3 n.s. (January 1842): 181–84.

Norris, George W. "Statistical Account of the Cases of Amputation performed at the Pennsylvania Hospital from Jan. 1, 1831, to Jan. 1, 1838." *AJMS* 22 (1838):356–65.

———. "Statistical Account of the Cases of Amputation performed at the Pennsylvania Hospital from Jan. 1, 1838, to Jan. 1, 1840." *AJMS* 26 (1840):35–36.

Noyes, Henry D. "Tucker against Noyes." *MR* 19 (1881):25–26.

O'Dea, James J. "Duties of a Medical Witness in Cases of Malpractice." *MR* 2 (1867–1868):474.

———. "Medico-Legal Science A Sketch of its Progress, Especially in the United States." In *Papers Read Before the Medico-Legal Society of New York*, 3rd ser. New York: Medico-Legal Society, 1886.

Ordronaux, John. *The Jurisprudence of Medicine*. Philadelphia: T. and J. W. Johnson, 1869; reprint, Arno Press, 1973.

Ormsby, O. B. "Fracture of the Humerous, with Injury of the Musculo-Spiral Nerve: Suit for Malpractice." *MSR* 38 (1877):447–48.

Parker, Joel. "Extract from a Lecture on the Rights and Liabilities of the Physician and Surgeon." *WMSJ* 31 (March 1855):217–19.

Parkman, Samuel. "On the Relations of the Medical Witness with the Law and the Lawyer." *AJMS* 23 (January 1852):126–34.

———, and Calvin P. Fiske. "Report on the Causes and Prevention of Suits for Mal-Practice." *MCMMS* (appendix) 8 (1853):123–32.

Perkins, N. R. "A Suit for Malpractice Resulting from a Case of Fracture of the Femur, with a Verdict of Judgment for Defendants." *New England Medical Gazette* 32 (1897):116–21.

Pillsbury, A. E. "Ignorance as a Legal Excuse for Malpractice." *Transactions of the Massachusetts Medico-Legal Society* 1 (1878–1884):191–95.

Pott, Percival. *Treatise on Compound Fractures*, vol. 1. Philadelphia, 1819.

Powell, A. M. "Surgical Malpractice." *Saint Louis Medical and Surgical Journal* 42 (March 1882):231–36.

Price, Mordecai. "Remarks on Suits for Malpractice." *NYMJ* 65 (15 May 1897):676–78.

R. M. K. O. "Trial for Mal-Practice." *BMSJ* 41 (17 October 1849):216–19.

———. "Trial for Mal-Practice." *BMSJ* 41 (23 January 1850):500–502.

———. "Suit for Mal-Practice in Vermont." *BMSJ* 44 (11 June 1851):377–78.

Reamy, Thaddeus A. "Suit for Alleged Mal-Practice." *OMSJ* 10 (1857–1858):13–24.

Redfield, Amasa A., and Thomas G. Shearman. *A Treatise on the Law of Negligence*. Baker, Voorhis, 1870.

Reese, John J. "Case of Alleged Malpractice." *MT* 1 (1 December 1870):73–74.

Rice, Nathan P. *Trials of a Public Benefactor*. New York: Pudney and Russell, 1859.

Robinson, Conway. *The Practice of Courts of Justice*. Richmond: A. Morris, 1855.

Sanger, E. F. "Report on Malpractice." *BMSJ* 100 (2 January 1879):14–23.

———. "Report on Malpractice." *BMSJ* 100 (9 January 1879):41–50.

Saunders, John Simcoe. *The Law of Pleading and Evidence in Civil Actions.* Philadelphia: Robert Small, 1844.

Sheldon, James. "Report of Trial for Malpractice." *BufMJMR* 4 (August 1848):131–54.

Shipman, Azaiah Booth, *A Report of the Circumstances Relating to a Case of Compound Fracture and Prosecution for Mal-Practice.* Cortlandville, N.Y.: Cortland Democrat, 1841.

Shrady, J. "The Civil and Criminal Responsibility of Physicians for Malpractice." *Bulletin of the Medico-Legal Society of New York* 1 (1878–1879):65–84.

Sims, J. Marion. *The Story of My Life.* New York: Da Capo Press, 1968.

Smith, Stephen. "[Review of John Elwell's *Treatise on Malpractice*]." *AJMS* 40 (July 1860):153–66.

———. *Doctor in Medicine and Other Papers on Professional Subjects.* New York: William Wood, 1872; reprint, Arno Press, 1972.

———. "On the Legal Responsibilities of Medical Men." *OMSJ* 1 n.s. (1876):46–50, 148–52; *OMSJ* 2 n.s. (1877):63–67.

Souwers, G. F. "The Laws of Malpractice." *MSR* 4 (1 October 1881):386–88, 414–16.

Stockwell, J. K. "Suits for Malpractice." *MR* 17 (1880):161–62.

Taylor, O. H. "On the Obvious Decline in the Respectability of Public for the Medical Profession . . ." *MSR* 11 (July 1858):460–69.

Vinnedge, W. W. "*Groenendyke v. Thos. W. Fry, M.D.*" *Transactions of the Indiana Medical Society* 26 (1874):107–12.

Wade, Martin J. *A Selection of Cases on Malpractice of Physicians, Surgeons, and Dentists.* St. Louis: Medico-Legal, 1909.

Waggoner, F. R. "Alleged Malpractice—Case of *Russel v. Wardner.*" *MSR* 24 (20 May 1871):410–11.

Walker, Timothy. *Introduction to American Law, Designed as a First Book for Students.* Philadelphia: P. H. Nicklin and T. Johnson, 1837; reprint, DaCapo Press, 1972.

Walker, William J. "On the Treatment of Compound and Complicated Fractures." *MCMMS* 7 (1842–1848):171–215.

Walsh, David. *The Röentgen Rays in Medical Work.* New York: William Wood, 1898.

Warren, Edward. *A Doctor's Experiences in Three Continents.* Baltimore: Cushings and Bailey, 1885.

Warren, John Collins. *A Letter to the Hon. Isaac Parker, Chief Justice of the Supreme Court of Massachusetts, Containing Remarks on the Dislocation of the Hip Joint . . .* Cambridge: Hillard and Metcalf, 1826.

Weinschenk, L. "Malpractice." *DTJM* 5 (1889–1890):208–22.

Weist, J. R. "Civil Malpractice Suits. How can the physician protect himself against them?" *AP* 30 (1884):160–74; *Transactions of the Indiana Medical*

Society 34 (1884):132–46; *Fort Wayne Journal of Medical Science* 4 (1884–1885):154–66; and *Indiana Medical Journal* 3 (1884):1–11.

Wey, C. William. "Medical Responsibility and Malpractice. Anniversary Address Delivered before the Medical Society." *TSMSNY* (1872):65–89.

Whitman, Walt. *Leaves of Grass: The First (1855) Edition.* Edited, with an introduction by Malcolm Cowley. New York: Viking Press, 1960.

Wilding, R. J. "The Necessity of an Amendment in the Law Governing Medical Evidence in Malpractice Suits." *Transactions of the Medical Society of the State of New York* (1891):390–94.

Winthrop, John. *Winthrop's Journal: History of New England, 1630–1649.* 2 vols. Edited by James Kendall Hosmer. New York: Charles Scribner's Sons, 1908.

Wood, William M. "Thoughts on Suits for Malpractice, Suggested by Certain Judicial Proceedings in Erie County, Pennsylvania." *AJMS* 18 (October 1849):395–400.

———. "A Statement of Two Suits for Malpractice, Tried in November and December 1850, in the Court of Erie County, Pa." *AJMS* 22 (July 1851): 43–50.

Young, Alexander. "The Law of Malpractice." *BMSJ* 5 (9 June 1870):425–43.

———. "Criminal Malpractice." *BMSJ* 7 n.s. (5 January 1871):1–12.

AMERICAN MALPRACTICE APELLATE CASES

These cases constitute only a portion of the 216 appellate malpractice decisions in the nineteenth century.

Cross v. Guthery 1 Amer. Dec. 61 (Conn. 1794)
Grannis v. Branden 5 Day 260 (Conn. 1812)
Landon v. Humphrey 9 Day 209 (Conn. 1832)
Bliss v. Long 1 Wright 351 (Ohio 1833)
Gallaher v. Thompson 1 Wright 466 (Ohio 1833)
Bemus v. Howard 3 Watts 255 (Penn. 1834)
Grindle v. Rush 7 Ohio 123 (1836)
McClallen v. Adams 19 Pick. 333 (Mass. 1837)
Mertz v. Detweiler 8 Watts & Sargent 376 (Penn. 1845)
Bowman v. Woods 1 Green 441 (Iowa 1848)
Howard v. Grover 28 Me. 97 (1848)
Piper v. Menifee 51 Ky. 465 (1851)
Ballard v. Russell 33 Me. 196 (1851)
Adler v. Buckley 1 Swan. 69 (Tenn. 1851)
Moody v. Sabin 63 Mass. 505 (1852)
Twombly v. Leach 65 Mass. 397 (1853)
McCandless v. McWha 22 Penn. 261 (1853)

Leighton v. Sargent 7 Foster 460 (N.H. 1853)
Moor v. Teed 3 Cal. 190 (1853)
Reynolds v. Graves 3 Wisc. 416 (1854)
Leighton V. Sargent 31 N.H. 119 (1855)
Fowler v. Sergent 1 Grant 355 (Penn. 1856)
Clapp v. Wood 4 Sneed 65 (Tenn. 1856)
Graham v. Gautier 21 Tx. 111 (1858)
Ritchey v. West 23 Ill. 385 (1860)
Smith v. Overby 30 Ga. 241 (1860)
Piles v. Hughes 10 Iowa 579 (1860)
Belinger v. Craig 31 Bar. 534 (N.Y. 1860)
McCrory v. Skinner 2 Ohio 268 (1860)
Woodward v. Hancock 1 Quarterly Law Review 385 (N.C. 1860)
West v. Martin 31 Mo. 375 (1861)
Cochran v. Miller 13 Iowa 128 (1862)
Patten v. Wiggin 51 Me. 594 (1862)
Wilmot v. Howard 39 Vt. 447 (1863)
Chamberlain v. Porter 9 Minn. 260 (1864)
McNevins v. Lowe 40 Ill. 209 (1866)
Craig v. Chambers 17 Ohio 254 (1867)
Hyatt v. Adams 16 Mich. 174 (1867)
Teft v. Wilcox 6 Kan. 46 (1870)
Chamberlin v. Morgan 68 Penn. 168 (1871)
Hibbard v. Thompson 109 Mass. 286 (1872)
Smothers v. Hanks 34 Iowa 287 (1872)
Almond v. Nugent 34 Iowa 300 (1872)
Branner v. Stormont 9 Kan. 51 (1872)
Scudder et al. v. Crossan 43 Ind. 343 (1873)
Kendall v. Brown 74 Ill. 232 (1874)
Ballou v. Prescott 64 Me. 305 (1874)
Getchell v. Hill et al. 21 Minn. 464 (1875)
Wenger v. Calder 78 Ill. 275 (1875)
Hathorn v. Richmond 48 Vt. 557 (1876)
Musser v. Chase 29 Ohio 577 (1876)
McDonald v. Mass. General Hospital 120 Mass. 432 (1876)
Gramm v. Boener 56 Ind. 497 (1877)
Hoener v. Koch 84 Ill. 408 (1877)
Fisher et al. v. Niccolls 2 Ill. App. 484 (1877)
Quinn v. Donovan 85 Ill. 194 (1877)
Carpenter v. Blake 75 N.Y. 12 (1878)
Higgins v. McCabe 126 Mass. 13 (1878)
Hitchcock v. Burgett 38 Mich. 501 (1878)
Potter v. Warner 91 Penn. 362 (1879)
Small v. Howard 128 Mass. 131 (1880)

De May v. Roberts 46 Mich. 160 (1881)
Ressequie v. Byers 52 Wisc. 651 (1881)
Gobel v. Dillon 86 Ind. 327 (1882)
Mallen v. Boynton 132 Mass. 443 (1882)
Kesle v. Hay 84 Ind. 189 (1882)
Brooke v. Clarke 57 Tx. 1905 (1882)
Jones v. Angell 95 Ind. 376 (1883)
O'Hara v. Wells 14 Neb. 403 (1883)
Secord v. St. Paul, M. & M. RY. Co. 18 Fed. Rep. 221 (1883)
Hyrne v. Erwin 23 S.C. 226 (1885)
Whittaker v. Collins 34 Minn. 299 (1885)
Quinn v. Higgins 63 Wisc. 664 (1885)
Holtzman v. Hoy 118 Ill. 534 (1886)
Mayo v. Wright 63 Mich. 32 (1886)
Gates v. Fleischer 67 Wisc. 504 (1886)
Vanhoover v. Berghoff 90 Mo. 488 (1887)
Reber v. Herring 115 Penn. 599 (1887)
Davis v. Spencer 27 Mo. App. 279 (1887)
Lower v. Franks 115 Ind. 334 (1888)
Bute v. Potts 76 Cal. 304 (1888)
Nelson v. Harrington 72 Wisc. 592 (1888)
Ayers v. Russell 3 N.Y. Supp. 338 (1888)
Graves v. Santway 6 N.Y. Supp. 892 (1889)
Sanderson v. Holland 39 Mo. App. 233 (1889)
Beck v. German Klinik 78 Iowa 696 (1889)
Hess v. Lowery 122 Ind. 225 (1889)
Spaulding v. Bliss 83 Mich. 311 (1890)
Gores v. Graff 77 Wisc. 174 (1890)
Langford v. Jones 18 Ore. 307 (1890)
DuBois v. Decker 130 N.Y. 325 (1891)
Pettigrew v. Lewis 46 Kan. 78 (1891)
Stevenson v. Gelsthorpe 10 Mont. 563 (1891)
Sims v. Parker 41 Ill. App. 284 (1891)
Link v. Sheldon. 136 N.Y. 1 (1892)
Lawson v. Conaway 37 W.Vir. 159 (1892)
Lewis v. Dwinell 84 Me. 497 (1892)
Hewitt v. Eisenbart 36 Neb. 794 (1893)
Mitchell v. Hindman 47 Ill. App. 431 (1893)
Carpenter v. McDavitt 53 Mo. App. 393 (1893)
Peck v. Hutchinson 88 Iowa 320 (1893)
Force v. Gregory 63 Conn. 167 (1893)
Cayford v. Wilbur 86 Me. 414 (1894)
Mucci v. Houghton 89 Iowa 608 (1894)
Downes v. Harper Hospital 101 Mich. 555 (1894)

Styles v. Tyler 64 Conn. 433 (1894)
Swanson v. French 92 Iowa 695 (1894)
Union Pacific Ry. Co. v. Artist 60 Fed. Rep. 365 (1894)
Yunker v. Marshall & Daly 65 Ill. App. 667 (1895)
Jackson v. Burnham 20 Col. 533 (1895)
Hedin v. Minn. Med. & Sur. Inst. 62 Minn. 146 (1895)
Eighmy v. Union Pacific Ry. Co. 93 Iowa 538 (1895)
Hearns v. Waterbury Hospital 66 Conn. 93 (1895)
Moratzky v. Wirth 67 Minn. 46 (1896)
Dashiell v. Grifith 84 Md. 363 (1896)
Harriott v. Plimpton 166 Mass. (1896)
Feeney v. Spalding 89 Me. 111 (1896)
Jones v. Vroom 8 Col. App. 143 (1896)
Wurdemann v. Barnes 92 Wisc. 206 (1896)
Richards v. Willard 176 Penn. 181 (1896)
Griswold v. Hutchinson 47 Neb. 727 (1896)
Pelky v. Palmer 109 Mich. 561 (1896)
Whitesell v. Hill 101 Iowa 630 (1897)
Pike v. Honsiger 49 NE 760 (N.Y. 1898)

Secondary Sources

Ackernecht, Erwin. "Elisha Bartlett and the Philosophy of the Paris Clinical School." *BHM* 24 (1950):49–60.

Armstrong, David D. "Medical Malpractice — The 'Locality Rule' and the 'Conspiracy of Silence.' " *SCLR* 22 (1970):811–21.

Atiyah, P. S. *The Rise and Fall of Freedom of Contract.* Oxford: Clarendon Press, 1979.

Auerbach, Jerold S. *Unequal Justice: Lawyers and Social Change in America.* New York: Oxford University Press, 1976.

———. *Justice Without Law?* New York: Oxford University Press, 1983.

Ayers, Edward L. *Vengeance and Justice, Crime and Punishment in the Nineteenth-Century American South.* New York: Oxford University Press, 1984.

Bailyn, Bernard. *Education and the Forming of American Society.* New York: Vintage, 1960.

Barker-Benfield, G. *Horrors of a Half-Known Life.* New York: Harper and Row, 1976.

Becker, Carl L. *The Declaration of Independence: A Study in the History of Political Ideas.* New York: Random House, 1921.

Beecher, Henry K., and Mark D. Altschule. *Medicine at Harvard: The First Three Hundred Years.* Hanover: University Press of New England, 1977.

Bellah, Robert N., Richard Madsen, William M. Sullivan, Ann Swindler, and Steven M. Tipton. *Habits of the Heart: Individualism and Commitment in American Life.* Berkeley: University of California Press, 1985.

Bender, Thomas. *Community and Social Change in America*. New Brunswick: Rutgers University Press, 1979.

Berman, Alex. "The Thomsonian Movement and Its Relation to American Pharmacy and Medicine." *BHM* 25 (September–October 1951):405–28.

Bernstein, Samuel. "The Impact of the Paris Commune in the United States." *MassR* 12 (1971):435–45.

Berthoff, Rowland. *An Unsettled People: Social Order and Disorder in American History*. New York: Harper and Row, 1971.

Betts, John R. "Mind and Body in Early American Thought." *JAH* 54 (March 1968):787–805.

Black, Henry Campbell. *Black's Law Dictionary*. 5th ed. St. Paul: West Publishing, 1979.

Blake, John. "From Buchan to Fishbein: The Literature of Domestic Medicine." In *Medicine Without Doctors*, edited by Guenter B. Risse, Ronald L. Numbers, and Judith Walzer Leavitt. New York: Science History Publications, 1977.

———. "Anatomy." In *The Education of American Physicians*, edited by Ronald L. Numbers. Berkeley: University of California Press, 1980.

Boles, John B. *The Great Revival, 1787–1805*. Lexington: University Press of Kentucky, 1972.

———. "Evangelical Protestantism in the Old South: From Religious Dissent to Cultural Dominance." In *Religion in the Old South*, edited by Charles Reagan Wilson. Jackson: University Press of Mississippi, 1985.

Brecher, Edward and Ruth. *The Rays: A History of Radiology in America*. Baltimore: William and Wilkins, 1969.

Breeden, James Otis. "Thomsonianism in Virginia." *VMHB* 82 (1974):150–8.

———. "Body Snatchers and Anatomy Professors: Medical Education in Nineteenth-Century Virginia." *VMHB* 83 (1975):321–45.

Bremner, Robert. *American Philanthropy*. Chicago: University of Chicago Press, 1960.

———. *From the Depths: The Discovery of Poverty in the United States*. New York: New York University Press, 1956.

Brieger, Gert H. "American Surgery and the Germ Theory of Disease." *BHM* 40 (1966):135–45.

Brieger, Gert H. "Therapeutic Conflicts and the American Medical Profession in the 1860s." *BHM* 41 (1967):215–22.

———, ed. *Medical America in the Nineteenth Century: Readings from the Literature*. Baltimore: Johns Hopkins University Press, 1972.

Broekhoff, Jan. "Physical Education and the Reification of the Human Body." *Gym* 9 (1972):4–11.

Brown, Richard. "Modernization and the Modern Personality in Early America, 1600–1865: A Sketch of a Sythesis." *Journal of Interdisciplinary History* 11 (Winter 1972):201–28.

———. *Modernization: The Transformation of American Life, 1600–1865*. New York: Hill and Wang, 1976.

Burnham, John C. "Change in Popularization of Health in the United States." *BHM* 58 (1984):185–97.

Burns: Chester R. "Malpractice Suits in American Medicine Before the Civil War." *BHM* 43 (1969):41–56.

———. "Medical Ethics in the United States Before the Civil War." Ph.D. dissertation. Johns Hopkins University, 1969.

———. "Medical Ethics and Jurisprudence." In *Education of American Physicians*, edited by Ronald L. Numbers. Berkeley: University of California Press, 1980.

———. "Medical Malpractice Law and the Public's Health in the United States During the Nineteenth Century." *Actes Proceedings, XXVIIIᵉ Congrès International d'Histoire de la Médecine* 1 (1982):75–77.

Bushman, Richard. *From Puritan to Yankee: Character and the Social Order in Connecticut, 1690–1765*. Cambridge: Harvard University Press, 1967.

Cash, Wilber J. *The Mind of the South*. New York: Random House, 1941.

Cashdollar, Charles D. "European Positivism and the American Unitarianism." *CH* 45 (1976):490–97.

———. "Social Implications of the Doctrine of Divine Providence: A Nineteenth-Century Debate in American Theology." *HTR* 71 (1978):265–84.

———. *The Transformation of Theology, 1830–1890: Positivism and Protestant Thought in Britain and America*. Princeton University Press, 1989.

Cassedy, James H. "Why Self-Help? Americans Alone with Their Diseases, 1800–1850." In *Medicine Without Doctors: Home Health Care in American History*. Edited by Guenter B. Risse, Ronald L. Numbers, and Judith Walzer Leavitt. New York: Science History Publications, 1977.

———. *American Medicine and Statistical Thinking, 1800–1860*. Cambridge: Harvard University Press, 1984.

———. *Medicine and American Growth, 1800–1860* Madison: University of Wisconsin Press, 1986.

Caton, Donald. "The Secularization of Pain." *Anesthesiology* 62 (1985):493–501.

Chapman, Carlton. *Physicians, Ethics, and the Law*. New York: New York University Press, 1984.

Christianson, Eric H. "Medicine in New England." In *Medicine in the New World*, edited by Ronald L. Numbers. Knoxville: University of Tennessee Press, 1987.

Cirincione, Sandra. "The History of Medical Malpractice in New York State: A Perspective from the Publications of the Medical Society of New York." *NYSJM* 86 (1986):361–69.

Clapesattle, Helen. *The Doctors Mayo*. New York: Simon and Schuster, 1970.

Clark, Charles Edwin. "Science, Reason, and an Angry God: The Literature of an Earthquake." *NEQ* 38 (1965):340–62.

Cluff, Leighton E. "America's Romance with Medicine and Medical Science." *Daedalus* 115 (Spring 1986):137–59.

Cochran, Thomas C., and William Miller. *The Age of Enterprise: A Social History of Industrial America*. New York: Harper and Row, 1961.

Commager, Henry Steele. "The Nationalism of Joseph Story." In *The Bacon Lectures on the Constitution of the United States*. Boston: Boston University Press, 1953.

Cross, Whitney R. *The Burned Over District: The Social and Intellectual History of Enthusiastic Religion in Western New York, 1800–1850*. New York: Harper and Row, 1965.

Curren, William J. "The Unwanted Suitor: Law and the Use of Health Care Technology." In *Machine at the Bedside: Strategies for Using Technology in Patient Care*, edited by Stanley Joel Reiser and Michael Anbar. Cambridge: Cambridge University Press, 1984.

Dargo, George. *Law in the New Republic: Private Law and Public Estate*. New York: Alfred A. Knopf, 1983.

Demos, John. *A Little Commonwealth: Family Life in Plymouth Colony*. New York: Oxford University Press, 1982.

De Moulin, Daniel. "A Historical-Phenomenonological Study of Bodily Pain in Western Man." *BHM* 48 (1974):540–71.

Duffy, John. *Epidemics in Colonial America*. Baton Rouge: Lousiania State University, 1953.

———. "Anglo-American Reaction to Obstetrical Anesthesia." *BHM* 38 (1964):32–44.

———. "American Perceptions of the Medical, Legal, and Theological Professions." *BHM* 58 (1984):1–15.

———, ed. *History of Medicine in Louisiana*. 2 vols. Baton Rouge: Louisiana State University Press, 1950, 1962.

Eaton, Clement. *The Freedom of Thought Struggle in the Old South*. New York: Harper and Row, 1964.

———. *The Mind of the Old South*. Baton Rouge: Louisiana State University Press, 1964.

Edwards, Linden F. "Resurrection Riots During the Heroic Age of Anatomy in America." *BHM* 25 (1951):178–84.

Ekirch, Arthur Alphonse. *The Idea of Progress in America, 1815–1860*. New York: Peter Smith, 1951.

Engel, David. "Oven Bird's Song: Insiders, Outsiders, and Personal Injuries in an American Community." *LSR* 18 (1984):551–61.

English, Peter C. *Shock, Physiological Surgery, and George Washington Creel: Medical Innovation in the Progressive Era*. Westport, Conn.: Greenwood Press, 1980.

Epstein, Richard A. "Medical Malpractice: The Case for Contract." *ABFRJ* (1976):87–149.

———. "Market and Regulatory Approaches to Medical Malpractice: The Virginia Obstetrical No-Fault Statute." *VLR* 74 (1988):1451–74.

Featherstone, Mike. "The Body in Consumer Culture." *Theory, Culture, and Society* 1 (1982):18–33.

Fellman, Anita Clair, and Michael Fellman. *Making Sense of Self: Medical Advice Literature in Late Nineteenth-Century America*. Philadelphia: University of Pennsylvania Press, 1981.

Fifoot, C. H. S. *History and Sources of the Common Law*. New York: Greenwood Press, 1970.

Flexner, James Thomas. *Doctors on Horseback: Pioneers of American Medicine*. New York: Dover 1968.

Folgelman, Morris J., and Elinor Reinmiller. "1880–1890: A Creative Decade in World Surgery." *American Journal of Surgery* 115 (1968):812–24.

Friedman, Lawrence M. *Contract Law in America: A Social and Economic Case Study*. Madison: University of Wisconsin Press, 1965.

———. *A History of American Law*. New York: Simon and Schuster, 1973.

———. *Total Justice*. New York: Russell Sage, 1985.

———, and Jack Ladinsky. "Social Change and the Law of Industrial Accidents." *Columbia Law Review* 67 (1967):151–82.

Frisch, Michael H. *Town into City: Springfield, Massachusetts, and the Meaning of Community, 1840–1880*. Cambridge: Harvard University Press, 1972.

Galanter, Marc. "Reading the Landscape of Disputes: What We Know and Don't Know (and Think We Know) About Our Allegedly Contentious and Litigious Society." *UCLA Law Review* 31 (1983):4–71.

Garrison, Fielding H. *An Introduction to the History of Medicine*. Philadelphia: W. B. Saunders, 1914.

Genovese, Elizabeth Fox, and Eugene Genovese. "The Divine Sanction of Social Order: Religious Foundations of the Southern Slaveholder's World." *JAAR* 55 (Summer 1987):211–33.

Gibson, H. B. *Pain and its Conquest*. London: Peter Owen, 1982.

Gideion, Siegfried. *Mechanization Takes Command: A Contribution to Anonymous History*. New York: Norton 1978.

Gilmore, Grant. *The Death of Contract*. Columbus: Ohio State University Press, 1974.

Gordon, Robert. "Accounting for Legal Change in American Legal History." In *Law in the American Revolution and the Revolution in Law*, edited by Hedrick Hartog. New York: New York University Press, 1981.

Gorn, Elliot J. " 'Gouge and Bite, Pull Hair and Scratch': The Social Significance of Fighting in the Southern Backcountry." *AHR* 90 (1985):18–43.

Graveson, R. H. "The Movement from Status to Contract." *MLR* 4 (1941):261–67.

Green, Harvey. *Fit for America: Health, Fitness, Sport, and American Society*. New York: Pantheon, 1986.

Greenhouse, Carol. "Nature is to Culture as Praying is to Suing: Legal Pluralism in an American Suburb." *JLP* 20 (1982):17–35.

———. "Interpreting American Litigiousness." Paper presented at the Wenner-Gren Foundation for Anthropological Research, Bellagio, Italy, 10–18 August 1985.

———. *Praying for Justice: Faith, Order, and Community in an American Town.* Ithaca: Cornell University Press, 1986.

Gregory, Charles O. "Trespass to Negligence to Absolute Liability." *VLR* 37 (1951):359–98.

Gribbin, William. "Divine Providence or Miasma? The Yellow Fever Epidemic of 1822." *NYH* 53 (1972):283–98.

Griffin, Charles W. "Physical Fitness." In *Concise Histories of American Popular Culture*, edited by M. Thomas Inge. Westport, Conn.: Greenwood Press, 1982.

Grob, Gerald N. "The Social History of Medicine and Disease: Problems and Possibilities." *JSocH* 10 (1977):393–405.

Hall, Kermit. *The Magic Mirror.* New York: Oxford University Press, 1989.

Hall, Peter Dobkin. "The Social Foundations of Professional Credibility: Linking the Medical Profession to Higher Education in Connecticut and Massachusetts." In *The Authority of Experts: Studies in History and Theory*, edited by Thomas L. Haskell. Bloomington: Indiana University Press, 1984.

Haller, John S. *American Medicine in Transition, 1840–1910.* Urbana: University of Illinois Press, 1981.

Halley, Bruce. *The Healthy Body and Victorian Culture.* Cambridge: Harvard University Press, 1978.

Halliday, Terrance C. "Six Score and Ten: Demographic Transitions in the American Legal Profession." *LSR* 20 (1986):53–77.

Harrison, Louis B., Melvin H. Worth, Jr., and Michael A. Carlucci. "The Development of the Principles of Medical Malpractice in the United States." *PBM* 29 (Autumn 1985):41–72.

Haskell, Thomas. *The Emergence of Professional Social Science.* Urbana: University of Illinois Press, 1977.

Heath, Clark. "How Abraham Lincoln Dealt with a Malpractice Suit." *NEJM* 295:735–36.

Heitman, Elizabeth. "Caring for the Silent Stranger: Ethical Hospital Care for Non-English Speaking Patients." Ph.D. dissertation, Rice University, 1988.

Henretta, James A. *The Evolution of American Society, 1700–1815: An Interdisciplinary Analysis.* Lexington, Mass.: D. C. Heath, 1973.

Higham, John. "The Reorientation of American Culture in the 1890s." In *Writing American History: Essays in Modern Scholarship.* Bloomington: Indiana University Press, 1970.

Hilton, Boyd. *The Age of Atonement: The Influence of Evangelicalism on Social and Economic Thought, 1795–1865.* Oxford: Clarendon Press, 1988.

Hofstadter, Richard. *Anti-Intellectualism in American Life.* New York: Vintage Books, 1962.

Horwitz, Morton J. "The Emergence of an Instrumental Conception of American Law, 1780–1820." In *Law and American History*, edited by Bernard Bailyn and Donald Fleming. (Boston: Little, Brown, 1971).

Horwitz, Morton J. *The Transformation of American Law, 1780–1860*. Cambridge: Harvard University Press, 1977.

Hurst, J. Willard. *The Growth of American Law: The Law Makers*. Boston: Little, Brown, 1950.

Hylton, Joseph Gordon. "The Virginia Lawyer from Reconstruction to the Great Depression." Ph.D. dissertation. Harvard University, 1986.

Hyman, Harold M. *A More Perfect Union: The Impact of the Civil War and Reconstruction on the Constitution*. New York: Alfred A. Knopf, 1973.

Illich, Ivan. *Medical Nemesis: The Expropriation of Health*. New York: Pantheon, 1976.

Johnson, Herbert A. "Civil Procedure in John Jay's New York." *AJLH* 11 (1967):69–80.

Johnson, Paul E. *A Shopkeeper's Millennium: Society and Revivals in Rochester, New York, 1815–1837*. New York: Hill and Wang, 1978.

Joy, Robert T. J. "The Natural Bonesetters with Special Reference to the Sweet Family of Rhode Island." *BHM* 28 (1954):416–41.

Kaufman, Martin. *Homeopathy in America: The Rise and Fall of a Medical Heresy*. Baltimore: Johns Hopkins University Press, 1971.

————. "American Medical Education." In *The Education of American Physicians* edited by Ronald L. Numbers. Berkeley: University of California Press, 1980.

Kaufman, Walter. "Suffering and the Bible." In *The Faith of a Heretic*. Garden City, N.Y.: Doubleday, 1961.

Kelly, Howard. *A Cyclopedia of American Medical Biography: Comprising the Lives of Eminent Deceased Physicians and Surgeons 1610–1900*, vol. 2. Philadelphia: W. B. Saunders, 1912.

Kett, Joseph. *The Formation of the American Medical Profession, 1780–1860*. New Haven: Yale University Press, 1968.

Kinkead, Gwen. "Humana's Hard Sell Hospitals." *For* (17 November 1980):68–81.

Koffler, Joseph H., and Alison Reppy. *Handbook of Common Law Pleading*. St. Paul: West Publishing, 1969.

Larson, Magali Sarfatti. *The Rise of Professionalism: A Sociological Analysis*. Berkeley: University of California Press, 1977.

Lears, T. J. Jackson. *No Place of Grace: Antimodernism and the Transformation of America, 1880–1920*. New York: Pantheon, 1981.

————. "From Salvation to Self-Realization: Advertising and the Therapeutic Roots of Consumer Culture." In *The Culture of Consumption: Critical Essays in American History, 1880–1980*, edited by Richard Wightman Fox and T. J. Jackson Lears. New York: Pantheon, 1983.

Leavitt, Judith. *Brought to Bed: Childbearing in America, 1750–1950*. New York: Oxford University Press, 1986.

Levy, Leonard. *The Law of the Commonwealth and Chief Justice Shaw*. Cambridge: Harvard University Press, 1957.

Light, Donald W. "Corporate Medicine for Profit." *SA* 255 (December 1986):38–45.

Lockhart, Ailene S., and Betty Spears, eds. *Chronicle of American Physical Education: Selected Readings, 1855–1930.* Dubuque, Iowa: William C. Brown, 1972.

Lockridge, Kenneth A. *A New England Town: The First Hundred Years.* New York: Norton, 1970.

Longo, Laurence D. "The Rise and Fall of Batty's Operation: A Fashion in Surgery." *BHM* 53 (1979):244–67.

Loveland, Anne C. *Southern Evangelicals and the Social Order, 1800–1860.* Baton Rouge: Louisiana State University Press, 1980.

Ludmerer, Kenneth. *Learning to Heal: The Development of American Medical Education.* New York: Basic Books, 1985.

Maine, Henry. *Ancient Law.* New York: Henry Holt, 1884.

MacKinnon, F. B. *Contingent Fees for Legal Services.* Chicago: Aldine, 1964.

McLoughlin, William G. "Introduction to Charles G. Finney, *Lectures on Revivals of Religion.*" In *Essays on Jacksonian America.* Edited by Frank Otto Gatell. New York: Holt, Rinehart and Winston, 1970.

Malone, Wex. "The Genesis of Wrongful Death." *SLR* 17 (1965):1043–76.

———. *Essays on Torts.* Baton Rouge: Paul M. Herbert, 1986.

Marty, Martin E. *Righteous Empire: The Protestant Experience in America.* New York: Dial Press, 1970.

Marx, Leo. *The Machine in the Garden: Technology and the Pastoral Ideal in America.* New York: Oxford University Press, 1973.

May, Henry F. "The Decline of Providence?" In *Ideas, Faiths, and Feelings: Essays on American Intellectual and Religious History, 1952–1982.* New York: Oxford University Press, 1983.

May, William. *The Physician's Covenant: Images of the Healer in Medical Ethics.* Philadelphia: Westminister Press, 1983.

———. "Adversarialism in America and the Professions." In *Community in America: The Challenge of Habits of the Heart,* edited by Charles H. Reynolds and Ralph V. Norman. Berkeley: University of California Press, 1988.

Meier, Hugo A. "Technology and Democracy, 1800–1860." *MVHR* 43 (1956–1957):618–40.

Merry, Sally Engle, and Susan S. Sibley. "What Do Plaintiffs Want? Re-examining the Concept of Dispute." *JSJ* 9 (1984):151–78.

Meyers, Marvin. *The Jacksonian Persuasion: Politics and Belief.* New York: Vintage, 1960.

Millar, Robert Wyness. *Civil Procedure of the Trial Court in Historical Perspective.* New York: Law Center for New York University, 1952.

Miller, Perry. *The New England Mind: The Seventeenth Century.* Cambridge: Harvard University Press, 1939.

———. *The New England Mind: From Colony to Province.* Cambridge: Harvard University Press, 1953.

Miller, Perry, ed. *The Legal Mind in America: From Independence to the Civil War.* Garden City, N.Y.: Doubleday, 1962.

Moore, Winfred B., Joseph F. Tripp, and Lyon G. Tyler, eds. *Developing Dixie: Modernization in a Traditional Society.* Wesport, Conn.: Greenwood Press, 1988.

Morris, Richard B. "Responsibility for Tortious Acts in Early American Law." In *Studies in the History of American Law* Philadelphia: J. M. Mitchell, 1959.

Morris, Richard B. "Responsibility for Tortious Acts in Early American Law." In *Studies in the History of American Law.* Philadelphia: J. M. Mitchell, 1959.

Nelson, William E. *The Americanization of the Common Law: The Impact of Legal Change on Massachusetts Society, 1760–1830.* Cambridge: Harvard University Press, 1975.

———. *Dispute and Conflict Resolution in Plymouth County, Massachusetts, 1723–1825.* Chapel Hill: University of North Carolina Press, 1981.

Newmyer, R. Kent. *Supreme Court Justice Joseph Story: Statesman of the Old Republic.* Chapel Hill: University of North Carolina Press, 1985.

Numbers, Ronald L. "The History of American Medicine: A Field in Ferment." *RAH* 10 (1982):245–52.

———, ed. *The Education of American Physicians.* Berkeley: University of California Press, 1980.

———, and Ronald C. Sawyer. "Medicine and Christianity in the Modern World." In *Health/Medicine and the Faith Traditions: An Inquiry into Religion and Medicine,* edited by Martin E. Marty and Kenneth Vaux. Philadelphia: Fortress Press, 1982.

Nye, Russel Blaine. *Society and Culture in America, 1830–1860.* New York: Harper and Row, 1974.

Owsley, Frank Lawrence. *Plain Folk of the Old South.* Baton Rouge: Louisiana State University Press, 1960.

Park, Roberta J. "The Attitudes of Leading New England Transcendentalists Toward Healthful Exercise, Active Recreations, and Proper Care of the Body, 1830–1860." *JSH* 4 (1977):34–50.

———. " 'Embodied Selves': The Rise and Development of Concern for Physical Education, Active Games, and Recreation for American Women, 1776–1865." *JSH* 5 (Summer 1978):34–50.

Pernick, Martin. *A Calculus of Suffering: Pain, Professionalism, and Anesthesia in Nineteenth-Century America.* New York: Columbia University Press, 1985.

Porter, Thomas M. *The Rise of Statistical Thinking, 1820–1900.* Princeton: Princeton University Press, 1986.

Post, Albert. *Popular Freethought in America, 1825–1850.* New York: Columbia University Press, 1943.

Potter, David M. "Social Cohesion and the Crisis of Law." In *American Law and the Constitutional Order: Historical Perspectives,* edited by Lawrence M.

Friedman and Harry M. Scheiber. Cambridge: Harvard University Press, 1978.

Powell, John Harvey. *Bring Out Your Dead*. Philadelphia: University of Pennsylvania Press, 1949.

Pratt, Harry E. "The Famous 'Chicken Bone' Case." *JISHS* 45 (Summer 1952):164–67.

Reed, E. A. "Understanding Tort Law: The Historical Basis of Medical Liability." *JLM* 5 (1977):50–53.

Reiser, Stanley Joel. *Medicine and the Reign of Technology*. New York: Cambridge University Press, 1978.

Rieff, Philip. *The Triumph of the Therapeutic*. New York: Harper and Row, 1966.

Risse, Guenter B., Ronald L. Numbers, and Judith Walzer Leavitt, eds. *Medicine Without Doctors: Home Health Care in American History*. New York: Science History Publications, 1977.

Rogers, Tommy W. "Dr. Fredrick Ross and the Presbyterian Defense of Slavery." *JPH* 45 (1967):112–24.

Rosen, George. *Fees and Fee Bills: Some Economic Aspects of Medical Practice in Nineteenth Century America*. Supplement to the *Bulletin of the History of Medicine*, no. 6. Baltimore: Johns Hopkins University Press, 1946.

Rosenberg, Charles E. "The American Medical Profession: Mid–Nineteenth Century." *MA* 44 (1962):163–71.

———. *The Cholera Years: The United States in 1832, 1849, and 1866*. Chicago: University of Chicago Press, 1962.

———. "The Therapeutic Revolution: Medicine, Meaning, and Social Change in Nineteenth-Century America." In *The Therapeutic Revolution: Medicine, Meaning, and Change in Nineteenth-Century America*, edited by Morris J. Vogel and Charles E. Rosenberg. Philadelphia: University of Pennsylvania Press, 1979.

———. "Medical Text and Social Context: Explaining William Buchan's *Domestic Medicine*." *BHM* 57 (1983):22–42.

———. *The Care of Strangers: The Rise of America's Hospital System*. New York: Basic Books, 1987.

Rothstein, William G. *American Physicians in the Nineteenth Century*. Baltimore: Johns Hopkins University Press, 1972.

Sandor, Andrew A. "The History of Professional Liability Suits in the United States." *JAMA* 163 (1957):459–66.

Sandusk, Joseph F. "Analysis of Profesional Factors in Medical Malpractice Claims." *JAMA* 161 (2 June 1956):442–47.

Saum, Lewis O. "Providence in the Popular Mind of Pre–Civil War America." *IMH* 72 (1976):315–46.

———. *The Popular Mind of Pre–Civil War America*. Westport, Conn.: Greenwood Press, 1980.

Savitt, Todd L. "The Use of Blacks for Medical Experimentation and

Demonstration in the Old South," *Journal of Southern History* 48 (1982): 331–48.

Schlesinger, Arthur M. *The Age of Jackson.* Boston: Little, Brown, 1945.

Shafer, Henry Burnell. *The American Medical Profession, 1783–1850.* New York: AMS Press, 1968.

Shikes, Robert H. *Rocky Mountain Medicine: Doctors, Drugs, and Disease in Early Colorado.* Boulder, Colo.: Johnson Books, 1986.

Shryock, Richard Harrison. *Medicine and Society in America, 1660–1860.* Ithaca: Cornell University Press, 1960.

———. *Medical Licensing in America, 1650–1965.* Baltimore: Johns Hopkins University Press, 1967.

Simpson, A. W. B. *Legal Theory and Legal History: Essays on the Common Law.* London: Hambledon Press, 1987.

Smith, Hubert Winston. "Legal Responsibility for Medical Malpractice." *JAMA* 116 (1941):942–47, 2149–59; 2670–79; and *JAMA* 117 (1941):23–33.

Speer, James B. "Malpractice: The Historical Viewpoint." In *Proceedings of the Malpractice Conference: The Interaction of Medicine and Justice Through Public Policy.* Edited by Donnie J. Self. N.P.: East Virginia Medical School, Old Dominion University, 1976.

Stage, Sarah. *Female Complaints: Lydia Pinkham and the Business of Women's Medicine.* New York: Norton, 1971.

Starr, Paul. "Medicine, Economy, and Society in Nineteenth-Century America." *JSocH* 10 (1977):588–607.

———. *The Social Transformation of American Medicine.* New York: Basic Books, 1982.

Stetler, Joseph C. "The History of Reported Medical Professional Liability Cases." *TLQ* 30 (1957):366–83.

Sunderland, Edson R. *Cases on Procedure Annotated, Code Pleading.* Philadelphia: Callaghan, 1913.

———. *Cases on Procedure Code Pleading.* Chicago: Callaghan, 1923.

Schwartz, Bernard. *Law in America.* New York: McGraw-Hill, 1974.

Thomas, John L. "Romantic Reform in America, 1815–1865." *American Quarterly* 17 (Winter 1965):656–81.

Thomas, Keith. *Religion and the Decline of Magic: Studies in Popular Beliefs in the Sixteenth and Seventeenth Centuries in England.* London: Weidenfeld, 1971.

Tilton, Eleanor M. "Lightning Rods and the Earthquake of 1755." *NEQ* 13 (1940):85–97.

Tomlins, Christopher L. "A Mysterious Power: Industrial Accidents and the Legal Construction of Employee Relations in Massachusetts, 1800–1850." *LHR* 6 (Fall 1988):375–438.

Turner, James. *Reckoning with the Beast: Animals, Pain, and Humanity in the Victorian Mind.* Baltimore: Johns Hopkins University Press, 1980.

Verbrugge, Martha J. *Able-Bodied Womanhood: Personal Health and Social Change in Nineteenth-Century Boston.* New York: Oxford University Press, 1988.

Waiz, Jon R. "The Rise and Gradual Fall of the Locality Rule in Medical Malpractice Litigation." *DPLR* 17 (1969):408–21.

Walters, Ronald G. *American Reformers, 1815–1860*. New York: Hill and Wang, 1978.

Ward, John William. *Andrew Jackson—Symbol for an Age*. New York: Oxford University Press, 1953.

Waring, Joseph I. "Charleston Medicine, 1800–1860." *JHMAS* 31 (July 1976):320–342.

Warner, John Harley. "Southern Medical Reform: The Meaning of the Antebellum Argument for Southern Medical Education." *BHM* 57 (Fall 1983): 364–81.

———. *The Therapeutic Perspective: Medical Practice, Knowledge, and Professional Identity in America, 1820–1885*. Cambridge: Harvard University Press, 1986.

Warren, Charles. *A History of the American Bar*. Boston: Little, Brown, 1911.

Weaver, R. M. "The Older Religiousness in the South." *SR* 51 (1943):237–49.

Weigel, Charles J. "Medical Malpractice in America's Middle Years." *TRBM* 32 (1974):191–205.

Welter, Rush. *The Mind of America, 1820–1860*. New York: Columbia University Press, 1975.

Westfall, Richard S. *The Construction of Modern Science Mechanisms and Mechanics*. New York: John Wiley, 1971.

White, G. Edward. *Tort Law in America: An Intellectual History*. New York: Oxford University Press, 1980.

Whorton, James C. *Crusaders for Fitness: The History of American Health Reformers*. Princeton: Princeton University Press, 1982.

Wiebe, Robert H. *The Search for Order, 1877–1920*. New York: Hill and Wang, 1967.

Williams, Mitchell G. "Pleading Reform in Nineteenth-Century America: The Joinder of Actions at Common Law Under the Codes." *JLH* 6 (1985): 299–335.

Wilson, Major L. "Paradox Lost: Order in Evangelical Thought of Mid–Nineteenth-Century America." *CH* 44 (1975):352–66.

Winfield, Percy H. *The Province of Tort*. Cambridge: Cambridge University Press, 1931.

Wood, Gordon. *The Creation of the American Republic, 1776–1787*. New York: Norton, 1969.

Woodward, C. Vann. *The Burden of Southern History*. Baton Rouge: Louisiana State University Press, 1968.

Wyatt-Brown, Bertram. *Southern Honor: Ethics and Behavior in the Old South*. New York: Oxford University Press, 1982.

Young, James Harvey. *The Toadstool Millionaires: A Social History of Patent Medicines in America before Federal Regulation*. Princeton: Princeton University Press, 1961.

Zuckerman, Michael. *Peaceable Kingdoms: New England Towns in the Eighteenth Century*. New York: Random House, 1970.

Index